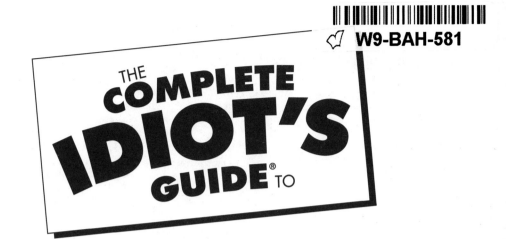

THE COMPLETE IDIOT'S GUIDE® TO

Understanding Catholicism

Second Edition

by Bob O'Gorman, Ph.D.
and Mary Faulkner, M.A.

ALPHA

A member of Penguin Group (USA) Inc.

International Standard Book Number: 1-59257-085-2
Library of Congress Catalog Card Number: 2003105469

05 04 03   8 7 6 5 4 3 2 1

Interpretation of the printing code: The rightmost number of the first series of numbers is the year of the book's printing; the rightmost number of the second series of numbers is the number of the book's printing. For example, a printing code of 03-1 shows that the first printing occurred in 2003.

Printed in the United States of America

Note: This publication contains the opinions and ideas of its authors. It is intended to provide helpful and informative material on the subject matter covered. It is sold with the understanding that the authors and publisher are not engaged in rendering professional services in the book. If the reader requires personal assistance or advice, a competent professional should be consulted.

The authors and publisher specifically disclaim any responsibility for any liability, loss, or risk, personal or otherwise, which is incurred as a consequence, directly or indirectly, of the use and application of any of the contents of this book.

Most Alpha books are available at special quantity discounts for bulk purchases for sales promotions, premiums, fund-raising, or educational use. Special books, or book excerpts, can also be created to fit specific needs.

For details, write: Special Markets, Alpha Books, 375 Hudson Street, New York, NY 10014.

Publisher: *Marie Butler-Knight*
Product Manager: *Phil Kitchel*
Senior Managing Editor: *Jennifer Chisholm*
Senior Acquisitions Editor: *Randy Ladenheim-Gil*
Development Editor: *Suzanne LeVert*
Senior Production Editor: *Katherin Bidwell*
Copy Editor: *Cari Luna*
Illustrator: *Jody P. Schaeffer*
Cover/Book Designer: *Trina Wurst*
Indexer: *Jennifer Rushing-Schurr*
Layout/Proofreading: *Angela Calvert, John Etchison, Donna Martin*

Contents at a Glance

Contents

Foreword

The underlying idea behind "idiot" in Greek (*idiotes*) is "a private individual" not holding public office. This usage got extended to mean "common person," the lay man or woman who is not a professional, not a specialist. Snobs later downgraded private, common, lay individuals into what most people think idiot means: imbecile, dunderhead.

This book rescues and re-elevates the term so that it is no longer an insult. In fact, it applies to most of us, since most are not professionals or specialists in Catholic life and thought. For that matter, it applies to virtually all of us, since it is almost impossible to be informed about the whole range of topics in this book. We are all common lay people in respect to some themes. (All right, I'll exempt the up to a half-dozen producers of single-author encyclopedias of Catholicism. It's their job to match the knowledge, skills, ambition, and industry of Bob O'Gorman and Mary Faulkner here.)

The authors succeed admirably in teasing us into the many chambers of the house Catholic, taking us toward the beginnings of the many Catholic trails, tantalizing us with the glimpses of what the Catholic vision is all about, and letting us sense the Catholic sensibility.

They have their own *shtick*, their own ways of getting attention and accenting favored themes. They acknowledge the influence of Andrew M. Greeley and Virgilio Elizondo, for instance. That means that they do not dwell on the grim downside of Catholic life. They communicate, in the midst of the realism about life and church, a sense of exuberance and an impartation of hope. That's all to the good in an age when Catholicism often gets lumped with "organized religion" as some sort of grumpy, tyrannizing force.

Professionals, specialists, in knowledge of things Catholic, they are also expert at telling stories, holding attention, and ministering to a hungry Catholic (and surrounding) world, where many "prefer" or "identify with" Catholicism but have a hard time gaining access to knowledge of what it's all about. This book is about "what it's all about."

—Professor Martin E. Marty

Professor Martin E. Marty is the Fairfax M. Cone Distinguished Service Professor (Emeritus) of the History of Modern Christianity Divinity School, University of Chicago.

Foreword

The best way of introducing this marvelous book, which I know will enrich the lives of anyone who reads it, is by exploring it in terms of why I love being a Catholic. This is the religion of my parents and ancestors, and it connects me with the very origins of my life and existence.

Being a Catholic is great fun, and this book celebrates the fun of this religion. Jesus started his public ministry with the feast at Cana—enjoying himself with family, friends, and other guests. Throughout his life, he loved going to the festivals in Jerusalem and having a good time with anyone and everyone. Mexican Catholicism is festive. It allows us to experience in very vivid ways the deepest mysteries of our faith, of God's love for us, of the life of Jesus, the Son of God made human for us, Mary, the sorrowful mother, and the saints who were sinners like us but achieved great virtue. For every mystery of the faith, there is a festive and elaborate celebration allowing us to enter into the mystery as if it was taking place in our own backyard.

Catholicism is colorful, it's sensual, it's emotional, it's dramatic, and it's fun. As this book helps you see, you can take part and benefit from the great celebrations of the faith like Guadalupe, Christmas Posadas, Midnight Mass, Ash Wednesday, Holy Week rituals, Day of the Dead, and many others. These popular festive celebrations allow everyone and anyone to enter into a collective mystical experience of the sacred as it is present among us here and now today.

The book tells you how Catholics have so many ways of being in touch with God throughout the day wherever we happen to be. Medals, holy cards, scapulars, rosaries, holy water, candles, home shrines, and other simple things put us in immediate contact with God, just like the picture of a loved one in my wallet helps to put me in their presence even when they are far away or even gone to heaven. These simple objects allow us, as the book points out, to touch God and feel God's touch even when we don't know much about God.

I love being a Catholic because much more than a religion, it seems to be a large, extended family, or as the book says, a tribe! We find ourselves at home wherever we go in the world, and even though the language and some of the details may be different, the basic symbols are the same and we immediately recognize ourselves to be among family. When people travel or migrate to other countries, we can immediately find a religious home in a local Catholic church.

I love being a Catholic because our Catholic story, as this book does such a good and balanced job of saying, is so human and divine at the same time. Human because of the many crazy, stupid, weird, and even cruel things we have done, as well as the many heroic acts and movements of charity, mercy, and compassion. Through all this weakness, I see all the good and beautiful things the Church has done throughout history and continues to do today: orphanages, lepresoriums, schools, universities, hospitals, community-organizing, social justice initiatives, visitation of the sick, aid to immigrants, and on.

The Complete Idiot's Guide to Understanding Catholicism, Second Edition, is wonderful and stimulating. It is brief while exposing substantial matter in an attractive way. I am honored to have been asked to introduce this book, which will definitely reach many more people than some of the best theological works or even the official catechism of the Catholic Church. It is written in a simple and attractive way, it is easy and exciting to read, and the authors have managed to distill and condense very technical matter into a very cohesive book.

—Father Virgilio Elizondo
The Mexican American Cultural Center, San Antonio, Texas

Introduction

Today's Catholic Church seems to be a Church in conflict. There is the obvious sexual conflict manifested in the scandals and the scramble to cover it up by Church leaders. In addition, there is great disagreement over birth control, the absolute ban on abortion, mandatory celibacy, women's ordination, and even about war. The Church seems split down the middle between conservatives and progressives. Underneath all the apparent quarreling, there is a people united through history and through sacramental practices. In this second edition, we look at the whole issue of authority, as the twenty-first century Catholic takes ownership of their religion. There isn't much doubt that the Church will survive ... but what will it look like in the future?

In almost every way, the history of the Catholic Church is the story of Western civilization, and for 1,100 years, all Christians shared its story. Today, there are over a billion Catholics worldwide, making it the largest denomination in the world. For most of its 2,000-year history, it has been wrapped in mystery. Its rituals and prayers were chanted in Latin. Its statues, candles, incense, and many other practices have enthralled many and frightened some. However, in the early 1960s, a radical change occurred within the Church, and since that time, it has uncloaked some of its own mystery and opened itself to the world. Now, forty years later, what changes have actually made it into Church law? How different is the institutional Church?

In telling the story of the Church, we are clearly telling two stories: one that existed when the twentieth century began and one that exists as the twenty-first century dawns. We talk about the Church from both the perspective that many older Catholics remember and the perspective of the emerging Church.

We look at the Church from many angles: its history and vision, its unique character, and the similarities and differences among Catholics. The book is about the people and their beliefs. It's about their prayers and practices. It's about the contemporary world and the challenges that the Church faces in the future.

Who are Catholics and how are they different from the rest of the folks? Answering this question engages the paradox of being unique and belonging to a world community. This is a delicate matter for Catholics, because in the past they have claimed that theirs is the only true religion. We have not made that claim for Catholicism; however, we have acknowledged that to be Catholic is to be different. The purpose of this book is to discover what is unique and what is different about being Catholic.

Sacraments are at the heart and soul of what it means to be a Catholic, and we look at them in detail in this book. To be Catholic is to see, hear, taste, touch, and smell the presence of God. For Catholics, this experience happens through the sacraments, which most distinguish Catholicism from other religions and other Christian denominations. Catholics have a tradition of prayers and practices, statues, medals, rosaries, and more that is part of their everyday life. This rich collection has been accumulating for some 2,000 years and comes from many cultures.

Perhaps the most recognizable Catholic figure is Mary. She is often the face of Catholicism to the world. The relationship between a Catholic and Mary embodies a special emotional bond of grace itself. The book explores the many roles of Mary and what she means to Catholics.

Catholics are everywhere. However, they have some particular gathering places where you are more apt to find them. The neighborhood parish is one of them. This is where Catholics come together on a weekly basis to celebrate the Mass. During the week, they participate in a number of social, recreational, educational, and outreach activities centered there. Catholic parishes are led by priests, sisters, and other professional Church ministers. You'll meet this special group of people in this book.

Another characteristic of Catholics is their sense of unity, their "tribal" nature. Catholics belong to a neighborhood community and a worldwide Church. The Catholic Church is a highly structured institution with a lot of people managing it. For Catholics, there is a sense of connection to the worldwide community, and this sense brings into being the vision that we are all God's people.

Catholic unity has a powerful potential to influence the world. Perhaps at no other time in history is this influence more apparent than with the present pope, John Paul II. His tireless world travels have symbolized religious truth for many. His presence magnifies the witness of the "body of Christ" all over the world. Electronic communication through television, the World Wide Web, and newswires, along with global travel, has made fulfilling the mission of the Church to announce the presence of God throughout the world a greater possibility than in any other era.

This book tells the Catholic story from its beginning with the tongues of fire on the feast of Pentecost to its present-day position in the modern world. It explores the Church's rich mysticism and its varied forms of spirituality, as well as highlights its traditional and contemporary theologies.

In this book, we focus more on the faith story of the people than the institutional story. You'll get an inside glimpse of the everyday practices of Catholics: their prayer life, the rich history of the saints, and the way they live out the holy seasons of the year from the springtime of Easter to the autumn of All Souls' Day and the winter renewal of Christmas. We trace the Church's rituals back to their roots in the earth itself.

Today Catholicism comes in many shapes and sizes. It's grown beyond the old stereotypes, yet the character of being Catholic is still very much intact. As we pass along our knowledge and stories to the next generation, we look at the challenges the Church will face and the resources it has to survive and remain meaningful to the people and faithful to Jesus.

The first edition took us up to the edge of the third millennium. We were aware of much unrest in the Church—strong differences between conservative and liberal Catholics. We were aware of a new generation much less knowledgeable of things Catholic, due to the loss of many of the strong institutional aspects of the Church.

Our attempt was to make this religion more accessible. Our expectations for the book have been exceeded. However, what we did not anticipate was just how much Catholicism would be "in your face" these past two years. It would not be an exaggeration to say that more information about the Catholic Church was in the news and on the air in 2002 alone than in the last half of the twentieth century. We know sex sells newspapers. Yet the national and international interest in the incredible abuse scandals reveals that Catholicism has truly, as we said previously, "been wrapped in mystery." It is, we believe, the fascination of seeing mystery exposed that has made the interest in this particular religion so engaging.

In this second edition we have re-examined Catholicism from the perspective of its humanness—a Church in process.

What You'll Discover in This Book

The book is divided into seven sections:

Part 1, "What's a Catholic?" provides a profile of Catholics and a peek at their practices and prayers. You'll get inside the workings of the Vatican and learn all about the Church's revolution, Vatican II.

Part 2, "Putting the 'Ism' in Catholicism: Becoming Catholic, Becoming Different," explores the roots of Catholicism in the earth, the Bible, and in Jesus, and Catholicism's emergence as a religion.

Part 3, "The Sensuous Side of Catholicism: How Catholics Experience God," lets you in on the way Catholics taste, touch, hear, smell, and see God through their sacramental practices and how Catholics experience Jesus. In this part, you'll learn all about Mary and Catholics' relationship to her.

Part 4, "Imagination and Prayer," takes you into the world of Catholics, their statues and holy cards, their liturgical cycle of seasons, their Rosary, their sacred music, their contemplative life, and most important, the Mass.

Part 5, "Catholic Identity: What Makes a Catholic?" looks at the center of Catholic life: its parishes and its schools and charities. You'll find out about key Catholic teachings and who determines them. You'll meet the hierarchy of the Church as well as its foot soldiers.

Part 6, "The Church's History," begins with a visit to the Roman Empire and looks at important people who had a hand in shaping the early Church. You will see the Church grow and struggle through the Middle Ages. You'll hear all about the miracle that brought Catholicism to the New World.

Part 7, "A Look to the Future," takes up the challenges that the Church faces in the third millennium. First, we look at the future for women in leadership. Then you'll see how the center of gravity for the Church moved from Europe to Africa, Latin America, and Asia, and meet a new generation of Catholics who will carry the

Church into the future. Finally, we look at the sex scandals that are currently shaking up the Church and shocking the community. We look at deeper issues about Church structure that may (or may not) contribute to a climate where abuse can fester. And we'll look at the potential for a "new" kind of Catholic and a "new" kind of Church to emerge out of the rubble.

In the appendixes, we have included information that will provide you with some interesting and useful details. There is a glossary for you to quickly check terms used in the book. There is a list of the books and sources we have drawn from and others that you might find helpful for further reading. There is a chart of religious symbols that show how Catholic rituals connect to the elements of the earth. Finally, we have included a list of fascinating but lesser known popes the Church has had, as well as a story on an alleged female pope.

Helpful Hints for the Reader

Throughout the text, you will find helpful and interesting information to spice up your journey through Catholicism.

S'ter Says _____

The Catholic religion has a language of its own. Information provided in this sidebar will give you a quick grasp of terms that may be new to you.

For Heaven's Sake! _____

This information is designed to help keep you on the straight and narrow and alert you to common misunderstandings about the Church.

Saints Preserve Us

In these boxes, you'll learn the stories of some well-known and not-so-well-known saints, their feast days, and who and what they watch over.

Epiphanies

These boxes offer a quick study of interesting Catholic tidbits. Use this information as a resource to impress your Catholic friends.

Your Guardian Angel _____

The Catholic Church is known for its mysterious practices. These boxes contain suggestions for the reader on how to easily participate regardless of whether you are a believer, along with helpful tips.

Acknowledgments

We've got a lot of people to thank. Some of the ones who were indispensable were Linda Roghaar, our agent; Suzanne LeVert, our primary editor; Jim Mallett, our religious editor; and Dan O'Gorman, our historical editor. We had great technical help from Dean Caskey, our personal photographer, and Valerie Harrell, who did our graphics, Cherri Kowalchuk and Matt Lohmeier, our Gen X'ers, and Scott Weiss, who untangled the computer. We had special consultation from Margaret Ann Crain, Jack Seymour, Joe Glab, Sheila Bourelly, and Lynn Westfield. Our perspectives in writing this book were greatly influenced by two people who have made major contributions to the study of Catholicism, Andrew M. Greeley, professor of Social Science, University of Chicago, and Virgilio Elizondo, founder of the Mexico-American Cultural Center, San Antonio, Texas.

Our families and friends helped us, too, including Mary Lou, Tim, John, Lucile (who prayed a lot), Elizabeth, Susan, John, Martha Leigh, Dorothy, Lilyleone, Noris, Claudia (for picking up the slack at the office), Paul Dokecki, and Bob Newbrough (for patience and support), The Ladies of Nashville Circle, and Darby.

Our thanks also go to all the words and thoughts of others both written and spoken that have worked their way into this book.

Special Thanks to the Technical Reviewer

The Complete Idiot's Guide to Understanding Catholicism, Second Edition, was reviewed by an expert who double-checked the accuracy of what you'll learn here, to help us ensure that this book gives you everything you need to know about Catholicism. Special thanks are extended to Rev. James K. Mallett, Pastor of Christ the King Church, Nashville, Tennessee.

Trademarks

All terms mentioned in this book that are known to be or are suspected of being trademarks or service marks have been appropriately capitalized. Alpha Books and Penguin Group (USA) Inc. cannot attest to the accuracy of this information. Use of a term in this book should not be regarded as affecting the validity of any trademark or service mark.

Part 1

What's a Catholic?

A pop image of Catholics exists in the world of movies, television, and books: the Irish cop, the spunky nun, and a priest who refuses to break the seal of confession. Nostalgic remembrances, stereotypes, prejudice, and just plain curiosity surround this somewhat mysterious religion. Candles, incense, processions, statues, and visions of Mary … We'll look at what is fact and what is fiction regarding Catholics and their practices.

There also exists an image of the Catholic as a political, social, and economic force in society. In most cities, there is an abundance of Catholic institutions: schools, hospitals, homes for the aged, and other vital social agencies. The Church exists in many countries and among many nationalities. It has a colorful mix of cultures.

Can You Judge a Catholic by the Cover?

In This Chapter

- ◆ What is a Catholic?
- ◆ The basics of the beliefs
- ◆ What Catholics do
- ◆ The curiosity of the Catholic world
- ◆ The Catholic "tribe"

Can you identify Catholics by how they look, what they believe, or how they act in the world? One way of answering this question is to point to the great diversity that exists within the religion. Yet, Catholicism also exists as a distinct culture, almost tribal. For many it forms a deep identity that goes all the way to the bone; it is intrinsic to their sense of being. And the Catholic Church is the kind of church that if you ever leave it, you never leave it behind; you forever bear its mark. For many, to be a Catholic is to be formed by a cadre of dedicated teachers whose life work it is to study and transmit the deep meanings of spirituality.

There is an "insider and outsider" character to the Church, captured by the language, rituals, songs, and beliefs of the religion, all of which serve to make Catholics distinct from other groups. Probably the best answer to the question "Can you judge a Catholic by his or her cover?" is to say sometimes yes and sometimes no.

This chapter highlights how Catholics are both of one mind and also differ. By doing so, it will give you an idea of who Catholics are today.

Why You Might Be Interested

Have you ever wanted to know more about this religion whose leader, the pope, has diplomatic relations with almost every country in the world and who receives weekly visits by heads of state? His frequent trips draw dramatic crowds everywhere he goes, from Uganda to Uruguay, from Paris to Papua New Guinea. Pope John Paul II, for example, has traveled to more than 129 different countries, logging more than 750,000 frequent flyer miles, which is approximately three times the distance to the moon. According to estimates, over the course of this pope's reign, more than 17 million people have attended his weekly audiences in Rome.

Every cityscape reveals churches, hospitals, schools, office buildings, and cemeteries that are statements of the Catholic presence in the culture. When you were in school, you probably encountered this religion in your World History class, because the history of the Catholic Church is a major part of the story of the Western world. All Christian religions share a common history with the Catholic Church for their first 1,100 to 1,500 years.

Catholicism is a religion with a high media profile. Hardly a week goes by that there is not something about it in the newspaper or on the television. From protests to papal appearances, it makes the front pages of newspapers all over the world. In the United States during the 1960s, men and women in Roman collars and black and white habits stood with civil rights protesters in Alabama. In the 1970s, they blocked the passage of "the White Train" that carried nuclear material across the country. Every January, Catholics walk up the steps of the Supreme Court to protest the Supreme Court's decision legalizing abortion. And, unfortunately, not all the publicity has been good. Most recently, sexual abuse scandals have been rattling the Vatican doors. Let's find out more about this fascinating faith that has held so many people together for so long.

Catholics Here, There, Everywhere

Perhaps you're reading this book because you were baptized a *Catholic* as a child but never practiced your religion. Perhaps you practice but don't fully understand the richness of your religion's culture and traditions.

Or maybe you're reading this book because you aren't Catholic but your daughter is about to marry one, or your boss has invited you to attend her son's baptism, or you're attending a Catholic funeral. What is it like to enter this religious world? Will you be expected to participate? If so, how? What will be the meaning of the ceremonies you'll be witnessing? What will it be like to mingle with these people in their own world? Catholicism has produced majesty, controversy, disgrace, and sometimes fear. This book will help you separate fact from fiction and prejudice from truth and be more at ease with your encounters with this denomination.

Catholics are the largest single denomination of any religious group within the United States population, and the second-largest group is made up of former Catholics. Think about it for a moment. How long would it take you to name five Catholics that you personally interacted with in the last 24 hours? Even if you aren't Catholic, when you go back through your family tree, chances are, if you are Christian, you'll find Catholic blood. Catholics are everywhere.

S'ter Says

Catholic is a Greek word literally meaning "toward the whole" or "one" and refers to the fact that the Catholic Church is found all over the world and all its members follow a set of common beliefs.

You're So Catholic If ...

- ◆ You have a St. Christopher medal in your car.

- ◆ You know more than 15 recipes for preparing tuna fish.

- ◆ You bury a statue of St. Joseph upside down in your yard when you are selling your house.

- ◆ You can name all of Ethel Kennedy's kids.

- ◆ You name your first daughter "Mary."

- ◆ You reach in your pocket for your handkerchief to cover a sneeze, and your rosary falls out.

- ◆ You still think twice about ordering a steak on Friday.

- ◆ You refer to other religions as "non-Catholic."

- ◆ You have mistakenly genuflected before taking your seat in the theater.

- ◆ You put J.M.J. at the top of your expense report before turning it in to your boss.

- ◆ You make the sign of the cross before shooting a basket.

- ◆ You suffer from free-floating guilt.

- ◆ You have braided palm leaves stuck behind the corner of the crucifix in your bedroom.

- ◆ You have pinned a tissue to the top of your head to go to church.

- ◆ You know the difference between a C-rated movie and an X-rated one.

- ◆ You have ransomed a "pagan baby."

- ◆ You know that a spiritual bouquet isn't something you buy at the neighborhood florist.

What You Have to Believe

Throughout this book, we'll be discussing and exploring the various religious concepts and practices of the Catholic faith in some detail, including the ones mentioned in this chapter. In short, however, the basis of Catholicism is a belief both in God as present in the world and a belief in God as bigger and more inclusive than the creation. This is stated as God immanent (God present within human existence, all of creation) and God transcendent (God beyond the limits of human experience and creation). Catholics' devotional life centers on reinforcing God's availability and presence to the people.

In addition, a list of characteristics Catholics would have in common (although these characteristics are not necessarily unique to Catholics) would include the following:

- ◆ The belief in the physical incarnation of God as Jesus Christ

- ◆ A shared history and common traditions

- ◆ A hierarchical governing structure with obedience to the pope regarding matters of faith

- ◆ The use of prescribed rituals called sacraments and a strong commitment to Holy Communion

- ◆ A belief in Mary, the mother of God, as intercessor, and reverence for the saints

- ◆ A rich tradition of spirituality and contemplative prayer, monasticism, and religious orders

- ◆ The use of statues, pictures, and other religious and artistic symbols and a shared tradition of music

- A deep appreciation for both faith as a set of beliefs that are not approached through pure reason and reason as a means of faith

- An emphasis on community as an essential ingredient of the faith journey

- A social doctrine based on the dignity of the human person

- A sense of responsibility for social justice and outreach

Besides a lot of standing and kneeling during ceremonies, one of the distinguishing characteristics of Catholic religious life is its use of sacraments, statues, incense, sacred music, holy water, rosaries, candles, processions, and colorful priestly robes. These and many other traditional practices symbolize, celebrate, and reinforce the belief in God's presence in the human faith journey. *Genuflection*, a practice of going down on one knee before taking one's seat in church in order to acknowledge the presence of Jesus, is one practice that might surprise a visitor. For instance, a Baptist woman who was engaged to marry a Catholic man was invited by her prospective mother-in-law to attend Mass. She had never been inside a Catholic church, and was trying to take it all in as she followed her mom-to-be up the aisle. Suddenly, without any warning, the mother-in-law stopped and genuflected before entering the pew. The visitor fell over her, knocking her down, and both of them spilled out across the floor. What an introduction to an already formidable situation!

Catholics believe that the faithful departed, as well as the living, are members of the Church body. For this reason, Catholics pay respect to and seek the counsel of saints, especially Mary, the mother of Jesus, who has a particularly high place of honor. Catholics believe that a fellowship exists among the Church's current members on earth, all members who have gone before, and those yet to come. Catholics have a rich tradition of mysticism, which means a personal religious encounter that usually occurs during prayer or meditation. During these encounters, a few people report visions of Christ, Mary, angels, or saints. However, mysticism is simply a time of being silent with God, and visions don't con-stitute the norm for Catholics. Catholic experiences for the most part are communal and happen in the context of organized Church services.

The Catholic Church believes in both grace (the gift of God's presence in our life) and our own good nature. Redemption does not come through belief in God alone; faith and good works are necessary as well. The beliefs and

CAUTION

For Heaven's Sake!

To be a good Catholic, you must avoid sin, but Catholicism has not been a "hell scared" religion for a long time. The present focus is on God's love and availability to the people—not on his judgment.

traditions of the Catholic Church change as time goes on. For example, the Catholic understanding of heaven, hell, sin, and redemption is much softer now than it once was and is one of the areas where you will find a lot of different views expressed. We will go into this subject in greater detail later in the book.

The Richness of Catholic Tradition

Tradition means more than just a long history; it refers to the faith experience of the many people who have made up the Catholic Church over time. Catholic sacred literature forms the spiritual heritage of Christianity. Tradition combines what has been discerned, received in revelation, lived, and handed down by the faithful members over the years. Catholic tradition, although it may appear to move slowly, is not static (fixed); it is always dynamic (in process). Tradition is open to new scholarly work of theologians, new witness of prophetic voices of the people, and the insight of the leadership. Although the Church sometimes finds itself at odds with the world of science—as science challenges Church doctrine—its comprehensive approach fosters the belief that science also leads to God. The physical world is seen as sacred, rather than in opposition to the spiritual. God's spirit is seen as active throughout creation. Creation is believed to be essentially good because it is reflective of the divine.

> **S'ter Says**
>
> **Tradition** is both the process of handing down the faith to others and the material that has been handed down. Tradition refers to the scriptures, Church doctrines, writings of the Church teachers, and the liturgical life of the Church down through the centuries; additionally, tradition refers to the everyday customs and practices of the Church.

Aren't All Catholics the Same?

If you ask any Catholic what he believes, you will hear as many different answers as people you have asked. Beliefs, like people, come in a lot of different shapes and sizes. Beliefs are about faith, and faith is a process. Catholic beliefs exist on a wide spectrum and must be considered on different levels. Although most Christians hold very similar beliefs, one of the differences between Catholics and other Christians is the Catholics' faith in the Church itself. Catholics believe that the Church has the divine authority to discern God's will and is the guardian of the basic truths of the religion. It represents the continuation of Jesus' presence as the active mediator of redemption.

The Catholic Church believes that God is the Creator and that Jesus is the Son of God who was born on earth, preached God's message, and brought God's love to the people. Jesus died and rose from the dead. Catholics believe that the Church is the continuation of Jesus' presence through the Holy Spirit. They believe that the Church holds the authority, through its leaders, the pope and the bishops, to teach and continue to discern the will of God. There is faith that life continues after death. Catholics believe the Bible contains sacred revelation from God forming the basis of their beliefs and morality.

Although these beliefs have formed the essential fiber of Catholicism throughout its 2,000-year history, a reform movement called Vatican II, held in the middle of the twentieth century, radically altered how modern Catholics interpret these beliefs and act upon them. Emerging Catholicism is characterized by the following:

♦ A shift in emphasis from the institution of the Church to the people

♦ Reconnecting to the foundation of Catholicism in Scripture

♦ Greater participation in the services and ceremonies

♦ Embracing the whole world: its people, their beliefs, culture, social and economic concerns, and an emphasis on world peace

♦ Cooperation with other religions and respect for the validity of their beliefs

♦ A call for an end to anti-Semitism and for a true respect for Judaism

♦ Valuing the role of the individual Catholic layperson as an emissary of Catholic values in society

♦ An end to discrimination of all kinds, recognition of the innate dignity of all people and all creation

♦ Upholding of the individual conscience as the norm for morality

What You Have to Do

Catholics define their beliefs as much through their actions as by their verbal statements. For example, Catholics celebrate their central belief of God's presence in Jesus by attending weekly Mass.

Although the media portray Catholics as all following a prescribed set of beliefs, the focus within the Catholic Church has shifted toward a personal sense of responsibility. The incubator for this sense of responsibility is Catholic schooling. Reading, writing, and arithmetic, along with values, heritage, and Catholic imagination, are taught to the tune of a hickory stick. For more on Catholic imagination and how it is transmitted, see Parts 3 and 4. The *liturgical* calendar reflects the seasons and cycles of the year and connects religious services with the events of one's life. Daily reminders of saintly ancestors model Catholic ideals of faithfulness to God.

Mass on Sunday

It is the tradition among Christians to follow the biblical commandment: "Keep holy the Lord's day." This tradition perhaps stems from the sacred story about the creation of the world in which God designates one day for rest. *Mass* is the term used to describe Catholic Church services. It is required to attend Mass on Sunday. (Mass is explained in detail in Chapter 15.)

Indeed, one of the things that distinguishes Catholic practice is the obligation to attend Mass weekly (and on other specified holy days during the year). This requirement is a very serious one, sometimes described as an obligation "under pain of sin," and for years it was considered a grave sin to miss Mass. In past years, no amount of effort was seen as too great for a Catholic to get to church on Sunday. For example, one person who grew up in the 1950s remembers summer vacations in the far reaches of Canada. The family would get up before dawn to travel many miles by boat to attend services at the tiny log church tucked in the pine forest beside the water. Missing Sunday Mass was not an option, even while on vacation.

Even though the percentage of Catholics fulfilling their Sunday obligation has slipped from 60 percent to 40 percent over the past 30 years, it is still higher than the national average for other Christians in the United States. Attending Sunday Mass is still considered an important part of being Catholic.

Parochial School on Monday

Although not as serious an obligation as weekly Mass attendance, going to *parochial school* certainly puts you one rung up on the Catholic ladder. Catholic schools give form and meaning to Catholic life. In addition to the religious values, many people, including some non-Catholics, are attracted by the sense of discipline and order these schools provide.

The Catholic school not only inculcates manners and respect, but also a sense of loyalty and identity to a particular way of life—part of being a special "tribe." The wardrobe is immediately identifiable: boys in shirts and ties and girls in jumpers.

At the high point of the glory days of Catholic parochial education, 1967, almost one out of every two Catholic churches boasted having its own school. Presently, there are 8,100 Catholic grade schools and high schools educating more than 2,600,000 youth—still impressive figures, but clearly on the decline. Yet, Catholic schools today make a strong social statement: More than 26 percent of the students are minorities and more than 13 percent are non-Catholic.

S'ter Says

Parochial schools are private schools run by the parish church.

A Saint for Every Day of the Year

Catholics have a saint and a prayer for every day and all occasions. Saints are people who have lived exemplary Catholic lives and who the Church declares worthy of special honor. Their goodness and holiness have been witnessed by others and ruled on by the Church through a special process. Saints represent particular values. Their lives hold up a model for good living.

Most of us turn to prayer when we need something. For children especially, God can sometimes seem impersonal and distant, like the big boss. To approach him can sometimes feel intimidating. Saints are friends of God who have proven their sincerity and reaped the rewards of their good lives. They are in heaven and have the power to help us. It never hurts to have friends in high places, and it is often smart to have someone speak on your behalf. Saints offer intercession.

Patron saints are believed to have influence over certain situations because of some special circumstances of their lives. For example, Jerome Emiliani, born in 1481, was an abandoned prisoner of war miraculously set free after praying to the Virgin Mary. He then dedicated his life to caring for abandoned children and establishing orphanages. By doing so, he became the patron saint of orphans. Catholics traditionally name their children after saints.

Many Catholics will choose a particular saint as their patron because they feel a connection to this person. It is an understatement to say there are saints for many diverse matters. For example, some watch over funeral directors, gallstones, uncontrolled gambling, garage workers, gardeners, and glandular disorders. Some saints are remembered for particular causes. You call on St. Anthony to help find lost objects; St. Jude is the saint for impossible cases. On February 3, Catholics have their throats blessed in honor of St. Blase, who was a philosopher and a physician. On his intercession, a child was healed of a throat ailment. Since then, those in similar situations have sought his aid.

Saints Preserve Us

St. Maria Goretti, July 6, Patron of Youth

St. Maria Goretti was born on a small farm in Italy in 1890. She was happy, good, openhearted, and serious beyond her years. In her parents' words, she was a prayerful and obedient child. Alexander, a neighborhood thug, began to harass the eleven-year-old Maria. She rebuffed his unwarranted advances. Six months later, he attacked her. She fought off his advances, and when she would not yield to him, he stabbed her. In the hospital, she forgave him and prayed for his repentance. The next day, Maria died of her wounds. She was made a saint in 1950. Apparently Maria's prayers were effective. After eight years of being unrepentant and imprisoned, Alexander had a complete change of heart. He was later released for good behavior and became a lay brother, working for the Church. He testified at the inquiry process that led to Maria Goretti's canonization. She is the patroness of youth, and her story is told to many a Catholic boy and girl in school. Her feast day is July 6.

On October 4, the feast of St. Francis, animals are blessed because he loved all of nature. A well-known prayer of young women seeking husbands is short and to the point: "Dear St. Anne, please send me a man." Everyone has a favorite saint. Perhaps you are named for one—Catholics are given the name of a saint at baptism. Perhaps it is the life story or virtue of the saint that attracts you. When the day of your particular saint comes around, you celebrate it in a special way. Catholic devotion to saints reaches beyond the Church into all cultures. Everyone knows about St. Valentine's Day and St. Patrick's Day, and the ever-popular Santa Claus is old St. Nick, a bishop of Myra who handed out goodies to the needy.

Follow the Rules Every Day

Certain requirements go along with membership in the Catholic Church, and Catholics are often identified by those requirements. Up until about 30 years ago, all Catholics tended to march to the same beat. The statistics on Catholics using birth control and their stand against abortion differed substantially from non-Catholics. That is not true today. Not too long ago, you could spot Catholics in a restaurant at the end of the workweek eating fish on Friday. That's not the case any longer. However, popular images of being Catholic persist, and a vast number of Catholics elect to continue to observe these practices that were rules for many years.

Modern-day Catholicism has begun to shift away from the authoritarian model on which it was once based toward a religion offering many more choices. Many spiritual practices—such as fasting before receiving the Eucharist, and Lenten fasts—that once were mandatory are now optional.

Obeying a set of laws guaranteed your status as one who lived a moral life. This mechanical form of morality is giving way to a creative model. Yet, not every Catholic is comfortable with this change. The old model meant going by the rules to avoid sin rather than exploring options to find the best way to do good. The new model is based on finding a loving response. With regard to Lenten practices, Catholics are now urged to incorporate a spiritual practice into their daily life, rather to give something up as was encouraged previously.

Science and technology present challenges about the basic dignity and right to life that did not exist previously. Examples of today's moral challenges include surrogate parenthood, in vitro fertilization, stem cell research, organ transplants, life support systems, and dying with dignity, along with political/moral issues such as abortion, capital punishment, nuclear weapons, and AIDS.

Epiphanies
In 1995, 49 percent of Catholics considered themselves pro-choice on the matter of abortion, and 41 percent considered themselves pro-life. Three years later, those figures were nearly reversed, with 48 percent of Catholics calling themselves pro-life and 41 percent calling themselves pro-choice. This shift mirrored the national shift in the same direction. Catholic beliefs are not all that different from the culture at large.

Church leaders once made decisions about these types of concerns and the followers simply obeyed the rules. The moral baton has been passed, and people must now work to resolve issues in the context of the Church's faith structures, regulations, and rules. Catholics use prayer, meditation, and reflection on the teachings of the Church as a way of coming to decisions and establishing moral priorities.

Catholic Ways

Community is a major part of what it is to be a Catholic. This sense of community produces a characteristic respect for leaders and tribal laws, including the importance of reaching out to the less fortunate and extending an invitation to all to be included.

Bingo, Raffles, and Pancake Breakfasts

Catholic identity is often connected to eating fish on Friday. However, second to that, it's playing bingo. In order to support their institutions, Catholics conduct many fund-raising events, such as bingos, raffles, and breakfasts, which not only provide an opportunity to raise money but also offer churchgoers some good times and community spirit. Although many think of church as a place you show up on Sunday, most Catholic parishes have a social structure that is as important as worship. In the original communities established in the early years of Christianity, the religion emphasized its identity as a new family for its members. Meetings were held in homes, and meals were shared. Today this tradition can be played out in a different way: the pancake breakfast.

A Catholic may spend all Saturday with the Boy Scouts, for example, as they shop for ingredients, deliver them to the church, set up chairs, cover tables with white butcher paper, wrap silverware in napkins, and stack plates. Bright and early Sunday morning, families of the Scouts are in the kitchen frying sausages, waiting for the crowd to show up. And show up it does. Between the 9:30 A.M. and 11:00 A.M. Masses, long lines of parishioners talk as they wait for their turn at the table. The priest moves in and out, working the crowd.

For Heaven's Sake!

Don't think being a Catholic means blind obedience. Just following the rules won't do it. You have to use your moral judgment.

These regular occasions provide opportunities for parishioners to check up on each other, renew relationships, and meet the new people in the parish. The next week's Sunday bulletin will tell how much money the church raised, but the real reward of such breakfasts is the development and nurture of the church family. This activity and others like it remain a distinctive mark of Catholic communities and strengthen "tribal" bonds.

Charity Away from Home

In addition to supporting the membership of the local parish through social activities, Catholics have always had a strong tradition of social outreach. A common practice among Catholics growing up in the 1950s was to "ransom pagan babies" by saving money to send to foreign missions. Politically incorrect as such terminology is today, the underlying message was about developing a social conscience and reaching out to others. Missions are churches, schools, hospitals, and other services operated by the Church to bring the word of God and serve the poor.

Catholics have always understood that outreach was as much about offering material and physical comfort as it was about religious concerns. The Catholic presence as a social support system is impressive. Catholic hospitals, orphanages, refugee resettlements, homes for the elderly, and immigration services are vital to the world community. Catholic Relief Services (CRS) is a major worldwide charity that has an impressive presence in war-torn areas and provides services to refugees.

Although these major forms of social outreach are a function of the institutional structure of the Church, the individual Catholic participates in outreach by a number of "second collections." Second collections not only support missions, but also educate the parish about charity as a faith expression. This idea is reinforced by sermons on those particular Sundays. A focus on charity encourages Catholics to examine deeper issues of justice. This justice orientation has resulted in significant statements by the leadership of the Church on matters such as disarmament, the economy, ecology, and racism.

Dazzled by Habits, Collars, and Other Funny Clothes

There is no doubt about who the religious tribal leaders are because their dress sets them apart from the crowd. The structure of male leadership in the Catholic Church is hierarchical. At the top is the bishop of the diocese, designated by the color purple. When the bishop presides at Mass, he walks down the aisle holding a large, gold-plated shepherd's staff called a *crosier* and wearing a tall, pointed hat called a *miter* (with a purple skullcap underneath).

The priest's color is black. He is most easily recognized by his Roman collar, which is a white, two-inch-wide band at the throat. If the priest is a monsignor, who is a notch up the ladder, he will have purple piping on his robe and on his collar.

Although the distinctive dress of nuns has become modernized in current times, most people think of them as still wearing the black habits with white collars. Many nuns still choose to wear these traditional outfits. Stiffly starched collars and exotic headdresses caused that venerable religious order, The Daughters of Charity, to be dubbed, "God's Geese."

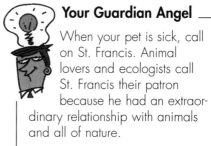

Your Guardian Angel

When your pet is sick, call on St. Francis. Animal lovers and ecologists call St. Francis their patron because he had an extraordinary relationship with animals and all of nature.

Monks' clothes have not changed for centuries. Some Franciscans, for example, still wear brown robes with the characteristic pointed hoods and rope belt just as they and their founder, St. Francis, did in the 1100s. At that time, his clothes were those of a beggar, and he wore sandals, as do the modern-day Franciscans.

Religious dress sets the leaders apart and enchants Catholics, who see them as different from ordinary folks. This manner of dress connotes timelessness and otherworldliness, setting leaders apart from the affairs of the world, and speaks to their spiritual availability.

Marry Another Catholic

The customs and taboos a people follow set them apart from others. For Catholics, one of the strongest customs was marrying their own, and the strongest taboo was against marrying outside the faith. Although this practice is much less important to most Catholics today than it was a generation ago, the point is that to be Catholic means to live up to a particular set of expectations. If a Catholic married a non-Catholic but wanted the Church to recognize the marriage, they had to be married by a priest in a Catholic ceremony and the non-Catholic had to promise to raise the children Catholic. The Catholic spouse was obligated to pray for his or her partner's conversion to the Catholic faith. Today, non-Catholic spouses are not obliged to make any promise, and the bishop may permit these marriages to be held in a non-Catholic church.

In more recent years, Church teaching encourages its members to honor other religious beliefs and practices. Although tribal expectations and taboos still exist in Catholicism as they do in any religious group, the choice to follow them is much more an individual decision. We talk more about these issues in Chapter 18. There is a heartfelt concern among some of the tribe as the laws and teachings are weakened and people become more personally responsible for decisions. They raise the question: Will the tribe survive?

The Classic Definition

Having looked at the beliefs and practices as they play out in everyday life, let's now consider a textbook definition of the Catholic Church. Just what is the Catholic Church? Let's begin with the word "church." The Catechism, the official book of definitions, says church is a convocation or assembly of people, gathered together for religious purposes.

S'ter Says

Ecclesiastical is a term used to describe church stuff. Like "civil" describes things that relate to government, ecclesiastical describes things that belong to an established institutional church.

The Catholic Church is a specific Christian denomination that declares its religious purpose is to follow the teachings of Jesus Christ. The word "catholic" means *toward the whole*. Catholics understand this to mean that God invites all people all over the earth to be a part of one community of followers. "Catholic" also means *universal*—they profess a unified faith, a common set of beliefs and practices. This unity is maintained through an *ecclesiastical* structure, under the leadership of the pope.

There are three primary ways the word "church" is used:

- ◆ Church is a building where members gather for religious services, as in "We went to church to pray."

- ◆ Church describes the group of people gathered together to support one another on the faith journey, as in "The church gathered clothing to aid flood victims of hurricane Camilla."

- ◆ Church is the governing authority that unites all the parishes throughout the world, as in "The Catholic Church has declared a new saint."

The word "catholic" was first used by Ignatius of Antioch around the year 110 C.E. It is from the Greek word *katholikos*, which means "whole." Ignatius was suggesting that the Church should be one body or membership, just as it was when Jesus Christ was alive and his followers were one.

Augustine, a Church theologian writing in the 400s, used the word "Catholic" to mean all membership, present everywhere, as one Church. Over the next several hundred years, the term gradually narrowed to distinguish what was considered the "one true Church" from groups who had separated from it. Today the term "Catholic" refers to the fact that this religion teaches the same doctrine everywhere, and it includes all classes of people.

Now that you've had a bird's eye view of Catholicism, we will go on to look at the variety of people and cultures in the Catholic Church.

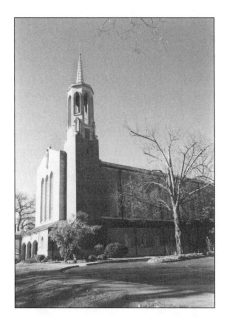

Christ the King Catholic Church, Nashville, Tennessee.

(Courtesy of H. L. [Dean] Caskey)

The Least You Need to Know

- ◆ The Catholic Church is the largest single denomination in Christianity.

- ◆ A major rebirth happened to the Church in the middle of the twentieth century.

- ◆ There is diversity of thought within the Catholic religion.

- ◆ Catholics value and connect to their ancestors through a practice of honoring the saints.

- ◆ Outreach, charity, and social justice are central to Catholicism.

- ◆ Catholicism is both a culture and a religion; it is tribal.

The People: Many Faces, Many Flags

In This Chapter

- ◆ Participate in an old-fashioned Irish wake
- ◆ Visit a Mexican cemetery
- ◆ Attend an African American Mass
- ◆ Facts and figures about the Catholic population

Right from the beginning, the mission of the Catholic Church has been to make the religion available to all people. As we learned in Chapter 1, "Catholic" means moving toward wholeness or, as it is often interpreted, "universal," and that term describes the Church very well. The Catholic Church includes many nationalities and exists in almost every country in the world.

Would I Know One if I Saw One?

The Church draws on a rich cultural heritage. Beyond the stereotypical image of a Catholic lies a diverse palette of cultural expressions of the religion. Particularly since Vatican II, the Church has encouraged all cultures to include their unique music, art, dance, dress, and values in the Mass and other religious services. This process is called *indigenization*. It has resulted in expressions of Catholicism that differ greatly from those that many "traditional" Catholics are accustomed to. These expressions may surprise you.

An Irish Catholic Wake

Perhaps no other cultural tradition carries more mystique than the Irish wake. Although the tradition has changed somewhat, many Irish Catholic families still observe it. In the "old country" of Ireland, the wake took place between the time of death and the time the body was carried to the church, which was usually the evening before the day of burial. Neighboring women gathered at the house, washed the body, and dressed it. They placed a crucifix on the breast and entwined rosary beads in the fingers of the dead one. They also tied the two big toes together, which they believed would prevent the deceased from returning as a ghost. They placed a pair of boots at the feet to help the deceased walk through *purgatory*. The deceased was laid out on a wooden slab supported by four kitchen chairs, and covered with a linen sheet, except for the face, hands, and toes. Candles were lighted and placed in candlestick holders around the body.

S'ter Says

Purgatory had traditionally been thought of as a place, like hell, where people spend time to suffer for their sins and are later released to heaven. More recently, the pope has clarified that purgatory is the condition of the soul of a person who at the time of death has not completely repented for wrongdoing.

The women who prepared the body led the mourning. Muffled sobs or loud wailing, depending on the dimension of the loss, filled the house and could be heard outside as well. For example, a dead parent who left a large family might elicit more crying than the passing of an elderly person. Neighbors would arrive. Their task was to pull the mourners away from the deceased and console them.

In the meantime, men of the village would order the coffin and bring the supplies for the wake: bread, meat, all other types of food, whiskey, stout, wine, pipes, tobacco, and snuff. Once the house was full of visitors, a plate of snuff would be passed around for all to take a pinch. Pipes were filled with tobacco, and food and drinks were served. The clocks were stopped as a mark of respect. All mirrors were turned to the wall or covered. Salt was sprinkled around to ward off the evil spirits who, it was believed, might steal the soul of the dead. The bed of the deceased person was taken out immediately and burned.

A woman attended the corpse by sitting beside it all evening. As the neighbors entered, they made their way to the side of the body, knelt down to recite a few prayers, and expressed sympathy to the family. Guests exchanged remarks about the deceased, and then wandered into another room where food and drink was laid out. The men gathered in the kitchen or outside. The corpse was in the parlor, kept separate from the celebration that was going on. Visitation lasted until midnight. The rosary was recited several times, led by an important person in the community, a teacher, for example. Most of the visitors left at midnight. Close neighbors remained until morning drinking tea or whiskey and relating stories of times passed with the deceased.

The next morning as the body was lifted, the four supporting chairs were kicked over, and the body left the house feet first. The corpse was placed in a wooden box, shouldered by the men, and carried to the church. The family walked behind the pallbearers, behind them came the men carrying spades, and behind them followed the rest of the family and relatives. As they neared the church, the priest approached wearing special death vestments embroidered by the women. Chanting and sprinkling holy water, he turned, leading the way to the church.

After Mass, the coffin was carried to the graveyard and set down into the ground and covered. Mourners passed by, placing a stone on the casket. Relatives and a few neighbors returned to the house where things were put back in order.

The practices of the Irish wake in the United States today are much more refined than those held in the old country. Typically they are no longer held in the home, but in the funeral parlor. But once again, they become major opportunities for the community to gather and tell stories. An Irish funeral home will typically provide a main room for the casket and several anterooms for the gathering of relatives and friends so that they can do the business of mourning and storytelling. In the United States, Irish Catholics pray and say the rosary in the funeral home, and then the body is moved to the church for a funeral Mass and burial the next day.

A Mexican Cemetery

In the Mexican Catholic culture, death is seen as a part of the cycle of life, and it is met with humor and joy as well as sorrow, a contrast to a somber or tragic view of death held by many people in other cultures. The dead are honored during a time of celebration known as the Day of the Dead.

Part of the Mexican celebration of the Day of the Dead includes eating special bread. Here is a recipe:

Pan de Muerto (Bread of the Dead)

(A Folk Recipe)

Mix together:

2 cups flour

$^2/_3$ cup sugar

1 tsp. and a pinch of salt

1 TB. anise seed

2 packages dry yeast

Combine in a saucepan:

$^2/_3$ cup milk

$^2/_3$ cup water

$^2/_3$ cup butter

Set aside for later:

5 eggs

$4^1/_2$ cups flour

Ingredients for glaze:

$^1/_2$ cup sugar

$^1/_3$ cup orange juice, fresh-squeezed and strained

2 TB. grated orange peel

Set oven at moderate (350°F) and pre-heat. Mix dry ingredients, adding warm liquid, and beat. Gradually blend in remaining flour. Sprinkle flour on a board and knead dough for about 10 minutes. Let it rise in a greased bowl, setting it in a warm place for one to two hours, until it doubles in size. Punch dough down and make into shapes of skulls and figures. Let it rise again for about one hour. Bake at 350°F for 40 minutes. Boil the glaze ingredients for about two minutes, and apply to warm shapes.

For Heaven's Sake!

Check your local newspaper to find out if there are any Day of the Dead celebrations in your part of the country. You might find them at a local museum or cultural center. You might use this day to visit the cemetery where someone you love is buried. You might honor them with a small altar at home on which their picture is displayed.

In Mexico and in many parts of the southwestern United States, markets are filled with bright orange marigolds, candy skulls, and figures of skeletons that are sold to grace home altars and graves. Every home, as well as many of the businesses and public buildings, has altars. In some towns in Mexico, the church builds an altar in the town square for "homeless" spirits. Families buy Pan de Muerto (Bread of the Dead) and other edibles that they place on the altar and serve to visitors. This is a time to gather at the local cemetery and clean the graves. Flower petals are strewn between the cemeteries and homes to show the spirits the way. Their favorite foods await them on the altars.

The Day of the Dead is the time for the whole family to come together for a celebration. During these two days, Catholics believe that the spirits of the dead return and spend several hours with the family. The family tells stories to share the events of the past year with the spirit of the loved one.

The celebration serves as a reminder that death comes as a natural part of life. It also dispels fear of death by poking fun at it. Skeletons are used as decorations, and the children play with them. There are sugar skulls to eat with one's own name written on them. A favorite game is to write a humorous obituary of a prominent townsperson and then read it out loud. Everyone enjoys a good laugh. The next day there is a Mass said for the dead.

The Day of the Dead festivities combine pre-Christian and European Catholic traditions. It occurs at the same time of the year as an old Aztec celebration of death, and dates back to pre-Christian Druid religion. Today, in the United States, Catholics honor the dead in two days of religious celebration. On *All Saints Day*, November 1, the souls of the dead who are believed to be in heaven are remembered. On November 2, All Souls Day, the souls of all the departed who are believed to be in purgatory are remembered.

> **Epiphanies**
>
> Marigolds are called **flor de muerto,** or flower of death, and Mexican Catholics use them to decorate altars and graves at the feast of the Day of the Dead. Some say the flowers smell of incense and bones. Others say the cycle of life and death is shown in the marigolds' bright orange color, which is reminiscent of the sunrise and sunset.

An African American Mass

Although African Americans make up a small percentage of the Catholic population in the United States, they have unique celebrations and worship services, and their cultural statement is strong. With the renewal of Catholic liturgy in the middle of this century, particular ethnic expression of the Mass was encouraged, offering quite a contrast to the uniformity that was the custom.

If you attend a Catholic African American Mass, expect to participate in a two-hour ceremony. African American spirituality celebrates a sense of God's presence everywhere, and it is met with a powerful emotional response. Sunday Mass is a family gathering, which brings together the gifts of all the people.

> **S'ter Says**
>
> All Saints Day is also known as the feast of All Hallows. The night before became known as All Hallows Eve, or Halloween. So when the "spooks" come to your door, they are honoring an old tradition as well as having a good night of fun.

Musically, hand clapping, tambourines, drums, and foot tapping set the tone. Everybody—the choir, the readers, the priest, and the servers—all move in the African rhythms that have been held sacred for generations. The congregation praises the Lord with body and soul. Several choirs made up of people of different ages join in song. The music varies from traditional hymns to spirituals to contemporary songs. It is an expression of the African American soul: alive and spontaneous.

The priest delivers the gospel, speaking to the people with drama and passion. He usually talks about things that reflect the lives of the people: black pride, racism, poverty, and social and family values. Responses from the people punctuate the message: "Hallelujah! Thank you, Jesus!" Hands wave throughout the church. At the sign of peace, the time during the Mass when worshippers exchange handshakes, parishioners and the priest move throughout the church, greeting and hugging every member.

Often, members of the congregation furnish the art displayed in the church, which reflects their lives and experiences. African colors of red, black, and green adorn the altar and are worn as vestments by the priest as a sign of black pride and solidarity with the African people. Although the celebration typically lasts two hours, the parishioners generally remain after the service to visit and conduct church business. The rich cultural heritage of the African American people is expressed within the honored traditions of Catholicism.

> **Your Guardian Angel**
>
> Learn more about the African American branch of the Catholic family by reading one or more of the several African American Bibles available. These Bibles feature devotions that celebrate the social experience and cultural heritage of black Christians. Many have illustrations that depict Jesus and the apostles as Africans.

A Rural Catholic Parish

When the Spanish arrived in the area now known as New Mexico, they found the native people living in permanent earth structures made of mud bricks in villages all along the Rio Grande. The Spanish called these settlements *pueblos* and named each of them for a saint who then became the patron saint of the village. Nineteen of these pueblos (considered parishes) still exist, and each one boasts a Catholic church. Over the years, the Native American people have adapted Christian practices and symbols to their native beliefs, creating a unique cultural blend of both religions.

The Southwestern Catholics regularly offer Masses on Christmas, New Year's Day, the Birthday of Mary, and Candlemas Day (the day on which the Church blesses the candles that will be used for the year). On St. Joseph's feast day and on the feast days of the patron saints, these parishes hold native dances and ceremonies as part of the religious feasts. The dances are prayers, not performances. One in particular, called the Deer or Matachina Dance, is a traditional, symbolic animal dance and is performed at San Ildefonso Pueblo on January 23. The night before the feast, *luminarios* (paper sacks partially filled with sand and containing a candle) glow, and their soft light illuminates the village.

In the large plaza, the Catholic church stands at one corner and an adobe-style *kiva*, a traditional native temple, stands in another. Fiesta *vespers* are held in the church at sundown. Afterward, people gather around juniper fires burning in the town square. They hold an all-night vigil in honor of the feast day. The medicine man, in traditional dress, makes a brief appearance, preparing the space for the festivities that will soon follow. Men dressed in traditional Native American costumes drum and chant.

At first light of day, figures appear on the horizon of the hill just outside of the town. They seem to be walking on stick legs, and they wave heavy antlers over their heads. They are the deer men. They descend in a noisy procession accompanied by painted and feathered costumed dancers. The drums accompany ancient songs that honor the deer and buffalo. A Mass is offered in the church as part of the ceremonies.

S'ter Says

The word **vespers** means "evening star," and Catholics use this term to describe prayers traditionally said at sundown. Vespers are the sixth of seven prayers said throughout the day and night in the Catholic Church.

The Taos Pueblo Catholic Church

Taos Pueblo is said to be one of the oldest towns in the United States, populated continuously since the 1400s. The Native Americans in Taos have created a religious system that combines their own deeply spiritual beliefs with Christianity in a way that works for them.

In the center of the village sits the Catholic church that the villagers still refer to as the "new" church, even though it was built more than 150 years ago. The church has no electricity, but is lit by gas lamps along the walls. In the center of the altar in the place where you would usually find a crucifix is a large statue of the Earth Mother. She is dressed in a beautiful satin gown, the color of which changes to match each season. In the spring, for instance, she wears green. The other statues and the altar are draped in a similar fabric. A large casket covered with matching cloth stands at the side of the altar. The casket is where Christ resides and is a reminder to the congregation, which is mostly Native American, that Christ died for them, and it serves to remind the congregation that a lot of them died for Christ, too.

San José de Gracia Catholic Church in Las Trampas, New Mexico.

(Courtesy of Bob O'Gorman and Mary Faulkner)

So Where Would I Find a Catholic?

You can find Catholics everywhere. In its long history, Catholicism has become a global religion. Although there are certain regions that have high Catholic populations, there are no countries that do not include Catholics in their populations.

The Americas: Close to Home

There are several lively Catholic centers in North and South America. The Catholic Church in Canada, for instance, exists under two separate but parallel hierarchies: French-speaking and English-speaking. Overall, Catholics account for more than 45 percent of the total Canadian population, about 13.5 million people. The majority of Canadian Catholics live in the province of Quebec; French-speaking Catholics comprise more than 95 percent of Quebec city's population.

Farther south, Mexico City became a diocese of the Catholic Church in 1530. A very Catholic country, with 125 million Catholics (almost 90 percent of the population), Mexico's unique history makes its relationship with the Catholic Church interesting. In 1820, Mexico won its independence from Spain, which conquered it in 1521. When it overthrew Catholic Spain, Mexico also overthrew the rule of the Catholic Church. The Catholic Church was not allowed to operate with full legal rights after the war of independence. Only as recently as 1992 have Mexico and the Vatican established full diplomatic relations.

Another heavily Catholic nation to the south is Nicaragua in Central America. Its five million Catholics make up more than 80 percent of the total population. The history of Catholicism in Nicaragua goes back to the Spanish conquest in 1524.

Cuba's relationship with Catholicism began in 1514, and Cuba today has a Catholic population of six million, which comprises about 55 percent of the total population. When communist Fidel Castro took control of the government in 1959, he nationalized Catholic schools and expelled more than 100 priests. The visit of Pope John Paul II highlighted the Catholic presence on this island and invigorated the Church. In response to the popularity of this visit, the government improved its relationship with the Church.

The Caribbean nation of the Dominican Republic has been a Catholic country since Columbus arrived there in 1492. Today the Catholic population of seven million represents about 90 percent of the total population, and Catholicism is the state religion.

Your Guardian Angel

Spanish-speaking communities in the United States are served by the Institute of Hispanic Liturgy, a national organization of liturgists, musicians, artists, and pastoral agents. It publishes liturgical material and promotes the development of liturgical spirituality among Hispanics. The Mexican-American Cultural Center in San Antonio, Texas, is a center where Hispanic leadership is developed and cultural materials are available.

The largest Catholic population in the world lives in the South American nation of Brazil. First celebrating the Mass in 1500, Brazil is a country in which a significant number of clergy and lay Catholics have been active in movements for social reform. More than 144 million Catholics, making up 80 percent of the population, call Brazil home.

Because of the tightly woven relationship between the colonial governments and the Church in Latin America, politics and religion have remained closely connected. As a result, many Church leaders, both clerical and lay, take an activist role in the politics of Latin Americans.

Compared with Brazil, the United States has a relatively small Catholic population of just 62 million people, or 22.5 percent of the total population. Here's where most U.S. Catholics live:

◆ Los Angeles has 4 million Catholics, making up 38 percent of the population.

◆ Chicago has 4 million Catholics, representing 41 percent of the population.

◆ New Orleans has almost 500,000 Catholics, making up 37 percent of its population.

- Boston has two million Catholics, representing 53 percent of its population.

- New York City has almost 4 million Catholics, which is 45 percent of its population.

- El Paso has 630,000 Catholics, which represents 79 percent of the population.

The Rest of the World

Here is a random selection of Catholic populations around the world.

Country	Catholic History	Catholic Population	Percent of Population
Belgium	Introduced to Catholicism as early as the year 325. It was a Catholic land from about 730.	8.1 million	79 percent
Czech Republic	Christianity spread by the martyrdom of Prince Wenceslaus in 929. Continuousparish system since the thirteenth century.	4.3 million	41 percent
Croatia	Christian since the seventh century. Independent republic in 1991, formerly under Yugoslavia.	3.8 million	72 percent
Iceland	An island republic first visited by Irish hermits in the 700s. Catholicism was officially accepted about the year 1000.	4,000	1 percent
Ireland	This island received Catholicism from St. Patrick in the middle of the 400s.	4 million	77 percent
Poland	Presence of Church from later ninth century. First bishop 968. Suffered through two world wars and the rise of Communism. Birthplace of John Paul II.	34.6 million	96 percent
Philippines	The Spanish introduced Catholicism in 1564.	66.8 million	82 percent
Uganda	Catholic missionaries arrived in 1879. In its short history of Catholicism, 22 of its first converts were martyred. These people were declared saints in 1964.	10 million	45 percent

Country	Catholic History	Catholic Population	Percent of Population
Australia	The first Catholics in the country were Irish convicts sent by the British.	5 million	28 percent
Israel	It all began here.	94,000	1.5 percent

Worldwide Catholic Population by Continent

There are one billion Catholics in the world, or about 18 percent of the world's population. Nearly one in every five people in the world is Catholic.

- Africa: 12.9 percent

- Asia: 11 percent

- North America: 23.9 percent

- Central America: 85.5 percent

- South America: 87.3 percent

- Europe: 27 percent

- Oceania: .8 percent

As you can see, Catholicism comes in many colors, shapes, and sizes. There is also a great diversity in how it is practiced. Paradoxically, the diversity of the Catholic Church is sustained by following the same leadership—the office of the pope in Rome. In the following chapter, we'll look at some well-known Catholics who represent a wide range of individual spiritual expression.

The Least You Need to Know

- There's no such thing as a typical Catholic.

- The Catholic Church is a cultural mixing bowl of color, music, art, dance, and tradition.

- Inhabiting every region of the globe, Catholics comprise nearly one in every five people.

- The Catholic Church has diversity that is maintained through a common allegiance to the office of the pope of Rome.

Chapter 3

Catholicism: It's a Big Tent

In This Chapter

- Faith in action
- Getting involved
- Living in the moment
- Charity and militancy
- Forgiveness: doing right

Spirituality is the heart of religion. Spirituality is both the way we believe and how we express our beliefs through action. As we know, the Holy Spirit moves freely and refuses to be shut up in a box. So one of the things every organization must inevitably struggle with is maintaining corporate identity and dealing with the individual expression of this identity through its members

While the Church still uses its authority to call members on the carpet if they are perceived to be too far out of line, it primarily uses censure only when the person is acting as a representative of the Church in an official way, and only when his or her comments are public and seen to be a threat to the people's faith. Within the Church there is much individual diversity of expression—many ways people put action to what they consider important values. As in secular politics, spiritual expression includes voicing opposition to the authority of the institution. Our political history as well as religious history generally has given its artists and creative thinkers a wider berth in this regard—or maybe those creative souls are willing to take more risks.

We have selected some well-known modern day Catholics who represent a variety of spiritual positions. Beneath their unique spiritual expressions lies a communal base, a common ground upon which they all stand. For a church that is often characterized by an image of strict uniformity, these diverse approaches to Catholic life show that quite the opposite is true. In this chapter, we'll explore that diversity with you by introducing some famous Catholics and their contributions. Over the last three years, some readers have let us know how strongly they disagree with the spirituality of some of the folks we've chosen, and an equal number have said just the opposite. That proves our point. Uncomfortable as disagreement can be, you will hear us say throughout the book, "catholic" means embracing the whole—in itself, a challenging spiritual task. The Church is a living institution—held together by both people and institution. The institution has shaped history, and history continues to shape the institution.

From Bishop Sheen to Dan Berrigan

Two very important characteristics of the Catholic Church are its logical side and its passion for justice. During the 1950s, the leadership of the Church focused on the reason side of the equation; in the 1960s, there was a radical shift into the realm of social justice. The Catholic leaders of these times reflected these trends.

The Good Ambassador

In the mid-1950s, a common topic of conversation at work and in the grocery store centered on Bishop Sheen's talk the evening before on his phenomenally popular television show, *Life Is Worth Living*. Mingling religious ideas with secular life, Sheen had an audience of millions. He became a kind of pop culture icon for the Catholic Church and established himself as the best-known and most popular Catholic in 1950s America.

Through his television show, he moved Catholicism into mainstream American life, as well as redefined the Church within the larger society by telling Catholic stories that had continuity both with other Christian communities and with Judaism. He made the social and political world of Catholics part of the American mainstream. His aim was to mediate between rather than divide denominations. He was responsible for many people choosing to become Catholic: Claire Booth Luce, Henry

Ford II, and violinist Fritz Kreisler, among others, converted to Catholicism under Bishop Sheen's influence.

Sheen's approach to faith always provoked thought. He popularized philosophy. He took on a mission to preach against the evils of atheistic communism, and he focused Catholic spirituality in the 1950s on that mission. Working with his sharpest tools—logic, reason, and humor—he was the premier anticommunist.

In England, Sheen had met and was inspired by G. K. Chesterton, a Catholic who held weekly radio broadcasts in the 1930s on the BBC touting the Catholic Church as the center of reason in the modern world. Sheen saw reason as the best cure for family and social difficulties and the breakdown of morality in the culture. In his carefully crafted talks, he made philosophic reasoning work for the world, not just for the university.

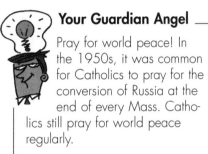

Your Guardian Angel

Pray for world peace! In the 1950s, it was common for Catholics to pray for the conversion of Russia at the end of every Mass. Catholics still pray for world peace regularly.

Religious Outlaw

Much to the surprise of both Catholics and the public, the turbulent 1960s revealed a liberal, activist side of Catholicism. For many, the spiritual awakening during this time continued through the next several decades and is still a vital part of their religious expression. At the center of this awakening was Daniel Berrigan, a *Jesuit*. He was one of the first clerics in the Church to draw the media's attention to what he considered to be an important moral dimension to the political protest against the United States' role in the Vietnam War. In 1968, he and his brother Philip, also a priest, stormed the building housing draft records in Catonsville, Maryland. Using homemade napalm, he torched hundreds of files within 10 minutes.

He was sentenced to three years in prison, but he went underground for several months until federal authorities arrested him on Block Island, located off the coast of Rhode Island. He used his time on the lam to publicly teach and lecture, showing up at various antiwar protests. His every move made sensational news. He even managed to slip out a side door at Cornell University after giving a speech to a crowded auditorium with FBI agents sprinkled

S'ter Says

Jesuit is the common name for a religious order of priests and brothers in the Catholic Church. The official name is the Society of Jesus, and hence the initials after a member's name are "S.J."

throughout the audience. What was the trick that allowed him to pull off such a feat? He hid in a larger-than-life papier-mâché puppet of an apostle. After 18 months in prison, Berrigan was paroled in 1972.

Dan Berrigan's radical leftist beliefs created great controversy within the Catholic Church. He pushed the Church's theory of just war to the limits, and many say he pushed it past the limits. The Church has a theory that limited war is acceptable only under a certain set of circumstances. We talk more about this in Chapter 19. Berrigan has written that "the death of a single human being is too great a price to pay for the vindication of any principle."

To this day, the political activism of Dan Berrigan and others is seen by some Catholics as a positive outgrowth of the true principles of the Church and by others as totally inappropriate radicalism. Indeed, those who are incensed by such politics consider clerics like the Berrigans to be traitors hiding behind the religious collar. Those who agree with their motives and their methods consider them to be brave saints. Regardless of where you come down on the issues, the Berrigans focused Catholic spirituality in the 1970s on confronting injustice.

Epiphanies

Martin Sheen, who plays the U.S. president in the NBC series *The West Wing*, recently addressed the Los Angeles Religious Educators Congress and said for Catholics being a peacemaker is not a role, but a calling. In a *Los Angeles Times* interview (Teresa Watanabe, March 2, 2003), he said, "Spirituality is not safe. It leads you down uncharted waters. If it didn't cost you anything, you'd have to question its value." Sheen professes belief in a "non-violent Jesus," dedicating himself to the cause of peace and spirituality. His first protest was at the age of nine when he organized caddies to strike for wages. He opposed the "Star Wars" missile defense program with the Berrigan Brothers, marched with Cesar Chavez, and protested U.S. aid to El Salvador's right-wing government. Born Ramon Estevez, he connects with the poor and oppressed with whom he shares a common history. He works in soup kitchens and visits prisons and juvenile detention halls. Sheen attends Mass regularly, and carries a rosary in his pocket.

From Cesar Chavez to Clarence Thomas

Although theology and Church beliefs are often defined in the Vatican chambers and universities, the average Catholic learns his religion in the home and transmits it by the way he lives in the real world. Two Catholic men, both from poor beginnings, developed very different ways of expressing their spirituality and helping their fellow workers during two different political eras (one in the 1960s and one in the 1990s). One chose the way of self-reliance, and the other chose community action.

Grapes of Wrath

Cesar Chavez was born in 1927 in Yuma, Arizona. His family worked its small farm until 1939, when unpaid taxes forced them into the migrant labor stream. The year 1952 found Chavez working in a lumberyard in the San Jose barrio called Sal Si Puedes, which means, ironically, "get out if you can." There he met a Catholic priest who worked with migrant farm laborers. This priest immersed Chavez in the social activism side of the Catholic Church, particularly the pope's teachings on the right of labor to organize. Chavez also came under the influence of a community organizer who taught him how to apply the Church's social philosophy to the community around him.

In 1962, Chavez began organizing California's migrant workers into a union. His strategy was economic boycott. In 1968, Chavez led a boycott of table grapes. The response of the Church and community groups in boycotting supermarkets who carried nonunion grapes resulted in contracts for the union for 85 percent of the table grapes market. Although his methods were political and economic, Chavez espoused a fundamental and absolute affirmation of the dignity of the human person and a firm commitment to nonviolence. He based his philosophy on the teachings of Jesus, St. Francis, Gandhi, and Martin Luther King Jr.

Your Guardian Angel

Look for the union label on all your grapes! Chavez and the many others who worked with him fought a long and hard battle to get better pay and working conditions for the migrant laborers who picked crops. They formed a union. You can join in the support of the dignity of the workers by buying union grapes.

Chavez himself was a deeply religious man, thanks in large part to the influence of his mother. Fasting and daily Mass accompanied his protests. He named one of his largest marches a *peregrine* (pilgrimage, a religious term signifying the holy walk of a people). In addition to the union banner and the United States flag, he and his followers carried banners depicting the Mexican Lady of Guadalupe and the Aztec eagle. His actions on behalf of justice gave new meaning to the concept of spirituality to his generation and the ones that followed. This spirituality consisted of a profound conviction of the absolute value of each individual, a firm commitment to nonviolence, and untiring work on behalf of the dispossessed.

Dirt Poor in Georgia to the Supreme Court

Despite growing up in poverty and facing racial oppression, Clarence Thomas, who is now a Supreme Court justice, took advantage of the sacrifices that his family made for him to receive a good education. Thomas's family sent him to Catholic schools whose teachers taught him that with hard work and self-reliance, he could overcome the obstacles of discrimination. In the end, he would, but the road was never easy. Although he entered a Catholic seminary, he dropped out because of intolerable racial remarks made by classmates at the time of Martin Luther King Jr.'s death.

Epiphanies

There are many biblical references to the poor, and it is clear that the God of the Scriptures loves the poor, but not the condition of poverty. God's people, especially the leaders, are given the responsibility to care for the poor. They are a necessary part of bringing God's reign, and are a constant reminder that God's will is not yet fully accomplished. Their presence reminds the faithful of the responsibility we have for one another. The help of the poor is the hope of the Church.

Thomas attended the Jesuit Holy Cross College, graduating cum laude, and was elected to Alpha Sigma Nu, the Jesuit national honor society. From there, he received his law degree from Yale University, and then went on to serve the government in legal positions under conservative Republican administrations at the state and national levels. He was nominated and approved as a justice of the United States Supreme Court, October 16, 1991.

Thomas's conservative views on public policy evolved from his grandfather's self-reliance and independence. His grandfather was anti-welfare, holding that, "Man ain't got no business on welfare as long as he can work." Thomas's independence of spirit and strong belief in hard work and self-reliance articulate an American belief that everyone can succeed and speak to the spiritual belief that humans can overcome the odds and excel.

From Bing Crosby to Madonna

Spirituality does not exist solely in the realm of academics, intellectuals, and politicians. Indeed, for most modern Americans, the media has the greatest effect on our religious imagination. Music, television, and film provide much of today's spiritual message. During the 1950s, some singers sang songs about the importance of living right. During the 1990s, the message was a different one, but it was a message just the same. Two of the most popular singers of these eras had one thing in common: being Catholic.

The Good Priest

Harry Lillis, better known as the singer and actor Bing Crosby, was born in 1903 in Tacoma, Washington, graduated from Gonzaga High School in Spokane, and received an honorary doctorate from Gonzaga University. His first recording was "I've Got the Girl" in 1926, which began his career as a top pop vocalist for the next 50 years. He starred in 55 films and earned three Academy Award nominations. He won best actor in 1945 for his portrayal of a priest, Father O'Malley, in *Going My Way*.

Going My Way was the top box office draw of the year, and the film earned nine nominations and seven awards, including the award for Best Picture. The immensely popular film and its songs made a deep impression on the Catholic imagination in the 1940s and on the public's imagination of Catholics as well.

Your Guardian Angel

Rent a video to catch a glimpse of the social history of the Catholic Church. Many films made in the 1940s and 1950s portray the pre-Vatican II Catholic life in America. Check your video store classics.

In this magical version of priestliness, Father O'Malley solves every problem great and small, from the finances of St. Dominic's to the threat of street gangs—and he does so with a cool nonchalance. The film's presentation of a nonsexualized version of male power created a paradigm for priests for generations to come. His black clerical dress topped with a straw hat created a mixture of religious restraint and jauntiness. Father O'Malley was a priest and a real okay guy at the same time.

The spirituality of the film and the music celebrates a hope-filled belief that right acting and right thinking will produce right results. To borrow from the old poem, "God is in his heaven and all is right with the world." The spirituality is focused on the accomplishment of goals as a virtue rather than the journey. It shows a world in which reason, order, and logic will prevail. Virtually everyone knew the songs from this movie by heart, particularly "Would You Like to Swing on a Star?" The songs spoke of delayed gratification while exploring the basic themes of self-improvement through education—this "you can do" thinking was both personally and culturally uplifting.

Wild Child, Modern Mystic, Existentialist

Madonna Ciccone, the rock star better known by her single first name, Madonna, was born near Detroit in 1958. She was the third of eight children. Her mother died of cancer when she was six years old, creating a void she has never filled. She says of herself, "I always considered myself an utterly motherless child." And probably no

S'ter Says

Mystic comes from the Greek word meaning mystery. The term describes a person whose prayer life includes meditation from which he or she gains spiritual understanding and new insight.

For Heaven's Sake!

Sexuality and spirituality are not two separate things. Although many religious thinkers over the ages have tended to separate the physical body from the spiritual soul, we know today that it is all one. Today's spirituality mends the soul/body separation that has characterized much of the Church's teachings. Today's spirituality sees sex as very much a part of the human story and therefore part of the human spirit.

one, including Madonna herself, would argue that she also was a wild child. In the tradition of the Church *mystics* who explore that void through prayer and meditation, Madonna explores it through her art.

Madonna earned a scholarship to study dance at the University of Michigan. After two years, she struck out for New York and joined acclaimed dance troupes. She switched from dance to music, and in 1982, Warner Brothers signed her to a recording contract. Since that time, her music, her videos, her books, and her public appearances have created a great deal of controversy and made her one of the most well-known and provocative performers of the time.

In creating her art, Madonna enters and moves through a forbidden world where eroticism and religion meet. She brings the darkest part of her soul forward and puts it in the public's face. Is her work discomforting? Yes. Interesting? Absolutely. Fear-producing? Of course. Her work is also, by its very nature, distasteful to some and intriguing to many. Her uncharted expedition to the dark waters of the human soul dramatizes how dangerous truth can be, and she dares us to explore it. She reminds us that joy and pain are intertwined.

Madonna's Catholicism is reflected throughout this mystical journey. She says about Catholicism, "it's very sensual, and it's all about what you're not supposed to do … forbidden stuff … the confessional … heavy green drapes … stained glass windows … the rituals … the kneeling … there is something very erotic about all that."

Madonna grew up in what she calls a "very strict" Catholic household, and she attended Mass every morning before school. At the age of 17, she broke away from this regime, leaving both her family and the Church behind. However, she soon found out that "The Church pretty much stays with you. I have never stopped being a religious person." Today, she is drawn back into the silence of the Church. The candles, the incense, the smells, and the rituals of Catholicism are grist for her videos. The Church offers her a real sense of solitude and tranquility. In her own words, she says, "I reek of Catholicism."

Before a performance begins, you can find Madonna in a circle with her dancers and crew, leading them in prayer, urging them to treat one another with compassion, kindness, and respect, reminding them that there is already too much pain in the world. Madonna believes that prayer is found in the way we relate to one another.

Mystics don't take others' word for what God is like or what spirituality is. They go inside and find it for themselves. Madonna is an artistic mystic. She relentlessly explores through her music and dance. The mystical message Madonna offers for the millennium explores the erotic connections among sexuality, spirituality, and religion. For her, the Church is both very sensual and mysterious. Her spirituality is of self-reflection. In her corner of the Catholic tent, you can find people who are looking within, redefining God and religion, and forging a new relationship between them.

Your Guardian Angel

Try composing your own prayer. For a long time Catholics relied solely on prayers they memorized as children. Today's Catholics are more adventurous in their prayer life, creating prayers to fit the moment.

From Mother Teresa to Mother Angelica

Representing a spirituality of volunteerism with a clear vision and a clear message, Mother Teresa demonstrated a long tradition of serving the poor. A very different approach is Mother Angelica's concern for the loss of religious clarity in times of confusion and change.

A Saint in the Making

Agnes Gonxha Bojaxhiu, better known as Mother Teresa, was born in 1910 in Macedonia. She was the daughter of an Albanian grocer. By the age of 12, Agnes had developed a special interest in overseas missions and realized her vocation was to help the poor. She joined an order of sisters that ran schools in India. For 17 years, she was a teacher and principal at a Catholic high school in Calcutta. Responding to a spiritual call to serve Christ in the slums among the poorest of the poor, she asked the pope for permission to start a religious order devoted to this charity. Although she began with 12 members, there are now over 4,000 Missionaries of Charity worldwide.

Mother Teresa's first act was to establish the Home for Dying Destitutes. Finding a woman half-eaten by maggots and rats lying in front of a Calcutta hospital, she sat with her until she died. It was then that she made her mission the act of caring for the human cast-offs who the world wanted to forget. During her lifetime, she created a global network of homes for the poor from Calcutta to New York, including one of the first hospices for AIDS victims. Today, her order operates more than 500 missions in more than 100 countries.

Mother Teresa, winner of the Noble Peace Prize, worked with the dying in the streets of Calcutta.

(Courtesy of Photofest/Icon Archives)

Mother Teresa's life and work is not without controversy. In 1994, British television produced a documentary entitled *Hell's Angel: Mother Teresa of Calcutta* that accused her of taking donations without questioning where they came from, including the likes of Haitian dictator Jean-Claude Duvalier. Inside the Church, there were concerns that Mother Teresa did not bother to examine the social causes of poverty, but instead chose to direct her attention to bandaging up the victims of an unquestionably oppressive system of economics and politics. An article raising the question of the difference between charity and justice led with the headline "Mother, Why Are They Poor?"

Your Guardian Angel

Take a stand! The issues of charity and justice are closely linked. Many find they are drawn to work at the level of charity by taking care of the poor. Others are drawn to seeking justice through changing the social structures. They are two sides of a coin.

In her defense, Mother Teresa did not see that it was her job to ask "Why?" Her spirituality was based in charity and love rather than politics. It was of the heart, not of the mind or intellect. She was charismatic, and she crossed all political boundaries. More important, she commanded the attention of all religious denominations and all classes of people. She inspired hundreds, both highborn and common, to join in her work at her hospice for the dying in India.

Radical and Right

The largest religious cable broadcasting network in the world, Eternal Word Television Network (EWTN), resides in Irondale, Alabama. With more than 1,600 affiliates, the network reaches 54 million homes in 34 different countries. The dynamo in front of the camera is Mother Angelica, a nun dressed in full Franciscan habit who, in best *Tonight Show* style, interviews a different guest every night. The network also broadcasts a Mass every day, complete with the Latin *Tantum Ergo* (a favorite Catholic hymn) as well as a live recitation of the Rosary. The network also features a full series of lectures by priests and showcases Catholic events, especially the travels of the pope.

The mission of Mother Angelica is to present strict, hard-line Catholic belief. She is determined to uphold and highlight a traditional, conservative understanding of Catholic doctrine, culture, and discipline. She not only sees her mission as one of bringing the "true light" of *faith* to the common person, but she also wants to expose the liberal tradition of Catholicism, which she considers negative. She attacks personal speculation about religious beliefs. She cites what she considers to be liturgical abuses and doctrinal deviations. According to Mother Angelica, "The faithful need a solid and unambiguous doctrinal foundation upon which to build their Christian lives." She believes that she serves the people who are marginalized by the current trends in Catholicism.

S'ter Says

In the Catholic religion, **faith** has many aspects. One meaning of the word "faith" describes the way in which a person responds to Christ in their daily life. Faith is the presence of God within (grace) and the interior presence of the Holy Spirit moving the heart and turning it to God.

Mother Angelica's philosophy and approach have upset members of the Catholic leadership, but she fails to back down even in the face of some bishops, whom she characterizes as "wolves, preying upon people brought up to obey." To one angry bishop who questioned, "By what authority do you operate?" she responded, "I own the network."

The spirituality she represents appeals to those desiring a solid and unambiguous doctrinal foundation on which to build their religious lives. They are tired of questions, and they want answers. She expresses a side of Catholicism that has always been present in the church, albeit somewhat uncomfortably so: absolute certainty. It responds to a basic human condition that longs for assurance.

From Ted Kennedy to Pat Buchanan

Catholics also express and experience their spirituality through both political ideals and practical politics. Indeed, Catholics have never been strangers to the political arena. Entering the ring from two different corners are two Catholic born and bred politicians, each with a passion and a mission, each playing their mission out in very different ways.

The "Bleeding Heart"

Senator Edward M. (Ted) Kennedy was born in Boston in 1932, the youngest of the nine children of Joseph and Rose Kennedy. He was first elected to the U.S. Senate in 1962 when he took over the seat formerly held by his brother John F. Kennedy, who had been elected president of the United States in 1960.

Epiphanies

John Fitzgerald Kennedy, the only Catholic elected to the presidency of the United States, broke an enduring stereotype of Catholics as being unthinking, superstitious, clannish, and separatist. Prior to Kennedy, a Catholic could not expect to sit in the chair that administers the highest office of the United States, indeed of the world. One of the key battles to overcome was the lack of public acceptance and the fear that Catholics could not be trusted because of their loyalty to the pope and to Rome. In a memorable 1960 speech before the greater Houston Ministerial Association, Kennedy called upon the best in Catholic intellectual thought to show that good Catholic beliefs did not interfere with good citizenship.

For more than 35 years, Ted Kennedy has stood for the best in Democratic liberalism, consistently supporting social programs for the poor, such as welfare, universal health insurance, and civil rights. In these efforts, he represents a Catholic tradition of social consciousness.

For Heaven's Sake!

Do something, because faith without works is dead! Catholics have a strong belief in putting their faith into action. You might even want to show a commitment to living your faith in the world by running for political office.

Today, Ted Kennedy has become the patriarch of the Kennedy clan and continues to lead this powerful political and cultural family. The media spotlight that continues to shine on Ted Kennedy and his family reveals not only the family's glamour and influence, but also reveals their Catholic faith, particularly at times of tragedy and death.

As prominently displayed as his banner of liberalism and Catholic family heritage is his personal vulnerability. He reveals a Catholic characteristic of embracing what it means to be human by asking forgiveness and understanding. The Kennedy legacy has revealed a Catholic spirituality of endurance, faithfulness, loyalty, and of giving back to society, as well as human frailty.

Fighting for the Soul

Patrick Buchanan was a speech writer in the Nixon administration, and during the Reagan administration he rose to political prominence as a TV commentator on *Cross-Fire* where he represented the conservative position. In the 1990s, he ran for the Republican presidential nomination and attracted the most right-wing element of the party. He holds an uncompromising stand against abortion. Additionally, he is a proponent of United States isolationism in such matters as international trade agreements. In a recent book, he stated that the United States should not have joined the Second World War.

Born in 1938 in Washington, D.C., Patrick Buchanan did his undergraduate work at Catholic Jesuit Georgetown University before serving as a senior advisor in the Nixon administration. He attended four summits with President Nixon, including the one held during Nixon's historic trip to China in 1972. During the 1980s, Buchanan served as President Ronald Reagan's communication director, which allowed him to attend the Reagan-Gorbachev summit in 1986.

Buchanan's skills as a communicator expanded when he became a syndicated columnist. He has published several books in which he expresses his conservative political philosophy. He has been a formidable candidate for nomination at the Republican presidential convention for several years.

Buchanan focuses his politics and his faith on his moral principles. "There is a religious war going on in this country," he explained. "It is a cultural war as critical to the kind of nation we shall be as the cold war itself, for this war is for the soul of America." The religious war to which he refers is between people who hold very different ideas of what is sacred and what is ultimately true and good.

Buchanan is a deeply conservative Catholic who was imbued early on with the religion of his stern father. In his own words, he calls himself a "soldier in the war for America's soul." He is determined to preserve the American worker's standard of living by protecting the borders against illegal immigration. He favors trade protection. He is a pro-life conservative. He calls forth a strong populace base.

Buchanan presents a militant Catholic spirituality in the tradition of the Jesuits by whom he was educated. His spirituality encompasses respect for law and order, adherence to certain principles, and esteem for the rules. He presents a clearly drawn line between right and wrong. He is against privilege and identifies with the plight of the common man.

This chapter has shown how a variety of Catholic beliefs are played out in the public arena. The next chapter explains more about how these beliefs are shaped. You'll learn about the Church's structure and guiding principles.

The Least You Need to Know

- Spirituality is the way we express our values to the world.

- Coming from the same Catholic principles, there is a wide variety of spiritual expressions and a wide variety of people to express them.

- Spirituality plays out not only in different forms of religious practice, but also in a variety of arenas: politics, music, and the nightly news, for example.

- There is elasticity to the Church that allows for a diverse membership, but the Church also has a strong commitment to unity and common ground.

Chapter 4

The Vatican: The Church That's a Country

In This Chapter

- ◆ Meet the Church's leader
- ◆ Learn whether the pope can make a mistake
- ◆ Explore Vatican City
- ◆ Understand the Church's organizational structure

The Catholic Church is a study in contrasts. It consists of more than a billion members throughout the world, but it has the ability to speak with one voice. It is made up of thousands of parish churches, yet these houses of worship all follow the same faith. How is this unity accomplished? That's the focus of the chapter, which starts by introducing you to the leader of this massive organization: the pope.

Just Who Is the Pope?

Pilgrims from all over the world travel to fill the square outside this man's window every day and wait hours to catch a glimpse of him. Dignitaries from every country request an audience with him. On his worldwide visits, millions of people gather to cheer and witness his presence. Seldom does a week go by that there isn't international coverage on his whereabouts or pronouncements.

Who is the man who commands this much attention? It is the pope, the leader of one of the biggest and most complex organizations in the world: the Catholic Church. In Latin, the word *pope* means "papa" or "father." The pope is the spiritual father or head of the Church. He is the focal point of unity among its members and has diplomatic relations with every country in the world.

Pope John Paul II was the first non-Italian man elected pope in almost 500 years. This popular pope comes from Poland.

(Courtesy of Photofest/Icon Archives)

All of this attention and power in the hands of one man may seem extraordinary. It may seem less so when you consider that Catholics believe that he is the physical representative of Christ on Earth and that his office is the storehouse for the truths of the Church.

Since the ninth century, *pope* has been the designated title of the bishop of Rome, *Vicar of Christ*, a title the pope shares with all other bishops, referring to the claim that they stand as representatives of Jesus Christ and act with his authority in the Church. Catholics have traditionally claimed St. Peter as the first of the Roman bishops and trace the succession of popes in a direct line back to this apostle. They believe the authority of the Church rests on the commission given by Jesus to Peter found in Matthew 16:18–19:

> You are Peter, and upon this rock I will build my church, and the gates of hell shall not prevail against it. I will give you the keys of the kingdom of heaven, and whatever you bind on earth will be bound in heaven, and whatever you loose on earth will be loosed in heaven.

New scholarship explores the Church's historic connection to St. Peter, making the matter of linear descent a debatable issue. There certainly was no formal papal office in the first centuries of the Church. Originally, apostolic described the early communities that were formed during the lifetime of the apostles. Only one of the six of these first communities was in the West—Rome. The other five—Antioch, Philipi, Ephesus, Corinth, and Thessalonica—were in the East. These large communities were geographical centers for groups of smaller communities. Official teaching depended on what the larger communities, representing the smaller ones, agreed on. This process developed as a way of securing the teaching of Jesus, keeping it separate from the personal revelations that were popular in communities—which had a more charismatic character. The early Church communities mentioned above were not hierarchal, but operated by the principle of agreement.

Issues of identity arise at critical junctures throughout history, and are responded to differently at different times under different leaders. Popes have a strong influence on the Catholic religion; however, not all popes interpret Church law the same. Different popes place different emphasis on how much collegiality there will be during their reign—popes leave a personal mark on the Church. Traditionalists cry heresy when questions about long-held, treasured beliefs are questioned; and progressives push the boundaries. Just where that balance is struck depends on who's in the Vatican sitting on St. Peter's chair.

Catholics believe that the office of the pope is infallible. Papal *infallibility* means that the pope cannot make a mistake when defining a doctrine, or formal belief, of faith or morals for the Catholic Church. The pope speaks infallibly only when he claims to be using his authority according to the established process, when he speaks in regard to official beliefs of the Church, and when he speaks about articles of faith or morals.

Today, as well as throughout history, questions arise from the people and from the clergy that eventually stir the theological waters. Issues are debated, and those that make it up to the top are finally wrangled out among the bishops. The pope eventually rules on what is acceptable and what is not. We talk more about this process in Chapter 17.

The pope works with the bishops in a shared decision-making process called collegiality. The pope, in communion with the bishops, is the highest teaching authority of the Church. Together they make up what is known as the *magisterium*, which is the Church's teaching authority. Collegiality is one of the most important pronouncements of the Second Vatican Council. It turned upside down the old way of looking at Church hierarchy.

In reality, the pope seldom uses his power of infallibility. The last time an infallible doctrine was declared was in 1950 when Mary's assumption into heaven was proclaimed an article of faith, which Chapter 12 discusses in more detail. In other words, rather than being some mystical power of the pope, infallibility means the Church allows the office of the pope to be the ruling agent in deciding what will be accepted as formal beliefs in the Church.

S'ter Says

Infallibility is a gift of the Holy Spirit to protect the Church's teachings from error. Papal infallibility is the Church belief that when the pope defines a doctrine of faith and morals that must be held by the whole Church, the Holy Spirit grants him infallibility. **Magisterium** is from the Latin word for "teacher" and refers to the teaching function of the Church.

What's His Address?

The pope, bishop of Rome, resides in the Vatican. Vatican City is the smallest sovereign state in the world, covering an area no larger than 108.7 acres. The Basilica (or church) of St. Peter is the focal point of Vatican City and is the mother church of Catholics and the largest church in the Christian world. About 1,000 people live in the Vatican, and another 4,000 work there every day. In addition to being the home of the spiritual leader of the Catholic Church, the Vatican has an enormous library of sacred books and a vast collection of religious art.

S'ter Says

The **College of Cardinals** is a collection of cardinals that offers counsel to the pope, elects new popes, and governs the Church in between popes. There are approximately 130 members of the college.

At one time, the small city-state of the Vatican comprised several states in central Italy known as the Papal States. Although the size of the Vatican is now greatly reduced, it still maintains the accoutrements of a large country—for example, having formal diplomatic relations with 182 countries, plus the United Nations. The Vatican issues its own stamps and coins, and there is a remnant of the papal army represented by colorful Swiss guards who maintain a vigil that at least symbolically guards the pope.

St. Peter's Basilica in Rome, Christianity's largest church, is the Mother church of Catholics.

(Courtesy of Alinari/Art Resource, New York)

Smoke Signals

The pope is elected by the *College of Cardinals* during a council called to order no sooner than 15 days and no later than 20 days after the death of his predecessor. A cardinal is a bishop of high rank appointed by the pope. All cardinals under the age of 80 are eligible to take part in the election. Election is permitted by a voice vote, but the usual manner is the tradition of secret ballot.

Ballots that fail to produce the necessary two-thirds majority are burned in a small stove inside the counsel chambers, along with straw that will make dark smoke. The dark smoke announces to the waiting crowds that a pope has not yet been elected. When the necessary majority is acquired, the ballots are burned without straw, producing the white smoke that signifies election of the pope.

The Big Church and the Little Church

At the base of the organizational structure of the Catholic Church is the local diocese, which is under the direction of the bishop. A diocese is a group of parishes under the direction of the priest, called the pastor. Provinces, or archdioceses, join dioceses throughout a country. They are under the direction of an archbishop. Over all of this is the central administration of the Church, the Vatican.

Structure	Geographical Divisions
Pope	Vatican
Cardinals	Provinces or Archdioceses
Archbishops	Dioceses
Bishops	Parishes
Priests	

The parish is the whole Church as far as most Catholics are concerned. The various types of parishes include large suburban parishes, poor inner-city parishes, urban neighborhood parishes, and rural parishes. Additionally, ethnic parishes serve new immigrant groups in their native languages and customs.

At the center of a typical parish, you'll find the church itself, which is often named for a saint, such as St. Michael or St. Elizabeth. Various styles of architecture are represented in churches across the country from tiny little chapels to huge cathedrals. The church is the center of Catholics' faith life. They attend Mass there on a regular basis, they are married there, their children are baptized there, and family funerals take place there.

Next to the church, you might find a rectory, or house where the priests live. Many Catholic parishes also have parochial school buildings. Parochial means "belonging to the parish" and is used to describe Catholic schools. If this school is conducted by a religious order of sisters, there will probably be a house for them on the parish property, too.

Another building you might find in a parish today is the parish center. This center is where the people gather: scouts, the Knights of Columbus, and prayer and scripture study groups. The center also provides a place for lectures or films. It contains the parish library and a full kitchen where weekly parish dinners happen. Some parishes use their center for homeless people in cold weather and offer the use of the building for community meetings such as Alcoholics Anonymous. Many parishes offer complete sports programs, so you might also find a basketball court and sports field for baseball or football.

Rules and Regulations

As we discussed in Chapter 1, the basis of Catholic morality is life in Christ, and the primary knowledge of Christ comes from the Scriptures. This morality involves, among other things, the observance of the Ten Commandments. In the fulfillment of these commandments, special emphasis is placed on what is called the twofold law of love of God and neighbor, which Jesus said was the most important commandment. Other important sources for Catholic teaching come from the Bible's Sermon on the Mount, where Jesus pointed out the basics of moral behavior.

The Ten Commandments

Collectively, the Ten Commandments are also called the Decalogue, which comes from the Hebrew phrase meaning "10 words." Taken from the Old Testament Scriptures Exodus 34:28 and Deuteronomy 4:13; 10:4, the Ten Commandments are believed to have been given to Moses by God on Mount Sinai.

For Heaven's Sake!

Don't get caught up in the rules! Remember, love is the first law, and motivates one toward good. "You shall love the Lord your God with all your heart, with all your soul, with all your mind, and all your strength." (Mark 12:30, Deuteronomy 6:5) Likewise, "Love your neighbor as yourself." This is the basis for the whole moral law.

The requirements set down in the commandments are not unique to the Jewish people; they can also be found in other texts of the ancient Near East. Nowhere, however, are they so clearly and concisely stated or expressed so personally and as intimately as having been given by God as laws to live by. As described in the Scriptures, God gives the Ten Commandments directly to the Jewish people in his own voice. It is said that they were written by God's own hand on two tablets of stone, the first containing the commandments that directly refer to our relationship to God and the second governing our relations with one other. The Ten Commandments constitute the foundation of Christian law and ethics.

Here are the Ten Commandments as they appear in Catholic teaching:

1. I am the Lord your God. You shall not have strange gods before me.

2. You shall not take the name of the Lord thy God in vain.

3. Keep holy the Sabbath.

4. Honor your father and your mother.

5. You shall not kill.

6. You shall not commit adultery.

7. You shall not steal.

8. You shall not bear false witness against your neighbor.

9. You shall not covet your neighbor's spouse.

10. You shall not covet your neighbor's goods.

The Ten Commandments play an important role in a Catholic's life. One of the first tasks of a young Catholic is not only to memorize them, but also to understand what it means to live by them.

The Six Precepts

In addition to the Ten Commandments, the Church has six rules, called *precepts*, for membership:

1. Attend Mass on Sunday and on the six other established holy days of obligation.

2. Observe the fast days as established by the Church.

3. Confess any grave sins at least once a year.

4. Receive Communion at least once a year, preferably during the Easter season.

5. Contribute to the support of the Church.

6. Observe the Church's laws concerning marriage.

The 1,752 Canons

From the very earliest times up to the present, the Church has compiled a complex system of rules called *Canon law*. These rules are compiled and reviewed regularly. As of the current revision, there are 1,752 Canon laws. Canon law functions in service of the people. It defines internal structures and describes the rights and obligations for its members in relationship to their religious life. Canon law provides the operational principles and structure of the Church.

S'ter Says

The term **canon** comes from the Greek word **kanon**, which means a "measuring stick of life." It is used to describe the rules governing the Church, or Church law.

Canon law affects the everyday Catholic by regulating how the faith should be lived. For example, Canon law regulates how and when marriages take place, sets the rules for fasting, states the requirements for church attendance, and establishes the process by which leaders and teachers are chosen. For the most part, Canon is Church law, not moral law, which is contained in the Ten Commandments.

The Beatitudes

The spirit of the Church laws is expressed in the Beatitudes, which lie at the heart of the Church's teachings. They provide examples of Jesus' love for the people and provide a map for Christian life. They sustain hope and proclaim the blessings and rewards of life in Christ. The Beatitudes teach that true happiness is not found in riches or well-being, fame, power, or material achievement, but in our good relations with one another. The following Beatitudes are taken from the New Testament of the Bible in Matthew (5:3–12) and are Jesus' teachings from the Sermon on the Mount:

- Blessed are the poor in spirit, for theirs is the kingdom of heaven.

- Blessed are those who mourn, for they shall be comforted.

- Blessed are the meek, for they shall inherit the earth.

- Blessed are those who hunger and thirst for justice, for they shall be satisfied.

- Blessed are the merciful, for they will receive mercy.

- Blessed are the pure in heart, for they shall see God.

- Blessed are the peacemakers, for they shall be called the children of God.

- Blessed are those who are persecuted for righteousness' sake, for theirs is the kingdom of heaven.

- Blessed are you when people revile you and persecute you and utter all kinds of evil against you falsely on my account. Rejoice and be glad, for your reward is great in heaven, for in the same way they persecuted the prophets who were before you.

As we began this section, we pointed out that Jesus came to bring us the law of love that he expressed as love of God and neighbor. And this is the basis of all Catholic rules and regulations. With all of the laws and even the Beatitudes, the individual ultimately stands responsible for his or her actions.

Conscience, Virtue, and Grace

Catholics believe that moral conscience is present at the heart of a person, assisting in each person's choices by approving those that are good and denouncing those that are not. Catholics believe that when you listen to your conscience, you hear God speaking, and that voice is your conscience. The Church teaches that it is important for every person to be present enough to hear and follow the voice of the conscience.

Prudence results when we choose actions that conform to what our inner moral compass suggests. The Church teaches that we have the right and responsibility to make our personal moral decisions. A person must not be forced to act against what he or she determines to be the right action for themselves. The Church also requires that the conscience be educated and sees this as a lifelong process.

A virtue is the habit of doing the right thing. Virtues are developed through practice. In addition to the virtues we develop, there are virtues that are characteristic of our soul, the Holy Spirit of God within us. They lead us toward good and help steer us away from things that will harm us. The Church calls these faith, hope, and love. These three virtues support us in the development of all others.

- By faith we intuitively understand that there is a God and actively seek to know and do God's will.

- Through hope we desire God regardless of the circumstances of our life at any given moment.

- Charity allows us to experience God's love, love ourselves, and love our neighbors.

Here are four key virtues we acquire through practice. They develop our inner compass:

- Prudence is following our "inborn" common sense.

- Justice is respecting others' rights and working for the common good.

- Courage ensures firmness in our pursuit of good.

- Temperance moderates our pursuit of life's pleasures, assuring balance.

Catholic spiritual life is formed in acquiring and honing these virtues. Catholic spirituality involves the practice of them in everyday interactions in the community with family, friends, and the society as a whole. To be a practicing Catholic means following these principles to the best of one's ability. The emphasis is on practice! The Church is the people of God striving to live according to spiritual principles. To do this requires grace.

There are many definitions of grace. In the broadest sense, you could say grace is the gift of God's faithfulness to us. It is reflected in God's constant and unfailing love for us even when we fail to get it exactly right.

We've looked at the heart of the Catholic Church and the organizational structure that holds that core in place. In the next chapter we'll look at a shift in this organizational structure and some new challenges Catholics have been given to live their religious principles.

The Least You Need to Know

- The Catholic Church expresses its unity through the office of the pope.
- The doctrine of infallibility is seldom evoked.
- The Church is administered from a central headquarters with a worldwide network.
- The local parish is the seat of activity for Church members.
- The Church bases its moral laws on the Bible and tradition.

The '60s: Seeds of Revolution

In This Chapter

- ◆ The Catholic Church throws open the windows, and a lot of people catch cold
- ◆ Galileo forgiven: faith and science talk
- ◆ The Church gets a new name
- ◆ The 1960s: the sexual revolution and Church politics
- ◆ How we lost a few of our favorite things

Before getting any further into our exploration of Catholicism, let's take a look at what many consider the most formative event in the life of the Church, the Church council called Vatican II. Although you'll learn much more about the history of the Church in Part 6, right now it's important to understand this pivotal event that took place in 1960. During that year, the pope summoned the Church leaders to begin to reform and update Church policy and practice. Although many leaders of this revolution viewed this as a golden time for Catholicism, others resisted, preferring that it never happen.

Young Catholics have most likely heard their parents and grandparents refer to being a pre-Vatican II Catholic almost like they belonged to a totally different Church. While the Church itself is the same Church, the experience of living through that change was monumental. The 1960s molded a new Catholicism—it set the Church in a new direction, and not everyone wanted to go that way. The tension between liberals and conservatives that began at that tumultuous time in history continues to characterize Catholicism today. This chapter tells the story behind this tension.

The Stillness Before the Storm

Just as the bland sweetness of Wally and Beaver Cleaver represented the surface of America of the 1950s on television, growing up Catholic in the 1940s and 1950s had a similar innocence and order to it. It probably involved attending a Catholic grade school, which was most likely located right across the street from the public school. Other than a brief encounter at the crosswalks, the Catholics didn't mix much with the public school kids. Catholic schools were named things like Visitation, Incarnation, and Resurrection. They had their own ball teams, textbooks, library, and, of course, their own church.

Girls wore blue jumpers and white blouses for school. They kept their heads covered while they were in church, pinning on a tissue with a bobby pin in the absence of a proper scarf or hat. They always wore dresses to church and wore gloves on Sunday. Boys wore shirts and ties to school and suit coats to Mass. The sisters who taught school wore starched habits and long ropes of rosary beads that jangled (giving fair warning of their arrival) as they glided down clean, waxed corridors. The answers to all moral questions were neatly contained in the *Baltimore Catechism*, the little paperback book that held all the rules and beliefs of the Church. Every Catholic child memorized it.

The popular images of this time in history were merely a thin veneer covering issues of social, political, and spiritual unrest that emerged in the 1960s. For better or worse, the world would never be the same again.

Vatican II: A Radical Departure and a Rebirth

Characterized by Woodstock, political assassination, and America's seemingly endless and controversial involvement in Southeast Asia, the United States of the 1960s was in the throes of cultural and social revolution. As if the political questions being raised were not enough to shake the very ground of being, the Catholic Church chose this moment to come together to raise many of the same issues in the arena of religion that were being asked in the political world. Pope John XXIII, elected in 1958, called a *council* to update the Church and to open it up to the modern world.

Ironically, Pope John XXIII was regarded as a transitional pope, someone who would fill the space between Pope Pius XII, a scholarly and aloof man, and the next strong leader yet to emerge from the ranks. Although Pope John XXIII's time at the helm was indeed short—an all-too-brief five years—the Church soon realized this very energetic man with an instinctual connection to the people and a far-reaching vision for the Church was to occupy a particularly crucial place in history. He was possibly the most popular pope of modern times, perhaps of any time, and he consistently demonstrated such warmth, simplicity, and charm that he won the hearts of Catholics, Protestants, and non-Christians alike.

The Second Vatican Council, or Vatican II, opened on October 11, 1962. By this time, the pope knew of his own fatal illness. His death came more than three years before the council ended. The council continued, and the changes that were effected are still unfolding, influencing, and changing the face of Catholicism in the post-modern world.

S'ter Says

A **council** is an assembly of representatives from the whole Church called together by the pope to make decisions. The preceding council, Vatican I, was held from 1869 to 1870.

Lighting the Council Fires

As the Catholic Church moved into the second half of the twentieth century, it found itself in perhaps the most powerful position in its history in terms of numbers of followers, influence on the international scene, and respect. And yet, it found itself too often locked in old battles, fighting against false beliefs and confronting the influence of Protestantism; these issues had been the focus of past councils. Vatican II was the first council called for the purpose of initiating change from within rather than combating heresy, pronouncing new dogma, or marshaling the Church against hostile forces.

More than 900 million Catholics were living at the time of Vatican II, making it the world's largest religion. The revolution begun by Pope John XXIII with Vatican II put into motion ideas and forces that would come to affect a major portion of the world's population.

Church councils are rare; there had been only 20 in the nearly 2,000 years of Catholic history. Simply by summoning Vatican II to renew the Catholic Church, Pope John caused a major impact. Although councils are rare, revolutions in Catholicism are even more rare. The last one of any consequence happened more than 400 years ago and resulted in a major split when Protestantism was born (you'll read more about that in Part 6). In the 1960s, Pope John's historic mission was aimed at revitalizing the Church's spirit, not only to bring the mother church of Christendom into closer touch with the modern world, but also to end the division that had fractured Jesus' message for four centuries.

By stretching out his hand in friendship to non-Catholic Christians, calling them "separated brethren," Pope John made history. He showed us that the walls that divided Christians could be broken down and that it was possible to align the Church's life with the worlds of science, economics, and politics. Under his leadership, the Church was to become more Catholic and less Roman, making a huge leap toward that distant and elusive goal of Christian unity. The Church's revolution brought it into the world and onto the front pages of newspapers, often outranking the secular concerns of the day. The Church's monolithic and absolutist character was forever changed.

Your Guardian Angel

Do justice, love kindness, and walk humbly. A prophetic message from the past given to the Jewish people by Micah is as pertinent to the Church today as it was then: "What does Yahweh require of you but to do justice and to love kindness, and walk humbly with your God?" (Micah 6:8)

Prophets have always existed and are part of religious history. We know their names from the Old Testament: Isaiah, Amos, Micah, and Elijah to name a few. Their voices often alerted the leaders to look where they were going; they cried out for change. In the 1960s, a revived spirit cried out for change and was heard. Perhaps the most revolutionary mark of Vatican II was the tacit acknowledgement of Catholicism's modern-day prophets. It recognized that those who had difficulty with the Church, even those who had left it, may well have had good reasons for doing so.

Pope John invited the bishops to Rome to speak freely. He encouraged what he called "holy liberty." The bishops, who had long considered the pope as the sole source of power and authority in the Church, discovered that they, and not just the pope, constituted the leadership of the Church.

Pope John's unique gift of perception opened the way for change in the Church. Most Protestant and Catholic clergymen and theologians, as well as many non-Christians, agree that Catholicism is a much stronger, more effective, and more positive influence today than it was when World War II ended. The Church had finally begun to recognize and address the problems that had cut off much of its communication with the modern world.

Epiphanies

A story that captures the spirit of the changing times in both the arena of politics and religion involves Jacqueline Kennedy's visit to Pope John XXIII. He asked his secretary what would be the proper way to address her. The secretary replied, "Mrs. Kennedy or just Madame, since she is of French origin and has lived in France." Waiting in his private library, the pope went over the options, trying to decide which one to use: "Mrs. Kennedy, Madame; Madame, Mrs. Kennedy." Then the doors opened, and the First Lady entered. He stood up, extended his arms, and cried "Jacqueline!"

In the five years of the council, Church leaders pounded out a new definition of the Church and a new way for the Church to relate to the world. Catholics, who for more than 500 years had come to believe that the eternal truth resided only inside their religion, now found themselves in a new Church that admitted that truth may indeed be found elsewhere as well. A major goal of Vatican II was to create a Church less focused on its institutional structure and more focused on its people. Vatican II invited all Church members to become full participants. The institutions and structures of the Church, triumphantly expressed in buildings, fine liturgical vestments, and the reigning hierarchy, gave way to a Church of the people.

Indeed, the old understanding for the Church had focused on its institutional structure. It was guided by the image of the Church as "the perfect society," self-sufficient, independent, and separate from the world around it.

Vatican II heralded a new model of Church. "People of God" became the defining image. This image is from the Old Testament covenant relationship between God and his creation. The council understood this image to refer to the whole human race. Internally, the Church shifted from seeing itself as a hierarchical institution that organized and ruled people to Church as a community of people with co-responsibility. The hierarchy still exists as the organizational structure, but its purpose is to empower the people.

Externally, the Church shifted from seeing itself as the only means of salvation to developing its relationship to the larger community—the whole people of God. It began to take down many of the walls that existed between Catholics and the rest of the world. In doing this, the council examined the following areas of the Church:

- Liturgy: the prayers, songs, and the Mass
- The role of the laity: from spectators to participants
- The role of the Church in the political and social world
- Religious freedom and respect for other spiritual paths

Core issues of Catholic identity were fundamentally challenged; the rules changed. We'll take a look at these changes next.

The Altar Rail Comes Down, The Priest Turns Around

For years, the priest faced the altar with his back to the people while he said Mass. A railing separated the people from the front of the church where the altar was located. No one other than the priest or the servers was allowed near the altar except in rare times during particular ceremonies.

To the average Catholic, the changes in Church ceremony after Vatican II were nothing less than shocking. The altar was moved forward. The priest now faced the people during Mass. The altar railing that separated him from the people came down. Members of the congregation walked up to the altar and read the Scripture at Mass. The Mass was no longer said in Latin, and during the service, members of the congregation turned to one another with a handshake. Even the priest left the altar to walk up and down the aisle and greet members of the crowd by name.

Like the culture around it, the Church reflected the atmosphere of informality that characterized the 1960s. Worshippers wore jeans to church, and sometimes folk music played in the background. In some churches, you might have seen a bareheaded young woman and her longhaired boyfriend carrying the Communion bread and wine up to the altar to be consecrated. Perhaps most striking of all, the priest handed the bread of Communion to Church members rather than placing it on their tongues. In the past, only the priest, whose hands had been consecrated, was allowed to touch the Communion host.

In addition to these very public changes, Vatican II also fundamentally altered the organizational structure and authority of the Church. It began to move away from a highly centralized power structure into which it had evolved over the years to a broader power base. Prior to Vatican II, a "father-knows-best" attitude prevailed throughout the Church. All decisions were made on the highest level by the pope and handed down to the bishops, who handed them down to the priests. In the parish, the priest made the decisions and handed them down to the people. Now, in the post-Vatican II Church, laity were invited to participate in Church governance through *parish councils*.

S'ter Says

A **parish council** is an elected group of Church members whose job it is to plan and secure the resources for the mission of the parish.

Councils were also established to work with the bishop at the level of the diocese. These councils were composed of both priests and lay members of the Church. In a similar fashion, at the highest level of the Church in Rome, the bishops worked in a more collaborative relationship with the pope than had ever existed in the history of the Church. Although many people still tend to think that the pope holds all authority in the Catholic Church, in reality Vatican II changed all that.

The Rosary Gives Way to the Bible

Another crucial change for Catholics after Vatican II involved the role of Scripture. Prior to Vatican II, the Church did not emphasize it. In fact, Catholics were cautioned against private interpretation of the Bible and instead were directed toward the Catechism, a book of Catholic teachings. Over the years, this lack of emphasis had translated into an unofficial, but very definite, lack of biblical familiarity among Catholics. They found they had to bow to the expertise of the Protestants when it came to quoting chapter and verse. After Vatican II, Catholic education began to focus on Scripture rather than on memorizing the Catechism.

In addition to the changes in the Mass, popular devotions changed dramatically after Vatican II. Prior to 1960, Catholics might celebrate the month of May by marching through the streets of their town in a rosary procession; after 1960, Catholics were more likely to gather in the church for the Liturgy of the Word, commonly called a Bible Vigil—a ceremony in which the Bible is prominently displayed on the church altar and the service consists of reading and reflection on biblical texts.

Today, many people choose to share their faith in small gatherings in homes during which they read from the Scripture, a tradition that departs radically from what had always been the "Catholic way." One result of Vatican II was to promote the concept of God's presence in the sacred word of the Scripture as well as in the sacraments, where the emphasis had been placed prior to the council.

Church as Listener

Perhaps the most revolutionary concept to come out of Vatican II identified the Church as a listener. Its new relationship to the culture demanded that it pay attention to the times—a direct reversal of what had been centuries of Church antagonism toward cultural changes. The pre-Vatican II Church's position was to inform culture, not to learn from it. The new direction was to listen and learn.

The world of science was one of the arenas upon which this age-old conflict clashed most dramatically. People lived in two worlds that did not connect: the world of matter (science) and the world of spirit (religion). The rift between faith and science was wide and deep. Remember that it was the Catholic Church that placed astronomer Galileo, one of the greatest scientists in history, under house arrest back in the 1600s.

In the spirit of Vatican II, the Church issued a long overdue apology to Galileo, recognizing him posthumously as a great scientist and removing their sanctions against him. Although this apology may seem totally ridiculous to the present-day reader, it represented a complete change in Church policy. Popes, like kings and queens and many other political and religious leaders, traditionally did not—and still do not—apologize. To do so showed a complete change of protocol. This expression alone represented one of the most remarkable and revolutionary changes of identity that resulted from Vatican II.

Epiphanies

Galileo (1564–1642), Italian mathematician, physicist, and astronomer, was one of the first men to emphasize scientific observation rather than philosophical speculation to learn how the natural world works. He invented many instruments and was able to apply mathematical laws to determine that the earth moves around the sun rather than the reverse, which was the popular belief of Europeans and the Church of his day. He was brought before the Church authorities in 1633, where he was forced to take back his teachings and was put under permanent "house arrest." As he left the court, it is said he murmured, "and yet it moves," referring to the earth's revolution around the sun.

Science and Faith Reach a Compromise

One of the ways the Church has begun to reflect its new role as listener is by paying attention to some of the visionaries in its ranks. Pierre Teilhard de Chardin, who lived from 1881 to 1955, was a visionary who bridged the gap between the two worlds of science and religion in his writings and teachings in modern time. He was a paleontologist and a French Jesuit theologian.

Chardin's writings ended the mind/body duality for both the secular world and the Church. His positive vision helped to set aside conflicts between religion and science and inspired the spiritual journeys of many men and women in search of a worldview that is beyond the conflicts of dualism.

Chardin told of his two loves, one for the world of matter known by science and the other for the world of spirit revealed by faith. He said that at one time they were like two stars that divided his allegiance. Through his love and devotion to both science and religion, he eventually reconciled the two, seeing matter and spirit as indivisible and evolving together.

From the Sanctuary to Selma

Change and surprise characterized the voice of the Church's visionaries in the 1960s. In opening the Church's windows, the Vatican Council gave the green light to active involvement in the world's culture. The world the Church stepped into was one in massive turmoil over almost every social issue: race relations, international relations, and sexual relations. Every hot topic was being examined from the Catholic perspective.

Suddenly, priests were joining protest marches and advocating for social and political change from their pulpits, activities almost unheard of in the United States before the 1960s. This radical confrontation with the real world was often shocking to the image many Catholics had held of their clergy. But Catholics had to learn to overcome their shock during the six o'clock news on television, where they saw not only young people dragged off and arrested by police, but also their beloved nuns, priests, and bishops.

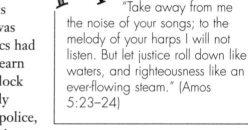

For Heaven's Sake!

"Take away from me the noise of your songs; to the melody of your harps I will not listen. But let justice roll down like waters, and righteousness like an ever-flowing steam." (Amos 5:23–24)

Although Catholics always had a strong presence in charitable work through building institutions to care for the poor, aged, and orphans, they began to look below the surface to examine the very structures of the society. There was a shift in focus from charity to justice. Rather than simply helping the poor, Catholics began to push their leaders to look at the causes of poverty.

Indeed, after Vatican II, a profound change came in the way that Catholics practiced the faith. Social justice became a core focus—to be a Catholic was to be involved with the issues of the world and to seek justice. In the United States of the 1970s and 1980s, Church leaders talked, wrote, and preached about peace, justice, racism, poverty, nuclear war, and ecology. In Latin America, clergy seeking justice for their people risked torture and death to challenge what they considered to be unjust authorities. Previously, the voice of the Church restricted itself to spiritual matters or Church rules, but Catholics in great numbers overcame the dualism of faith in God and the desire for change in the world after Vatican II.

Your Guardian Angel

Use inclusive language. Rather than saying someone is a non-Catholic, acknowledge his or her denomination by referring to the person as a Methodist, Baptist, or Lutheran, for example.

Ecumenism: Catholics' Relationship to Other Christians

Ecumenism is a term that describes the oneness of all Christian believers. Prior to Vatican II, Catholics divided the world into two distinct categories: Catholics and non-Catholics. After Vatican II, in the spirit of John XXIII, they referred to other Christians as "separated brethren," a marked shift in the Church's belief that it was the only true church. The Vatican Council declared that the term *church* included all Christians, not just those who practiced the Catholic faith.

Ecumenism has very practical consequences for average Catholics. In the past, the Church placed major restrictions that discouraged marriage between Catholics and others. For example, if a Catholic married a Protestant, the service was often performed in the privacy of the priest's office rather than in the church. Very little public recognition was given to "mixed" marriages.

Today, not only can mixed marriages take place in the sanctuary, but often the priest also invites the partner's minister or rabbi to witness the ceremony. With the permission of the bishop, the marriage can take place before another Christian minister or rabbi. Today it would not be uncommon for the partner of a Catholic to participate in Catholic Church services and functions, including being a member of the parish council.

Many commissions and dialogues have been established to improve communication and bring about greater understanding among all Christians. Preachers from other Christian faiths have been invited to speak in Catholic churches. Cooperative ventures in social justice efforts such as "Room at the Inn," a program to house homeless people in the winter, bring many churches together to open their doors to each other as well as to the needy.

Expanding Interfaith Relationships

Vatican II not only took a more open stance toward other Christians, it also reached out to mend relationships with other faiths, particularly the Jewish people. For example, the Church removed prayers from the liturgy that implied Jewish culpability in the death of Jesus. For centuries past, these prayers and the attitudes they represented contributed to anti-Semitism on the part of the Catholic Church and many Catholics.

In addition, efforts have been made in the religious education curriculum to revise prejudicial stands toward the Jews and to teach about the Hebrew faith. This new attitude toward the Jewish faith has led Church scholars to encourage a deeper respect for sacred Hebrew literature, referring to the Old Testament as the "Hebrew

Scriptures" or "The First Testament." These writings are seen as important to the faith on their own, not just as an introduction to the "Christian Scripture" or New Testament.

A major effort of the Church since Vatican II has been to reevaluate the Catholic Church's role in the Holocaust. Pope Pius XII has been criticized by many for failure to take a stand against Nazi Germany's persecution of the Jews. Pope John Paul II has spoken out on this matter, offering an apology to the Jewish people for the Church's conduct. Clearly, much more investigation and explanation is necessary before any moves toward reparation can be meaningful.

In addition to attempts to repair relations with the Jewish people, the Church has reached out to Muslims, meeting with Muslim leaders and delegations in Rome and around the world. The pope has spoken to large gatherings of Muslims in Morocco, Indonesia, Mali, and elsewhere. Formal dialogues have been held from time to time with Islamic organizations to promote good relations between the Christian world and the Islamic world.

Within Catholic monastic life, the hand of friendship has been extended to members of Buddhism, Hinduism, Confucianism, Taoism, and Shinto. Buddhist and Catholic monks have joined together in practices and studies of the mystical life. Thomas Merton, a popular twentieth-century Catholic mystic, met with Buddhists to talk about the mystical life and social justice issues during the Vietnam War before he died in Thailand in 1968.

We Throw Open Heaven's Gate: Religious Liberty

Vatican II issued "The Declaration on Religious Liberty." In this important paper, the council declared that all people have the right to religious freedom. This means that all men and women should be free from coercion regarding religious choices. No one can be forced to act against personal convictions in choice of religion and practices.

This document held particular importance to U.S. Catholics, because the United States was the first Western country to be constitutionally founded on religious freedom. During his campaign for president, John F. Kennedy made it clear that Catholics championed this separation.

"The Declaration on Religious Liberty" also had a profound effect on Catholic missionary activity. No longer was it acceptable to disregard the beliefs of others. As a result, mission efforts have been much more concerned with sharing beliefs rather than imposing the Catholic faith.

Conscience Reigns Supreme

Catholic teaching has always taught that you must obey your conscience. Vatican II strengthened that stand. Prior to Vatican II, Catholics generally would seek and follow the advice of their priest in moral matters. Since Vatican II, they have been urged to search their own hearts and minds to come to their own informed moral decisions.

For Heaven's Sake!

Take responsibility for yourself and your actions. The post-Vatican II Catholic Church emphasizes personal responsibility for moral decisions, which means that you cannot simply follow directions. You must seek instruction, pray and meditate, and make your own moral choices.

Here is an example of the way the changes might be seen in the life of everyday Catholics. Theresa (let's call her) was a Catholic mother during the 1960s. She and her husband had been practicing the rhythm method, the only means of birth control condoned by the Catholic Church. They have three "rhythm" babies: the youngest is six weeks old, and the oldest is five years. Theresa and her husband do not feel they can bring any more babies into their family, and a life of celibacy together does not seem like a good idea to either of them.

This devout Catholic couple decided to practice birth control, even though they knew they were on dangerous theological grounds. One Saturday afternoon, Theresa brought her moral dilemma to the confessional. Laying the situation out to her confessor, she found that her decision had already been made. Rather than confess birth control as a sin, she informed him of her choice to use it. Surprisingly, the priest sympathized with her. He understood the difficulty of the choices Theresa had to make and encouraged her to pray, search her heart, and only then to make a moral decision about what she believed was God's will for her in this situation. The priest would not have offered such advice before Vatican II. Before Vatican II, it would have been very difficult to find a priest who would offer such advice.

A Painful Side Effect of Vatican II: Loss of Tradition

Although Vatican II brought positive changes to the lives of Catholics, many of the faithful felt a deep loss as traditional and beloved beliefs and practices were altered or dropped altogether in an effort to update the Church. In addition, the Church lost some of its uniqueness. Once so clearly defined by their difference from other faiths, and characterized by separation from the world, many Catholics were left with a vague sense of the Church being "less Catholic" than it used to be.

Mea Culpa, Mea Culpa, Mea Maxima Culpa

Mea culpa, mea culpa, mea maxima culpa is Latin for "I am sorry, I am sorry, I am heartily sorry." It was a line from a prayer said at the beginning of the Mass, but it also spoke to the sentiment of many Catholics who regretted the loss of their Latin prayers. Until Vatican II, all Catholics heard the Mass in this ancient language. Thus, it was possible to attend Mass in any Catholic church in the world and hear the prayers said in exactly the same way. In the pre-Vatican II days, uniformity was the rule, and diversity and individuality were discouraged.

Because Church music was written and performed in Latin, when the language of the Mass was changed to the vernacular, meaning the language of the country, the music changed, too. Music had been a central gathering point for many in the Church, and as the choir was deemphasized and the congregation was urged to sing, many felt a painful loss of their religious identity.

For example, before Vatican II, choir practice was a very special ritual. One woman recalls going to choir practice every Wednesday evening and Saturday afternoon for as long as she could remember. The whole week revolved around Sunday morning. "We arrived at 9:30 in the morning to prepare for the 11 o'clock service," she reminisces. "We didn't finish until at least 1:00 in the afternoon. Afterward we went to lunch together. There were other events, too—potluck suppers, parties, and the annual choir picnic. Lifelong friendships were formed—it was all about the music and about the religion."

Then suddenly everything changed with Vatican II. "They came in and took our sheet music and carted it away, stacks and stacks of Gregorian chant. We had spent years collecting it, and it was all destroyed in a day. The choir was replaced by a fellow with a guitar in the front of the church who tried to lead us in songs not only that no one knew, but songs many of us believed did not belong in church."

Until this point, the Catholic Mass relied heavily on the Gregorian chant and classical music in addition to hymns and psalms sung in Latin. Their loss after Vatican II was deeply felt by many Catholics. Churches are now following what they believe the council recommended by making a sincere attempt to update the songbooks and having congregational singing.

Fasting and Fish Rules Relaxed

One of the more derogatory insults flung at Catholics was the nickname "mackerel-snappers." This moniker derived from the fact that Catholics were forbidden to eat meat on Friday to honor the day Christ died—a rule most Catholics held as absolute to their identity.

Another pre-Vatican II dietary rule involved the fasting requirements for Lent and in preparation for holy days. Basically, a Catholic could not have more than one complete meal on the specified days. In a similar way, Catholics observed a complete fast from all food and water from midnight until they received Communion the next morning. There were many sad stories of the little boy or girl who made a mistake on First Communion Day and took a drink of water from the fountain as his or her classmates gathered in the school for the procession over to the church. Doing so meant he or she couldn't receive Communion with the class, which was not only embarrassing but meant that he or she couldn't share in the joy of the celebration of the day. Often, nuns would tie off all the drinking fountains with white rags to avoid such mishaps.

Your Guardian Angel

Make Friday your fish day. Every Catholic over the age of 50 knows at least 10 recipes for tuna casserole. Here is a favorite one: Mix one large can drained tuna fish with one can cream of mushroom soup, add two cups cooked macaroni or rice, and top with crushed potato chips. Bake for 20 minutes in a moderate oven. Deeeeeelicious!

Today, such dietary restrictions have been relaxed so that Friday meat abstinence is urged only during Lent (the 40-day period of preparation for Easter) and fasting before Communion can be limited to one hour before reception. Some wonder if this relaxation does not take the "Holy" out of "Holy Communion," make Catholics forgetful of the Lord, and diminish the celebration of Easter.

Shifting Prayers and Practices

Several practices once considered an integral part of the Catholic faith and ritual either have been eliminated or their importance has been diminished. Let's take a look at some of the practices that once characterized a Catholic:

- ◆ **Spiritual bouquets.** A spiritual bouquet is the name for a gift of prayers that one might pledge to say as a present for another person. They could include 10 Hail Marys, 10 Our Fathers, 15 Glory Bes, 1 Rosary, 5 Masses, and 5 Communions. The one offering the bouquet writes down the prayers that will be said and signs the piece of paper as a promise.

- ◆ **Scapulars.** Still popular with some Catholics, these brown and white pieces of cloth worn around the neck looked like oversized postage stamps connected by two strings. Representing a monk's robe, the scapular is meant to remind the person who wears it that he or she has been called to a life of prayer.

◆ **Ransoming pagan babies.** This was the common term for a practice that introduced children to the missionary activities of the Church. Children were encouraged to save nickels, dimes, and quarters until they had $5. With this amount, they could select the name of a child in Asia or Africa whom the missionaries would baptize in exchange for the donation.

◆ **May Day.** On a spring day in May near the end of the school year, everyone gathered for the May Day ceremony. The boys wore white pants, white shirts, and white ties. The girls dressed in beautiful white dresses with veils. One girl would be selected to climb the ladder and place a crown of flowers on a statue of Mary while the entire congregation sang, "Oh, Mary we crown you with blossoms, today. Queen of the Angels, Queen of the May …"

These ceremonies, practiced faithfully for decades, gave Catholics a clear image of what it meant to belong to a particular tribe of people—to be Catholic. With the passing of time, many of these practices have been dropped from the Catholic portfolio, and for many people, the loss of these ceremonies has resulted in the blurring of their image of what it means to be Catholic.

Attendance at Mass has dropped and, as the definitions about sin have been softened, people no longer line up outside the confessional on Saturday afternoon, as was once the weekend ritual. Catholicism lost its absolutism, and for many it also lost its certainty.

Mary Loses Center Stage

Prior to Vatican II, people often asked Catholics why they worshipped Mary. The answer was that Catholics didn't worship her, they honored her. The reason someone might have asked this question was the extremely high profile she had in Catholic life. Devotions to her often rivaled all other services. Every Saturday Mass was dedicated to her. Many of the major feasts in the Church calendar are devoted to her. Typically, the first girl in a Catholic family was named Mary.

The prayer most closely associated with Mary is the Rosary, and it has long been the favorite prayer for many Catholics. Often people opted to pray the Rosary during Mass rather than read along in their prayer book. You can find out more about this very Catholic and very popular devotion in Chapter 14.

At Vatican II, the Church attempted to de-emphasize Mary, putting her in her place, so to speak. With the focus on the Mass as the primary Catholic devotion, Catholics were discouraged from praying the Rosary during Mass. Devotions to her were greatly reduced, because the new liturgy emphasized Christ and the scriptures.

Here is a spiritual bouquet a child might have given to her mother.

(Courtesy of Bob O'Gorman and Mary Faulkner)

A SPIRITUAL BOUQUET

TO MOTHER

10 Hail Marys
10 Our Fathers
15 Glory Bes
1 Rosary
5 Masses
5 Communions

Love,
Maria

The Saints Suffer

Devotion to the saints has long been a favorite Catholic practice. There is a saint for every day of the year, and a saint is designated as the patron of almost everything from countries to careers to conditions. At Vatican II, the Church attempted to clean up its roster of saints, determining which ones had a historical basis and which ones were simply part of the folk legends of the people. In the process, they removed many saints from the records. In doing this, Church leaders discovered that the people were not willing to let the saints go.

Regardless of whether there was a historical basis for these saints, the virtues represented in the stories about them were important to the people. They had become part of the fabric of Church mythology, and the Church leaders could not unravel it. St. Christopher, a beloved character in Catholic mythology and popular with non-Catholics, too, was one of the saints who was declared to be no longer part of the official directory. However, devotion to him has continued. Today, as always, people keep St. Christopher medals in their cars and feel protection under his care.

Dress Code: Defrocking the Clerics

With the changes of Vatican II came changes in the relationship between the clergy and the people they served. This change was most obviously apparent in the way the clergy and other religious members dressed. Before Vatican II, priests wore black suits with the Roman collar as we described earlier. They seldom appeared in public without their formal attire. Even more distinctive was the elaborate dress of the nuns.

After Vatican II, dress codes were relaxed. Many nuns moved out of the convents into other living arrangements; some even took secular jobs. There has been a mixed response to these changes. Catholics liked the fact that their religious leaders could be so easily identified and that the greater community showed them respect. Many people feel the change in dress code resulted in a general lack of regard for the Church and its leaders. Others feel that the old style of dress set religious leaders apart too much and emphasized separation of the religious leaders from the people they were to serve.

Numbers Tell the Story

Numbers told the story of the changing face of the Church. In the pre-Vatican II days, a large parish typically would have four or five priests. Today, very few parishes have more than one in residence. Often the parishes are much larger. There has been a big exodus of priests, nuns, and brothers from the Church ministry since the 1960s, and the numbers of people entering religious life has dropped. This downsizing of clerical ministers is seen both as a sign of the times and a result of Vatican II's strict adherence to celibacy. Many persons had expected a change in this regulation.

Sister Mary Catherine, CSJ (Congregation of St. Joseph), in the traditional pre-Vatican II habit of her order.

(Courtesy of Bob O'Gorman and Mary Faulkner)

Here Sister Mary Catherine appears in a post-Vatican II style of dress.

(Courtesy of Bob O'Gorman and Mary Faulkner)

The reduction in religious vocations is a great challenge the Church faces in the post-Vatican II time. Many feel that the shortage will eventually cause the Church to rethink its stand on celibacy and on the ordination of women. In addition, a major focus of the council was toward giving more responsibility to the people. The reduction in Church staff has certainly resulted in more participation by the lay members of the Church. We'll look in detail at some of the ways this is happening in Chapter 19.

We've just taken a quick look at the Church both before and after Vatican II. Now we're going to go back in time to the beginnings of the religion and see how it developed. We'll look at its roots, the Bible, Jesus, and the beginning of his followers' journey.

The Least You Need to Know

- Vatican II was an important turning point for Catholics.
- The Church focused the religion less on institutional structure and more on the people.
- Better relations between Catholics and Protestants, Catholics and Jews, and Catholics and the rest of the world were fostered.
- In updating the Church, some traditions that were important to many Catholics were lost.
- The Church continues to change as a result of Vatican II.

Part **2**

Putting the "Ism" in Catholicism: Becoming Catholic, Becoming Different

In *Fiddler on the Roof*, the character Tevia sings about a very important word, "tradition." As with our Jewish forebears, tradition is an important part of Catholicism. Tradition is the composite teachings of the Church, compiled over the last two thousand years, and Catholics believe that both the revelations within tradition as well as the Bible must be taken into account as faith directives. For many Protestants, the focus must be on Scripture alone.

Catholic tradition, as you will see, is deep and wide, going to the center of the earth as well as stretching to its four corners. Just what constitutes official Catholic teaching (Catholic tradition) and traditional practices? These issues are the core of religion and are as alive and elusive today as they were yesterday—which can mean two thousand years ago in this very old Church. At the same time, the story of this religion is the story of the progressive development called tradition. You'll learn about all this in Part 2.

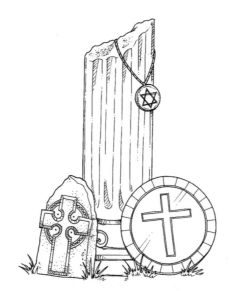

Chapter 6

"It's Elementary, My Dear Watson"

In This Chapter

- ◆ The roots of Catholicism are in the earth
- ◆ Catholicism draws its identity from the Jewish Scripture
- ◆ Greek learning gives Catholicism a heady start
- ◆ Catholics gain power and might from the Roman tradition
- ◆ The Celts pave the way for a rich mythology

In this chapter, you'll see how the Catholic religion came upon the scene within the context of human history. We'll explore the experiences, images, stories, and gatherings that make up the ritual, creed, and code of the Catholic Church. You might be surprised to find the sources of its ritual in the earth, air, fire, and water ceremonies of ancient people. We'll look at the culture and religion of the Jews, Greeks, Romans, and Celtic people and see how they influenced the formation of the early Church and how their influence is still present in the modern Church.

The Church's official birthday is Pentecost, the day the Scriptures tell us the followers of Jesus went out into the community to tell of their experience with him. But the story has much deeper roots than that. The Church is a composite of many quite ancient rituals that speak to the heart, mind, and actions of its members.

Ritual: The Old Religion, Roots, and Renewal

One of the hallmarks of Catholics is their long tradition of ritual and ceremony. In order to understand the religion, it helps to understand how rituals work to transmit spiritual truths. We don't know exactly how that happens, but we do know that rituals work to reveal deep spiritual meanings to those who participate in them.

Earth is the first church. To get to the core of the Catholic religion, we're going to go on a very deep journey into the heart of our planet. The roots of this old tradition go to the very beginnings of the human story, back to birth, death, and regeneration. Ever since humans conceived of some power or spirit beyond themselves, they have enacted and re-enacted elementary themes of life and death in what is called *ritual*. Ritual began as our way of reinforcing what we intuitively knew.

The term *Judeo-Christian* describes Catholics' connection to the Jewish religion and acknowledges our common history. Yet even farther back than this tradition is a culture developed by the people who lived in the Fertile Crescent, an ancient region made up of what is today the Middle East, Turkey, and Greece. The people of this culture, sometimes called *pagans*, had well-developed societies, raised children, built towns, made pottery, worked with metal, said prayers, and enjoyed productive, artistic lives. Some were monotheistic, believing in one God, and others were polytheistic, believing that God takes many forms. Many of these tribal people were assimilated into Judaism and Christianity. The tribal religions of Europe survived for hundreds of years into the Christian era and a cultural exchange went on between the two cultures that influenced Church practices and rituals we still use today.

> **For Heaven's Sake!**
>
> Watch your language! The word pagan can be a derogatory term. If you're talking about someone who believes in more than one god, you may be better off using the word polytheistic, if that is what you mean.

Pagan is a word that was originally used as a derogatory term to describe one who lived in the country (the "sticks") rather than the city. Another term for pagan would have been country bumpkin. The meaning was further shortened to describe anyone who is not a Christian, Moslem, or a Jew, as these religions developed in the cities. The term pagan is often used to describe the religions of the Greeks and Romans—distinguishing them from Jews or Christians, and is sometimes applied to indigenous cultures today. Heathen originally described those who lived on the heath. It is now applied to the people regarded as worshipping "false gods." In light of modern scholarship, both terms are considered culturally insensitive.

Elementally Speaking

To revisit these people and explore their faith is vital to the understanding of Catholicism because, fundamentally, all religion is about understanding who we are and our connection to the Creator, as well as understanding the way humans have interacted in the world throughout history. The word *religion* comes from the Latin *religare*, which means "to bind back, to bind together." Understanding religion, then, means connecting to the past and learning the story of the communities of people on earth who came before us. Their simpler, peaceful societies are an important contribution to the human story. We can't go forward until we go backward and connect their stories with our own.

S'ter Says _____

Religion concerns what exists beyond our comprehension. It is different from philosophy in that it operates from faith or intuition rather than reason.

The words **ceremony** and **ritual** are often used to describe the same thing: a formal act or set of formal acts established by custom or authority as proper to a special occasion, such as a wedding or other formality. They describe the process by which we observe something that we want to honor as important or sacred.

For many thousands of years, it was believed that all physical matter was composed of four elements: earth, air, fire, and water. These elements symbolized God's real presence in creation. The seasons and cycles of nature translated to our own human spiritual process. Our creativity was connected to the Creator and reflected in the earth's abundance. Crops planted in the earth would be nourished by the sun and rain and would produce food. Winter was like a death: inevitable and a part of life. Nature shut down and regenerated itself again in spring. To die was to be reborn. Ceremonies celebrating the seasons of the year were deeply rooted in the human psyche; they affirmed that life would continue. (Consult Appendix C.)

A Visit to Antiquity

Imagine you're a member of a tribe living thousands of years ago. Summer is ending. The days grow shorter. A distinct chill fills the morning air. The vines no longer produce their fruits. You're concerned about the food supply. (Remember that this is before the age of microwaves and corner grocery stores. When the food is gone, it's gone!) If the winter is as long and cold as it was the previous year, will there be enough food? Will the old people and the children stay warm enough; will they survive the winter? Winter connects us to thoughts of death and also to renewal.

Today, as well as in ancient times, rituals and rites explore these themes. In the past, drummers gathered in a circle outside the cave and beat their drums in rhythms that matched the human heartbeat to make the spirit strong for winter. Then dancers circled the fire, echoing the beat and pounding the experience of hope renewed, moving it up through the legs into the body and into their hearts.

Hope is strengthened through the rhythms of *ritual* and enactment of *ceremony*. In Baptism, for example, we light the candle, which is our ritual fire. We are immersed in water, and through it we are born into the new life of the spirit just as God once gave us physical life through our mother. We are connected in a sacramental way to God's renewing spirit. We are reborn.

Within the Catholic Church, the rituals and ceremonies celebrate not the passing of seasons as they did in ancient times but rather the physical presence of Christ on earth. His availability to human beings, walking and talking with them in their everyday experiences, is a key belief for Catholics. They believe he showed us that God is, was, and will always be present to his people. We can realize his presence through all of creation. We can understand that we are loved and cared for in all ways. God is in the earth, providing food, shelter, and all the material things we need to sustain us.

Catholics connect to the earthly presence of God by enacting rituals. Through rituals, they're able to physically touch and be touched by God's presence. The Communion bread is made of the wheat that grows in the fields. The Communion ritual says: "I am here with you. This is my body. I will feed and nourish you. This is how I am intimate with you." This earthy ritual manifests the physicality of God.

Rituals are tribal events. They're acted out in a community. It is only when we find a connection to the symbols of hope with others that we become certain of their validity.

"Yada, Yada, Yada"

As we stated earlier, Catholics share a common history with the Jews. In Hebrew, the word for faith is *yada*, which the Greeks translated as *gnoskin*, meaning "to know." For Judeo-Christians, *yada* (knowing) is something we do more with our hearts than with our minds. *Yada* comes from having earthy experiences, not by standing back from the world at an intellectual distance. Indeed, faith and knowing are action words that require a lot of living to achieve. A Catholic's faith is expressed through action in the world, and its roots stem from the Jewish tradition of *yada*.

To strengthen and develop this faith, both Jews and Catholics look to Scripture. The term *Bible* is commonly used to designate the sacred writings of the Christians, but it contains both the Jewish and the Christian scriptures. In fact, the word *Bible* comes from the Greek *ta biblia* meaning "the books," which describes its contents rather accurately. When the term was translated into Latin, the plural was dropped, making it the singular "The Book" we know today. (Chapter 7 explores the Bible further.)

For Heaven's Sake!

The "Old Testament" is old, but not out of date. It is called old in relationship to the "New Testament" that begins with the life of Christ. The stories continue to give us fresh meaning and insight, and are integral to the religious understanding of both Christians and Jews.

Epiphanies

The abbreviations B.C. (before Christ) and A.D. (**Anno Domini,** which means "in the year of our Lord") have been in existence a long time and are widely accepted by the entire world, but they are strictly Christian in origin. Many believe these abbreviations are insensitive to non-Christians. Sometime in the last century, people began using the new terms B.C.E. (before the common era) and C.E. (common era). Jewish people, Moslems, Buddhists, Hindus, and many other religious groups agree that these new terms are more accurate for all people. We'll use them in this book.

To Catholics and Jews, Scriptures are inspired, meaning that they have divine origin and provide guidance and comfort as well as the special sense of connection with the divine. Scriptures contain common themes, stories, and characters that give an identity to a religion and by which a religion can interpret the unfolding events of the day. These stories and characters provide a mirror in which people look to see who they are and where they came from, as well as where they are headed.

For Heaven's Sake!

Don't think the Genesis creation story is the only one available. There are more than 20,000 known creation stories. Virtually every group of people has a story about how the world was created and how its culture came into being.

Paradise Lost, and Paradise Found

To gain a quick understanding of any culture in the world, note how it describes its own creation. A culture's creation story gives you the basics on what the people of that culture believe about God, the world, and themselves. The Judeo-Christian creation story begins in the Garden of Eden.

Genesis, the first book of the Jewish Scripture, explains that God has been involved in a huge project called Creation. God created the earth, the sea, the sky, the animals, Adam (the first man), and Eve (the first woman). In this book, God places humans in a beautiful garden and cares for their needs. The humans walk and talk with God on a regular basis. Right from the beginning of the story, God is shown to be personal and caring.

God puts only one stipulation on Adam and Eve. He tells them not to eat the fruit of a certain tree. A serpent, representing evil, enters the garden and tempts them to eat the forbidden fruit. As they eat the fruit, they immediately experience terrible consequences. They are cut off from the very close relationship they enjoyed with God, and they are, as the Scripture says, "cast out of the garden." However, later in Genesis, God promises the people that he will not forget them.

The human journey depicted in Genesis begins in travail and loss, but also with promise of reunion. Christians believe that Jesus brings the long-sought-after reunion with God, the reunion God promised. Here's what the story of Genesis means to Catholics' understanding of their relationship to God and relationships among men and women on earth:

1. Creation has a master plan. It has meaning.

2. We are created in God's image, which means we are intelligent, compassionate, and creative.

3. There are sacred laws and rules that we must follow.

4. We have free choice, and our choices carry responsibility.

5. God is compassionate and will stay with us. He has a covenant relationship with the people.

The creation story in Genesis conveys both a sense of loss and of promise. This theme runs throughout Christianity. In Judaism, it is expressed as the covenant relationship between God and the people. Christians believe Jesus fulfills the covenant.

The Covenant

The idea of the *covenant* is the central theme in the Hebrew scriptures of the Old Testament. In the covenant relationship between God and the Jewish people, God promises to stay faithful to his people, and the people promise their faithfulness to him. This theme of covenant is expressed in the following stories.

In the story of Noah (found in Genesis 9:9–11), God sends a flood to punish the people. Noah is saved because God judged him and his family to be just. When the flood is over, God places a rainbow in the sky as a symbol of his promise to the people, the animals, and the earth that he will never send another flood to destroy them:

> I will establish my covenant with you and with your descendants after you; and with every living creature that is with you, the birds, the cattle, and every wild animal with you; all that came out of the ark, even the wild animals. I establish my covenant with you. Never again shall all living things be destroyed by the waters of the flood; never again shall there be a flood to destroy the earth." And God said, "This is the token of the covenant; I set it between me and you and every living creature that is with you, for all generations to come. I will set my rainbow in the clouds, and it shall be a token of the covenant between me and the earth." (Genesis 9:9–13)

S'ter Says

A **covenant** is made of two separate agreements. Each party agrees to abide by certain rules of the covenant. If one party fails to keep the covenant, the other party is still obligated. This makes a covenant different than a contract, because in contracts default can take place. Covenants have no default.

In a later story, God tests Abraham by asking him to offer his son, Isaac, as a sacrifice. Abraham is grief-stricken but obeys God and prepares to kill his son. God stops him and forms a covenant, promising Abraham that because he has obeyed, he will become the father of a great nation and that the land of Canaan will be its permanent possession. (Genesis 22:1–19)

Moses Receives the Law

At Mount Sinai, God seals a special covenant with the entire people of Israel through Moses as he gives Moses the law. Catholics believe in the covenant relationship as it is presented in the Hebrew Scriptures. Both Judaism and Catholicism are based on the understanding that God is constant and available and that we have a choice in entering into relationship with him. To be in this relationship means we have the responsibility to live in accordance with his laws.

Law is the second central theme of Jewish identity. The Ten Commandments are the core of Jewish law. God gave them to the people through one of their leaders, Moses. Jews do not experience the law as an external obligation, but as an expression of God's care. God gives his people the law as an act of love, as his side of the covenant. The people respond to it as their side of the covenant. It is through obeying the law (right action) that the Jewish people know of God's love.

The Jews were a wandering nomadic people who had no homeland. They carried the presence of God with them on a portable throne contained in an object called an ark. The ark housed the throne and the Scriptures that contained the law, their covenant with God. Eventually, when they established a homeland, the Ark of the Covenant was placed in the holiest part of the temple. The temple, then, became the place where Jews could be in physical contact with the sacred relationship that was signified by God's law.

Epiphanies

The Ark of the Covenant resided in the most holy place in the Jewish temple. It was entered on one day only per year, the Day of Atonement (Yom Kippur). Access was restricted to one person, the high priest. The ark itself was a small box made of acacia wood, overlaid with gold. Two long bars, also made of the same wood overlaid with gold, carried it. It contained three sacred items of the Jewish religion: the two stone tablets of the law given to Moses, Aaron's rod that budded, and the golden pot of hidden manna. Catholics keep the Communion bread in a similarly sized box, which they call the tabernacle. The tabernacle occupies a place of honor near the altar.

The Hebrew Scriptures talk of "knowing the Lord." This means that God takes the initiative, and the people respond to this encounter as it happens in events, in relationships, and in creation. In other words, such knowledge is gained here and now, not in an otherworldly way. Knowledge of the Lord is knowledge of the law and demands obedience to God's will.

In following this tradition, a Catholic's knowledge of God is not a fixed possession but is an activity. Knowledge develops in the life of the Catholic as lasting obedience and reflection. Faith is not a defined set of beliefs; it is an ongoing relationship with God.

A Summary of Jewish Influence

These important aspects of Catholic identity come from the Hebrew Scriptures:

◆ **Monotheism** The belief in one all-knowing God is central to both Catholicism and Judaism. Unfortunately, monotheism carries with it an intolerance of other religions.

◆ **God's presence** Judaism's central theme is the covenant between God and the people. Faith is a living response.

◆ **Free will** Catholics and Jews believe that we are all personally responsible for our actions. Actions bear consequences.

◆ **Moral law** The Old Testament forms the basis for Christian morality as it does for the Jewish people.

The key difference between Judaism and Catholicism is that Catholics believe that Jesus came as the fulfillment of the Old Testament covenant Scriptures.

Influences of the Greeks, Romans, and Indigenous Peoples

Although the influence of the Jewish faith is most easily recognized because Catholics and Jews share common sacred writings, two prominent cultural philosophies (the Greek and the Roman) also affected the formation of the early Church. Less prominent, yet equally important, were the indigenous peoples of the Middle East and their understanding of mystery.

The Greeks Decapitate the Mind from the Body

What is called the Golden Age of Greece had been in full glory, influencing Jerusalem and the surrounding areas, for at least 300 years before Christianity. The view of the world held by the ancient Greeks is paradoxical. On the one hand, they contributed much of what is considered Western civilization in the way of art, education, health, philosophy, and mathematics; Greek order and beauty as well as Greek love of thought are the foundation of our understanding of culture.

On the other hand, the official religion of Greece was one based in power struggles and domination in which the god Zeus established and maintained his supremacy through acts of cruelty and barbarism. Greek philosophy was based on the belief that humans are ruthless, grasping, and self-centered. The Greeks had a very strict class system that required force to uphold—a force the Greeks believed was natural and right. The most influential thinker of the time was Plato. His perfect society was one in which the strong dominated the weak, and it became the model for Greek culture.

Plato was a Greek philosopher who lived 400 years before Christ. His thinking greatly influenced both the Greek and Roman world at that time and for the next 1,500 years. The Church reflected Plato's teachings in its own way. Plato believed that the human soul is eternal and that learning occurs when the soul remembers its former life. It then becomes one with the eternal perfect idea.

Plato believed God was the ideal form of Good and that the goal of humans was to become more like God. His ideal world was composed of incorruptible, perfect forms held as ideas. The physical world contrasted sharply and was considered inferior to his perfect world of ideas.

Plato's philosophy is dualistic in that it sharply divides reality into two separate parts: either mind or matter, rather than both mind and matter. The shift in thinking from either/or to both that has occurred in more recent eras may seem like a small shift now, but it had major impact on the cultural development of the *Western world*.

This duality between the spiritual world and the physical world began to infiltrate the church right from the beginning. As Christianity moved out of the Jewish world and into the Greek world, it met the dualistic mind. According to Plato's philosophy, to progress toward accomplishing union with God, we must move away from the imperfection of the material world of the physical body into the more perfect world of the mind. This philosophy put Christians at war with the physical body. Rather than being sacred in itself, the body was considered an impediment to the spiritual nature.

S'ter Says

The **Western world** separates from the Eastern world in Istanbul, Turkey. Lands to the east are called the Eastern world, and to the west lies the Western world.

Roman Power and Might

Although the Greeks certainly left a philosophical mark on the development of Western civilization, Rome ruled the world by the time of Christ. This was the world in which the Church developed. "All roads lead to Rome" was a saying of the time. Roman roads flowed both ways. As people and goods flowed into Rome from elsewhere, Roman ideas and Roman soldiers traveled outward, influencing all areas of the known world. When you think about it, Catholicism spread largely because of the work of Roman road-builders.

The Romans borrowed much from Greek culture. In addition, they developed technology, architecture, administration, trade, and law. This combination established the foundations of Western civilization. However, some of the destructive elements of Roman rule were found in its militaristic mentality. The Romans developed a competitive, patriarchal culture in which the greatest value was placed upon accomplishment in battle, physical strength, and fearlessness. In addition, self-denial and service to the state were ways to achieve excellence in this society.

The warrior aspect of the Roman world influenced the culture at the time of the early Church in three main ways. First, Rome ruled by its undisputed power and might. What it decreed became law. Second, Rome was able to back up its laws with the authority of its military. Finally, Rome had a hierarchical ranking system upon which all militaries are formed.

In its first 100 years, the new Church struggled for survival in the midst of Roman chaos. As we shall see in Chapter 20, when Catholicism became the religion of the Roman Empire, the Church modeled itself on Greek ideas and the Roman sense of law.

The Church adapted a hierarchical and patriarchal ranking system for its clergy, placing them above the people they served. At the top of the hierarchy was the Bishop of Rome, as Rome was the center of all things. Roman influences brought strength and unity to the newly developing Church, and created problems as well.

Two major concepts that were woven into the Church in its early years are patriarchy and hierarchy. Patriarchy is a society led by older men having authority over members. Hierarchy describes a ranking system where a group of persons or things are arranged in order of rank, grade, or class, and thus are accorded privilege.

Problems inherited from the patriarchal and hierarchical paradigm are the social, religious, and ecological forms of domination it created. This worldview supports and promotes the strong conquering the weak, the rich exploiting the poor, males ruling over females and children, and human society dominating the earth. It found racial expression in the dominance of light-skinned people over dark-skinned.

In the hierarchical worldview, each order has sovereignty over those below it. Power flows from the top down, exclusively. It can be compared to a communal worldview using a circle. The circle represents the Divine and contains all the other groups. The eight pieces of the pie represent each of the kingdoms: mineral, plant, animal, child, woman, man, saints, and angels. The circle worldview is relational; all the groups meet in the center. It is based in equality and shared power.

The hierarchical worldview is less relational as each individual kingdom only touches the one next to it. The early Church formed in communities that are represented by the communal paradigm. As the Church became increasingly influenced by Roman politics, its institution developed according to the hierarchical form.

The hierarchical and communal worldviews.

(Courtesy of Bob O'Gorman and Mary Faulkner)

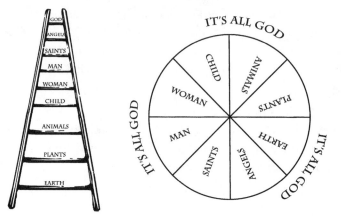

Indigenous Peoples of Western Europe

Anyone who has family roots in central and western Europe probably shares a common heritage. Tribal people living on the edge of the Roman world existed more than 3,000 years ago across most of Europe. They were constantly being taken into the empire as it expanded into their lands. Many were captured and served as slaves, joining the households of their captors. Although the tribes were in no way unified, they shared similar beliefs, languages, and practices.

Each tribe was distinct from the others and had its own community identity and its own gods, laws, and customs. Unlike the Romans and the Greeks, these people had an integrated worldview. They did not separate religion from the activities of daily life, but they instead celebrated God's mystical presence in the natural world. The concept of the presence of God in daily life was a reality to them, because their gods and goddesses lived with them in nature.

What the indigenous people contributed to the early formation of the Catholic Church was a mystical understanding of the world in which logic and order did not always prevail. This understanding is the basis of a faith structure that believes in God's presence through his son, Jesus Christ. Such a belief defies science and cannot be thoroughly substantiated by history. In many ways, the Catholic Church, although it has a highly developed theological base, remains what is called a mystery religion. What is meant by that is that Catholics fully accept that many of their doctrines cannot be understood or accepted other than by faith.

Cultural Influences

The influence of other traditions and cultures on the development of the early Catholic Church is outlined in the following chart.

Cultural Influences	Time Span	Contributions
Judaism	1800 B.C.E.–70 C.E.	Love of the law, patriarchal structure, monotheism, God present to his people, a rich written tradition in the Hebrew Scripture
Greek	332 B.C.E.–141 C.E.	Love of thinking, dualism, hierarchical structure, a better world awaits us elsewhere, authority outside of self, a loss of intuitive knowing
Roman	63 B.C.E.–600 C.E.	Authority, militaristic enforcement of the rules, hierarchical structure, ability to reach many people through Roman expansion
Indigenous	3000 B.C.E.–300 C.E.	Love and loyalty to leaders; mystery, tribes, myth, and symbol; real presence of God in the world; community; intuitive knowing

Now that you understand the major points that surrounded the beginning of the Catholic Church, you're ready to see just how it developed into a major world religion. But first let's take a look at the source for Catholics' story of their religion: the Bible.

The Least You Need to Know

- To get to the origins of the Catholic religion, you need to revisit history and look at the collage of cultural influences that affected it.

- At the heart of the Catholic religion is its ceremonies with their elementary expressions of earth, air, fire, and water.

- Judeo-Christian is a term used to describe the shared world of Jews and Christians. Catholics draw on the Hebrew Scripture for a basic understanding of their religion.

- ◆ The Greeks gave us Plato and his belief that things of the material world are bad, and things of the spiritual world are good and that these two worlds are separate.

- ◆ At the time of Christ, Rome ruled the known world and was a warrior culture. The Roman character of power and might had a profound influence on the Church.

- ◆ Indigenous people influenced the Catholic Church's mythology and the understanding of God's real presence.

Chapter 7

The Bible

In This Chapter

- ◆ The Jewish people and Christians share a common Scripture base
- ◆ The Old Testament represents at least four basic sources
- ◆ Four different communities of people wrote the Gospels called Matthew, Mark, Luke, and John
- ◆ A Catholic view of the Bible

The last chapter explained how the stories of the Old Testament created the basis for Catholics' understanding of their relationship to God. This chapter provides a glimpse of how the Bible works as the storehouse of sacred information for the Church. Who wrote the sacred texts? What were their reasons for writing them? How did the Church decide on what would be included as sacred texts? To find out the answers to these questions, read on!

Sacred Scriptures

The *Bible* is the sacred book or Scriptures of Jews and Christians. The Bible as we know it today is divided into two parts. The first part, the Hebrew Scriptures or the Old Testament, is the written record of the Jewish people from Abraham (1800 B.C.E.) until Maccabees (168 B.C.E.).

The second part of the Christian Bible is the New Testament, which contains the life and work of Jesus, as well as the faith experience of the early Christians until about 100 C.E.

S'ter Says

The word **Bible** is derived through Latin from the Greek **biblia**, or "books," the diminutive form of **byblos**, the word for "papyrus" or "paper," which was exported from the ancient Phoenician port city of Biblos.

Your Guardian Angel

A good way to approach the Bible is to see it as a faith history. The stories teach how to handle life's experiences. The events in the Bible are the recorded wisdom of those who have gone before. Through these stories, experiences are kept alive, and important moments are preserved.

The word *testament* means agreement and refers to the belief that God, the Creator of life, has initiated a personal relationship with his creatures. The Old Testament is the Christian name for the agreement God made with the Hebrew people that they would be his special people in whom he would reveal his love. Christians believe that in Jesus, God has revealed himself in a new way. They believe Jesus is both human (completely accessible to everyone) and divine (fully acting as God). They believe that what Jesus teaches about God and his care for humanity is a new testament. Catholics believe the Bible is the "word of God," inspired by the Holy Spirit and written by humans. They consider both testaments as one Bible, not two.

Like all good stories, the Bible has a plot. The basic plot revolves around God's love for the people and his willingness to be with them. It begins in Genesis with God speaking, "Let there be light." It ends in the book of Revelation with a prayer, "Come Lord Jesus!" In between, there is a constant dialogue between God and the people, rich stories, and an amazing cast of characters.

The Old Testament

The Old Testament is not called "old" because it is out of date; it refers to its position as coming before the "new" testament. It's an essential part of sacred scripture for Catholics, and they believe the books that comprise it are divinely inspired. To avoid any confusion, it is sometimes called the Hebrew Scriptures. The Old Testament is more than a book of history or culture. It is a book of religion: Israel's witness to its encounter with God and its faithful response to him. As the faith journey of the Jewish people, the Old Testament is a sacred history to both Jews and Christians. They turn to these stories for guidance in life's events. Ultimately, the stories disclose the meaning of human life. The 46 books of the Old Testament contain a wealth of teaching on God, as well as wisdom about the affairs of human life. They are a treasure house of prayers.

The Old Testament was formed gradually; its books were composed over many centuries. The *Pentateuch* is the first five books of the Old Testament: Genesis, Exodus, Leviticus, Numbers, and Deuteronomy. The Hebrew name for these five books is *Torah*. Torah is a difficult word to capture in translation, but a close meaning is law, and a better one might be "teaching." It contains the divine guidance given by God for the historical pilgrimage of the Jewish people. The teachings stand for all time. Most of all, Torah is an expression of God's care. It is summed up in the phrase: "I will be your God, and you will be my people." As such, then, the law of God is the Jews' expression of care and response.

S'ter Says

Pentateuch is a word based on a Greek term referring to "the book of the five scrolls (the **pentateuchos biblos**)," also known as the **Torah**. Moses commanded that the Torah be placed in the Ark of the Covenant. The book of Joshua and the Torah were placed in the ark, and these sacred books were kept there during the wilderness journey.

Jewish, Protestant, and Catholic scholars agree that the books known as the Pentateuch are a composite of several sources. Nearly 200 years of study have determined four main literary strands, which are identified as follows:

A Judaean source, using the divine name Yahweh and written about 950 B.C.E.

A North Israelite source that favors the use of the divine name Elohim and was written about 850 B.C.E.

A source reflecting the style and theology of the period of Josiah's reform about 650 B.C.E. and later

A source from the time of the Babylonian Exile, 550 B.C.E.

These different strands, each having a different perspective on the stories, were woven together in a final form that emerged in about 400 B.C.E. (For more information on the themes and stories referenced here, we suggest consulting a more detailed resource. See Appendix B.) The Old Testament ends in what some have described as an incomplete drama. According to the beliefs of many Jewish people, it leads to the Talmud (the authoritative writings of Jewish tradition) and a continued wait for the Messiah. According to the Christians, the story leads to Jesus Christ who came not to destroy, but to fulfill the law.

The New Testament

The New Testament is the story of God's son Jesus Christ, his teachings, the story of his death and resurrection, and the Church's first 100 years of life. Like the Old Testament, the New Testament also developed gradually. As Christian communities began to spread to other parts of the Roman Empire, specifically the lands around the Mediterranean basin, the followers of Jesus took with them their memories of their time with him. They had been firsthand witnesses to the events, and they taught others about Jesus' life and works from their experiences. However, they wrote none of it down. As the first witnesses were dying, it became apparent that someone had to record the information.

The first written material consisted of the letters written by Paul to the various faith communities; the early Christians circulated these letters. Paul was a convert to the new religion. He was the first missionary, founding churches all over the Mediterranean. He wrote letters to these communities offering guidance. These letters were written about 52 C.E. to 64 C.E. and are the earliest works of the New Testament. His letters, called *epistles*, offer valuable and practical instructions to the new Church for living out Christ's teachings.

Next came the Gospels, which are the books of Matthew, Mark, Luke, and John. The Gospels form the heart of the New Testament. Gospel is a word meaning "good news," and the Gospels of the Bible contain important stories of Jesus' life and teaching. Between the years 70 C.E. and 100 C.E., the community acknowledged four Gospels to be the most authentic because they appeared to be written by those who were most intimately connected with the apostles. Scholars believe they were developed in four major communities of the Christian world. Mark was written in Rome; Matthew in Jerusalem; Luke in Antioch; and John in Ephesus.

The communities that produced the New Testament material operated as writers and editors, and they were inspired in this regard. The roles of the writers (evangelists) were understood to be the following:

1. **Selectors**   From the many things Jesus did, they chose what they wanted to include and emphasize.

2. **Arrangers**   They organized the material in blocks, often by themes rather than chronologically.

3. **Shapers**   They adapted their sources and told the stories in ways that would emphasize what they wanted to stress.

4. **Theologians**   They reflected on the meaning and significance of the events in light of their belief in God and in Jesus.

S'ter Says

Synoptic means seeing with one lens. Matthew, Mark, and Luke all give a common view of Jesus, and they are called the Synoptic Gospels. John has a different perspective.

Matthew, Mark, and Luke constitute the *Synoptic Gospels*. That means they are looking at the same events and describing them in similar ways. Scholars generally agree that all four gospels were written in Greek and drew on the stories that were being told about Jesus and his life.

John's Gospel reports several incidents not mentioned in the other stories. Likewise, some of the events mentioned in the Synoptic Gospels do not appear in John. He gives a different order to the events and gives different dates for the Last Supper and Crucifixion. It is generally believed that John's material was written after the Synoptic Gospels. He may or may not have been aware of them when he wrote.

All the Gospels differ from one another in terms of author, time of writing, audience, and purpose. Although each Gospel is a separate and unique portrait of Jesus, no one Gospel tells us everything we need to know about him. To gain a fuller understanding of Jesus, we must consider all four Gospels together.

Around 70 C.E., a companion of the apostle Peter named Mark, sometimes referred to as John Mark, probably wrote the Gospel attributed to Mark. It is the earliest Gospel. It's called "the Gospel of action" because Jesus is always on the move. It emphasizes the humanity and suffering of Jesus and portrays him as the unrecognized Messiah. It was directed toward Gentile members of the Church living in Rome.

For Heaven's Sake!

Don't make the mistake of thinking that the four evangelists—Matthew, Mark, Luke, and John—wrote all their own material. The Gospels were a composite of writings gathered by their respective communities.

A Gentile doctor around 85 C.E. possibly wrote Luke. This Gospel stresses the central role of the Holy Spirit in Jesus' life. It shows Jesus' compassion, mercy, and concern for sinners in the miracle stories. It is the first part of a two-part work; part two is the Acts of the Apostles (the story of the beginning of the Church). It appears to have been written for Gentile Christians and perhaps for well-to-do ones, at that. Its message seems to be about the universality of Christianity. It shows women and poor people in important roles.

Matthew, written around 90 C.E. for Jews who were converting to Christianity, emphasizes Jesus as the fulfillment of promises made by God in the Hebrew Scriptures. It demonstrates Jesus' role as a teacher and preacher and talks about the responsibilities of Jesus' followers.

John was probably written by followers of this beloved disciple of Jesus and was written around 95 C.E. It reflects theological sophistication and is considered to be more poetic and more spiritual in nature than the other accounts. It presents Jesus as "the Word of God" and highlights God's presence as flesh and blood with us—his incarnation. It urges the reader toward faith, emphasizing that faith comes from God and is most present when the believer is without visible evidence of God. John creates poetic and memorable images of Jesus such as the vine and the good shepherd.

The Canon: How Are We Sure What Texts Are Sacred?

The canon of the Bible refers to the definitive list of the books that are considered to be divine revelation and are included in the text. Slightly different books were selected for the Catholic canon than for the Protestant canon. Catholics include 46 books in the Old Testament, and Protestants have 39. Both groups accept 27 books for the New Testament, for a total of 73 and 66 books, respectively.

S'ter Says

Canon, from the Greek **kanon,** means "a reed, a straight rod or bar, a measuring stick, or something serving to determine, rule, or measure." The word is used to designate those writings that came to be accepted as authentic Biblical texts.

How did the disciples' writings come together to form the New Testament canon, the collection of books that the Church acknowledges as genuine and inspired Holy Scripture? The leaders, guided by the authority of the Spirit, determined which books God inspired. The actual canonization process took a long time. There were many questionable gospels and epistles circulating. Careful, prayerful, and deliberate examination proved which books were genuine and which were false. Pope Damasus at the Council of Rome in 382 listed the books of today's canon. At that time, the canon was closed, and no more books were entered. Here's what it includes:

The Old Testament

- ◆ **The Pentateuch**   Genesis, Exodus, Leviticus, Numbers, and Deuteronomy

- ◆ **The historical books**   Joshua, Judges, Ruth, 1 and 2 Samuel, 1 and 2 Kings, 1 and 2 Chronicles, Ezra, Nehemiah, Tobit, Judith, Esther, and 1 and 2 Maccabees

- ◆ **The wisdom books**   Job, Psalms, Proverbs, Ecclesiastes, the Song of Songs, the Wisdom of Solomon, and Sirach (also called Ecclesiasticus)

- ◆ **The prophets**   Isaiah, Jeremiah, Lamentations, Baruch, Ezekiel, Daniel, Hosea, Joel, Amos, Obadiah, Jonah, Micah, Nahum, Habakkuk, Zephaniah, Haggai, Zachariah, and Malachi

The New Testament (in parentheses: total number of chapters/total number of verses for each book)

- **The Gospels** according to Matthew (28/1,071), Mark (16/678), Luke (24/1,151), and John (21/878)

- **The Acts of the Apostles** (28/1,008)

- **Thirteen letters attributed to Paul,** written to particular communities and individuals in the following cities: to the Romans (16/433), 1 (16/437) and 2 (13/257) Corinthians, Galatians (6/149), Ephesians (6/155), Philippians (4/104), Colossians (4/95), and 1 (5/89) and 2 (3/47) Thessalonians

- **Letters to individual Christian leaders** (the first three are called the Pastoral Letters): 1 (6/113) and 2 (4/83) Timothy, Titus (3/46), and Philemon (1/25)

- **One biblical sermon,** for which neither the author nor the audience is explicitly mentioned: Hebrews (13/303)

- **Seven epistles** that are attributed to early apostles and written to more general audiences: the Letter of James (5/108), Peter 1 (5/105) and 2 (3/61), John 1 (5/105), 2 (1/13), and 3 (1/14)

- **The Letter of Jude** (1/25)

- **The Apocalypse** in the Book of Revelation (22/404)

Catholic Beliefs Regarding the Bible

Catholics hold these beliefs regarding the Bible:

- The Bible contains both the Hebrew Scriptures and the Christian Scriptures as one book.

- The sacred Scriptures are the inspired word of God. God is the author because he inspired their human authors.

- The Catholic Church accepts and venerates as inspired the 46 books of the Old Testament and the 27 books of the New Testament.

- The four Gospels occupy a central place in the Bible because Jesus Christ is their focus.

- The unity of the two testaments reveals the whole of God's plan.

There are no copies of the original Scriptures. The early manuscripts were written on scrolls and later copied by monks. When Latin became the commonly used language, the manuscripts were translated into Latin from Greek texts.

The Septuagint is the third century B.C.E. Greek translation of the Jewish Scriptures from Alexandria, Egypt, and was used heavily in the early Church. It contains texts that are not included in the Hebrew canon, and is still used by Greek Catholics.

Since Vatican II, new translations of the Bible are available for Catholics, and Bible study is encouraged. New research continues to add to the body of knowledge around these sacred texts. Today, Bibles are composed by the collaboration of Jewish, Catholic, and Protestant scholars. Rather than a means of separation, the Bible has become an interfaith event.

What Place Does the Bible Hold for Catholics?

Catholics constantly find nourishment and strength in the scriptures. The four Gospels hold a unique place in the Church and are read each time that the Mass is offered.

The Catholic Church understands that in sacred Scripture, God speaks in a human way. To interpret Scripture correctly, you must listen for what the human authors wanted to say and what God wanted to reveal through their words. To do this you must know something about the culture, writing style, and times in which it was written.

The Church distinguishes between two interpretations of Scripture: literary and spiritual. The literary (or scholarly) meaning is discovered by following the rules of sound interpretation. The spiritual meaning comes through understanding the allegorical, moral, and symbolic levels of the Scriptural stories.

The Scriptures are understood to have parallel (allegorical) meanings: Thus, the crossing of the Red Sea could be a sign of Christ's victory and also of Christian baptism. They are also understood in the moral sense by leading us toward right action. Finally, the symbolic level reveals an ultimate spiritual or mystical meaning.

The Catholic Church teaches that interpreting Scripture is ultimately up to the judgment of the Church. It believes that it is the task of Scripture scholars to work toward a better understanding and explanation of the meaning of sacred Scripture.

Now that you have a fairly basic understanding of the Bible as the faith source for Catholics, let's move on and meet the one from whom Catholicism truly emerged: Jesus.

The Least You Need to Know

- The Old and New Testaments work together to create the Bible.

- The Bible was written over a long period of time and has many authors; it was inspired by the Holy Spirit and written by human hands.

- The four Gospels work together to give us different perspectives of Jesus' life and work.

- At a certain point in time, the Church decided which books were authentic and which were not and closed the canon. No new books can be added.

- Catholics do not believe in simply a literal interpretation of the Bible.

Birth and Spirit of a New Religion

In This Chapter

- ◆ Finding the roots of the Church in Jesus
- ◆ The Christian stories: Christmas, Easter, and Pentecost
- ◆ The persecution of the early Church
- ◆ The Church's first organizational structures

As established and powerful as the Catholic Church may seem today, it had a rocky start, and its history is a long and fascinating one with lots of ups and downs. (You'll learn more about it in Part 6.) This chapter focuses on Jesus and shows you how his message became a religion, how this religion became organized, and how it survived persecution. We will take you to the point where it became the established religion of and the key force in Western civilization.

How We Know What We Know About Jesus

As you read in Chapter 7, followers of Jesus compiled the historical references to Jesus and his teachings, but these references weren't formally

Your Guardian Angel

For many years, it was the custom to capitalize all pronouns that refer to Jesus: He, Him, His. One of the major developments of Vatican II was to emphasize the human side of Jesus. As a result, religious writers now generally use lowercase pronouns when referring to Jesus. The reasoning behind this is to recognize Jesus' likeness to us.

written down until a generation or two after his death. These written accounts were interpretations of the experiences his followers had of him and of his teachings.

Very few facts are known about the true history of Jesus. We know that someone like him lived and preached in Galilee, a region in northern Israel, and in Jerusalem. Someone like him was crucified in Jerusalem, probably on a combination of charges of blasphemy against the Jewish religious leaders and treason against the Roman authorities. The rest of what is known of him comes to us through the stories that his followers told about him and what they believed the stories to mean.

The Wellspring of Galilee

Who was Jesus? Jesus was a Jewish preacher and teacher who lived and taught in Galilee. But "Jesus Christ" is more of a description than a name. Jesus is a Latin version of the Greek *Iesous*, itself a form of a Hebrew name, *Y'shua*. Christ is not a name, but a title. It comes from the Greek word, *Christos*, which in Hebrew means "the

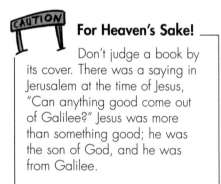

For Heaven's Sake!

Don't judge a book by its cover. There was a saying in Jerusalem at the time of Jesus, "Can anything good come out of Galilee?" Jesus was more than something good; he was the son of God, and he was from Galilee.

anointed one," translated from the Hebrew word *messiah*. Messiah is a term used to describe a figure of great importance chosen or "anointed" by God. As Jesus' name already shows, he lived in the Jewish, Greek, and Roman worlds.

Unlike Jerusalem, Galilee was not a particularly important cultural or religious center for the Jews. In fact, Jews who lived so far away from the temple in Jerusalem were thought to be ignorant and lax in religious matters. In the society of the time, the Jews were scorned, and even the Jews of Jerusalem scorned a Galilean Jew like Jesus.

Yet, in its own way, Galilee was a natural geographic region to spawn a new religion. It was a natural crossing place for international travel routes, and people of many nations gathered there: Phoenicians, Syrians, Arabs, Greeks, and Asians, as well as Jews. These international contacts meant that ideas flowed in from the four corners of the known world. Its distance from Jerusalem, where the Jewish law and teachings prevailed, gave it a freedom of thought that would not have been available nearer the temple. Its people were relatively unschooled in Jewish law, but were ruled by common sense and wisdom. The people practiced a Jewish faith that was simpler and more spontaneous than the more conservative faith of the Jerusalem intelligentsia, and these qualities greatly influenced Jesus' teachings.

Jesus the Jew

Jesus himself was a bit of a character. Growing up with diverse people and cultures, he invited diversity into his inner circle. He broke class and cultural rules, bringing fishermen, tax collectors, and women into his ranks.

But make no mistake: Jesus was born, lived, and died a Jew. His community, the Jews, related to God in two ways: in observing the law and in visiting the temple. Jesus and his followers came out of this intense experience of Judaism's personal and faithful relationship with God.

What did the people find so interesting about Jesus and his teachings? Jesus claimed to have a special experience of God, which he said he could share with everyone. This new level of relationship was captured in the very intimate way he addressed God as *Abba* ("my dear papa"). His relationship with God was simple and direct, and most important, he made it available to all. The followers of Jesus saw themselves as the ones who shared this special intimacy or presence of God as Jesus did.

The love of God that Jesus experienced was so compelling that he spent his whole life on earth bringing it to others in what he called the "reign (the will) of God." First, his preaching addressed the evils of his society: poverty, hunger, illness, and injustice. Second, he demonstrated a willingness to be with people. He lived and walked among them. He didn't seem to require anything of them and spoke to them of how much they were loved by God. People began to take notice, and he acquired a band of loyal followers.

The Key Stories of the Christians

All religions have their great stories. Chapter 6 outlined several stories that were important to the Jews: Adam and Eve and the creation story, Abraham and the covenant, and Moses and the law. Christians, too, have their stories that reveal something special and deep in the recorded historical events. Christians have three great stories of Jesus: his birth, his death and resurrection, and his abiding presence in the community that lives after him.

Jesus' Birthday: Christmas

The story goes that Jesus was born in Bethlehem of simple parents named Mary and Joseph, who were a young couple from Galilee. This story makes it clear right from its start that something very important was happening. The night Jesus was born, angels burst into song. Shepherds heard them and came to the place where the baby lay. They bowed, knowing instinctively that they were in the presence of a "great one." News of his birth traveled far and wide. Kings and wise men from distant lands saw a star in the Eastern sky, and they came in search of him.

Jesus' father, Joseph, made a living with his hands as a carpenter. We assume that Jesus grew up working in his father's shop. Jesus did not receive a formal education. However, when he visited the temple in Jerusalem at the age of 12, the story says that he impressed the Jewish scholars with his knowledge and understanding of Jewish law. We don't hear much more about him until he began his public life of preaching at the age of 30. Most of the events of his public life took place in and around Galilee and on the road to Jerusalem. His life ended at the age of 33.

His Mission, Death, and Resurrection

From the beginning of his public life, Jesus astonished all who came into contact with him. To the leaders of the Jews, he was an uneducated upstart, a hayseed from the boondocks of Galilee. Yet he astounded others with his knowledge and wisdom. His attitude of welcoming those people whom society had rejected challenged the convictions of the Jewish leaders of the time. The Jews had endured much and survived as a culture and religion by making sure they remained pure and true to the Law. Jesus invited everyone into a relationship with God and opened his teachings to all who wanted them. He had a message of liberation, and he lived it in his attitude, which was friendly, unassuming, and caring.

Epiphanies

Christmas takes its name from the central act of Catholic worship, the Mass. Christmas means "Christ's Mass," a ritual that celebrates his birth as a human. Most languages, except English, use a word signifying nativity or birthday of Christ to designate the feast of Christmas: in Latin, **Dies Natalis;** in Italian, **Il Natale;** and in French, **Noel.** Wherever you are and whatever language you speak, what is being celebrated is the birth of Christ. The way this event is commemorated and renewed in Catholicism is the Mass. Legend says that Christ was born moments past midnight on December 25, and Catholics celebrate this occasion by the tradition of Midnight Mass.

The stories tell that he worked *miracles*. His first miracle occurred at a wedding feast in Cana where he turned jugs of water into wine to prevent the embarrassment of his host, who was running out of wine for the guests. His followers, some of them fishermen, tell that he had power to calm the sea, walk on water, and know where fisherman should place their nets in order to catch the most fish. It was reported that he turned a small amount of fish and bread into enough food to feed 5,000 people who had gathered to hear him speak. He cured others from physical illness, even bringing them back from the dead. After three years of preaching and teaching in Galilee, Jesus went from the outskirts of the Jewish world to Jerusalem.

S'ter Says

A **miracle** is an event that breaks through the laws of nature. Miracles are extraordinary happenings that provide a glimpse of God at work.

Jerusalem was the symbol of established power for the Jews. Everything about it had religious significance. It was the holy city, the site of the temple, and the reference point of Jewish identity and belonging. It was also elitist and the center of the powers that oppressed and excluded many of its people. Jesus took his message, which attacked the very concept of elitism, to Jerusalem to confront the leaders of the establishment. With his simple philosophy and nonconformist actions, he forced their hand, and they played it. The authorities had him arrested, charging him with political sedition because he challenged the Romans' power, and religious blasphemy because he claimed he was the Son of God. When he said this, he claimed that he had a special relationship with God—and that we all have this relationship, too. We are all sons and daughters of God.

Epiphanies

Crucifixion was a method of capital punishment practiced by the Greeks and Romans in ancient times. It was used frequently in putting down Jewish opposition to the Roman conquest of Israel. The Romans used wooden beams crossed like a T. Typically the one to be executed was scourged (whipped) and required to carry the cross to the site of the execution. The prisoner was either nailed or tied to the cross. Death came by asphyxiation. Crucifixion was abolished when the Roman Empire became Catholic.

Jesus' trial was swift, and he was sentenced to die by a common method of Roman execution called crucifixion. Most of his followers abandoned him at the hour of his death; only a handful remained with him. After his death, his body was hidden in a cave. Three days later, when some women in his close circle came to anoint his body for burial, they found an empty tomb. An angel appeared to them and told them that

Jesus had risen. During the next six weeks, there were a series of sightings of him, and then he was seen ascending into heaven. That was the end of the historical Jesus.

Pentecost: The Birthday of the Church

Fifty days after Jesus' death, his followers gathered together in the room where they used to meet with him for meals. Jesus had told them to wait there because he would send his Spirit to be with them.

A sudden storm began to rattle the shutters on the windows, and it grew dark. The room began to glow. Tongues of fire appeared over each of their heads. The people in the room said they experienced an inspiration to go and proclaim all the things they had seen and heard. They reported feeling especially strong. Jerusalem was filled with thousands who were gathered there for religious ceremonies. To their amazement, they could understand the apostles, each in their own language.

In a very bold action, Jesus' followers decided to tell the world their stories of him. Given that he was so recently put to death, telling these stories was a pretty risky thing to do. They began by saying that Jesus had risen from the dead and had walked among them and that he was the Messiah, the Son of God. The story says that 3,000 people were baptized as a conversion to Jesus' teaching. Jesus' followers were encouraged by this response and decided to gather together and actively pursue bringing Jesus' vision into being. As you shall soon see, although the followers had undergone a change, the society in which they began to preach had not.

Jesus Christ's followers came to believe he was both a human man and the divine Son of God. They believed he fulfilled a promise God made to the Jewish people. They believed he was the Messiah sent to help them and to fulfill the promise of the law. The followers believed he fulfilled the law in his teachings, which emphasized mercy and forgiveness.

Jesus' popular ministry, which challenged the accepted social and religious rules of the day, embraced sinners and social outcasts. His rather simple and straightforward message promoted love, tolerance, and belief in God. His core message seemed to be: "All people, especially the poor and rejected, are invited to come into the kingdom of my Father." This message, which was spiritual in nature and political in its effects, began to worry both the Jewish leaders and the Roman authorities.

In addition, Jesus' nontraditional teachings about equality revealed new insights into the understanding of God and what it meant to be a human. Almost all societies appear to have a way of accepting some people and rejecting others, thereby defining who will be the "in" group and who will be the "out" group. Most groups of people have classifications that determine who is a success and who is a failure, what it means to be good or bad, normal and abnormal. Jesus challenged many of the cultural assumptions of his day. His core message was one of unity. He taught that all are one in the Father.

Was Jesus the First Catholic?

The big question you might be asking about Catholicism is: Was it really founded by Jesus? Like all big questions, there is no simple answer to this one. We can find clues by looking at what his followers said about these early years.

On the surface, Jesus' ministry seemed to be a failure. He did not liberate the people from Roman oppression. Many of the people who had been part of his following lost interest and continued living their lives in very much the same way as they did before they knew him. A handful, however, were inspired to continue his work because they realized his teaching about the kingdom meant building the kingdom within and restoring human dignity. Jesus preached to the down and out, telling them they were God's sons and daughters. His followers banded together in small groups in order to keep his work and his memory alive. Nearly 2,000 years later, the work continues.

The Core Beliefs

Here are Jesus' main ideas:

♦ The law of the Old Testament is based in forgiveness and love.

♦ The kingdom (the will) of God is within and accessible to the individual.

♦ Everyone can have a personal relationship with God.

♦ Social class, education, and economics have little to do with God's love.

Jesus' core message was and continues to be that God is available to everyone. Jesus' followers believed that the real presence of God they had experienced in Jesus continued after he was physically gone.

The Calling

Jesus' followers did not immediately formalize a church. They lived in communities and met mostly in homes. They were simply called disciples at this time. Only later would they be called *Christians*. Their mission was to bring the "reign of God" to others the way that Jesus had brought it to them. Early writings use these terms in describing the followers: a household, a family, God's assembly, a new creation, and the body of Christ.

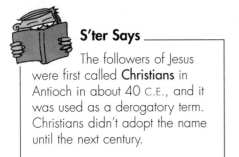

S'ter Says

The followers of Jesus were first called **Christians** in Antioch in about 40 C.E., and it was used as a derogatory term. Christians didn't adopt the name until the next century.

You met Paul in the last chapter. An early convert and a leading missionary, Paul spread the teaching of Jesus throughout the Mediterranean world. He established communities from Syria to Turkey, Greece, and Rome. Paul's most lasting influence has been felt through his writings to the communities, which, as we have noted, were the earliest and most extensive writings in the New Testament.

The spiritual tasks the followers dedicated themselves to were celebrating, teaching, and serving:

- **Celebration**   Jesus celebrated his relationship with the Father. He did this as he gathered with the common people, sharing meals and enjoying camaraderie. His followers remembered how special these times were, and they wanted this memory to be a part of their communities.

- **Teaching**   Jesus taught who God is and how good and loving he is. Perhaps his teaching is best captured by the prayer he taught his followers: the "Our Father," which is also known as the Lord's Prayer:

  > Our Father, who art in heaven,
  > hallowed be thy name;
  > thy kingdom come,
  > thy will be done,
  > on earth as it is in heaven.
  > Give us this day our daily bread,
  > and forgive us our trespasses,
  > as we forgive those who trespass against us;
  > and lead us not into temptation,
  > but deliver us from evil. Amen.

  Jesus declared that God was intimate and accessible to all. His followers gathered the memories of his teachings and passed them on.

- **Serving**   Jesus served the people, caring for their physical and spiritual needs. He healed the sick, cured the deaf and blind, and fed the hungry. His followers wanted to carry on these important ministries.

At first, Jesus' followers believed that he would come back to take them to the Father if they just managed to hold on for a few years. During prayer services, there was a part of the ritual where one person would leave the congregation to look up in the clouds to see if he was coming. When the person reported that Jesus was not coming, the service would continue. Eventually, they came to understand that he was not coming back in the form they thought he would, but that he was with them in spirit always.

We can answer our opening question about whether Jesus founded the Catholic Church by saying there was no institutionalized Catholic Church at the time of Jesus or for many years after. The early followers of Jesus were considered to be members of a sect of Judaism. They said they had a new experience of God's presence unlike any before. Knowing Jesus was so powerful that they banded together to keep his presence alive. As they realized he would not return in their lifetime, they began to build an institution to hold his memory.

Your Guardian Angel

Catholics end the Lord's prayer with the line "deliver us from evil." They don't say, "For Thine is the kingdom, the power and the glory forever," as is the Protestant custom. So if you're attending a Catholic service and are used to the Protestant version, don't get confused by this.

Catholics Separate from the Jews

For many years, the Jewish people had offered resistance to the growing oppression of the Romans and had suffered much at their hands. In the year 70 C.E., the Romans crushed a Jewish rebellion, which resulted in the destruction of much of Jerusalem, including the temple.

During the next few years, Jewish leaders met to reorganize. Some of this reorganization included expelling sects of Judaism they identified as heretical. When the Jews tightened their ranks, Jesus' followers were closed out of the circle, which encouraged them to emerge with an identity and authority separate from Judaism. Outcasts already, the followers of Christ further split from the Jewish religion as a result of this series of events. From this time forward, the religions were separate.

The Martyrs

In the beginning, few people converted to the new religion. Many came from the non-Jewish world. The new religion appealed largely to the urban poor, women, noncitizens, social outcasts, and slaves. The message was that they did not need money or education to belong to the kingdom. The idea that no man or woman could be a slave in God's world was appealing. They liked the idea of Jesus being a common man, a martyr with a message. They liked his promises of a better tomorrow and refuge from pain and suffering. The new, available God had infinitely more appeal than the distant gods of Greek and Roman mythology who gave the people no real guidance for morality. These early converts formed communities, giving whatever resources they had in exchange for security. The communities provided housing and food and cared for the elderly and widows.

Roman authorities viewed the spread of Christianity as a threat to the state. More and more, the lines between the emperors and the gods they worshipped blurred. Roman leaders had begun to perceive themselves as divine and required homage to be paid them. Christians were becoming separatists, and more and more often and in greater numbers they refused to burn incense before the emperor's statue. Increasingly, Christians became the targets of mockery and violence.

Technically, Christianity was an outlawed religion, although the authorities didn't always enforce the law against it. However, whenever acts of civil disruption against the Romans erupted, regardless of who was behind them, Christians were blamed, and punishment was severe. Christians were sometimes put into the arenas with *gladiators* or wild animals, which usually resulted in their martyrdom. Christians also suffered other forms of execution (crucifixion, for example). On and off, the early Church endured 300 years of persecution.

S'ter Says

Gladiators were slaves (including Christians) and prisoners of the Romans who were trained for the sport of hand-to-hand combat, as well as fighting wild beasts. The result of this combat was often death. **Martyr** is the Greek word for "witness." It describes people who are killed because of their religious beliefs. The Church considers martyrdom to be the highest form of witness to the faith; therefore, martyrs go straight to heaven and become saints.

Often Christians were offered a chance to recant, which meant they had to offer incense to the Roman gods. If they didn't, they were killed. Many opted to recant; however, many more chose death and became *martyrs*. They became the saints of the early Church.

The Greeks and Romans did not believe in burial and instead cremated their dead. Jews and Christians were allowed to bury their dead, but they had to do so outside of the city limits. Following the Jewish tradition, early Christians buried their dead in cemeteries called catacombs. They were extensive subterranean vaults and tunnels around Rome and other cities. Besides serving as places of burial, the catacombs became hiding places for Catholics fleeing persecution. Later, catacombs were honored as shrines to the saints and martyrs.

For Heaven's Sake!

Don't think that the candles on the altar are just for decoration! The church lights candles at every Mass, and it is the custom that a relic of the saints (a fragment of their bones) be contained in the altar as a reminder of the early martyrs.

Martyrdom for one's religious beliefs became an early part of Catholicism's identity. St. Stephen is believed to be the first martyr. Several of the 12 disciples closest to Christ were also put to death for their faith. The stories of the bravery of the early Christians nourished the young religion. Strangely, it became the source of many more conversions because people were curiously attracted to this new religion for which so many would willingly die.

Saints Preserve Us

St. Stephen, December 26, Patron of Stonemasons

St. Stephen, a disciple of Christ, was the first martyr. He was described as "full of grace and fortitude," and the effect of his work was great among the people. He was accused of blasphemy against Moses and against God and was brought before the authorities who condemned him to death by stoning. Kneeling down before his murderers, he cried out with a loud voice saying, "Lord, do not lay this sin against them." He was stoned to death in 35 C.E. His feast day is December 26, and he is the patron of stonemasons.

Designing the Structures

The next task that faced the developing Church was to design a structure that would hold them together. The goals of the Church founders were to carry on the work and keep the teachings consistent. Local communities gathered with other communities in the region under the guidance of leaders that they called *bishops*. The lines of authority and offices of leadership were slowly established. The followers believed that Jesus had selected Peter to lead them. He went to Rome, where the Church eventually established its center. His position as the bishop of Rome was later given the title pope. Catholics claim a direct line of succession of their leader, the pope, back to Peter.

S'ter Says

Bishop is from the Greek word **episcopos** and means "overseer." A bishop is in charge of the Church in a local area.

Although the Roman Empire was still the controlling force as Catholicism started, its decline as a world power had begun. Many forces contributed to its decline: increased invasions by warring tribes, the outrageous cost of maintaining the military, and the growing decadence of the aristocrats. As taxes continued to increase alarmingly, more people grew disenchanted with the state and turned instead to religion. The Church's more austere lifestyle and moral code was attractive by contrast, and the social services it offered were attractive as well. Christian communities offered care for widows and orphans, health care, and care for the elderly. As Rome declined, the Church grew.

The Desert Fathers and Mothers

During these early years of the Church's growth, a movement called the Desert Fathers and Mothers developed in the Egyptian desert. Rejecting everyday life with its many earthy and tedious concerns and distractions, and wanting to follow their new-found and deeply felt faith, many of the members of the new Church established communities in the desert where they meditated, prayed, and studied.

Anthony, the man who began this movement, lived in 251 C.E. and was the son of Christian parents. As a young man, the word of Jesus inspired him to give away all of his possessions to the poor and go to the desert. He lived the life of a hermit for many years, devoting himself to prayer and meditation. He began to attract hundreds of followers whom he guided in their spiritual life.

With this movement, an important tradition of monasticism and the contemplative life began within the Church. This tradition would grow and develop over the next centuries to become a strong core of Catholic life. Many of the early Christian thinkers who lived in these communities helped define and clarify Church teachings. These writings are still a part of Catholic life. Their observations and writings were crucial to establishing the spirituality of the Church.

The next chapter examines how the present-day Church keeps the message of Jesus alive and how it keeps his spirit present through ceremonies, rituals, and celebrations.

The Least You Need to Know

- Jesus invited all to participate in "the reign of God."

- The followers of Jesus formed the Church as a way of keeping his presence alive and bringing the reign of God to the people.

- The Church began as a persecuted community.

- The contemplative tradition is integral to the foundation of the Church.

Part 3

The Sensuous Side of Catholicism: How Catholics Experience God

Catholics believe God is present in all things. Sacraments awaken sacramental memory, the presence of God deep within us. They mark significant events in the spiritual life, celebrating and connecting the one receiving the sacrament to God's presence in life's events, birthing, nourishing, sustaining, and bonding the community of his followers. Their purpose is to develop sacramental awareness by sharpening the ability to sense the presence of God every day.

God's revelation is an inspiration, the spirit of God becoming available to humans. Jesus is the sacrament of God; the Church is the sacrament of Jesus; and Mary is the people's sacrament. We'll learn all about these sacraments in the following chapters.

Chapter **9**

Tasting, Touching, Smelling God

In This Chapter

- ◆ How the senses are God's gateway to the soul
- ◆ How Catholics use their whole brain
- ◆ How Catholics differ from Protestants
- ◆ What is Catholic imagination?

Catholic ritual at once seems mysterious and magical, perplexing and intimidating. It can enthrall and even scare a visitor or newcomer. Ritual opens many levels of knowing. On the surface, Catholic ritual engages the senses (sound, sight, smell, touch) and the emotions that are evoked. At a much deeper level, it opens the religious imagination, the deep place in the human psyche where we connect with the sacred. In this chapter we'll explore the very complex practice of Catholic ritual, and learn how people use it to connect to the sacred.

Feeling Faith

Faith is often described as trust in someone or something without proof. You've probably heard Catholics refer to their religion as "the faith," but religion itself isn't faith. Instead, religion gathers the faith experiences of the followers, assists in interpreting these experiences, and codifies the information into rules and regulations that tell newer members what has been learned about life from these experiences. It is the body in which the faith of the people is incorporated.

Faith often comes as the result of a spiritual experience—a time when the sacred reaches through into the material world, and God's presence is *felt*. Religion is built on faith, as there is something in the human mind that eventually needs to interpret and more fully understand the faith experiences. Religion becomes the system by which faith is examined and understood, and action is determined. It involves …

 ♦ Feeling: experiencing the spiritual.

 ♦ Thinking: figuring out what the experience meant.

 ♦ Being: responding with action.

In the beginning, the followers of Jesus had an experience that resulted in a new understanding of God. They came to believe that life on earth could be different. This is what we know as faith. These folks wanted to keep their experience alive, to share it with others. They did this mainly by getting together, talking about the stories he told them, eating a ritual meal, and doing good works in the community. In essence, they created the early ritual Catholics follow today.

The Church uses ritual to reconnect the original experience of Jesus on earth, and the spiritual experience of his continued presence in our midst—assuring one another that he continues to be involved in our human struggle. Catholic ceremonies are the means of creating an experience of the sacred, not something to be proven, but something to be felt. Later the experience is translated into beliefs or doctrine through an analytical process called theology—the science that works out the "how's" and "why's" of the religion. But faith itself starts as a spiritual experience.

Now You See Him, Now You Don't: How God Is Present

Every religion has to wrestle with just how present God is to his creatures. The classical terms used to talk about this issue are *transcendence* and *immanence*. Transcendence refers to how far away or different God is from creation. Immanence refers to how close or alike God is to creation. All classical religions offer basic positions on this issue. Christianity goes further than any with its insistence on Jesus' nature as both human and divine—both immanent and transcendent. Within Christianity itself, Protestants (a general name for other denominations within Christianity) and Catholics can be characterized by their different emphasis on God's closeness to creation. (Part 6 contains an extensive explanation of the differences between Catholics and Protestants.)

S'ter Says _____

Transcendence describes the belief that God exists on a higher plane, such as heaven. God is beyond humans' ability to perceive. **Immanence** describes the belief that God exists throughout all of creation and that humans can experience God's presence on earth.

Protestants Worship from the Neck Up/Catholics Do It from the Neck Down

Do Catholics have a particular kind of religious sensibility or particular way they relate to God that contrasts with that of other religions? The question isn't meant to ascertain which way is "better," but rather only to ask whether there are different and distinctive ways of relating to God. It is quite obvious, almost at first glance, that something different goes on in Catholic Masses than what happens during Protestant services. One big difference is ritual. Dorothy Day, a twentieth-century U.S. Catholic hero, in her autobiography, *The Long Loneliness*, exclaimed, "Ritual, how could we do without it!" She further observed, "We have too little ritual in our lives."

Catholicism is more "right-brained" than Protestantism. (We'll discuss that later in this chapter.) Take the two important religious symbols used in both churches—the cross and the crucifix. As you enter most Protestant churches you will notice a cross usually centered on the wall over the altar. The cross does not have Christ's body on it. In a Catholic church, in the same place, you'll find the crucifix, which is a cross with the body of Christ on it. The body of Christ on the cross gives the symbol its essential Catholic sacramental character. Catholic experience of God begins with a sensual connection, which elicits an emotional response. The crucifix is meant to convey God's closeness to us here, within creation, through the presence of Jesus. When you contemplate the cross (without the body), you *think about* the crucifixion, with a bit of distance that allows some objectivity. As you contemplate the body of Jesus on a crucifix, on the other hand, you *feel* the crucifixion and have an emotional, rather than intellectual, reaction. Often the emotion it triggers is both uncomfortable and inescapable: It is unsettling at best to see the Son of God on the cross. In those moments, most experience a disquieting shiver, and God seems very real and imminently present.

The Cathedral of the Incarnation, Nashville, Tennessee.

(Courtesy of H. L. [Dean] Caskey)

Protestants are concerned about Catholic idolatry, superstition, and magic; they tend to have a real fear of identifying God too closely with nature. Thus, they emphasize God's otherness or difference from the world. Perhaps the best example of the vitality of Catholic imagery is the Catholic affection for Mary, which may well be the place where Protestants and Catholics most differ. Through Mary, Catholics experience the female face of God. She is a mother, loving, relational, and most of all, flesh and blood. So when you enter a Catholic church and see Jesus hanging on the cross, you have a powerful sensual impulse, a feeling that brings a reaction. This is Mary's child, our brother. The crucifix depicts a real person, not just an "idea" of God. For Catholics, the world is a sign (a sacrament) of God. God is in the world and is accessible to us through it.

The Hound of Heaven

The difference between Protestants and Catholics is further captured in what is called in theology the "Protestant Principle." This principle refers to the way of talking about God by defining what God is not. Protestant writings emphasize how God is different from objects, events, experiences, and persons in the natural world. The "Catholic Principle," however, looks for similarity and likeness, often by making an analogy. When Catholics talk about God, they are more likely to do it by saying how God is like objects, events, experiences, and persons in the natural world. A famous poem for Catholics is Francis Thompson's "The Hound of Heaven." In this poem,

> **Epiphanies**
>
> The magical term "hocus-pocus" comes from the most sacred moment in Catholic ritual: the consecration of the bread as the body of Christ by speaking the words "This is my Body," which in Latin is *"Hoc est Enim Corpus Meum"*

the author declares without any qualification: God is the hound of heaven chasing you down the paths of life until you are his. Protestantism originated in the age of the printing press, and it tends to use words and concepts as the first language describing God; image is the first language of Catholics.

The Touchy Feely Stuff

To sum things up, Catholic sacraments, ritual, and ceremony make up what we know of as a Catholic imagination—the quality of viewing the events of your life through a religious or spiritual lens. A well-developed religious imagination experiences the world as God's realm.

We know each other through our senses. We see, hear, smell, and touch one another, and we feel the emotions that being close brings. Sensations are physical evidence that something or someone is present. Jesus, the flesh and blood manifestation of God, continues to walk among us. We experience our awareness of this sacred presence through the senses. Catholics activate the senses through ritual and ceremony and create a dialogue with God that occurs at the physical level. The more a Catholic's senses are awakened, the more awareness there is of God. For Catholics, spirituality is about developing increasing awareness. Now, how do they do this?

A Full-Bodied Experience

Many Catholic rituals flow out of Judaism. Before that they were rooted in the indigenous cultures of those who lived in the Middle East. In short, these rituals go back to the beginnings of time. As Christianity moved into Europe, it blended with indigenous tribal people whose spiritual understanding was inscribed in their rituals. Both the pre-Patriarchal people of the Middle East and the indigenous Europeans connected with the sacred in and through their connection to nature.

For Catholics, the everyday awareness of God's presence comes through the senses— touch, taste, smell, sight, and sound—the gateway to deep parts of the human mind and imagination. As mentioned in Chapter 1, people who have "left" the Church often talk about taking it with them; indeed, Catholicism is often described as being in the bones. Since the beginning of the Church, Catholics have placed an emphasis on ritual, perhaps even more than book learning, and certainly more than on preaching. Ritual is what encodes religion into the body and bones of Catholics, not merely as a metaphor, but in reality.

Catholics believe they can touch, taste, and feel God through the senses, that they can draw God in through the breath, and see God through the bright colors of the vestments and stained glass windows. Just inside a Catholic church, you find containers of holy water, where Catholics dip fingers and make the sign of the cross, touching their forehead, heart, and left and right shoulders, connecting the mind and body to the presence of the sacred. They genuflect before taking their place in the pews, again getting the body involved in the experience. During the Mass, often the pungent smell of incense fills the church and the nostrils and the body is further brought to conscious awareness of the holy presence. The priest wears vestments of various colors: purple during Advent and Lent, white at funeral masses celebrating the Resurrection, Easter, and Christmastime, and green on all other Sundays. These vibrant colors touch the eyes. Catholics call these things—holy water, incense, rosaries, and vestments—*sacramentals* or little sacraments.

S'ter Says

Sacramentals are sacred signs such as medals, holy water, and even actions like the "sign of the cross." Through them, Catholics feel God's grace.

If the imagination is not excited, the intellectual and philosophical underpinnings of religion are meaningless. The bells, beads, and candles used in Catholic rituals are not just decorations; they are essential to spirituality and to effective Catholicism. In Chapter 13 we talk about these practices in more detail. Here the emphasis is on how and why the senses are involved in ritual.

The Bell: Call to Worship

In the Catholic Church the sound of bells fills the ear. Bells get our attention; they awaken hearing and tune the ears for what God has to say. The ringing of bells has always marked Catholic experiences of worship. The church bells ring in the neighborhood to announce Mass, calling the people to worship. Traditionally, as the priest entered the sanctuary, another bell rang to signal his arrival. The congregation stood in reception. Altar servers ring bells to invite a sacred response at the moment the priest consecrates the bread and wine. Bells remind Catholics to pause and reflect on the great mysteries of God's presence.

Your Guardian Angel

When you hear the bells ring at Mass, it is a signal to be especially attentive to a sacred moment. Bells are used to get your attention.

In the early morning hours, as day breaks, the church bells toll the Angelus, a special prayer offered three times a day. The bells ring this prayer again at noon to mark midday and at six in the evening to signal the close of the day. The Angelus ends with a two- or three-minute full ringing of the bells:

> The angel of the Lord declared unto Mary.
> And she conceived of the Holy Spirit.

Hail Mary …
"Behold the handmaid of the Lord."
"Be it done unto me according to your word."
Hail Mary …
And the word was made flesh.
And dwelt among us.
Hail Mary …
Pray for us, holy mother of God.
That we may become worthy of the promises of Christ. Let us pray:
Lord, pour forth we beseech thee,
thy grace unto our hearts
that we, to whom the incarnation of Christ thy son
was made known by the message of the angel,
may be brought, by his passion and cross,
to the glory of his resurrection,
through the same Christ our Lord. Amen.

In his painting titled *The Angelus*, Jean François Millet depicts peasants pausing in the field and reflecting on the great mysteries of salvation and redemption (see the figure). In the foreground, a man and woman stand praying in response to the ringing of the bells of the distant church. In the work, Millet portrays the peasant as one close to God. The abundant dirt is a reference to creation. He has blended the figures into a tone almost equal to that of the ground.

Jean François Millet, The Angelus.

(Courtesy Alinari/Art Resource, New York)

You'll also hear a bell tolled once every few seconds as a beloved parishioner is carried into the church for the last time. As the hearse pulls away, the bell tolls again. Bells carry the voice of God.

Books and Beads: Touching the Word of God

When Catholics touch their rosaries, they touch their God. Beyond the specific prayers associated with the beads, the beads themselves transmit a spiritual meaning through touch.

Late one evening in his bed, an 82-year-old lifelong Catholic suffered a sudden loss of breath and was unable to speak. His son arrived just as the paramedics responded to his wife's frantic 911 call. As his son accompanied him to the ambulance, his father expressed a great frustration, wanting the son to get him something but being unable to speak. Although his words were unintelligible, the son knew that his father expected him to understand what he wanted. Both of them became more and more agitated. Finally, when they got to the hospital and the father received enough oxygen to speak, he unleashed his great frustration by blurting out: "Get me my rosary, damn it!"

The father wanted that rosary in his hand. He was a Catholic to the bone. Throughout his life he had partaken of the sacraments, said his Rosary, dipped his fingers in holy water each time he entered the church, and fervently walked to the altar to receive Communion on his tongue. Through his faithful practices God had become present to him. When he reached a moment of crisis, he wanted to reach out for God and he turned to what he knew and trusted: the Rosary. For Catholics, sacramentals make God present.

Candle: The Fire of Change

Fire has always been used in ceremony to symbolize transformation and signify the presence of the transcended. Likewise, fire is another important ingredient in Catholic ritual. The first thing Catholics see when they enter a church is the sanctuary lamp burning on the altar. Its eternal flame signals the sacramental presence of Jesus in the tabernacle, as shown in the figure. Candles are lit at every Mass. On a weekday morning, there may be only two small ones burning, but on a big feast day, there might be as many as 12.

Before leaving the church, some Catholics might place a few coins in a metal stand that holds 20 to 40 small candles (shown in the picture). Lighting a candle, they say a prayer for a special intention or for a loved one. The candle burns for several hours as representing the prayers being offered. It also tells God, "If I could stay longer, I would, but I have to go now, so I'll leave this little candle burning in my stead."

During the Easter Vigil, the most dramatic moment occurs outdoors as the priest announces Christ has arisen while simultaneously lighting the Easter candle from a bonfire called the "new fire." The Easter candle is carried into a completely dark church, and the flame is passed candle by candle to all who have come to witness the risen Christ. In no time, the church is ablaze with new light.

Fire accompanies Catholics at the beginning of their Church life and at the end. Throughout the year, baptismal candles are lit from the Easter candle. When a person dies, a vigil light, similar to the sanctuary lamp, is left burning beside the casket.

Sanctuary lamp signaling the sacramental presence of Jesus in the tabernacle. Cathedral of the Incarnation, Nashville, Tennessee.

(Courtesy of H. L. [Dean] Caskey)

A stand of vigil light candles. Christ the King Catholic Church, Nashville, Tennessee.

(Courtesy of H. L. [Dean] Caskey)

Epiphanies
A priest lights the new fire with flint and steel before the celebration of the Easter Vigil Mass. This dramatic ceremony takes place after sundown on Holy Saturday. Everyone gathers outside the darkened church, and the fire is lit and blessed. From this fire, the Easter candle, representing the risen Christ, is carried into the church and from it the candles of all the faithful are lit, lighting up the church.

The Right Brain/Left Brain of Catholics

A widely accepted and popular theory postulates that the brain knows things through a tandem process occurring first in the right hemisphere and then in the left hemisphere. This bicameral process begins as an event, a sensual experience that registers in the right hemisphere—this eventually sparks a new insight. The left hemisphere then reflects on the insight, connecting it with previous experiences, which are now informed by the "new" experience, thus bringing deeper meaning to life. An event is the primary function, and thinking about the event is secondary, as the mind must always reflect back "on" something that has happened—an experience.

Let's see how it works by looking at a child's birthday party. Brightly colored balloons, delicious cake, the joy and laughter of the games, and the singing of "Happy Birthday," stimulate the senses. Later, the child is lying in bed, feeling the emotions that the party created, and feeling loved, happy, proud, and cared for. The fullness of the party began with the sensuousness of the event, a ritual, and the emotional reaction to it. It is then given meaning, through a thought process or conclusion the child draws from the experience, "I am a worthwhile person."

Catholic religion begins in ritual. Catholic ritual engages the senses (the right hemisphere) and is considered by many to be a "right-brained" religion. This is partially true. It is right-brained because the senses and the emotions evoked in ritual register in the right hemisphere. However, it is more accurate to say that it is a "whole-brained" religion because it engages both hemispheres. As you remember from the discussion earlier in this chapter, Catholic ritual engages the senses, and it is meant to evoke an emotional response. From this response, an insight is generated. This insight is then sent to the left hemisphere where reflection goes on.

Now let's take a look at how this all affects the practice of Catholicism.

Spiritual Time

The right brain does not register time in the linear way that the left brain uses, which is how we ordinarily *think* of time. In the right brain, all time happens right now. For example, think of the way you get caught up in memories when you look through old photographs. If you lean back and close your eyes, you may go deeper into these memories, and soon it may seem as if you are there again. You see the people in your mind's eye, even hear their voices and laughter. Such an experience seems very real, and you are apt to walk around all day feeling as if you have one foot in that day long ago and one foot in today. Catholic rituals work the same way. They allow you to have one foot in today and one in the "other" world.

Spiritual experiences, going back though the ages, have been encoded in ritual and religious traditions. Color, sound, scent, holy pictures, smells, and even movement (the standing, sitting, and kneeling for which Catholics are so famous) transmit these experiences, as well as bring new insight. When you are involved in the ritual, it is as if you are experiencing the past, and indeed you are. Who is to say which one is the more "real" occurrence: the one you are experiencing in your mind and heart, or the numbers as they appear on the clock? In fact, both are going on at the same time, and people participating in a ritual are in at least two dimensions of time.

Thinking Things Over

In addition to the tradition of ritual, however, Catholics are also known to be pretty "left-brained." There is no better example of a product of the left brain of Catholicism than the *Summa Theologiae* of Thomas Aquinas, a five-book, rational treatise on the nature of God, the premier work of Catholic theology going back to the thirteenth century. All major Catholic universities and seminaries continue to teach "Thomism" and theologians and philosophers of religion of all denominations study it. Of St. Thomas's many works, these volumes present a systematic treatment of several hundred important theological questions, ranging from God, the Trinity, and the nature of Christ, to the nature and psychology of the human person and the nature and mission of the Church.

Down through the ages, people have reasoned their way to God using theology and the thinking aspect of the Catholic brain. Others have engaged the mystery of the religion. Mystics, poets, musicians, and artists have brought insight into the nature of God gained through the feeling part of the religion. Today's Catholic continues to enjoy a synthesis of body and mind (intellect and sensuality) in rituals such as the Eucharist (Catholic Mass), the sacraments, and the insight derived from these spiritual experiences. Catholics then translate these insights into Catholic thought that eventually defines Catholic action in the world.

Blue Monday

The de-spiritualized world can be a dismal place. A Catholic often lives a dual life: attending a colorful Church filled with rich pageantry and powerful rituals that engage and feed both body and soul, but living in the workaday world where the rational mind reigns supreme. One of the major challenges Catholics (and all others as well) face in contemporary cultures like the United States is how exclusively left-brained they are forced to become in modern society. Such exclusive reliance on left-brain functions such as "pure" reason, while excluding the right brain's more subjective and relational values often results in the mind-numbing repetition of tasks that are empty of meaning and bring no fresh insight to a spirit hungry for substance.

Rituals come naturally to humans. When rituals are detached from spiritual or religious significance, they become tedious and empty. Many people tell of how such a ritual happens daily when the alarm clock rings, and they roll over, turn it off, get up, perform the bathroom rites, and engage the commuter traffic, only to arrive to work at a job that has lost its connection to their real values. They speak of returning home exhausted only to do it again the next day. Without new insight and connection that come from the right brain, there is only repetition. After a while, whatever meaning was once part of the work ritual has been lost. The spirit suffers and dies a piece at a time. No wonder there are more heart attacks on Monday than any other day of the week!

The same can be true of Church rituals. When people are put in the role of passive observer, their imagination is not engaged. Even the most spiritually nourishing ritual can become ho-hum if the distance between the priestly role and the people's role is too great. A healthy congregation depends on the vital engagement of the community in the ceremonies and services. Healthy religious ritual brings balance by nourishing the spirit, which keeps the body healthy and strong and renews the whole self. Out of that fresh space balanced thinking comes, and one's actions in the world make sense.

Formal and Informal Rituals

The Church has formal rituals such as the sacraments (discussed in detail in Chapter 11), and it also has informal rituals such as the one we're about to describe. While Confirmation is a formal rite of passage, our description of a young person's first time to participate in the adult world of Midnight Mass shows how an important truth can be transmitted unconsciously through an informal ritual.

The Sensate Stuff: Opening the Catholic Spirit

Imagine a young Catholic encountering the first opportunity to serve Christmas Midnight Mass. This child, on the brink of puberty, is probably in third grade, and likely enjoying his or her first time staying up so late—younger brothers and sisters are at home in bed. Freshly scrubbed, hair shining, sporting new clothes from the skin out, a dash of cologne or perfume lingering in the air: All signifies that a rite of passage is about to take place. The church is one block away, so the child is allowed to walk there alone, definitely something new. The chilly night air is charged with excited anticipation. This night is special. The informal ritual has begun; the approaching formal ritual will enforce this movement from the world of childhood into the adult world.

As the youngster approaches the church, cars are already packed into the lot. When this young Catholic enters the sacristy, a room just before the sanctuary, a crowd of people is already buzzing around in preparation, including several servers (all older), three priests (vesting), and a group from the choir putting on their robes. Flowers, along with freshly starched and ironed altar linens, and extra collection baskets are whisked by, carried by other helpers. The organ is playing carols. All these things awaken the senses, telling the mind the importance of this occasion. Without the connection to the physical events, the spiritual significance would not be as deep.

The group is lined up to go out into the church when the priest calls the child up to the front of the procession and places the statue of the baby Jesus, wrapped in a white cloth, into eager and trembling small hands. The door opens, and the neophyte leads the large group out into the church just as the organ strikes the sounding note and the choir begins to sing "Silent Night." This is a time to take in all the experiences: seeing, hearing, smelling, and touching Christmas. Spiritual experiences are being stored in the child's memory—becoming part of the psyche—from which the meaning of being Catholic, and belonging to the community of the faithful, will unfold from now on.

Levels of Meaning

During events like these, important things are happening to each person. You may not be able to put words to the experience immediately, but by engaging the pomp and ceremony, we are bound into a community, and that community transcends time and space. Ritual allows the mind to leap the chasm between the small picture of Catholic (those present in this particular church at this moment in time), and the big picture of "catholic" (all people everywhere in all time). Thus the true meaning of catholic, which embraces the whole, is accomplished.

The community of all people all over the world—now, back through the ages to Jesus and the original followers, and even before, to the very first people—all stand in solidarity, united by the Holy Spirit of God innately present in each and every person. Catholics as well as many other Christians say the words, "Do this in memory of me," during the ritual of the Eucharist. Regular practice of ritual and ceremony stimulates the senses, awakens the memory, and reinforces our spiritual connection to God *in* as well as *to* all of us. A shift to a deeper state of consciousness has occurred, where all is connected, and we know unity through the experience of it.

God's Constant Comment: Catholics' Cup of Tea

Ritual changes our consciousness and puts our brain in a meditative, dreamlike state. Prayer is often described as a time we talk to God (usually presenting our requests). Meditation, a quiet state, is where God speaks to us.

The Bible is full of important dreams. Notable dream communication in the Bible includes the Genesis story of Joseph, Jacob's son, who dreamed that he would rule over his brothers (Genesis 37:5). The book of Matthew tells of the important dream of another Joseph that warns him of Herod's plot to kill all male babies after the birth of Jesus (Matthew 2:13).

Letting Go and Letting God

In fact, God speaks all the time. The challenge, as always, is taking time to hear. Catholic ritual creates time for the thinking mind to be quiet, making it more likely that God's "voice" can be heard. Following ritual, there is a deepening and a relaxing of the thinking mind, the part of our brain that likes to stay in control. As long as we are "in control," we can't take in anything new, no matter the source. As the thinking mind stills, inner awareness increases. In this quiet space within, we can receive a sacred communication. It can come as an insight, an inspiration, a desire, or a sudden or unexplained knowing.

Your Guardian Angel

Dreams can be an important part of your spiritual life. Throughout religious history, God has spoken to people through their dreams. Today people often share their dreams with a spiritual counselor for insight.

For example, in your meditation, for no apparent reason, you might find yourself remembering times you spent with an old friend. The memory might be quite vivid; as if your friend is there with you. As you emerge from your meditation, again for no apparent reason, you think about making a phone call to a different person you know, who has been going through a rough time. Even later, perhaps as you are driving across town, you begin to feel a strong connection to other folks in your life. You may make further realizations over the next days and weeks, until one day you find you are simply flooded with the feeling of loving and being loved. The whole delightful chain of events began as a result of being quiet, and in this case, allowing a memory of an old friend to surface out of the myriad of memories and emotions floating around in the unconscious mind. Why this memory at this particular time? That's God's business. The ultimate purpose of religion for Catholics is love, and they believe God's will calls them to respond to the world and the inhabitants of the world in that fashion. Catholicism by nature is relational, and relationship is a right-brain function. As you read earlier in this chapter, the presence of the Holy Spirit in all of us is reinforced through ritual, and the bonds of community with the whole world are strengthened.

Follow Your Conscience

Making a decision is not simply a rational act for Catholics. It begins in the body as a felt twinge, and it packs an emotional punch, too. When the feeling side of the brain is left out of moral decision-making, we are left with nothing but a lot of laws and rules that might take a long time to work through. And as everyone knows, you can apply reason and arrive at almost any conclusion. Remember Adam and Eve's emotional realization that they had messed up? They were filled with shame. Without the feeling that something isn't right with our plan, we are morally vulnerable. Also, that very necessary quality of moral discrimination, empathy, which is our natural emotional connection to others, is likewise a feeling thing, and is wired into the right brain. All of this is really what we know of as moral instinct, the ability to hear God's instructions from within. If you cannot feel your inborn sense of right and wrong, your conscience is kaput.

Saints Preserve Us

St. Peter, June 29, Patron of Fishermen and Watchmakers

St. Peter, the patron saint of fishermen and watchmakers, was a fisherman of Galilee named Simon who gave up his family and possessions to follow Christ. Christ changed his name to Peter, which means "rock," and made him the "rock" on which his church was to be built. Catholics recognize him as the first pope of the new Church. Peter was known for his humanness: his anger, his imperfect faith, his impetuosity. When Jesus was arrested and the soldiers asked Peter if he knew him, he denied it three times. Under Nero's reign in the year 67, he was crucified with his head downward, at his request, because he said he was not worthy to die as did his Divine Master.

Catholics have numerous codes of behavior, such as the Ten Commandments, Scripture stories, and the teachings of the Church, to inform them. Yet the Church has always said that the bottom line in making a moral decision is "to follow your conscience." The key to an informed conscience is when intuitive knowing and what we have learned, matches. In order to do this, you have to be in touch with your feelings, your inner self. Again, Catholicism's high degree of ritual and ceremony builds the bridge into this inner world.

We have taken a look at how Catholics use ritual to feel God's presence (how Catholics are wired) and next we will see how Jesus is the ultimate sense experience of God.

The Least You Need to Know

- ◆ Catholics connect to God through the senses in the rituals that are an important part of the religion.

- ◆ Ritual connects Catholics to an inner voice and calls them to a moral response.

- ◆ Catholics emphasize God's presence in creation.

- ◆ Catholics use analogy to talk about God, to describe what God is like.

- ◆ Catholicism is a whole-brained religion as it uses ritual as well as theological reasoning.

Chapter 10

Jesus: The Original Sacrament

In This Chapter

- The mysterious and untouchable God
- The available and touchable Jesus
- The explanation of sacraments
- The Church as a presence of Jesus
- The presence of God in all things

A song in the early 1960s titled "What's It All About, Alfie?" could be the motto for all of us as we struggle to know life's meaning. We wonder how much we really know about the people and events in our lives. We constantly strive to know what is real only to find out there is more than we thought. We conclude everything has a greater dimension than what we can imagine. Why can't we take it all in? Why can't we know what it's all about? The answer is because we can only know through what we taste, touch, hear, smell, and see. We can get in touch with "what it's all about" only through our senses, and the senses take in the surface, not the inner hidden dimension. However, the senses open the religious imagination, and that's where we can experience deeper or hidden dimensions of reality.

The Catholic Church began with a new experience of God that came through personal contact with the man called Jesus. Jesus brought a different experience of God, into the picture—an extremely intimate experience. He talked to him like a parent, calling him *Abba*, which actually means *papa*. He taught that we could be intimate with God, too. The Catholic Church is organized around the idea of making this intimate relationship of creature to creator available on a regular basis.

S'ter Says

Sacrament originally meant mystery, a sense of something hidden. Later, in Roman times, it was translated as the word for the oath a soldier took when entering the military. He was marked or branded with the symbol of the person he was to serve. He was "consecrated" for service.

The early Catholic community understood Jesus as the flesh-and-blood connection with a mysterious, elusive God. Jesus' surface dimension of flesh and blood revealed the inner and hidden dimensions of God's presence. Catholics refer to Jesus as "the sacrament of God." *Sacrament* means something sacred. Jesus as sacrament describes the ongoing presence of the hidden dimension of God in creation. This presence is available to us through the awareness evoked by sacred or sacramental rituals connected to Jesus. The Church refers to itself as "the sacrament of Jesus" in describing the presence of the sacred in the community of Jesus' followers. We focus on Jesus and "sacramental" presence in this chapter.

The Very Brief Story of Jesus

The story of the historical Jesus is very brief, not because he wasn't important, but because there isn't much actually known about him as a historical figure. There was a man who lived in and around Jerusalem about the same time Jesus probably lived. This man was charismatic, and people came to hear him speak. He was a Jew, and most of his teaching followed Jewish traditions, but not always Jewish law in the strict sense. This man was arrested and tried in a court of law, although it seems his offenses were more of a religious than a political nature. He was evidently found guilty of the charges brought against him and then was crucified, a cruel punishment common among the Romans. That pretty much ends the life of the historical Jesus. The rest is taken on faith.

Therefore, faith testimonies found in the writing of his followers tell us most of what we know about him after his death, and they also give us insight into what the experiences of being with him signified for the communities of followers. They report that his body was taken down and buried. After three days, when the women went to anoint him, there was no trace of him left. An angel appeared and said he had risen. He made several appearances to them: The first was to tell the women to spread the news that the Son of God lives on in the Spirit. Fifty days after his death (Pentecost), he came to the apostles and disciples and gave them instructions to continue his teaching. This is considered the birthday of the Church.

The gist of his message was about loving one another, and about bringing the reign of God into being, a time characterized by justice for all people. What may have been his fatal error was his claim to be the Son of God—the Messiah, or Anointed One predicted in the Hebrew Scriptures. His followers were both men and women primarily from the Jewish world. According to the reports, Greeks, Romans, and others later joined the movement spawned by this profound, yet simple teacher.

The early Church communities weren't structured. People met in homes to reenact the Passover meal as Jesus had done in his lifetime, and to do good works—the essential message of his ministry. As the communities grew, they organized into what we now call the Christian faith in its earliest form, the Catholic Church. Just as Jesus sacramentalized, or made us aware of the sacred presence of God in the world, the early Church community sacramentalized, testified, to the continued sacred presence of God in the people.

The significance of the gospel stories of Jesus to Catholics is encoded in the sacraments of the Church, and is passed on in the re-enactment of the rituals.

Just What Is a Sacrament?

It isn't necessary to understand exactly how ritual does this, as the subconscious mind knows how, and that's where the connection is made. By now, we hope you've grown to understand the importance of Catholic ritual in keeping the experience of Jesus alive in the minds and lives of his followers. The Catholic Church has a rich sacramental life, and it tosses the word *sacrament* around a lot, using it in many ways, which can cause confusion to those unfamiliar with the religion—and even some who are familiar with it. For instance, the Church refers to Jesus as the "sacrament of God," and it calls the Church "the sacrament of Jesus." It specifies seven rituals as sacraments, including the principal one, and perhaps the most imbued with symbolism, Holy Communion, which is a re-enactment of the Last Supper. To illustrate its importance, Holy Communion is itself sometimes referred to as "the sacrament." Finally, the Church describes things such as rosaries, statues, holy water, candles, and incense as sacramentals, or little sacraments.

Then, of course, we have to factor in that a sacrament is essentially a mystery that can't be fully known. Part of its essence totally escapes the logical mind, and is best understood by flashes of intuition. With all that in mind, we'll wade into what we just said can't really be known, with the hope of at least gaining some ground.

Getting from Here to There

In a sacrament, three elements are present. Specific words are said, promises are made, and a mark or symbol such as water, oil, bread, or wine is used. The third part, the symbol, is the mystery of the sacrament, the sense of the hidden dimension and its unknowable quality. Sacraments function at the symbolic level. The word *symbol* comes from the Greek noun *symbolon*, which means "pulling together." Symbols bridge the gulf between the concrete experience and the meaning, which goes beyond the experience. One reason that the exact meaning of sacrament or symbol defies exact definition is that it continues to work on a person's subconscious mind, going deeper and deeper into the psyche over time. In a sacrament, the mark or symbol makes a physical connection between the person and the spiritual meaning of the event.

As symbols, sacraments are mediators; they are rituals that act as a medium in transferring something from one place to another, in this case the transmission of grace. They connect the visible to the invisible and the exterior to the interior dimensions of reality. Jesus is the mediator who connects human beings to God. The Church is the body of believers who mediate or connect to Jesus. Sacraments are the symbolic system by which these connections are preserved by the institutional Church. You might say that the institutional Church is the governing body who keeps this all straight.

Jesus, God's Sensible Side

Before Jesus, God was thought to be untouchable. In fact, among the Hebrews, his name could not be spoken. They referred to God as Yahweh, literally, "I am who am," which is not a name but a description. Catholics understand Jesus as the one who came in flesh and blood to close the gap between heaven and earth. His physical presence confirmed God's physical connection to the people. Jesus is the word of God, existing in human form. Through his birth, Jesus became God's gift of himself. Jesus is the touchable reminder of God's constant presence in the world and is God's very real connection to the human story.

In the modern vernacular, Jesus was a spinmeister; Catholics believe that Jesus put a whole new spin on God. He did this through his actions and his teachings. He broke the rules, he changed the social boundaries, changing the way people related to each other—how they lived together. For example, he invited women into his close circle, something that wasn't acceptable practice at the time. This explains why he was particularly popular with women. They even left their homes to follow him. He hung out with the "wrong crowd": meaning the poor, the uneducated, and others who more traditional religious leaders did not consider qualified to understand religious matters. He taught his followers that the presence of God is within each person, which goes against the idea of God present only in the temple and the law. His message was that God is not separate from his creation and that his creatures should not be separate from each other.

Catholics believe not just that Jesus was a historical figure, but that his message about God's presence lives on.

Your Guardian Angel

Get out and help others. To be a Catholic is to reach out to others who are in need. A Catholic cannot ignore or refuse this mission and stay true to the teachings of Jesus.

The Church, Jesus' Sensible Side

When the resurrected Jesus appeared to his followers after his death, he appeared in a transformed state. He was obviously in spirit form, yet he was apparent, perceptible to them; they could see him, hear him, and even touch him. After he did this, he imparted his Holy Spirit to be in the hearts and minds of the community he had gathered. This community of followers became the Church. Catholics believe that the Church became the "body" that would now contain his Spirit. They call themselves the "new body of Christ."

As you read earlier, sacraments are symbolic; they aren't scientific events. They can and do defy reason; nonetheless, they are real. In the scientific world in which we grew up, we have come to understand that things are only real if they can be reproduced in a laboratory and proven, using scientific principles. However, the imagination is also real. Today, at the most sophisticated levels of science, the most advanced scientists recognize this. We talk about the unification of science and spirituality in Chapter 24. The growing field of quantum physics now gives scientific credence to spiritual principles that have long been understood through faith.

Epiphanies

The Holy Grail is the cup from which Christ drank with his disciples at the Last Supper. It passed into possession of Joseph of Arimathea, and he gathered the precious blood of Jesus when his body was taken from the cross. Romantic legend says that it came to England, and it was the task of the knights of King Arthur to find it.

Wonder Bread

A central Bible story for the Church is Jesus' last meal with his friends in Jerusalem the night before he died. In an upper room, where they had gathered to celebrate the Passover, he took bread, blessed it, broke it, shared it with them, and said, "This is my body." He did the same with a cup of wine. Since that day, Catholics have continually repeated this action with the belief that God becomes real through the ritual eating and drinking of bread and wine. When the Church gathers to share the ritual meal of bread and wine, as they once did with Jesus, the spirit of God is present. For Catholics, this spirit takes form under the appearance of bread and wine, literally becoming the body and blood of Jesus. We continue this discussion in Chapter 11.

In Jesus' culture, a shared meal was a sign of a community's true intimacy. It was based on peace, trust, and nurturing. During the Last Supper, Jesus connected God's gift of nourishment, in the form of bread and wine, with his own body and blood. In light of his death that soon followed, he speaks of himself as a sacrifice. The Latin word for sacrifice is "to make holy." He is bringing to a closure his time on earth. He is allowing his followers to continue to share in the intimacy they have had together and the intimacy with God that he has brought to them. He does this by instructing them to continue the ritual meal in his memory. As he breaks the bread, so his body will be broken. As the wine is poured out, his blood will be spilled. As he connected his physical suffering to the touchable elements of bread and wine, he created a sacrament.

Your Guardian Angel

At a Catholic Mass, Communion is offered as both bread and wine. However, it is not necessary to partake of the wine in order to experience the full sacrament of the Eucharist.

The Church as Sacrament

The experience of the Last Supper was so powerful for the apostles that it etched itself into their memories. Each time the ritual is enacted, the memory of it is enlivened. Ritual creates an emotional response that is felt in the body, thus the connection to the original event is kept alive and experienced again and again. As the ritual continues over the years, it keeps its link through time, and makes God present for future generations.

The ritual sharing of bread and wine is called the sacrament of the Eucharist. It celebrates the intimacy between the Church and Christ and intimate communion among the people within the Church, as well. The Last Supper became the ritual the disciples did together at meals after the Resurrection following Jesus' request: "Do this in remembrance of me." The Catholic Church becomes a sacrament as it continues to enact this ritual.

The Kingdom of God Is Within

We are spiritual beings in human form. Spirit resides throughout the rest of God's creation as well. As a person becomes increasingly aware of the sacredness of creation, her or his imagined separation between the self and God disappears. One is acutely aware of the interconnectedness of all life and the hidden presence of God in all things. The Church would say that a person with this awareness becomes a living sacrament.

Religion is not about becoming more spiritual, but rather it is about becoming more aware of your spiritual nature. Jesus made this point the central teaching of his Gospel when he said, "The kingdom of God is within." For Catholics, the major point of Jesus Christ's incarnation was not to see him as different from them, but to recognize his likeness in themselves and others. As the God who took human form to be with the people, he shows them that they have a divine nature, too. Going against the dualism of the time in which he lived and even of our time today, Jesus demonstrated that the sacred and the worldly are not separate and that God exists in all life forms. The mission, should we choose to accept it, is to become more aware of our own divine nature, as well as sacred presence within one another, and to lovingly embrace humanness, a place where God's divinity resides. This is called sacramental awareness.

S'ter Says

A **spiritual director** is a person trained to work with people spiritually, much like a psychologist works with someone emotionally. Spiritual directors work with individuals and with groups of people in retreats.

Ignatius Loyola's Spiritual Exercises: A Journey into Sensual Imagination

Spiritual exercise has a long history in Church tradition. It refers to a disciplined and systematic approach to spiritual development. It was found in the desert traditions, the monasteries, and the cloistered life of the Middle Ages. Such practice is a vital part of Catholic life today.

The key phrase for the spiritual exercises of St. Ignatius of Loyola is "allowing the creator to deal with the creature." St. Ignatius set the traditional form of these exercises in 1556, and they are more popular than ever with modern Catholics and others.

The participants in these spiritual exercises attend a retreat center away from their homes and observe silence for four weeks, sometimes less. The intention of these retreats is to break through old ideas that we continue to cling to, even when part of our mind knows they aren't true any longer. This is done so that new spiritual insight can feed the mind. Subsequent decisions will be clear and unencumbered by the old, "inordinate attachments," as they are called. Under the leadership of a *spiritual director*, participants are led through meditations and encouraged to "play" with God and Jesus through their imagination. The leader takes the participants on an inner journey of imagination by using Biblical stories.

If you were looking for an answer to a question in your life, for instance, you would take this question with you into a spiritual journey and ask Jesus for advice. In your meditation, you might walk with Jesus on the road to Emmaus. The leader would connect you to the experience through the senses, asking questions like: What does the countryside look like to you? What is the temperature there? What does the road feel like to your feet? What are you wearing? What colors do you see? Who, besides Jesus, is there with you? What does it feel like to be there with Jesus?

Saints Preserve Us

St. Ignatius of Loyola, July 31, Patron of Retreats

St. Ignatius of Loyola, patron saint of retreats, was born in 1491 in Spain. After having painful surgery performed on his legs, he began reading devotional books. In a radical transformation, he dedicated himself to Christ. A depression drove him inward where he began to develop his spiritual awareness. He formulated his process into the spiritual exercises that bear his name and are still practiced today. He founded the Jesuit order, and his feast day is July 31.

As the senses are engaged by the questions, your imagination is activated, and you go deeper into your inner world. You are directed to imagine asking Jesus for his advice on the situation you are struggling with and imagine Jesus' response. Through this process, you are able to encounter the divine spirit that resides within you and receive deep spiritual insight.

St. Ignatius believed that God speaks to us through our imagination. The leader, acting as a guide, does not give advice, but helps direct people into their inner worlds, where the spirit of God resides and the answers can be found.

In this chapter, we have looked at how God is present to Catholics through Jesus, whom the Church calls the "sacrament of God." In the next chapter, we will get into the seven sacraments that mark the life of Catholics.

The Least You Need to Know

◆ Jesus came to show the connection between creation and Creator, so that spiritual presence could be more fully experienced.

◆ Sacraments are symbols that connect the visible and invisible dimensions—the other world and this one.

◆ The Church understands itself as a sacrament as people filled with God's spirit, as keeper of the mysteries, and a place where God's presence can be experienced.

Chapter 11

Seven Sensual Sacraments

In This Chapter

- How the sacraments connect Catholics to the sacredness of everyday life
- Why Catholics baptize babies
- Why Catholics don't divorce
- How a priest keeps confidences
- How the sacrament of the dead became a sacrament of the living

The seven sacraments form the framework of Catholic spirituality. Catholic children learn them like the days of the week. Sacraments mark key transitions in life, bringing spiritual meaning and power to the individual, and binding Catholics together. They are the heart of the Catholic community.

As we discussed in Chapter 10, sacraments are physical as well as spiritual. Each sacrament has specific form: It uses certain words accompanied by a prescribed action, and involves the symbolic application of an element—fire, water, oil, bread, and wine—to effect spiritual meaning. Catholics celebrate seven significant spiritual events that are divided into three groups.

The first group of sacraments is the sacraments of initiation: baptism, Holy Eucharist, and confirmation. The second group is called sacraments of state of life, including marriage and Holy Orders. And the third group is called sacraments of healing, and they include reconciliation and anointing of the sick.

This chapter examines the sacraments and explains what roles they play in Catholic life and faith. We'll begin at the beginning—baptism.

Baptism: More Than Just Water on the Head

Baptism is a rite of initiation, and it starts a Catholic on the faith journey by bonding the child to the community. It is a naming ceremony following a Catholic tradition of naming the child after one of the saints. Baptism also introduces the new Catholic to the community among whom they will live and grow spiritually. Likewise, the community commits to be the baptized person's guide and companion on the journey, offering spiritual mentoring when needed.

Catholics believe in infant baptism, although adults who have not been baptized in another faith receive the sacrament when they enter the Catholic faith. This process, called the Rite of Christian Initiation (RCIA), is described in Chapter 16.

S'ter Says

The **baptismal font** is a large container of water often made of marble and placed at the entrance of the church. At it, the priest or deacon pours the water that is used in the baptism of the candidate entering the Church. In some churches there is a pool of water for immersion.

Water on the Head

At an infant baptism, you will see a young couple presenting their new baby at the *baptismal font*, along with several family members, the godparents, and the priest. After greeting the people, the priest "signs" the infant with the cross in what Catholics call the imprint of Christ. Scripture is read and the priest anoints the child's forehead, lips, throat, and chest with holy oil as a protection from spiritual harm.

The baptismal water is blessed and the climactic moment comes when he pours it over the child's head. He does this in three distinct gestures while saying the words, "Mary (the child's name), I baptize you in the name of the Father, and of the Son, and of the Holy Spirit." Next he takes perfumed oil to anoint the child as a symbol of the enlightenment of the Holy Spirit. Some Catholic churches offer baptism by emersion.

Godparents stand nearby, holding the child's special candle that has been lit from the Easter candle on the main altar of the church. Godparents are chosen by the parents to sponsor the new candidate as he or she enters the Church. In the case of infant baptism, which is the usual time for the sacrament, they speak for the child, accepting the faith by responding to a litany of beliefs and reciting the Lord's prayer, or as Catholics are more apt to say, the Our Father. With a solemn blessing, the priest concludes the ritual and congratulates the parents.

Baptismal font and pool. Here you see a baptismal font in the foreground. Behind it is a shallow pool for immersion. Notice the Easter candle. Cathedral of the Incarnation, Nashville, Tennessee.

(Courtesy of H. L. [Dean] Caskey)

Who Can Baptize?

Although a priest or deacon usually performs baptism ceremonies at the church, anyone can baptize in an emergency situation (a car wreck, for example). Any person (Catholic or not) can pour the water and say the words. The only requirement is to follow the wishes of the person you are baptizing. Virtually all Christian religions baptize in a very similar way and the Church recognizes the baptism of Christians from other denominations as valid and would not re-baptize them if they chose to become Catholic.

The Church teaches that children who die before baptism are in God's loving care. Previously it taught that babies who died before being baptized went to "Limbo." This was a "happy resting place," but not heaven.

How Do You Assist at a Baptism?

If you're invited to a baptism but are unfamiliar with Catholic ritual, accept the invitation and let yourself be dazzled by all the ceremony. You'll see the child dressed in white, the name bestowed, the candle lit, promises made, and the child anointed with oil. A baptism is a sensuous ceremony, understood more by symbols than by words. Pay more attention to what people are doing rather than saying and you will more fully experience this ritual. Thirty years ago, this ceremony was conducted in Latin and hardly anyone present except the priest followed the words.

The Origins of Baptism

Entrance rites or rites of initiation, or naming ceremonies are part of all cultures. Exactly what is being signified differs according to each culture's beliefs. The prototype of this rite in the Christian Church is John the Baptist's baptizing Jesus in the waters of the river Jordan. However, it must be noted that John was following Jewish custom. According to the Bible, the heavens opened, and those who were present saw the spirit of God descending like a dove upon Jesus. A voice from the heavens announced, "This is my beloved son with whom I am well pleased." (Matthew 3:16–17) This event teaches two important points: First, the Holy Spirit is present at baptism; and second, baptism recognizes the person being baptized as a child of God.

St. Paul understood baptism as a drowning or a death and rebirth as a new being. Catholics believe that baptism washes away all sins. The Church recognizes two other times where baptism is implied. One dates back to the time of the martyrs, and is called baptism by blood, which means anyone killed for their beliefs is considered baptized. The other is baptism by fire, which occurs when someone desires to be baptized, but dies before having the opportunity.

In the first centuries of the Church, adult baptism was the common form of the rite. Joining a new community that wasn't Roman, Greek, or Jewish meant a radical change in one's life. As the religion became part of the Roman Empire, both the numbers of people who were becoming Christian and the way whole pagan tribes converted caused a decline in emphasis on instruction. In a few generations, infant baptism became the norm. Catholics renew their baptismal promises at Easter Mass, acknowledging that faith continues to grow after baptism, and we are always "new."

Eucharist: It's More Than Just a Bite of Bread

The Catholic Church uses the term Eucharist in two ways: to describe the celebration of the Mass and to define the sacrament of the Eucharist, also called Holy Communion. In this section, we are going to talk about the sacrament of Holy Communion. (We'll talk about the Mass in Chapter 15.) Holy Communion is a ritual enactment of the Last Supper, during which Christ promised his ongoing presence to his disciples. During their last meal together, he blessed bread and wine, saying, "This is my body. This is my blood. Do this in memory of me." The priest repeats these same exact words as he consecrates the bread and wine. The Eucharist is the central ritual of the Church. Catholics believe that the priest changes the bread and wine into the actual body and blood of Christ.

Invited to the Grown-Ups' Table

Typically, Catholics receive the sacrament of the Eucharist for the first time at about the age of seven at the rite called the First Holy Communion. The Church recognizes that previous to the age of seven a child is not considered morally responsible. The sacrament of reconciliation, discussed later in this chapter, accompanies First Communion, and preparation for the First Communion includes instruction about confession, too. Both sacraments mark the time in a child's life when he or she will begin to assume moral responsibility.

A child's First Communion celebration is often held on Mother's Day, and creates a lifelong memory. If you were to go to a First Communion celebration, you would probably see little girls in white dresses, shoulder-length veils, white stockings, and white shoes. The boys would be wearing white suits, white shirts, and white ties. They might enter the church in a procession, sitting in the first several pews in front. This exciting time in the Catholic child's life is like being invited to sit at the grown-ups' table at Thanksgiving or Christmas. The children are being included in one of the most important rites of the Catholic Church. The ritual then becomes central to their spiritual life. Unlike the first two sacraments, baptism and confirmation, which are received only once, Catholics receive the Eucharist at every Mass.

Feeding the Spirit

The elements of the sacrament come from the earth—wheat that is specially made into bread and grapes made into wine. (By the way, Catholics use real wine, rather than the grape juice customary in most Protestant churches.) During the Mass, the priest speaks the words of consecration over the bread and wine, transforming it into the body and blood of Christ. This ritual is called transubstantiation, indicating that the elements of the sacrament, bread and wine, are substantively changed.

Those who are going to receive the Eucharist—usually almost everyone in the church—walk up the aisle to the priest or Eucharistic ministers, and are given the bread, called the host, and are offered a drink of wine out of a chalice. It is not necessary to take the wine, as either element (bread or wine) completes that part of the ritual. After receiving the sacrament, it's customary to return to your place, kneel down, and meditate or offer prayers of thanksgiving until everyone has received the sacrament and the rite is completed.

Prior to Vatican II, no one but the priest was allowed to touch the consecrated host; the priest placed it on the tongue of the person receiving it. Catholics continue to have a deep respect for the Eucharist, and there are special rules regarding how the consecrated elements must be handled. For example, Catholics refrain from eating or drinking anything but water for an hour before receiving Communion. Before Vatican II, it was the custom to abstain from all food and drink, even water, from midnight until they received the Eucharist. Today, lay members are allowed to touch the sacrament and those receiving it can take the host in their hands and place it in their mouth themselves. The priest or other Eucharistic minister will bring Communion to the home or hospital for the sick and homebound, where a prayer is said and thanksgiving is shared.

Eucharist: A Catholic's Thanksgiving

Eucharist means thanksgiving, and is rooted in an earlier Jewish ritual where the term described the practice of giving thanks during a meal for God's creation, redemption, and sanctification. Eucharist is a symbol of God's nurturing care, offering both physical and spiritual life to the people in the form of bread and wine. In Chapter 9 we described in detail how ritual awakens deep memory and connects those who participate back through time to all who have performed the ritual. The Eucharist reaches back through the ages to the Last Supper, connecting today's Catholics to the ritual Passover meal when Jesus first blessed bread and wine and instructed his followers to do as he did as a way of remembering him. It is the way Christ remains present and accessible to his Church.

Communion is also an important bonding ritual. Just as a family sits down at the table together regularly to secure their connection to one another and also their identity as a family, Catholic bonds are strengthened through this ritual. United with Christ in the Eucharist, the congregation is unified with each other, becoming one body. Because it is both physical and spiritual food, Communion serves as a reminder of the practice of charity toward others less fortunate, teaching compassion for the poor.

Catholics are encouraged to receive Communion every time they attend the Mass, but they must receive it at least once a year. It is reserved for people who are in full relationship with the Catholic Church, including Orthodox Christians. Usually, if you are a non-Catholic guest at a Catholic Mass, you do not partake of the Eucharist.

Confirmation: It's No Longer a Slap on the Face

A typical memory of growing up Catholic several decades ago includes being confirmed: being 12 years old and standing before the bishop, trembling with fear. You worried that you would be asked a question and not know the answer, even though there was little chance that would happen, because you had spent the year in preparation, memorizing the entire Baltimore catechism, and a list of prayers that covered all situations. And then there was the anticipation of the slap in the face to worry about. Although it was merely a token touch, it carried the warning that life could be tough, and you were expected to be tougher. Receiving this sacrament took you out of the child camp and put you in with the adults. Taking the slap was the sign you were ready to face the spiritual challenges that lay ahead.

Your Guardian Angel

If you're invited to a confirmation celebration, it is customary to give the guest of honor a small gift. (May we suggest a copy of *The Complete Idiot's Guide to Understanding Catholicism, Second Edition?*)

Origins of the Sacrament of Confirmation

Confirmation has its roots in the coming-of-age ceremonies found in most cultures, and was traditionally received at the age of puberty. It corresponds to the Jewish rite of passage, bar mitzvah for boys and bat mitzvah for girls, which is the ritual ceremony that marks the thirteenth birthday of a Jewish child, after which they are expected to take full responsibility for moral decisions and conduct. The biblical roots of confirmation are in the New Testament story of Jesus' baptism by John, Matthew 3:10-12 and the story of Pentecost, found in Acts 2.

In Matthew, John says, "As for me, I baptize you with water for repentance, but He who is coming after me is mightier than I, and I am not fit to remove His sandals; He will baptize you with the Holy Spirit and fire."

After rising from the grave, Christ promised his followers that he would send his Spirit to be with them. Pentecost means 50, and 50 days after the Resurrection, the followers were gathered together in a room attempting to continue the practice of a ritual meal. However, fear had gotten the best of them, and they couldn't imagine how they would be able to continue Jesus' work. A sudden storm began to blow, rattling the shutters on the room, further adding to their fear. Then the Holy Spirit came to them, appearing over their heads as tongues of fire. They were filled with inspiration and the strength to carry the teachings into the world. When they spoke, each person could hear them in their native language. Since the official ministries of the followers began that day, Pentecost is considered the birthday of the Church. Confirmation is the baptism of the Holy Spirit completing the water baptism.

Oil and Words and the Holy Spirit

Confirmation increases and deepens the process of initiation into the faith begun at baptism, this time with conscious awareness. Those seeking confirmation must be of age to understand what they are committing to, and must have completed a rigorous study of the religion. (Although in the Eastern Churches, confirmation is received in infancy, along with baptism). It bestows spiritual strength for the next leg of the journey, and also strengthens the bond between the individual and the community. Many parishes require candidates to take part in a service project in their community, such as working for a local agency like Meals on Wheels or Habitat for Humanity. This voluntarism demonstrates the candidate's willingness and ability to take Christian values out into the world.

Confirmation, the second rite of initiation, is also a naming ceremony. In baptism, the child was given a name. In the sacrament of confirmation, the young adult chooses his or her name, usually that of a saint whose life story reflects values that hold a particular meaning. Candidates choose a sponsor to stand up with them. This part of the ritual uses touch, as the adult sponsor places a hand on the candidate's shoulder, transmitting the physical sense of support. The message is that the youngster is going out into the world, but they are not alone, they are not without support. The sponsor is promising to provide lifelong guidance. Often, one of the baptismal godparents plays this role.

Those being confirmed stand in front of the congregation, and the bishop, who usually administers the sacrament, extends his hands over them while saying a prayer. In a tradition that goes back to the time of the apostles, extending of the bishop's hands signifies the awakening of the Holy Spirit.

Your Guardian Angel

Don't be fearful when you hear the phrase "fear of the Lord!" This gift of the Holy Spirit refers to the Old Testament idea of trembling in awe or wonder in the presence of God. Thus, its deep meaning is reverence for God, not being fearful of God.

The bishop says the new name as he anoints the forehead of each candidate with chrism (holy oil), followed by a laying on of hands, saying the words, "Be sealed with the gift of the Holy Spirit." The oil the bishop uses represents abundance and joy. Being sealed with oil means to be marked as belonging to Christ. It signifies the one receiving the seal is committing to align his or her will to the will of God. Oil also gives strength to the body. The very name

"Christian" means anointed, and this is why the confirmation rite is essentially an oil rite rather than a water rite like baptism. To conclude the rite, the bishop offers the sign of peace, which is a handshake, affirming union with the community.

The Seven Gifts

Catholics believe that confirmation awakens certain spiritual attributes called the seven gifts of the Holy Spirit, described in the Old Testament: Wisdom, Understanding, Right Judgment, Courage, Knowledge, Reverence, and Fear (awe) of the Lord. Catholics believe that all members are called to share in the priesthood of Christ in that they will be called to publicly and officially profess and mediate the faith of the Catholic Church at times in their lives. Confirmation is the sacrament that opens this "priestly" function.

> ### Epiphanies
>
> Confirmation corresponds to the appearance of the Holy Spirit to the apostles on Pentecost. In the first centuries, when baptism was generally administered to adults, confirmation accompanied it. This is still the case when an adult is brought into the Church today and in the Eastern Rite Catholic Churches. Eventually, as the practice of infant baptism grew, the time between the two sacraments lengthened to include the age of discernment, and it became the tradition of the bishop to administer it.

Menagé à Trois: It's More Than Just Two in a Marriage

In a Catholic marriage, three parties are involved: the husband, the wife, and Jesus Christ. Not only is marriage a lasting relationship between partners, it is also considered a covenant relationship, based on the covenant relationship between God and his people. Covenant relationships cannot be broken, and Catholic marriage is for life, with very few exceptions. Therefore, thoughtful preparation and prayer precede the marriage vows.

I Do! I Do!

A Catholic marriage usually takes place during a special "Nuptial Mass." Guests who are not forewarned can be surprised at the length of the ceremony! Usually, you will find liturgy books in the seats that will help you follow the service. The wedding party enters the church in a ceremonial way, taking places in the front of the church near the altar. Prayers and scripture readings for the service have been selected in advance by the couple. The celebration of the Mass begins, and vows are exchanged.

Your Guardian Angel

Check your Sunday bulletin for Wedding Banns! Catholic parishes announce the forthcoming weddings of their parishioners in what are called the "Wedding Banns." These are usually published in the Sunday bulletin.

Unlike the other six sacraments, the priest does not administer this sacrament, but rather the couple marries each other. The principle of consent is the central feature. Consent is fulfilled as the parties mutually agree to give themselves to each other. "I take you to be my wife." "I take you to be my husband." The priest or deacon is the official witness to the consent of the spouses and they give the blessing of the Church to the ceremony. The best man and maid of honor represent the connection of this marriage to the Church community.

A Covenant Relationship

A covenant is more than a civil agreement. It is also religious in nature, and religious covenants cannot be broken. Catholics believe that God enters into the covenant relationship with the couple, which means they will be given the spiritual support and insight to maintain the marriage as long as they keep the covenant. In other words, God gives the couple a spiritual guarantee to stay with them and provide the necessary grace to help them grow individually and together over their lifetimes. Their part of the covenant is the promise to hang in there, even when the times are tough, or, more traditionally stated, for better or for worse.

In forming the covenant, the couple enters a partnership with God in creation; this has traditionally meant that the prime intention of Catholic marriage is to have children. From the time of Augustine up until Vatican II, Church teachings specifically stated: "The primary end of marriage is the procreation and nurture of children; its secondary end has to do with sexual satisfaction."

Vatican II again restated both of these principles, but recognized the importance of the comforting and bonding aspects of sex, making them of equal importance.

For Heaven's Sake!

Look before you leap! Marriage is a lifelong partnership commitment, based in love, for the well-being of the spouses and for the purpose of having and nurturing children. It is absolutely dependent on the free consent of the couple.

This means having children and sexual enjoyment together constitute the primary intention of marriage. The fact that having children is still foundational to Catholic marriage does not mean that couples who can't have children are not fulfilling the contract. This same thing applies to couples who marry later in life, past their childbearing age. Such marriages carry the complete sacramental blessing. As you will learn in Chapter 18, Catholics are not allowed to practice artificial contraception of any kind.

Forever Is a Long Time

Because a Catholic marriage cannot be dissolved, and consent is key, there is a mandatory preparation for it known as the Pre-Cana sessions. These group sessions, typically six in number, include prayers and possibly a retreat weekend in which the religious and spiritual aspects of the marriage relationship are talked about in great detail. The sessions are practical as well. They include communication skills, finances, and lectures about human sexuality and health issues. Although the parish priest coordinates these sessions, parish laypersons facilitate them.

In the case of mixed marriages, where one party is Catholic and the other is not, further instruction and preparation is required. The purpose is to find helpful ways in which the couple can fully express their love and faith with spiritual unity.

The Church does not recognize divorce between any two baptized people of any denomination. It does acknowledge the need for physical separation, such as when there is violence in the marriage. However, the man and woman involved are never free to contract a new union.

Saints Preserve Us

St. Elizabeth of Portugal, July 4, Patron of Marital Problems

St. Elizabeth of Portugal (1271–1336) is invoked against marital problems because she had a reputation around town for interceding as a peacemaker in many marriages. After the death of her husband, Elizabeth joined a convent of the Sisters of St. Claire, which she had founded.

The Church also acknowledges situations when an invalid marriage has occurred; where there was not complete consent, or complete consent is compromised because of deception by either one of the couple. In this case, the word annulment is used because the marriage is not dissolved, but declared null—it didn't happen. Annulment is a lengthy and sometimes expensive process, handled by a Church court.

Holy Orders: It's More Than Just Oil on the Fingers

Holy Orders is the sacrament by which a man commits his life to serve the faith community. With this commitment, he is granted the responsibility and power to preside over sacred rituals, offering Mass, forgiving sins, giving blessings, administering sacraments, and attending to the spiritual life of the people he serves. Holy Orders is traditionally thought of as a higher calling, and those who accept the call are expected to live up to higher standards than the rest of the folks. The priest becomes a symbol of Christ's presence, which carries both privilege and responsibility.

The Church teaches that all Catholics share in the priesthood of Christ. At the same time, it recognizes that the ordained person must meet certain obligations of service of a higher degree than those who are not ordained. Two primary priestly responsibilities are care of the spiritual needs of the people, and care for the institutional Church, meaning its rules and regulations.

In the Beginning ...

In the early years of the Church, there was no ordination, no priests or bishops as we know them today. By the end of the first century, two important offices began to emerge: that of overseer, which would later become the office of the bishop, and that of presbyter, the position that became deacon and priest. In the second century, the terms ecclesiastical and priestly began to identify these roles as something apart from the laity. One of the early Church writers, Tertullian, considered these offices more institutional than spiritual. The spiritual quality was developed a bit later, but the tension between these two priestly identities continues today.

Eventually, the presbyters (priests) did more and more of the hands-on leadership, and the bishops confined themselves increasingly to administration. The Church recognized Holy Orders as a sacrament in the 1100s.

Although Holy Orders is a "one-time only" sacrament, it is received in levels as three separate ordinations, from deacon to priest to bishop:

- **Deacons** are assistants to the bishop and usually work in charities in the parishes where they are assigned. They perform a number of sacramental ministries, especially marriage and baptism.

- **Priests** celebrate the Eucharist. They are appointed as the pastors of parishes.

- **Bishops** celebrate the sacrament of ordination and appoint priests and deacons to parishes. They are in charge of the parishes that make up a diocese.

Epiphanies

There are two types of deacons. Prior to Vatican II, ordination as a deacon was only a stepping stone on the way to priesthood. A man would be ordained deacon about six months before he was to be ordained priest. Today that step continues for those going on to priesthood. These men are called "transitional deacons." However, the Church has restored the "permanent diaconate" of the early Church as an order of leadership and service in its own right. Presently, only men are candidates for this office. They can be married, but if their spouse dies, they may not remarry. They must be 35 years of age or older.

The Ceremony

Only bishops can administer the sacrament of ordination, and it takes three to ordain a new bishop. One officiates, and the other two are witnesses. The ritual of Holy Orders for all three levels follows essentially the same form. It is administered during a special Mass usually performed on Sunday in a cathedral with as many of the faithful taking part as is possible. It is a high celebration, with much pomp and circumstance.

The rites begin with a presentation of the candidates and a ritual "calling forth" of those who will be ordained, symbolizing the enactment of "vocation" or God's calling them to the priesthood. The common phrase describing a man's decision to enter the priesthood is *vocation;* the word is from the Latin and means calling, which signifies that God is the one who calls. This is followed by an "instruction" by the bishop, who tells them what is expected of them as they receive this office. The first quality of the priest is his openness and ability to listen to God's will or "call."

The bishop then asks a series of questions to examine the adequacy of the person seeking ordination. Again, the questioning is symbolic, because the preparation for this sacrament has been extensive. As in confirmation, there is a laying on of hands by the bishop. In addition to the symbolic calling, instructing, and laying on of hands, there are many other symbols used in the ritual. Candidates lie face down on the floor in front of the altar, symbolizing humility, service, and connection to the world, as well as the priesthood. Those being ordained as bishop are anointed with holy oil, given the book of the Gospels, a ring, a special hat (called a miter), and a staff (called a crosier). Priests are presented with a paten, which is a gold plate on which the Communion bread is placed during the Mass, and a chalice, which is the container for the Communion wine. Their fingers are anointed with holy oil because they will be handling the consecrated host. Deacons receive a book of the Gospels.

A Few Good Men

Ordination is the Catholic Church is reserved for men only. Many women also feel called to the priesthood, and must fulfill this calling through service or ministry by different means. Traditionally, women joined religious orders as nuns, where they often served as teachers and health-care workers, as well as orders where prayer and meditation is the focus. Today, women go to seminaries and prepare themselves for various Church leadership positions. We discuss this process in Chapter 24.

Ordination is considered lifelong, so there is a long process of discernment before one is admitted into the final stages of the process. It can take as long as four or five years of seminary training after college. A seminary is a graduate school that has two purposes: One is academic training, and the other is spiritual formation of the candidate. Not only must a man demonstrate his intellectual ability, but he must also show his spirituality and willingness to serve. The final decision is mutual, based on the personal willingness of the candidate to accept the role, and assessment of his fitness for the priesthood by Church officials.

Celibacy is mandatory for priests and bishops. Being celibate means you cannot get married or have sexual relations. Celibacy was instituted gradually over the first thousand years of the Church. There is an exception to this rule in the Eastern Rite for priests, who can marry. In addition, married clergy from other denominations who seek Catholic ordination can be accepted as married priests and remain married. Deacons also can be married.

There is much heated debate in the Church over both the issue of the all-male clergy and mandatory celibacy. The present pope has suspended official dialogue on both matters, but that has not quelled the unofficial fires. The recent attention drawn on the Church due to the sex scandals among the clergy has certainly poured gasoline on the fire. At the same time, there is no officially or universally recognized direct link between celibacy and sexual abuse of children, or to the existence of an all-male clergy. Both these topics and more on the subject are found in Chapters 19 and 25.

Penance: It's More Than Just a Kick in the Pants

Penance, now called "reconciliation," is better known among Catholics as "confession." Confession has always captured the public imagination—probably because of its very secretive nature; the whole idea of going into a dark little booth and telling someone your deepest faults seems strange to many. However, most people agree that confession is good for the soul. Great mystique surrounds the role of the priest, and many a good story has been spun about his refusing to break the seal of confession, refusing to betray the confessed, even when testifying in court.

For years, Catholics observed a weekly rite of examining their consciences, sorting out greater and lesser sins, and entering the confessional box to anonymously whisper them to the priest who sat on the other side of a tiny screen door. Today, most Catholics do not observe the weekly rite of confession, and the setting for the sacrament can include sitting face-to-face with a confessor in a room rather than the little black box. However, this sacrament remains an important part of Church practice. This section looks at the practice today.

Confession Is Good for the Soul

The sacrament of reconciliation has two parts: confessing your sins and forgiveness by the priest in Christ's name. Confession begins with a time of personal reflection, where Catholics examine the events of their lives, particularly their actions and reactions to the people and situations they are currently experiencing. In reflecting, they might assess themselves in light of the Christian principles most important to them. They determine where they are measuring up to their ideals and where they are falling short. As this assessment is made, they might discover particular thoughts, feelings, or actions that are out of alignment with what they know is right, asking questions such as the following:

◆ How could I have responded (in a given situation) in a more loving way?

◆ What habit or tendency do I have that needs to be changed?

◆ Where have I contributed to problems in my world?

◆ Where am I having problems in my spiritual life?

◆ Where do I need healing?

The process eventually leads to identifying patterns of behavior that need to be addressed. While confession once seemed to be focused on cataloging and measuring sins, it has always included a more positive process of self-reflection and moral housekeeping. That is certainly the emphasis today.

Sin, the "S" Word

At the same time, no discussion of confession would be complete without talking about *sin*. While some Catholics fear the Church has gone soft on sin, today it is more likely to be identified as simply falling short of the mark instead of something more evil. We commit a sin when we don't measure up to what we know is right.

The Catholic Church identifies two levels of sin based on the seriousness and pervasiveness of the offending behavior. Mortal sin is a consistent and pervasive action and fundamental negative disposition to God's will. It is an indication of serious moral decline and it carries serious consequences. Venial sins concern lesser offenses and carry lesser consequences, but are not to be ignored.

S'ter Says

Sin is a thought or an action that is contrary to the will of God. If left unchecked, it creates a pattern of problematic behaviors. The sacrament of reconciliation helps uncover the pattern and correct it.

Reconciliation is the point of this sacrament. Catholics understand that when a person is consistently acting contrary to what is accepted in the normal range of behavior either in the general community or within the Church community, there is a fundamental break in the relationship happening. Reconciliation means "to go with again;" it heals the brokenness caused by sin. The concepts of sin and forgiveness will be discussed in greater detail in Chapter 18.

Bless Me Father, for I Have Sinned ...

Following the time of self-reflection, also known as the examination of conscience, the penitent, the one going to confession, either enters the confessional or the reconciliation room where they will talk with the priest. Traditionally, the opening line of confession began with "Bless me father, for I have sinned." This is followed by ...

- Telling your sins to the priest.
- Expressing true sorrow.
- Making a firm commitment or promise to change your behavior.

In turn, the priest ...

- Extends the forgiveness of Christ through the position he holds as a priest in the Church.
- Determines the reparation or penance.

The penitent then ...

- Prays the Act of Contrition.
- Performs the penance given (after leaving the confessional).

Penance usually comes in the form of prayers or acts of charity the penitent must do. If reparation is appropriate, that, too, must be done. However, according to the teaching of St. Paul, the sinner is forgiven by God when still in the sin. Confession is the symbolic acting out of this belief. The priest acts symbolically as Christ, forgiving sins through God. His role is symbolized by the stole he wears—part of the priest's vestments.

The Little Black Box

Even to Catholics, the rite of confession seems mysterious and often uncomfortable. In the past, it was common to receive this sacrament in the confessional box, as shown in the illustration of a traditional confessional. The priest sat in the middle of three stalls. There was a small, screened sliding door on each side, opening to the other stalls. When the penitent on the right was confessing, the other door was closed so that others could not hear. There were no lights, conversation was whispered, and there was a sense of anonymity.

Today, Catholics have the option of face-to-face confession in a reconciliation room. In this style, a person sits down with the priest and confesses in a more conversational and interactive manner.

In addition to private confession, parishes hold communal penance services to emphasize the corporate nature of sin. Communal services emphasize the social consequences of all sin. In such a service, there are Bible readings and reflections about the correct Catholic response to social issues. Such a service concludes with the opportunity for individuals to go to confession privately.

A traditional confessional. Christ the King Catholic Church, Nashville, Tennessee.

(Courtesy of H. L. [Dean] Caskey)

Guilt: The Gift You Leave Behind

Reconciliation celebrates forgiveness and God's willingness to heal us, and it develops introspection and moral responsibility. The Church teaches that a person becomes responsible for their actions some time between the ages of 7 to 12, as the sense of right and wrong develops. From this age onward, Catholics must receive the sacrament of Eucharist and reconciliation, if necessary, at least once a year. The Church teaches that all sins are forgivable.

The sacrament of reconciliation recognizes that sin creates a block between us and God. The effect of reconciliation is to restore the person to a sense of intimate friendship with God. No sin is entirely private; it affects others. Sin is about broken relationships—between the self and God, self to self, and self to the community. It's not just the penitent who is affected by the sacrament, but also the sense of community and trust within the Church is restored.

Forgiveness absolves guilt. The penitent goes forward, unencumbered by the past, and participates more fully in life. Confession is usually followed by a feeling of peace and serenity, a strengthening of the spirit, and joy.

A contemporary confessional with the option of face-to-face confession, shown by the two chairs, or traditional confession with the screen. The Cathedral of the Incarnation, Nashville, Tennessee.

(Courtesy of H. L. [Dean] Caskey)

Anointing of the Sick: More Than a Simple Good-Bye

Before Vatican II, this sacrament of anointing the sick was commonly referred to as "the Last Rites," or "*Extreme Unction*," both suggesting a sense of finality. Many a story has been told of a Catholic waking up from a deep sleep during a serious illness only to find a priest administering the Last Rites. Because this sacrament was the spiritual equivalent of calling 911, or worse, throwing in the spiritual towel, you can imagine the devastating effect this might have had. Even today, chaplains report that when they go to visit a sick Catholic, they are often greeted by a hand signaling stay out, and the proclamation "You don't need to visit me today; I'm feeling just fine!"

Three for the Price of One!

The Last Rites are comprised of the three sacraments of reconciliation, Holy Eucharist, and the anointing of the sick. It was generally administered only at the point of death. The new name, anointing of the sick, makes it clear that this sacrament is about healing.

Under the reformed rite, use has grown to include this sacrament as a healing aid for those who are seriously ill, either physically or emotionally. It is given to people going into serious surgery, the elderly and frail, and even those who are victims of substance addiction and emotional or mental illnesses, as a means of strengthening the spirit and encouraging healing. The sacrament is now received more than one time.

Healing Body and Soul

The priest lays his hands on the sick and prays silently over them. He anoints the forehead with blessed oil (oil blessed by the bishop on Holy Thursday) praying, "Through this holy anointing may the Lord in his love and mercy help you with the grace of the Holy Spirit." He then anoints the hands of the sick person saying, "May the lord who frees you from sin save you and raise you up." The practice can be preceded by reconciliation and followed by Holy Eucharist.

S'ter Says

Extreme Unction was one of the former names of this sacrament of anointing of the sick. Extreme refers to the condition of those who are departing, and unction means oil. Receiving the Eucharist is part of the Last Rites. The sacrament of the Eucharist is called Viaticum when a dying person receives it. Viaticum is a Latin word meaning "on the way with you."

The sacrament honors both the physical and spiritual healing presence of Christ. It holds both strengthening and curative powers and brings wholeness and well-being to those who receive it. This sacrament brings the following gifts:

- Cures in the form of strengthening, peace, and courage to overcome the difficulties that go with serious illness or the frailty of old age

- The gift of finding spiritual meaning for health and physical struggles

- Preparation and fortification for the final journey

- Forgiveness of sins

Just as the sacraments of initiation (baptism and confirmation) begin the Catholic journey with anointing, this last sacrament points to the end of life's journey by strengthening through anointing.

Transformation for the Community

Before the reform of this sacrament at Vatican II, Extreme Unction was a very private affair between the priest and the dying person. Today, however, with a greater awareness of the effect of illness and death on the family and the community, friends and family are invited to be a part of this rite.

During the first 800 years of Catholicism, Catholics brought blessed oils home with them from Mass to anoint sick family members. Until Vatican II, anointing was restricted to the ministry of the priest and was kept for "deathbed situations." This restriction did not properly take into effect the physical as well as spiritual healing available through the sacrament. It has become quite common on given Sundays throughout the year to make anointing ceremonies part of the Mass. At these ceremonies, people in need of special healing come forward for anointing. The membership of the Church witnesses, prays, and supports the person's healing.

In such a setting, an intense transformation can take place when a large group of people prays for those who are sick. The event opens the participants to shifts of consciousness, resulting in a deeper sense of community and awareness of one's personal journey.

As you can see, the seven sacraments are essential to the life of devout Catholics, framing their spiritual life, and bringing strength to the challenges of "regular" life. In the next chapter, we'll tell you about Mary, who has been called "the people's sacrament."

The Least You Need to Know

♦ Sacraments mark natural passages and events in the lives of Catholics.

♦ Sacraments give spiritual and physical support in the life journey.

♦ Catholics practice seven sacraments honoring events from birth until death.

♦ Sacraments use specific elements and prescribed procedures that draw on both biblical and natural traditions.

♦ Sacraments transmit meaning, give grace, and give spiritual order to the Catholic's life. They represent the presence of the Risen Christ in the Church.

Chapter 12

Who Is Mary?

In This Chapter

- ◆ How a simple Jewish girl became the mother of God
- ◆ How the stories of many cultures meet in Mary
- ◆ How Mary functions as mediator and co-redeemer
- ◆ How Mary continues to appear to people all over the world
- ◆ How people pray to Mary

It would be impossible to imagine Catholicism without Mary. Her place in the Church is unrivaled. Just as Jesus is the sacrament of God, and the Church is the sacrament of Jesus, Mary is the people's sacrament. From the earliest years to present time, she has been celebrated in prayer, music, song, processions, devotions, and special Masses worldwide. The most famous cathedrals and basilicas in the world were built to honor her. Small roadside shrines where pilgrims hold vigils for her dot the countryside. All of this is testimony to the love that the people hold for her. Mary is the people's ambassador at large. She is deeply and tightly woven into the Catholic fabric. This chapter will explain the importance of Mary to the Catholic faith.

Do Catholics Worship Mary?

There are two central questions for most people regarding Mary and her place in the Catholic Church: First, who is Mary? And second, do Catholics worship her? Let's begin with the second question.

No, Catholics do not worship Mary. They are devoted to her, they venerate her, and they honor her as the mother of Jesus, but they do not worship her. Catholics worship only God in the three persons of the Trinity: the Father, Son, and Holy Spirit. Mary is revered because of her relationship with God through Jesus. Over time, she has been called the mother of Christ, the mother of God, the new Eve, virgin mother, mediator, co-redeemer, queen of heaven, and mother of the Church. She has many titles, fills many roles, and is a powerful character in a Catholic's spiritual life, but Catholics do not consider her divine, and so she is not worshipped like God. The question then arises: If Catholics do not worship Mary, what is her position in the Church?

Mary, the People's Choice

Just who is Mary? Much has been written about her, yet this question continues to perplex theologians and scholars today as it has for many centuries. It is perhaps easier for the common folk to comprehend her mystery than it is for the experts. For it is to the common people that Mary appears and speaks, and they intuitively understand her. Images, shrines, prayers, poetry, and great churches all over the world are built in her honor. Each year, thousands of pilgrimages are made to the places where she has appeared. Many who make these journeys claim that miracles take place there. Mary's connection to the folk is often a problem to the analytical, intellectual Catholic, but she cannot be explained away.

Mediator and Co-Redeemer

Mediator is a Latin word that means "one who goes between." In Christianity, Jesus is the mediator between humanity and God; Jesus is the redeemer. He came to Redeem the human race from the effects of Adam and Eve's sin, disobedience to God's direction not to eat the fruit of a particular tree in the Garden of Eden. Because of their sin, the gates of heaven were closed, breaking the relationship between God and his people. Catholics, like all Christians, believe that all humanity shares in the consequences of the disobedience of Adam and Eve in the Garden of Eden.

- She cooperated with God by knowingly and willingly saying yes to God's request to give birth to Jesus Christ.

- Mary birthed Jesus, thereby bringing redemptive grace to the people.

- As a mother witnessing her Son's death, she actively shared in Jesus' redeeming sacrifice.

The Church has used the title mediator for Mary for many hundreds of years when referring to her role as the one who cooperated with God in bringing Christ into the world. It has been applied to her in the East since the fifth century and in the West since the ninth. Her role in *redemption* is the subject of debate, however. The key question surrounding the issue is: Did what Mary endure in bringing Jesus into the world and being a part of his suffering, death, and resurrection constitute her as mediator and *co-redeemer* with her divine Son?

Mary's very special recognition in the Church as the mother of God has always earned her a prominent place in Catholic spiritual life. The title co-redeemer takes her position a step further. In recent times, a commission has been established to examine her status in this regard. No papal decision has as yet been declared, although the pope's writing refers to her as mediator many times.

S'ter Says

Mediator also refers to Mary, like Jesus, as "one who goes between" God and humans to speak for humans. **Co-redeemer** is a title celebrating Mary's part in the redemption. The term **redemption** describes the act that was accomplished by Jesus' life, death, and resurrection that bridged the gap between God and humanity caused by the sin of Adam and Eve.

Mary, the Mysterious Woman

Mary, a woman who is called the mother of God, is intricately connected to Catholic history. Nothing was written about her until 30 years after Christ's death. It is perhaps because of the very sketchiness and brevity of biblical references that Mary has grown in the hearts and minds of the people. She is a mystery and, as such, leaves much to the imagination.

The rise of Mary's popularity and the understanding of her roles in the Catholic Church are intricately connected to the cultures in which her legend grew. The gods and goddesses of ancient Greece and Rome were powerful archetypes in the minds of the people up through the first and second centuries. From the very beginning of Catholicism, their characteristics were assimilated into Mary's story.

Every period of history contains images of Mary, and through these images we can see reflections of religious faith. Yet, nowhere does there seem to be a complete picture: not in Scripture, not in theology, and not in popular writings. To understand Mary and the position she occupies in the Catholic Church, it is helpful to look at all these sources as well as the beliefs that existed in the pre-Christian cultures of North Africa, Greece, Rome, and Turkey. It helps to see the influence these beliefs had on the way Mary's role in the Church was understood and defined.

For example, images of Mary suspended in the heavens on the orb of a crescent moon with her head surrounded by a circle of stars were popular artistic expressions. These images are based on ancient beliefs and understandings. In the classical world, the moon is the archetypal female symbol. In these artistic representations, Mary, filled by the sun's light, held it in her essence until morning, where she released it to the morning sky, symbolizing her giving birth to the sun.

Virgin and Mother: Not a Problem

To understand the importance of the belief "Mary, ever virgin," let's look at a series of factors. In the Hebrew Bible, Isaiah first tells us "a virgin will bear a child." (Isaiah 7:14) The Hebrew word, which was translated to virgin, is actually *almah*. Properly translated, "almah" doesn't mean "virgin," but "young girl." As the text was translated into Matthew's Greek (Matthew 1:23), *parthenos* is used, which usually is understood as "virgin." Throughout the ages "virgin," rather than "young girl," became integral to the description and understanding of Mary.

In the cultures of North Africa, Greece, Rome, and Turkey where the events of the New Testament took place, the word "virgin" had a different meaning than it does today. Rather than having physical or moral connotations, it meant autonomy. It was a psychological quality signifying freedom of choice. In addition, a virgin birth often signaled a son's divinity. In other words, gods were born of virgins. Virginity is an important key to understanding Jesus' birth as the Son of God because it told the people in the way they would best understand it, that the child was conceived by divine origin rather than earthly. It said a miracle was taking place. Perhaps even more importantly, Mary's virginity shows us that she used her free will as she said "yes" to God's request. She gave full consent to making the Incarnation (the birth of God in Jesus Christ) possible.

Later, the importance of Mary's virginity as a symbol of purity developed at the time of Augustine (354 C.E.-430 C.E.). It was at this time that the Church began to emphasize the difference between the body and spirit. The spirit (our soul) was constantly pitted against the body. Matter (the body) was directly connected to our sexuality and was equated with sin. This dualistic view continued well into the twentieth century. Mary's virginity emphasized her lack of sexuality and therefore portrayed her as sinless.

Recent scholarship no longer supports the separation of body and spirit. New and better translations are available and new light has been shed on our cultural understanding of the definition of virgin. At the heart of the teaching about Mary is the belief that God is offering himself to us in the form of Jesus. In order for this gift to be realized, we must accept him into our lives. Mary does so in her freedom and totality, as "ever virgin." Mary is the people's ambassador at large as she enters into this relationship with God. She is the powerful symbol of our complete acceptance of his grace. She is our free and unforced positive response to God's gift—Jesus—when she says for us, "Thy will be done."

"Now and at the Hour of Our Death ..."

Two other important roles that Mary plays for Catholics are as mother and as queen of heaven. She was given the title "queen of heaven" to show her power over death. Catholics believe she defied death to be taken up into heaven body and soul because her body did not deteriorate in the grave as a human body would, but instead was preserved. This belief has been defined as the "assumption of Mary into heaven." Catholics believe Mary rules over death as the queen of heaven. This role came out of the Hellenistic mythology of Artemis (later called Diana by the Romans). The goddess Artemis presided over birth, nurturing the new mother and child. Artemis ruled over death as well. She was the one who was present at the end of the life journey, assuring safe passage to the other world.

Mary is the "mother of mercy, sweetness, and hope." Mary's role as mediator with her son Jesus gives strength to the living, but her greatest function is in the Catholic understanding of death and redemption. According to Catholics, because Mary is human and has the closet connection to Christ, Jesus cannot refuse her requests. Mary is the merciful one, the one who will not judge, but will simply love. In the last phrase of the Hail Mary, the plea, "pray for us sinners now, and at the hour of our death," expresses the popular belief in Mary's mercy and her particular association with death and heaven. Catholics turn to her to plead their case before God's justice. Mary gives God his human face in heaven as she did on earth. Mary has a way of touching God's heart. Through her, he becomes tangible as the "God of mercy."

Mary's Incomplete History

Again, who is Mary? The New Testament contains little information about her origins, family, birth, or even how she met Joseph. Joseph was a carpenter who was engaged to

Mary. When he discovered she was pregnant, he was concerned for her reputation lest she be treated as an adulteress. An angel appeared to him and told him the child was conceived by God. He married her and became her protector. Was Joseph an older man? He isn't mentioned after Jesus' infancy, and thus we don't know what happened to him. Was Joseph with Mary at the wedding feast of Cana?

How old was Mary at the time of the Annunciation, when the angel came to her and asked her to be the mother of God's Son? Did the Annunciation take place in the usual interval between engagement and marriage? How could a simple Jewish girl like Mary be as familiar with Hebrew Scripture as it appears she is in Luke 1:46–55 (in which Mary repeats the words of the prophet Isaiah and says: "My soul magnifies the Lord")? Did Jesus have brothers and sisters? We are left with many questions.

Mary's parents, Anne and Joachim, were old, possibly past the normal age of child-bearing. Mary's name has been said to be derived from the Hebrew word meaning myrrh and from the word for "bearer of light." St. Jerome called her *Stella Maris,* meaning a "Star of the Sea." This name later evolved into one of the many titles she bears, "Star of the Sea." Other sources connect the name Mary with Marah, the place of bitter water in the Exodus story. In this interpretation, her name would mean stubborn and even rebellious. It seems that even her name is a mystery.

Council of Ephesus

Despite how little is told about her in the Scriptures, Mary's legends continued to grow, especially around the city of Ephesus in Turkey, where the mother goddess was particularly popular. Pre-Christian legend says Artemis, a representation of the Great Mother, lived in the Arcadian forests, near Ephesus. Later Christian stories place Mary in the same area, living out her old age in Ephesus. It was also in Ephesus that Paul encountered the crowds cheering, "Great is Artemis of Ephesus," as he attempted to preach.

For Heaven's Sake!

The Catholic Church forbids anyone to ascribe any "divine" attributes to Mary. Although she is considered holy, it is by the grace of God, and she is still fully human. She possesses no characteristics beyond those of other women.

The Council of Ephesus took place in the year 431 C.E. in Turkey. The Church called it to settle the controversy around Mary and clarify Church beliefs regarding Jesus' dual nature. The essential question was: Did Christ have two natures, one human and one divine? Or did he have a single nature that was both human and divine?

This issue raises a very important question about Mary. Was she the mother of God or simply the mother of Jesus? If Mary were called only the mother of Jesus, separate from being the mother of God, it would separate Jesus' nature into two different natures: one human and the other divine. This issue was a difficult dilemma for the Church because it wanted to preserve its belief in Jesus' nature as being both human and divine.

The council decided on the doctrine that Jesus had one nature and was both true God and true man. It designated Mary as the mother of God, which elevated her to a central place in redemption. No longer was she simply a helper in God's plan, but her willingness to cooperate made human redemption possible.

Theotokos: Mother of God

Mary was given her official Church title, *Theotokos*, mother of God, which gave authentication to the growing popularity of liturgy, hymns, prayers, and stories coming out of the Eastern world. After this decision, theology and beliefs about Mary increased. It was believed that Mary was taken up body and soul by God to reign in heaven. This event is known as her Assumption. The Church declared this belief to be true, and it has become an essential belief or Church doctrine.

Mary evoked deep feelings in the people. The cultural flowering of the Middle Ages helped people fall in love with images of her, and then proclaim her reign as queen of heaven. What was central to the art of the East a few hundred years earlier became much of the focus of Western art. The Madonna and her divine child captured the cultural imagination. Mary became mother of humanity. Writers and thinkers of the time, including Thomas Aquinas, built the intellectual and theological framework that allowed her to be celebrated in the Church. And celebrated she was—art, statuary, painting, stained glass, and architecture depicted her and helped to create a huge community devoted to her. Mary is what is missing for many, the feminine face of God.

Apparitions: Here, There, and Everywhere

The Catholic Church defines an apparition as the appearance of a being in a supernatural state who would normally be beyond detection by the human senses. Generally speaking, then, an *apparition* is the appearance of someone who has died. Apparitions of Jesus, Mary, the angels, and saints are a part of Catholic culture. There have been numerous visions or appearances of Mary around the world. Some of the most celebrated are her appearances at Lourdes, France; Fatima, Portugal; and Guadalupe, Mexico.

After an extensive investigation, the Church can designate an apparition as authentic. When an apparition is declared authentic, this declaration does not bind Catholics to believe in the appearance. Instead, it means the Church does not believe its members will be harmed by such a belief. Such declarations of authenticity do not constitute an article of faith. *Articles of faith* are teachings Catholics have to believe and are found in the Church's creeds. They include foundational beliefs such as the Trinity, Immaculate Conception, and Incarnation. After an article of faith has been declared, it becomes part of the unifying faith statement of the Church. Apparitions are considered sources of grace and are understood as helpful to the worship of God.

Saints Preserve Us

St. Gabriel, September 29, Patron of Communications Workers

St. Gabriel the archangel was the angel who appeared to Zachariah to announce the birth of St. John the Baptist. He also announced to Mary that she would bear a son who would be conceived of the Holy Spirit. The name Gabriel means "man of God" or "God has shown himself mighty." The feast day for St. Gabriel is September 29, and he is the patron of communications workers.

Lourdes: Healing Waters

Lourdes is a town in the southwest of France where Mary appeared to Bernadette Soubirous several times between February 11 and March 25, 1858. During this time, Bernadette reported seeing 18 different appearances of a very beautiful lady. The lady directed Bernadette to uncover a flow of water and to drink of it and to bathe in it. She said it would have healing effects. The lady then asked Bernadette to have a church built nearby. On her final appearance, she told Bernadette, "I am the Immaculate Conception." Four years earlier, the doctrine of the Immaculate Conception, which refers to Mary's conception in her mother's womb free from original sin, was declared an article of faith by the pope.

Fatima: World Peace

Fatima is a small town in the middle of Portugal where, in 1915, three young children had a vision of a veiled figure. Three times in the next year, they saw an angel who told them he was the Angel of Peace. The angel urged them to pray to the hearts of Jesus and Mary. Following the angel's appearance, the children began to see the lady.

The lady appeared standing on a cloud in an evergreen tree near a small cove. During her visits with the children, she talked intimately with them. On the sixth and final visit, she identified herself as the lady of the rosary. She emphasized the importance of praying the rosary daily as a devotion to the Immaculate Heart of Mary in order to bring about world peace. "If people do not turn to prayer," she said, "more war will break out." She asked for Russia to be consecrated to her Immaculate Heart. Four months after her warning, the Russian Revolution began. Many popes have honored the shrine at Fatima.

At Fatima, Mary promised a sign to show the authenticity of what she was saying. Despite efforts by local authorities to discredit the children, word continued to spread, and on October 13, in front of a crowd of 50,000 people, she made the sun dance in the sky. It left its orbit and appeared to many in the crowd to plunge to earth.

Our Lady of Guadalupe: Patron of the Americas

The Lady of Guadalupe appeared in Mexico City in 1531 to an indigenous peasant, St. Juan Diego, recently canonized. Her image was imprinted on his cloak and hangs in the Basilica built in her honor. She has been named the patron of the Americas. Scientists from MIT have examined the image on the cloak and verified an interesting phenomenon that is part of the miracle. The reflections of the people who were present when the apparition first appeared can still be seen in her eyes. The cloth, made of a woven grass, remains in remarkable condition. Experts have noted that a similar cloth would have normally disintegrated by now. The Guadalupe shrine is a popular pilgrimage for people from all over the world. Her story can be found in Chapter 22.

Feasts and Devotions to Mary

There are 16 feasts of the Blessed Virgin throughout the liturgical year. In addition to these feast days, the months of May and October are dedicated to Mary and are the focus of many devotions. This section looks at seven of her major feasts.

Immaculate Conception of Mary: December 8, and Mary's Birthday: September 8

Many people mistakenly believe the term *Immaculate Conception* refers to Mary's sinless conception of Jesus, but it actually honors Mary's unique position of being conceived without original sin. It shows that she existed from her conception as prominent in God's redemption plan. God arranged sinlessness as a tribute to her and to prepare for the arrival of the Savior through her. The Feast of the Immaculate Conception became a holy day of obligation in 1854. Catholics in Spain celebrate this day by decorating houses with flowers and flags and burning candles in the windows the night before the feast.

Mary's birthday falls nine months later. This day honors Mary as God's gift to the people. Traditional feasts, which existed previous to this date and are now associated with the nativity of Mary, include thanksgiving celebrations, the beginning of Indian summer, and the fall planting season. Harvest blessings are given in many Catholic churches.

The Annunciation: March 25, and the Visitation: May 31

Near the vernal equinox, the Annunciation marks the celebration of the conception of Jesus in Mary's womb. It occurs nine months before the feast of Christmas, the birth of Christ.

In medieval Europe, pageants and processions marked the celebration of the Annunciation. A child, dressed as an angel and representing Mary, was suspended on a rope in midair. As the angel descended, mothers dropped candy in the pews for the children. The children believed that Gabriel had brought these goodies from heaven. In Russia, large wheaten wafers were blessed and distributed after the Mass. The people saved pieces of these wafers to be buried in the fields to assure a good crop, signifying the connection between Mary's fertility and the fertility of the earth.

The feast of the Visitation celebrates Mary's visit to Elizabeth immediately after the Annunciation where the baby in Elizabeth's womb, John the Baptist, stirred in recognition of the Messiah in Mary's womb.

Mary, Mother of God: January 1

"Mary, Mother of God" is a feast first instituted in Jerusalem as early as the middle of the fourth century. It was called the Presentation of the Child Jesus in the Temple and was celebrated on January 1, which followed the custom in Jewish law of presenting the baby in the temple on the eighth day following birth. The feast focused on the obedience of Mary and Jesus to Mosaic law. At one time, this feast was moved to February 2 and coincided with the pagan feast of lights. This feast day is also called the Solemnity of Mary.

The Assumption: August 15

The Assumption marks one of the oldest feasts of Mary and is an important date in the liturgical year. It celebrates Mary's body and soul being taken up into heaven and her coronation as queen of heaven. Liturgical processions began as early as 701 C.E. In some European cities, Mary's journey to heaven is symbolized by carrying her statue through town. Huge candles are taken to churches and lighted in a procession called candelieri.

The Blessing of the Herbs is a medieval tradition on the Assumption, and it was called "Lady's Herb Day." Blessings were given to the herbs to enhance their healing properties. First grapes were offered to her, and blessing of the fishing boats occurred on this day. In England and Ireland, an ancient tradition is to perform ritual bathing on this day to preserve good health. Catholics in the United States celebrate it on August 15.

Our Lady of Guadalupe, Mother of the Americas: December 12

Our Lady of Guadalupe is the patron saint of the Americas and is key to understanding the Catholicism of the New World. On December 12, Mary is remembered as patroness of the Americas. She is the mother of all the people and, because she was once poor, has particular favor for them. On this day, her appearance to Juan Diego near Mexico City in 1531 is honored.

Mary, as the universal mother symbol, is a reminder of the common relationship of all people. She offers her son, Jesus, to break through the old structures and categories of caste, class, religion, race, and gender by constantly reminding us that we are all children of the same God. More of her story is found in Chapter 22.

May Altars

In a Catholic schoolroom during the month of May, you might still find a May altar. A few years ago, it would have been a sure thing to find one. May altars were built in classrooms and in the homes of Catholics as part of the May devotions to Mary. May altars featured a statue or picture of Mary prominently displayed, often against a cloth backdrop, and surrounded by fresh flowers. It was the duty of the students to keep fresh flowers for Mary all month. In addition, a candle was kept burning in front of her. Another popular May devotion from the past was the May crowning ceremony, in which a statue of Mary was crowned with flowers.

Mary is one of the figures that Catholics are best known for. In this chapter, you have had a chance to learn a lot about her and the devotions that honor her. Part 4 describes other favorite Catholic devotions, sacramentals, and prayers. So if you have ever wondered what holy water, statues, mysticism, chanting, and a lot of other Catholic stuff is about, here is your chance to find out.

The Least You Need to Know

- The stories of Mary were drawn from the rich cultural heritage of many sources.

- Mary holds a unique place in salvation and devotion.

- Mary is revered as the mother of God.

- Our Lady of Guadalupe is the patroness of the Americas and brings with her a model for unity and peace.

Part 4

Imagination and Prayer

The imagination is a storehouse of all the sights, sounds, smells, sensations, and emotions we've experienced throughout our life. Imagination forms the lens through which we view life, and it forms our perspective on life. Imagination is also the place where God has traditionally spoken to the people, whether through dreams or from the insight gained in meditation.

In this part, we will look at Catholic imagination in terms of the words Catholics use, their music, and their everyday practices and rituals. Then we will focus on the central place where Catholic imagination and prayer are communally enacted: the Mass.

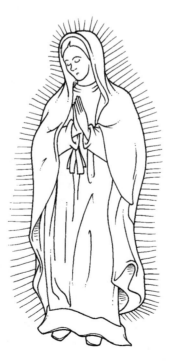

Chapter 13

Feeding the Imagination

In This Chapter

- ◆ Learn the difference between the cross and the crucifix

- ◆ Find out why Catholics use statues, holy cards, and other Catholic stuff

- ◆ Recognize some of the gestures that identify a Catholic

- ◆ Understand how the liturgical calendar keeps sacred time for Catholics

As we've discussed, Catholics relate to Jesus and God through the senses and through the imagination. Indeed, the Catholic imagination is filled with images that allow Catholics to understand the world from a spiritual perspective and respond to the world in prayer. In this chapter, we'll explore the use of sacramentals—"little" sacraments that help develop the *Catholic imagination* and make everyday life more spiritual. Sacramentals relate us to the immanence of God, his presence or touchability, as well as to his transcendent, otherworldly nature.

Sacramentals: Little Sacraments

If you walk into a Catholic church, you will see a crucifix, a cross with the image of Jesus on it. You might also notice lots of color, texture, smells, and shades of light in the church. You will find colorful stained glass windows that typically depict scenes from the life of Christ, angels, saints, or some modern art. In the church itself, you will find three or four shrines, in addition to the central or main altar, with statues or icons of St. Joseph, Mary, or others.

Stained glass window in a church, depicting the Annunciation. Christ the King Catholic Church, Nashville, Tennessee.

(Courtesy of H. L. [Dean] Caskey)

Almost everyone has a favorite object that belonged to a grandparent, parent, relative, or friend and that he or she holds sacred. When you see such an object or use it, you remember the stories that go with it. Like pictures of admired ancestors, holy pictures and statues connect us to the memories we hold of those being pictured. They connect us to what that person was all about, particularly the values they espoused.

For instance, you might have dishes or silverware that belonged to your mother. As you set the table, you remember the influence she had in your life and the values she represented. As you do so, her spirit comes alive for you. It is as if she could reach through time and space and be there with you again. The dishes are functioning in a sacramental way by connecting you to the things about the person you hold sacred.

The difference between official sacramentals and personal ones is that the Church's sacramentals relate to God and to the saints rather than to anyone's personal family archives. They connect the faithful to the life and times of Jesus.

Why Do Catholics Have Jesus on the Cross?

Probably the most widely used sacramental for Catholics is the crucifix. For Catholics, the crucifix is a sacramental because it connects them to the story of Jesus and the values he taught. Although most other Christian religions do not use the term sacramental, all use the symbol of the cross. But the cross you will see in the Protestant world differs from the Catholic crucifix. As you read in Chapter 9, a crucifix is a *cross* upon which the body of the crucified Christ is shown.

We talked about how Catholics prefer the crucifix to the plain cross because of the emotions it evokes—it helps them feel more connected to Jesus as human. For many non-Catholics, the image of Jesus' crucified body seems harsh. But for Catholics, the image of Jesus on the cross makes the story of his life, death, and resurrection come alive. Many Catholics also feel that the cross without Christ tends to become an idea rather than a real-life event that happened to a human man who was also the Son of God.

The history of the cross and the crucifix is a long one. Constantine, Roman emperor of the early 300s, dreamt of a cross and was told "in this sign you will conquer." He ordered the sign of the cross to be put on all the soldiers' shields, and then won the battle by which he became emperor of Rome. Although he wasn't Christian, he liberated the church, making Christianity a legal religion in the empire, and brought an end to the persecution of Christians.

Since then, the cross has been the universal symbol for Catholicism. There are some 400 varieties in use. Sometime in the Middle Ages, the body of Jesus was affixed to the cross and the image became known as a crucifix. It has become one of the most easily recognized symbols of the Catholic religion. Catholics display the crucifix prominently on the altar of the church, in their homes, and sometimes on pendants around the neck.

S'ter Says

A **cross** is made of two planks of timber, one placed across the other, like the picture shown in this section. It was the instrument of execution in Roman times, and Jesus was put to death on a cross.

Your Guardian Angel

Consider marking a special occasion with a holy card. You can remember a baptism, a First Communion, a wedding, or a funeral with a personalized printed holy card.

Crucifix prominently displayed over the altar. Christ the King Catholic Church, Nashville, Tennessee.

(Courtesy of H. L. [Dean] Caskey)

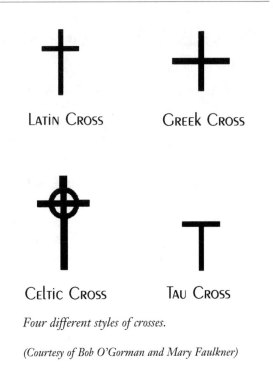

Four different styles of crosses.

(Courtesy of Bob O'Gorman and Mary Faulkner)

Catholic Stuff: Statues and Holy Cards

Statues are everywhere in the Catholic world: in church, in the home, out in the yard, and even mounted on the dashboard of the car. In the neighborhood where a friend's kids grew up, our favorite statue was one they called "Our Lady of the Birdbath." Enough said! On the side altars of Catholic churches, you'll see statues dedicated to saints: Mary, Joseph, the patron saint of the parish, St. Michael the Archangel, St. Anthony, and St. Teresa are particularly popular. A favorite statue in many churches is the Infant of Prague. It is a statue of the Christ Child represented as an infant king. The custom is to adorn the statue with elaborate robes.

Church statues range in size from 1 or 2 feet tall to 10 or 15 feet. They can be very modern pieces of art or traditional representations that have not changed since the Middle Ages. Since Vatican II, the presence of statues in Catholic churches has been deemphasized; however, for the most part, it remains a treasured tradition the people won't give up.

Another favorite sacramental is a holy card. In the past, students at a Catholic school might receive a holy card as a prize for getting the top grade in a quiz, or to mark some other honor. They are about the size of a playing card. On one side is a picture of a saint; on the other side is a prayer. A holy card illustrates events in the life of Jesus, Mary, angels, or saints. Beautiful in their presentation, holy cards are like gold-edged Catholic baseball cards. Young people collected them as such, sometimes using them as bookmarks in prayer books or trading them during church (until they got caught).

Perhaps the most common use of holy cards today is at the funeral parlor. As you sign the visitors' book, you will be offered a holy card with a picture on one side and a psalm or other prayer on the back with the name and dates of the deceased. These cards can be saved in your prayer book or at home in the family Bible as a reminder to pray for the deceased.

Another group of sacramentals includes medals, which are small, coinlike objects with an image of Christ, Mary, or a saint imprinted on them and worn on a chain around the neck. Like other objects, medals must be blessed in order to be considered holy objects. Medals make good gifts for religious occasions or holidays. Often the patron saint of the person is selected. The purpose of wearing a medal is to invoke the aid and protection of the saint whose image is on it.

Saints Preserve Us

St. Christopher, July 25, Patron of Travelers

St. Christopher is one of the most popular saints, and St. Christopher medals are among the most common sacramentals. Legend has it that Christopher was a giant of a man who made his living carrying people across a raging stream on his shoulders. One day his passenger was a small child who grew so heavy that Christopher feared they would drown. The child then revealed that he was Christ and that the heaviness was caused by the weight of the world he was carrying on his shoulders—hence his name, Christopher, which means Christ-bearer. Christopher is the patron saint of motorists and travelers and is invoked during storms. St. Christopher medals are typically affixed to the sun visor or dashboard of the car.

Advent Wreaths: O Come, O Come, Emanuel!

Advent wreaths are sacramentals that appear in Catholic life both at home and in church during Advent, the four-week period before Christmas. An Advent wreath is a green pine wreath with four candles placed at equal distances around the circle. Three of the candles are purple, and the fourth is pink. The four candles represent the four centuries people waited for the birth of Christ.

In church each week, the priest lights a candle and says special prayers preparing Catholics for the coming of Jesus. On the third week, he lights the pink candle. Its purpose is to uplift the spirit during the long, dark four weeks before Christmas. On the fourth week, all four candles are burning and your heart knows Christmas will soon arrive.

An Advent wreath. Christ the King Catholic Church, Nashville, Tennessee.

(Courtesy of H. L. [Dean] Caskey)

A large wreath is used in church; sometimes wreaths are suspended from the ceiling in the front of the altar. At home, Catholics place a wreath on the table where it is used as family devotion. It is customary for a parent to perform the blessing of the wreath before it is used. Before dinner, a member of the family lights a candle and says a prayer. Advent wreaths teach the spiritual meaning of the season and give children eager for Christmas something to do as they wait for the big day.

Sacramental Gestures

From the swirling Sufi dancers of the Islamic religion to the more staid Congregationalists of New England, all religions, including Catholicism, have certain gestures or movements they use in worship. Almost everyone who visits a Catholic church and attends Mass comes away amazed at how much standing, kneeling, and sitting goes on. This section describes some of the gestures and movements that define Catholics.

The Sign of the Cross

One of the most obvious gestures that identify Catholics is the sign of the cross. Indeed, one of the first things Catholic parents teach their children is how to bless themselves. It would be rare indeed to watch a basketball game without seeing someone using this gesture before shooting a basket.

The sign of the cross is made using the fingers of the opened right hand:

♦ You touch your forehead as you say, "In the name of the Father"

♦ You touch your heart as you say, "and the Son"

♦ You touch your left shoulder as you say, "and the Holy"

♦ You touch your right shoulder as you say, "Spirit"

♦ You bring your hands together as you say, "Amen."

Most prayers begin and end with the sign of the cross. The priest also uses this gesture as he gives his blessing to the people. The sign of the cross expresses one of the basic truths of the faith: the existence of the Father, Son, and Holy Spirit as Trinity.

Your Guardian Angel

Don't forget your blessings! Bless your food before you eat by making the sign of the cross over it.

Blessings for Everything!

We bless God for what he has done for us. In return we receive God's blessing. Catholics receive blessings from the priest, and the priest also blesses objects. What gets blessed? Name an object or being—boats, cars, bicycles, horses, dogs, cats, crops, fields, gardens—and there is probably a blessing for it and a special story to go with it. There's hardly anything that can't or doesn't get blessed.

Many parishes invite members to bring pets to church to be blessed on October 4, the feast of St. Francis. Stories of St. Francis's love of nature and all animals have captured the hearts and imaginations of people of all religious faiths. In farming communities, priests bless fields, tractors, and other equipment; in fishing communities, the boats are blessed; and in all communities, cars and homes are blessed.

Blessings are not just a Catholic practice. Probably most religions ask the divine to pay special attention in some way. Blessings acknowledge people's dependence on

God and confirm their belief that God concerns himself with their daily activities. Blessings connect Catholics more closely to God's *omnipresence*.

When a priest gives a blessing, he uses holy water, which is water that has been blessed and set aside for sacred use. He might sprinkle the person or object and will most likely make the sign of the cross on the head of the individual being blessed. If he is blessing an object or a crowd of people, he will make the gesture of a cross in the air with his hand. He says something like, "May God bless you and keep you safe in the name of the Father, the Son, and the Holy Spirit. Amen."

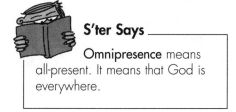

S'ter Says

Omnipresence means all-present. It means that God is everywhere.

The priest blesses all sacred objects before they are used sacramentally. The act of blessing reserves the object for use as a spiritual tool. From then on, those who use it must treat it with respect. Blessings change consciousness about the object; they change the understanding of it and the treatment of it. Crosses, beads, medals, and other Catholic stuff are just plain objects until a priest blesses them.

Hands, Knees, Heads, and Hats

Another sacred gesture involves the tradition of folding the hands together with fingers pointed upward as the common position for prayer. This hand position symbolizes that the one praying is focused on God. Some say the practice led to the shape of church steeples. Of course, prayer is acceptable in any posture at any time.

For Heaven's Sake!

Treat all sacramentals with respect when you're no longer using them. There is, for example, a protocol for retiring palm leaves. They are burned for distribution as ashes on Ash Wednesday.

As an earlier chapter described, Catholics genuflect before the altar to show respect for the presence of God. They usually do this just before taking their seats in church.

Kneeling is another Catholic practice, leading many visitors to remark on the ups and downs of a Catholic service. It's also customary to bow the head or even tip your hat when passing a church. The head is often bowed at the name of Jesus.

Sacred Elements: Earth, Air, Fire, and Water

As we discussed earlier, many of the Catholic rituals are rooted in the elements of air, earth, fire, and water. The elements connect Catholics to their physical world and remind them that God is present here and now, in the everyday world. The sacramental use of elements sanctifies Catholics' relationship with the earth, with one another, and with the Creator.

Palm Leaves and Ashes

We've talked about the use of fire and candles several times. Burning the palm leaves to make ashes for Ash Wednesday is another way the element of fire is used as a sacred practice.

Palm branches are sacramentals used once a year on Palm Sunday, the Sunday before Easter. On that day, Jesus rode into Jerusalem and the crowd waved palm leaves and placed them in his path as a sign of honor. In like manner, the Church distributes palms to be held during the reading of that Gospel story on Palm Sunday. Catholics traditionally braid the leaves and place them behind a holy picture or a crucifix in the home.

Ash Wednesday signals the beginning of Lent, which is the six-week period before Easter. The Ash Wednesday service starts with Mass, and attendance at this event is greater than any other day during the year. People come to participate in one of the favorite practices in the church: having their foreheads anointed with ashes.

Priests prepare the ashes by burning last year's palm leaves for this ceremony. At some point, either before or after Mass, the people come up to the front of the church. The priest dips his thumb into a small glass vial that contains the ashes and rubs a cross on each person's forehead as he gives the biblical reminder, "Remember that you are dust, and unto dust you shall return." (Genesis 3:19)

Garry Wills, a Catholic writer, talks about the very earthiness of this ceremony and describes it as a time when the Catholic comes face-to-face with death: "Certain feelings are not communicable. One cannot explain to others, or even to one's self, how burnt stuff rubbed on the forehead could be balm for the mind. The squeak of ash crumbled into ash marks the body down for death, yet makes this promise of the grave somehow comforting." During the day, activities slowly brush away the ashes, but perhaps a small cinder is left as a reminder of the ceremony.

Holy Water!

As a Catholic opens the doors of the church, he or she instinctively reaches out with the right hand to dip his or her fingers into the holy water font, which hangs on the wall just inside the door. The Catholic then blesses himself or herself with the holy water by making the sign of the cross. Holy water is water that has been blessed in a

Your Guardian Angel

Check your holy water supply. It is a Catholic custom to keep a bottle of holy water in the home. It can be used for blessing at the time of sickness and to protect the home against danger.

special ceremony as part of the Easter Vigil rituals and is used throughout the year.

The signing of the cross with water is a renewal of a Catholic's baptism. During the sacrament of baptism, the priest pours water over the forehead and makes the sign of the cross. Blessing yourself with holy water upon entering the church is a cleansing rite. It symbolically washes the outside world away and shows that you are entering sacred space.

Holy Oil!

Holy oil is blessed and set aside for use in administering several of the seven sacraments. Traditionally, oil is used as a healing balm, as a cleansing agent, and as a strengthener. In the Church, it is used in baptism, confirmation, Holy Orders, and the anointing of the sick.

The use of oil for anointing has become more common in the Church now than it used to be, because healing ceremonies have become more popular. In many parishes, one Sunday a month is set aside for the faithful to come to receive prayers and anointing to help with physical or emotional healing. The parish also may hold a special ceremony of consecration for someone who is about to volunteer for a year or so of mission service. That person would be blessed and anointed with oil.

Air as Holy Spirit

The Holy Spirit is symbolized as fire, and also as wind. The arrival of the Spirit on Pentecost was preceded by a wind that rattled the shutters! Incense, that very Catholic practice of filling the church with "holy smoke," is a way of sacramentalizing air. The smoke, charged with sacred meaning, fills the air, and is inhaled to become part of the body. The very intake of breath is called inspiration—or intake of Spirit. To be alive is to breathe, to be filled with God's presence in the Spirit. Today's quantum physics has added a new dimension to the understanding of air, and the presence of God or the Holy Spirit. Scientists have found that there is no such thing as a void. When they attempt to create one in the laboratory, it immediately fills with molecules that appear to bubble up out of nowhere and fill the space. The Spirit is present everywhere, constantly moving, changing, shaping, and creating. A Catholic definition of God's attributes includes omnipresence—all-present everywhere at the same time. That means in us and around us, filling the "space" between us. You can find more about this in Chapter 24.

Superstition or Sacred Tradition?

As we've said, Catholics believe that God is present in all things and is accessible in all of nature. Catholics' use of sacramentals often raises the question of superstition and idolatry. In response, Catholics answer that there is a need for the tactile in religious imagination. Sacramentals are a way of acknowledging God's presence in all things. It brings the very elusive and ethereal spiritual aspect of God into a form that humans can grasp. Sacramentals raise the awareness of Catholics to the fact that God is everywhere by putting that idea into concrete form.

As discussed in Chapter 9, involving the senses and the body in worship opens other levels of awareness in addition to listening to or reading sacred literature. One has only to attend a religious film or a play, listen to music, or visit an art museum to appreciate how images bring an additional dimension to the written word. No one would think of the famous paintings and sculpture of Michelangelo or da Vinci as superstitious, nor the music of Bach or Mozart or many other famous composers who first wrote and performed their music in church as part of the Mass. Sacramentals are just smaller representations of those aesthetics, and are infinitely more available.

The Liturgical Calendar: Sacred Time

If you are visiting relatives in Ireland and you are issued an invitation to a dinner, make sure you ask if the time specified is "Irish time." If the answer is yes, you would be wise not to be rushed by the movement of the hands on your watch. In their leisure, the Irish have a different meaning for time than they do during the workday. Every culture has different ways of experiencing time, and Catholics do, too, with regard to their sacred time.

The Sacred Wheel of Time

The Church follows time according to the birth and resurrection of Jesus by what it calls the liturgical calendar. This calendar establishes the pattern for the feasts and seasons that occur each year. It cycles around two major celebrations in the life of Christ: his birth at Christmas and his resurrection at Easter.

Your Guardian Angel

Get a liturgical calendar to hang next to your regular calendar. The liturgical calendar connects you to the spiritual seasons of the year. Liturgical calendars indicate the Scripture passages for each Sunday and are available from a Catholic bookstore.

- ◆ **Advent** begins the liturgical year with the first Sunday of Advent and goes to December 24.

◆ **Christmas** begins with the vigil of Christmas on December 24 and goes through the Sunday after January 6, the feast of *Epiphany*.

◆ **Ordinary time** begins after the Sunday following January 6 and continues through the day before Ash Wednesday.

◆ **Lent** begins on Ash Wednesday and lasts until the Holy Thursday Mass of the Lord's Supper.

S'ter Says

Epiphany is defined as a sudden intuitive perception or insight into the essential meaning of something. It marks the feast when the kings or wise men visited the Christ child in Bethlehem. It is celebrated on January 6. **Triduum** is most often used when referring to the Easter Triduum that includes the three days prior to Easter Sunday: Holy Thursday, Good Friday, and Holy Saturday.

◆ **The Easter *Triduum*** begins with the Mass of the Lord's Supper on Holy Thursday and lasts until Easter Sunday.

◆ **The Easter season** begins on Holy Thursday and lasts for 50 days until Pentecost. Easter is celebrated on the Sunday following the first full moon after March 21, the spring equinox. This system of determining Easter's date comes from the way the Jews calculated the feast of Passover.

◆ **Ordinary time** continues the day after Pentecost and ends the day before Advent. Ordinary time refers to the times between the major seasons of Christmas and Easter.

In addition to the Sunday cycle shown here, there are two other cycles of feasts on the Church calendar. The second cycle is composed of the saints' days, one for every day of the year. The third cycle is made up of Mary's feasts. This cycle is "unofficial," but popular. It consists of the months of May and October, which are devoted to special celebrations of Mary. Additionally, there are more than 15 feasts throughout the year celebrating her, beginning with the Immaculate Conception on December 8 through the Assumption on August 15.

Celebrating the Seasons

Catholics celebrate each of these seasons by reading the Bible texts appropriate to the feasts. Generally, there is a reading from the Old Testament, an Epistle, and a Gospel at each Mass. The readings revolve on a three-year rotation. The Gospels are drawn from Mark, Matthew, and Luke respectively. The color of the priest's vestments and the color of the various church decorations are changed according to the liturgical season. Naturally, the music of the Mass also changes with the season.

You've learned a lot about the sacred objects and practices of Catholics. In the next chapter, you'll find out about favorite Catholic prayers and sacred music.

The liturgical calendar of Church feasts shown on a wheel of the year.

(Courtesy of Bob O'Gorman and Mary Faulkner)

The Least You Need to Know

♦ Sacramentals are reminders of the sacredness of the everyday world.

♦ Catholics have the image of the crucified Christ on their cross as a reminder that he isn't just an idea, but the Son of God made man.

♦ The Church uses candles, holy water, ashes, and holy oil as sacramentals to ground spirituality in the physical world.

♦ Sacramentals are just objects until they are blessed, which is when they become sacred.

♦ The rituals of the Church follow the rhythm of the natural seasons according to the liturgical calendar.

Chapter 14

Catholic Prayers and Music: Tangible Poetry

In This Chapter

◆ How Catholics pray

◆ What a Rosary is

◆ The Church's mystical tradition

◆ Gregorian chant, the heart of the Church's music tradition

Prayer lifts our minds and hearts out of our everyday problems and opens the soul to receive God. Prayer is not simply an event, nor is it only words or actions. It is all of those things and more. As we become mindful of God's presence in us and in all things, our whole life becomes a prayer. Prayer opens us to our deepest level of being: our soul.

Prayer is like poetry offered to God. It becomes tangible when it is connected to certain objects such as rosary beads or to sacred music, such as Gregorian chant. Fingers touch beads while the mind evokes images of the mysteries of Christ's life. The sounds of psalms chanted awaken the ear. The mind quiets, contemplates, and is touched by God. There are many forms for prayer. In this chapter, we'll look at three prayer traditions: personal prayer; a favorite Catholic prayer, the Rosary; and mystical practices of prayer.

Personal Prayer

Since the beginning of time, people have experienced a hunger, a deep instinctual need, to make sense out of life. This sensation creates the idea that there is something with which we long to make contact. This recognition is a prayer in itself. You could begin to define prayer as the attentiveness to this primal urge.

Personal prayer represents an intimate, one-on-one relationship with God. It forms the foundation of spirituality. Although the Church has many formal community rituals and celebrations, the Mass being the most central of these, Catholics are urged to develop their personal prayer life.

The standard Catholic definition of prayer identifies four kinds of prayer:

♦ **Petition** is by far the most common type. Petition asks God for assistance in life's needs; it seeks God's intervention.

♦ **Gratitude** thanks God for blessings and gifts, both the asked for and the unexpected.

♦ **Adoration** expresses devotion, love, and recognition of a Catholic's absolute dependence on God.

♦ **Reparation** asks forgiveness, recognizes one's faults, and expresses sorrow.

The methods of personal prayer include the following:

♦ **Recitation,** such as the Rosary, litanies, the Way of the Cross, and other memorized prayers

♦ **Spiritual reading,** including passages from the Bible, particularly the Psalms

♦ **Recollection,** which is defined as taking a few moments throughout the day for a quick recall of God's presence in oneself and others

♦ **Contemplation,** including quiet time spent in inner reflection

♦ **Journaling,** or writing favorite passages and recording your interpretations and reflections on them

One way of praying is not better than another, and there is no one right way of praying. Traditional Catholic prayers include different types of prayers and different ways of praying. Prayer is personal and intimate. How one prays is not the point; that one prays at all is the more important concern!

The Rosary

The Rosary is perhaps the signature Catholic devotion. For example, if a filmmaker wanted to portray a character as Catholic, he or she might place a rosary in the actor's hands. The image of a Catholic kneeling in church, lips moving in silent prayer as beads slip through fingers, is a familiar one. Another is of nuns in traditional dress with large rosaries at their waist and looped down their side, nearly touching the floor; huge crosses tucked neatly in their belt, six-shooter style. Rosaries often hang from the rearview mirror of Catholics' cars. You'll know a Catholic at the end of his life because the rosary beads will be wrapped around his hands as he lies in his coffin; he will be buried with them.

Of all the Catholic prayers, the Rosary is perhaps the most popular devotion. The word *rosary* means "garland of roses." The rose is one of the flowers used to symbolize the Virgin Mary, and the prayer of the Rosary is very closely associated with her. A story says that Mary has revealed to several people that each time they say a "Hail Mary," they are giving her a beautiful rose. When you say a Rosary, it becomes a garland of roses.

The rosary itself is a string of beads that Catholics use to count the group of prayers known as the Rosary. The beads can be made out of wood, glass, gems, or even a knotted string. They range from very simple to very elegant in appearance. Rosaries are simply attractive objects until a priest blesses them. At that time, they become sacred and should be treated with respect.

For Heaven's Sake!

Treat your rosary with respect. Don't wear a rosary as a piece of jewelry or use it as a decorative object. While they are attractive, remember that they have been blessed for use in prayer.

As a ritual, the Rosary involves two elements: mental prayer and vocal prayer. The mental prayer consists of a meditation on the mysteries of the life and death of Jesus Christ and his mother Mary. The vocal prayer consists of saying the prescribed prayers shown in the following section. Together these elements create a focused meditation, which helps to quiet the mind.

Origins of the Rosary

A common Catholic story says St. Dominic (1170–1221), the founder of the Dominican order, received a vision of Mary in which she instructed him to encourage people to pray the Rosary to her as a means of invoking her aid. The Rosary was part of the monastic spiritual practices for centuries before Dominic. Prior to that, the custom of counting repeated prayers by using a string of beads, knots, or even pebbles in a bowl was in common use among the Moslems, the Buddhists, and other non-Christian religions.

Christian monks used beads to count the 150 psalms they chanted in Latin as part of their prayer life. Because some of the monks, as well as most of the common people, couldn't read Latin, they improvised a substitute for the 150 psalms. They began using beads to count 150 Our Fathers, divided into groups of 50. In time, Hail Marys were added to the prayer form. At that time, the Rosary was called Our Lady's Psalter, marking the 150 Hail Marys that corresponded to the 150 psalms.

Epiphanies

How did St. Dominic get the credit for starting the Rosary? It seems that during the years 1470 to 1475 a zealous Dominican preacher, Alan de Rupe, preached all over Europe and told the story of Mary's appearance to Dominic and how she gave him the Rosary. De Rupe was a born exaggerator, or perhaps he realized the value of a good story as a preaching device. His claims were taken as truth. Regardless of whether the story of St. Dominic and the Rosary is true, it has become part of the legend of the Rosary and has linked inextricably the Dominicans with this favorite tradition.

How to Say the Rosary

Of the many versions of the Rosary, the most popular is the Dominican one. In its complete form, the Rosary consists of saying 15 decades. *Decades* are groups of 10 beads on which a prayer is said. The common rosary has only five decades. The following illustration shows a picture of the rosary.

As we said earlier, the Rosary uses repetition and meditation—it is a spiritual practice. Here is how it is said:

1. While holding the crucifix, make the sign of the cross and then recite the Apostles' Creed.

2. Recite the Our Father prayer on the first large bead.

3. On each of the three small beads, recite a Hail Mary asking for an increase of faith, hope, and charity.

4. Recite the Glory Be to the Father before the Our Father on the next large bead.

5. Recall the first Rosary mystery and recite the Our Father on the next large bead.

6. On each of the adjacent 10 small beads, recite a Hail Mary while reflecting on the mystery. This completes a decade.

7. Each succeeding decade is prayed in a similar manner by recalling the appropriate mystery, reciting the Our Father, saying 10 Hail Marys and one Glory Be, and reflecting on the next mystery.

8. When the Rosary is completed, it is traditionally concluded with the prayer, "Hail Holy Queen."

Your Guardian Angel

Don't think you have to always say formal prayers. Your conversation with God is personal. Feel free to say what you need to say the way you need to say it.

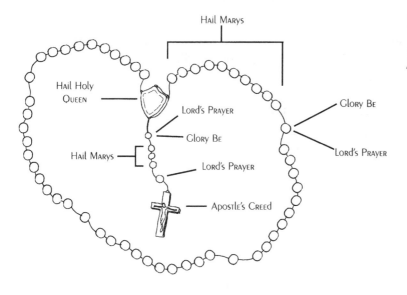

Hail Marys

Hail Holy Queen

Lord's Prayer

Glory Be

Hail Marys

Lord's Prayer

Apostle's Creed

Glory Be

Lord's Prayer

The Rosary.

(Courtesy of Bob O'Gorman and Mary Faulkner)

The Prayers of the Rosary

The following prayers make up the Rosary. Note that Catholics often refer to The Lord's Prayer as the Our Father; it's just one of those Catholic things.

♦ **The Our Father** Our Father, who art in heaven, hallowed be thy name. Thy kingdom come; thy will be done on earth as it is in heaven. Give us this day our daily bread; and forgive us our trespasses as we forgive those who trespass against us; and lead us not into temptation, but deliver us from evil. Amen.

♦ **The Hail Mary** Hail Mary full of grace, the Lord is with thee. Blessed art thou among women, and blessed is the fruit of thy womb, Jesus. Holy Mary, mother of God, pray for us sinners now and at the hour of our death. Amen.

- **Glory Be to the Father**   Glory be to the Father, to the Son, and to the Holy Spirit. As it was in the beginning, is now, and ever shall be, world without end. Amen.

- **The Apostles' Creed**   I believe in God, the Father almighty, Creator of heaven and earth. And in Jesus Christ, his only Son, our Lord; who was conceived by the Holy Spirit, born of the Virgin Mary, suffered under Pontius Pilate, was crucified, died, and was buried. He descended into hell; the third day he rose again from the dead; he ascended into heaven, sits at the right hand of God, the Father almighty; from thence he shall come to judge the living and the dead. I believe in the Holy Spirit, the holy Catholic Church, the communion of saints, the forgiveness of sins, the resurrection of the body, and life everlasting. Amen.

- **The Hail! Holy Queen**   Hail! Holy queen, mother of mercy, our life, our sweetness, and our hope. To you we cry, poor banished children of Eve. To you do we send up our sighs, mourning and weeping in this valley of tears. Turn then, O most gracious advocate, your eyes of mercy toward us, and after this our exile, show unto us the blessed fruit of your womb, Jesus. O clement! O loving! O sweet Virgin Mary! Pray for us, O holy mother of God, that we may be made worthy of the promises of Christ. Amen.

The Fifteen Mysteries of the Rosary

You will often hear the word *mystery* used in the Catholic religion. It describes important beliefs about God, Jesus, and Mary that are part of the religion but cannot be substantiated outside of religious belief. Another way of saying it is that they are important expressions of the faith of the people. The 15 mysteries of the Rosary are in three groups of five and represent joyful events, sorrowful events, and glorious events in the life of Jesus and Mary.

S'ter Says

Mysteries are beliefs of the religion that are taken on faith. They are events in the life of Christ that are vital to the spiritual life of Jesus' followers.

As stated earlier, the Rosary is a spiritual practice. It uses prayer and meditation. The repetition of the prayers quiets the mind and prepares it for contemplation on the events in the life of Christ. The beads soothe busy or nervous fingers, giving them something to do. Here are the stories or events upon which Catholics meditate or contemplate while saying the Rosary; they are the common stories of the religion.

The Joyful Mysteries

1. The Annunciation

2. The Visitation

3. The Nativity

4. The Presentation

5. The Finding of the Child Jesus in the Temple

The Sorrowful Mysteries

1. The Agony in the Garden

2. The Scourging at the Pillar

3. The Crowning of Thorns

4. The Carrying of the Cross

5. The Crucifixion

The Glorious Mysteries

1. The Resurrection

2. The Ascension

3. The Descent of the Holy Spirit

4. The Assumption of Mary

5. The Coronation of the Blessed Virgin Mary

Pope John Paul II instituted a change in the Rosary. He has added a fourth set of "mysteries" for contemplation, increasing the number from the fifteen mentioned above to twenty. The new mysteries focus on events of Christ's life:

The Luminous Mysteries

1. Jesus' baptism in the Jordan

2. Jesus' self-manifestation at the wedding of Cana

3. Jesus' proclamation of the Kingdom of God, with his call to conversion

4. Jesus' transfiguration

5. Jesus' institution of the Eucharist as the sacramental expression of the paschal mystery

In introducing this change, the first in centuries, the pope called for the "contemplation of Christ's face" through Mary's eyes. He proclaimed the year from October 2002 to October 2003 the *Year of the Rosary*.

When Is the Rosary Said?

The Rosary is both an individual prayer and a group devotion. The Church encourages families to use the Rosary as a family devotional practice during May and October, as well as throughout the year. May and October are months dedicated to Mary, and daily devotions using the Rosary are held in many parishes.

Your Guardian Angel

Any portion of the Rosary is a complete prayer! If you have time only for a single decade or even a single bead, it is still a prayer.

Besides praying the Rosary, the beads themselves have become a favorite devotional item. Catholics often carry them in their purse or pocket, keep them by the bedside, or hang them on sacred pictures. A priest blesses the rosaries in a ritual by which they become sacramental rather than simply secular beads. Many Catholics place special importance on rosaries that have been blessed by their bishop or the pope.

Praying the Rosary became a national enthusiasm after the appearance of Our Lady of Fatima. As you may remember from Chapter 12, Fatima instructed people to pray the Rosary for the conversion of Russia from communism and Catholics took up the cause. During May, Rosary processions were held in many cities. They involved tens of thousands of people who gathered and walked throughout the downtown area reciting the Rosary and singing hymns. Radio stations all over the country broadcast the Rosary in the early evening and families were encouraged to use this time for family prayer. Today, the Catholic Church broadcasts the Rosary on radio, television, and the Internet.

Monasteries, Mysticism, and Contemplative Prayer

Contemplative prayer is the practice of a Church tradition called *mysticism*. Mysticism and contemplative prayer developed as part of the prayer life in the monasteries. Of course, contemplation, mysticism, and even monasteries exist in other traditions as well.

In the Catholic Church, contemplative practice began back in the early years when many new believers went out into the desert to get away from the world and all its complication in order to pray and meditate without interruption. It has existed in every age of the Catholic Church: St. Augustine in the 400s; St. Hildegarde of Bingen in the Middle Ages; the English mystic of the 1500s, Julian of Norwich; a little later, Teresa of Ávila and St. John of the Cross; and in modern times, Thomas Merton. The mystic tradition of contemplation is still alive today in monasteries all over the world.

Monastic life lived in convents was one of the arenas in the Church where women were provided equal opportunity. It was their first chance to take an active role in the Church and society since the early years of the Church under the leadership of Jesus, where women were full participants in the inner circle. Convents became centers for learning, prayer, and good works.

S'ter Says

Contemplative prayer is a form of prayer developed in the monasteries. **Mysticism** describes the process of being contemplative. You are contemplative when you meditate and go within yourself to a quiet place where it is possible to experience God. **Monasticism** is the tradition of taking yourself away from the mainstream of society for the purpose of developing your spiritual practice.

Monasticism: The Great Getaway

The basic idea of *monasticism* is seclusion or withdrawal from the world or society. The object is to achieve a life whose ideal is different from the dominant culture. Monasticism is found in every religious system that has attained a high degree of ethical development and is often organized around simplicity, commitment to specific prayers, fasting, hard work, and sometimes even self-denial. Underlying its practices is a deep commitment to preserving a set of ideals.

Monasticism had its beginnings in the early years of the Church, as Christians felt the need to make a strong commitment to each other and to create a safe structure in which to operate. They took *vows* concerning life together. The life of the early monastic was often one of extreme deprivation and hardship. In the 500s, monasticism came under the influence of St. Benedict, and the emphasis on self-denial was tempered.

S'ter Says

Vows are the promises made when one goes into a religious order. They are like wedding vows. The principal three are poverty (giving up private ownership to the community), chastity (giving up the right to marry and have intimate sexual relationships in order to devote themselves to the Church), and obedience (submitting to the authority of superiors for assignments).

Liturgy of the Hours

All over the world, people of all religious traditions are praying 24 hours a day, 7 days a week, all year round. The form these prayers take in the Catholic Church is called the Liturgy of the Hours, and represents the acknowledgment of the sacred relationship between God and creation.

The Liturgy of the Hours honors the inherent powers of nature contained in times of the day and seasons of the year. The oldest documents of civilization describe sacred times of sunrise, noon, sunset, and night as times when prayers were offered and hymns were sung. The Jews adapted these practices from their neighbors, using the book of Psalms as the source of their daily prayers. Early Catholics followed the ancient tradition as a way of living the Biblical command to "pray constantly." Great events in Christianity follow the maps of ancient sacred times: Morning is the time of Resurrection, midmorning is the time of Pentecost, noon is the time of the Crucifixion, mid-afternoon is the death of Christ, and evening is the Last Supper.

The Liturgy of the Hours, along with the daily celebration of Mass, are part of the official prayers of the Church, which means that the clergy says them every day. In monasteries and convents this prayer is chanted in community according to its designated hours.

The Liturgy of the Hours is composed of hymns, psalms, Scripture, and prayers. The seven traditional Hours and their spiritual character follow:

- Matins or **Vigils** is the time of watching in the night. This prayer is celebrated at the midnight hour as one is enveloped in darkness in the silence of prayer and meditation while awaiting the coming of morning.

- Prime or **Lauds** is the prayer at daybreak; thanking God for the first light, as at the beginning of creation, and for the light of Christ's resurrection. New beginnings, awakened innocence, joy, and optimism are expressed in the prayers.

- **Terce** (Latin for third hour) is said at midmorning; the prayers call for strength as work begins and the day waxes strong. This hour is a reminder of Pentecost and the coming of the Holy Spirit, who strengthened the apostles.

- **Sext** (sixth hour) is prayed at noon when the sun burns directly overhead. One has become weary, and mindfulness of God is all but impossible. The prayer is a call for perseverance, and a reminder that Christ's crucifixion began at this hour.

- **None** (ninth hour) is prayed at midafternoon and calls for more perseverance and strength to continue as one exceeds his or her prime and must keep going. The sun is descending. By acknowledging this hour of Christ's death, one touches finitude.

- **Vespers** is celebrated at day's end. The evening light bathes the world in gold, transfiguring it. One sees beyond the struggles of the day. This is the hour of wisdom and rest in thanksgiving after the work of the day.

- **Compline** is from the Latin meaning "complete." It is the last prayer before retiring for the night. It foreshadows life's end and leads back to the darkness of night and the darkness of God's mystery. This prayer is a gentle daily exercise in the art of dying.

Mysticism: The Feminine Force in the Church

Mysticism literally means mystery and can be understood as the practice of meditation. It has been called the highest form of prayer. The practice of mysticism achieves a state of consciousness that takes the practitioner beyond the level of ordinary religious experience to a deep place within the self, where God is experienced intuitively. Mystics talk of exquisite sensations of burning desire for God. They report being consumed by his love in ways that are incomprehensible. A mystical experience is beyond reason, argumentation, or concern with proofs of God's existence. Through such an encounter, the mystic comes to know God's nature. Two women who had a great influence in mysticism and in convent life were St. Catherine and St. Teresa.

A Woman out of Her Place

If Catherine of Siena (1347–1380) were alive today, she would be described as a woman with an attitude! This spunky, spontaneous, fly-in-the-face of convention young woman told kings how to behave, rebuked cardinals, and chastised the pope—and lived to tell about it! Catherine had many mystical experiences she wrote about.

Catherine's writing took another form as well. She often wrote letters that she used for "counseling," and she did not seem to be shy about her mission. She wrote to Pope Gregory XI, who was caught up in a religious/political skirmish. She basically told him to let it go, to "… be not a timorous child, but manly," and to get back to work. She wrote to another pope telling him he needed to control his temper. Her letters provide a window into the history and culture of the period. They are valued in particular because they show that her activity extended far beyond the normal boundaries for women of her time and position in the Church and society.

Catherine's greatest gift may well be the gift of common sense she brought to the Church. She is known for the spiritual insight she provided into the caring nature of ministry. The keynote to Catherine's teaching is self-knowledge. Although she didn't learn to write until almost the end of her life, her writings earned her the title of Doctor of the Church. She died at the young age of 33 and was declared a saint only 81 years later.

Epiphanies

As a child, Catherine of Siena dreamed of dressing up like a man so that she could be accepted as a Dominican friar. From her earliest years, she knew she had a calling to religious life. She was born into a world that limited women in many ways, and although her parents opposed her vocation, they must have known their willful child would succeed in her goal. At 16, she entered the convent of the Sisters of St. Dominic. Her religious life centered on her numerous visions and ecstasies, and later she began writing.

Teresa of Ávila

Teresa of Ávila (1515–1582) was considered outrageously attractive, possessing a beauty matched only by her irascible spirit. Born to a wealthy Spanish family, she was at home in many worlds. She sang, danced, played a tambourine, was a shrewd businesswoman, cooked, practiced Zen meditation, and had an admirable knowledge of what ails and what heals the human body and spirit. She was a sixteenth-century Spanish nun who inspired a school of spirituality that is still followed today.

For Heaven's Sake!

Don't worry! Be happy! Teresa of Ávila said, "Let go, and let God! Surrender the intellect to a higher power." Teresa felt strongly that we should learn to "get out of our heads," meaning that we should slow down our minds and learn how to experience God's love by feeling it, not just thinking or talking about it.

Teresa may have been the first to espouse the "Let go and let God!" principle. Although she was an educated and intelligent woman and believed in reason and learning, she urged those she taught to lay reason aside and surrender the intellect to a higher power. She wrote about "knowing ourselves" and the great spirit of freedom we get by quieting the thinking self and joining with God. She was described as a warrior spirit with a fiery temperament. She was awarded the title of Doctor of the Church.

A major contribution of mysticism is the spiritual literature it produced and the deeper understanding it offered of the nurturing and loving nature of God. Like the Hebrew Song of Songs, mystical writings were sensuous, poetic, and filled with profound understandings of Christ's nature and ways to relate to him. Teresa's meditations brought a new understanding of God's relationship to us. She spoke of God seeking our friendship and needing our companionship. A great legacy is found in her writings, reflections, prayers, and poetry. In them, she dealt with the everyday human conditions of love and intimacy, friendship and family, dreams and nightmares, suffering, prayer, and the mystery of God. Her style has been characterized as lavish, elegant, extravagant, and flamboyant. In that regard, it matched her life and reflected her zest and enthusiasm.

Saints Preserve Us

John of the Cross, December 14, Patron of Mystics

A contemporary of Teresa of Ávila, John of the Cross lived from 1542 to 1591. He was a Catholic mystic, poet, and member of the Carmelite religious order. St. John suffered from depression and despair and wrote his greatest poetry during this time. His major work is "The Dark Night of the Soul," which describes his profound insight into how his depression and despair were lifted through his contemplative practice. "The Dark Night of the Soul" has become the modern metaphor for despair and the subsequent inner journey to healing that happens through meditation. St. John is a good reminder that the saints struggled with many of the same human conditions that are part of our journey, too. He is the patron saint of mystics, but he would also be a good patron saint for those suffering from depression.

Mysticism Today

Contemplation has been said to quiet the mind, still the body, and open the heart to God. It engages the whole self in the meditative process and moves the practitioner beyond thoughts, emotions, or words, into a state of true being. In this sacred space, practitioners are able to hear and feel God's presence within.

In present times, responding to an apparent deep hunger for spirituality, Catholics are having a renewed interest in contemplative prayer, and now this practice is no longer restricted to the monasteries. A contemporary contemplative practice is called *centering prayer* and comes from the tradition of John of the Cross. It awakens people to the presence of God within and builds contemplative attitudes of listening and receptivity. This practice is a synthesis of the wisdom of Zen (Buddhism) and Hindu traditions of meditation with the contemplative tradition of Catholicism.

This type of prayer often follows four steps:

1. Reading of sacred Scripture

2. Reflecting on the Scripture

3. Focusing on a key image

4. Resting in contemplation

Meditation is the practice of teaching the mind to stay pleasantly focused in the present moment. Many approaches to meditation can be grouped broadly as contemplative and mindful meditation. Contemplative meditation focuses on a single point (often the breath) and stills the mind. Mindful meditation opens the mind to observe the flow of thoughts, feelings, and sensations passing through one's awareness without thinking about them. Regardless of the type practiced, meditation's benefits to the whole self (body and spirit) are great. The body gains a deeper state of relaxation than that produced by sleep. Meditation increases awareness, intelligence, and creativity. Virtually all physiological systems are positively influenced by meditation. As a result, meditation is being taught in hospitals all over the country, for a wide variety of conditions. It normalizes many functions such as blood pressure, lifts depression, quiets anxiety, improves the immune system, and speeds recovery from surgery. When imagery is involved, it has cured cancer and healed burns.

Your Guardian Angel

When planning your Church celebrations (marriages, anniversaries, and funerals), choose music that sounds right for you and fits with the liturgical calendar. Talk with your priest if you have any questions.

In the past 15 years many books on Catholic contemplative practices have been published. Our bibliography in Appendix B cites many of these works. Catholic organizations for contemplative and centering prayer have developed across the country and throughout the world. Retreats and classes devoted to contemplative prayer are now widely available.

Sacred Music

Music is worship; it is prayer. It is an essential element to Catholic worship. Music used in worship services is called liturgical music. During Vatican II, when the Church reviewed its music along with other practices, it stressed music's importance in the worship service and identified its necessity as an integral part of the Mass. The council promoted full participation of the faithful in the Mass, especially by way of its music. Vatican II represented a major shift from music that was in Latin and performed by choirs to a new music in English that is sung by the people.

How Sacred Music Functions

In order for music to attain its liturgical purposes (to provide the listeners with spiritual sustenance), these qualities should be considered:

♦ **Aesthetic,** to connect the holy to the beautiful

♦ **Diversionary,** to eliminate boredom during tedious times during the Mass

♦ **Emotional,** to express hope and joy when words alone cannot do it

♦ **Enjoyable,** so that it is pleasurable to hear and perform

♦ **Involving,** so that it unites and draws people together into deeper participation in the Mass

♦ **Mood-setting,** to make the worship capable of addressing a wide range of human emotion

♦ **Revelatory,** so that it explores and reveals the religious experience

♦ **Text-enhancing,** to underscore the sacredness of certain texts

In most parishes, the choir director and the pastor work together to select music that matches the liturgical calendar and captures the meaning of the feasts.

Gregorian Chant

Once a definitive Catholic sound, Gregorian chant almost dropped out of use in the Catholic Church after Vatican II. Today, it's enjoying a resurgence of popularity throughout the culture. New understanding of its effects on the listener have found that its melodies quiet the mind, soothe the nerves, open the heart, and prepare one for worship. Several recordings of it have become best-sellers.

Named for Pope Gregory, Gregorian chant was compiled and arranged in the sixth century and was derived from chants sung in ancient Jerusalem. Many more chants were composed in later centuries. Gregorian chant was sung both in the cathedrals and in the monasteries, and credit for its survival is given to the Benedictine monks in northwest France, who began restoring the texts in the latter half of the nineteenth century.

Gregorian chant is also called plainsong or plainchant, which describes it quite well. It is a plain, monophonic, vocal music printed in square notes on a four-line staff. There is no chromatic scale or chromatic progression, and usually there is no modulation from one mode to another in the same melody. The melodies conform to the voice's natural range. Gregorian chant uses no defined rhythm. It functions as an extension of speech, as compared to metrical or

Your Guardian Angel

Chill out with chant! People believe that Gregorian chant assists in unifying body, soul, and spirit. It works its spiritual wonders both on the singers and the listeners. Chant creates a relaxed state in which the mind is stilled, the emotions are quieted, and the soul experiences a sense of peace.

rhythmic or polyphonic (Greek for "many voiced") music, in which two or more strands sound simultaneously. Notes are generally equal in time length in Gregorian chant, but the speed of singing is a matter of style preference.

Although Gregorian chant provides the foundation for Western music, it was designed for prayer and has a strong spiritual component. Key to its importance as a worship device is its close association with the psalms. Chant was designed as a means of singing them.

Saints Preserve Us

St. Cecelia, November 22, Patron of Musicians

St. Cecelia lived in Rome during the second century. She had made a vow of virginity to God; however, her parents forced her to marry. Her husband was not a Catholic, although he converted soon after their marriage. Cecelia reported hearing music from God all during her wedding. Both she and her husband were martyred. Church choirs have always remembered her name, and she is one of the saints mentioned in the prayers of the Mass. She is the patron of all musicians and of church music. Organ builders, composers, and poets all claim her as their patron as well.

In the Bible, Paul identifies three types of text sung during the early period of the church (Ephesians 5:18):

◆ Psalms

◆ Canticles, poems from the Bible

◆ Hymns, the earliest of which deal with the identity of Christ and the meaning of his life and death

Gregorian Chant Today

At the beginning of the twentieth century, the pope made a statement to the effect that Gregorian chant, and the polyphonic music that came from it, was the supreme model of liturgical music. After Vatican II, Gregorian chant almost disappeared, replaced by popular music and a renewed liturgy. It is important to note, however, that chant and liturgy developed together in an organic process. Chant is filled with the spirit of centuries of religious feeling and thought. Polyphonic music that developed out of Gregorian chant carries with it a similar spiritual content. The standoff between traditional and popular music may be near an end as the Church begins to consider its music history as a valuable theological tradition. Hopefully, a synthesis can be accomplished that would offer the best of both worlds.

Chant has many more effects than meets the ear. Beyond its theological application lies another surprising benefit. It seems as though it has a positive effect on physiology and emotions as well. A story circulating in the world of Church music tells that back in the 1960s, a French physician was summoned to a Benedictine monastery in the south of France to investigate a strange set of circumstances. The usually happy and productive monks had become despondent. In the wake of Vatican II, several hours a day of chanting had been suddenly eliminated from the daily routine. Following a hunch, the doctor told the abbot he would like to put the men back on their regular routine. The effect was dramatic. Within six months, they had become vigorous and happy again. They needed less sleep, and their monkish productivity increased. Gregorian chant lowers blood pressure, elevates the mood, and soothes the nerves. It seems it has something to offer the twenty-first century after all.

For Heaven's Sake!

Don't throw the music out with the bathwater! In the attempt to modernize, some mistakes may have been made. For centuries, people used chant as a form of prayer. Its simplicity allows the chanter to concentrate on the meaning of the psalm being sung rather than having to pay attention to complicated melodies.

We've looked at some favorite Catholic prayers and practices and touched on Gregorian chant. In the next chapter, you'll learn about some of the opportunities for spiritual growth in the Catholic Church.

The Least You Need to Know

- Prayer is one's personal relationship to God. It cannot be captured in any one prayer or contained in any one form.

- The Rosary is a popular Catholic prayer. Praying the Rosary is a spiritual practice that contains both contemplation and spoken prayer.

- Contemplation is a mystical practice that takes practitioners to their deepest center to experience their relationship with God.

- Gregorian chant has a long history in the Church. Its use of monotone unifies the body, mind, and spirit.

Chapter

The Mass: The Catholics' Big Dinner Party

In This Chapter

- ◆ What is a Catholic Mass?
- ◆ The two parts of the Mass and its seven activities
- ◆ What Catholics understand about Holy Communion
- ◆ How you can participate in the Mass

You've probably switched on the evening news only to be greeted by the image of the pope celebrating a Mass with 10,000 people in attendance. Other times the media reveals glimpses of the Catholic faith in practice is at a Catholic celebrity wedding or during a funeral when pallbearers carry a notable person's casket through the doors of a Catholic church after a funeral Mass.

More than any other practice, the Mass marks Catholicism. Why is this so? Just what is the Mass? What happens during it? What do you do if you attend it? This chapter looks inside the church doors at the somewhat mysterious Catholic worship service: the Mass.

Celebrating a Sacrifice: What Is the Mass?

Sometimes you'll hear Mass described as the Eucharist, or Holy Communion. The Catechism definition tells us that "Eucharist" is the Greek term used to describe the Jewish meal blessings that acknowledge God's creation and continuing care. Eucharist, which is a celebration of this continued presence, also specifically refers to the consecration and distribution of Holy Communion, the most important part of the Mass, and therefore Eucharist is the "official" term. Less commonly, it is called the Lord's Supper, the Breaking of Bread, or the Divine Liturgy, especially in the Eastern Church. All these names mean about the same thing and you can use the terms interchangeably. The most common name, however, is simply, "Mass."

For centuries, the Church used Latin for all prayers and services. The word "Mass" comes from the Latin phrase *Ite missa est*, "said at the end of the ritual," a phrase declaring that the liturgy was finished. The people were dismissed, or *missa* in Latin, which means sent out into the world with the instruction to do God's will in their daily lives.

Catholics will sometimes refer to Mass as the "sacrifice" of the Mass, and other times the "celebration" of the Mass. It is both these things—the re-enactment of the sacrifice Jesus made for us by his death on the cross, and the celebration of his resurrection and continued presence among us through the sacrament of the Eucharist. The key to Catholics' belief in the Eucharist is that Jesus Christ is not just a fact of history but is God's true presence with us now and always—and not simply present in memory or as a memorial, but sacramentally present, in "matter and form."

There is an old saying that is especially appropriate in seeing how important the Mass is to Catholics: What we act out is what we believe, and what we believe we act out. This is a great rule of thumb for examining any of our principles: personal, family, business, or political. What the Church "acts out" or does most often is the Mass.

Your Guardian Angel

If you are a person of another faith and are attending the Catholic Mass, it is acceptable to sit throughout the service. Or you can sit, stand, and kneel along with the other folks.

Mass is offered every day as well as several times each Sunday, and other special Holy Days throughout the year, when attendance is required. In fact, there is no hour of any day on this planet when a Catholic Mass is not being celebrated!

Catholics are rather well known for their standing, kneeling, and sitting that can confuse the newcomer. In the following discussion, you'll see that these various actions are not aerobic exercises, but designate the different activities of the Mass.

The Mass has two basic parts and a series of seven key activities:

Part I: Instruction: The Liturgy of the Word

- ♦ Gathering

- ♦ Proclaiming

- ♦ Explaining

- ♦ Praying

Part II: Breaking the Bread: The Liturgy of the Eucharist

- ♦ Offering

- ♦ Consecrating

- ♦ Communion

The New Testament story of the two disciples on the road to Emmaus the day of Jesus' resurrection (Luke 24:13–35) is reflected in the two parts of the Mass. In the first part of the story, Jesus walks with the disciples, but they do not recognize him. He gives them a hint by quoting the Jewish Scripture that tells about the coming of the Messiah. They still don't recognize him. Then he sits down to dinner with them, and he blesses and breaks bread, and they finally realize who he is. The two actions of Jesus in the story are enacted in Mass by the reading of the Scripture followed by the breaking of the bread. Let's begin at the beginning, with the first activity called the "gathering."

Gathering: The Guests Arrive

Gathering perhaps best captures the essence of what the Mass is all about. After Jesus' resurrection, his followers gathered together for the purpose of keeping his work alive. The gatherings of the early communities grew, and thus the Church was constituted. Gathering remains the primary function of the Church. If Catholics quit gathering, the entire Catholic Church would cease to exist.

As Mass begins, the people stand. They acknowledge their need for God's help, and their inability to lead a "perfect" life, by saying a prayer together, called by its Greek name, the *Kyrie:*

> Lord have mercy.
> Christ have mercy.
> Lord have mercy.

Next, the Gloria, a prayer praising God's greatness and the coming of the Lord, is either said or sung. It begins with the words of the Scripture the angels used to announce the birth of Jesus: "Glory to God in the highest!"

The priest then recites an opening prayer, which, like the Scripture readings, follows the cycle of the liturgical calendar. Themes change throughout the year depending on the season and particular feasts recorded on this Church calendar. The liturgical calendar appears in Chapter 13.

Proclaiming: The Word of God

After the priest's prayer, the people sit and several Scriptures are read by a layperson known as a lector. This first reading is often from the Hebrew Scripture or Old Testament. It is considered an honor to be a lector. They are members of the congregation who are selected or volunteer, and are formally commissioned in their job as Scripture readers in their parish church.

Next, the congregation either sings or recites one of the psalms. Usually a lector or cantor recites or sings a verse, to which the people respond with a verse from the psalm.

The second reading follows with a passage from one of the New Testament letters. After this reading, the people stand and sing "Alleluia!" proclaiming the word of God will now be spoken in the Gospel message. Gospel means "Good News," so there is an air of celebration as we approach this New Testament testimony. While lectors read the preceding scriptures, only the priest or a deacon reads the Gospel message.

Reflecting: A Word to the Wise

After the Gospel, the people sit for the priest's homily (or sermon) in which he comments on the various readings and their relation to everyday life. While the sermon in a Protestant church is often the focus of the service, in a Catholic Mass it represents a relatively small part, generally lasting about 10 to 15 minutes on a Sunday. During the weekday Mass, the homily, if one is given, is no more than five minutes.

Following the homily, the congregation takes a short time to reflect quietly on what the priest has said. The people then stand to recite the Nicene Creed together:

> We believe in one God,
> the Father, the Almighty,
> maker of heaven and earth,
> of all that is seen and unseen.

We believe in one Lord, Jesus Christ,
the only Son of God,
eternally begotten of the Father,
God from God, Light from Light,
true God from true God,
begotten, not made, one in Being with the Father.
Through him all things were made.
For us men and for our salvation
he came down from heaven:
by the power of the Holy Spirit
he was born of the Virgin Mary, and became man.

For our sake he was crucified under Pontius Pilate;
he suffered, died, and was buried.
On the third day he rose again
in fulfillment of the Scriptures;
he ascended into heaven
and is seated at the right hand of the Father.
He will come again in glory to judge the living
and the dead, and his kingdom will have no end.

We believe in the Holy Spirit, the Lord, the giver of life,
who proceeds from the Father and the Son.
With the Father and the Son he is worshipped
and glorified.
He has spoken through the Prophets.
We believe in one holy catholic
and apostolic Church.
We acknowledge one baptism
for the forgiveness of sins.
We look for the resurrection of the dead,
and the life of the world to come.

Amen.

The Nicene Creed dates back to the early 300s and is the most widely used statement of the Christian Faith. It is common to Orthodox, Anglicans, Lutherans, Presbyterians, and many other Christian groups.

Epiphanies

In a recent homily on the passage "Blessed are they who hunger for justice … " from the Sermon on the Mount, a priest suggested to the people of his parish that the Sermon on the Mount is a challenge to them to transform their world to Gospel values. He told stories about a visit some of the parishioners made to a parish in a poorer section of town during the past week. By doing so, he illustrated for the entire congregation that it was possible to begin to transform the world by putting up sheet rock, cleaning up the park, and helping kids learn to read, and explained how meaningful and spiritual such activities were at their heart.

The Prayers Go Out over the Land

The prayers of the faithful, in which the people pray for the needs of the world, follow the Creed. A lector will usually read a short intercession to which the people respond: "Lord, hear our prayer." The prayers specifically mention the pope, other Church leaders, political leaders, and members of the congregation who may be in need of special blessing such as sick family members, and friends or relatives who have recently died. To each of these prayers, the people respond out loud with a phrase like, "Lord, hear our prayer." The people then sit down for the offering.

There's No Free Lunch!

At this time, the congregation presents an offering in preparation for the second part of the Mass: the Eucharist. Members (quite often children or an entire family) take the gifts of water and wine up to the priest at the altar. The collection plate is passed, and the people are invited to give an offering of money that supports the operation of the Church. The collection basket is then taken up to the altar where the priest receives it along with the other gifts, blessing them, offering them to God "as the work and fruit of our hands." Often the choir sings a hymn or a musician plays music.

 For Heaven's Sake!

Use your envelopes. Most parishes ask parishioners to pledge a certain amount of money for the year and to use printed envelopes for the collection basket. It is easier on the parish bookkeeper and on you at tax time.

The priest prays that God will "cleanse him of all iniquity" and symbolically washes his fingers that will touch the bread. The people pray that God will accept the gifts "for the praise and glory of his name, for our good, and the good of all his church."

Blessing the Bread

During the next part of the Mass, Catholics' sacred rite of the Eucharist will be performed. All the activities point us in that direction. Bread and wine will be blessed or consecrated to become the body and blood of Christ. This part of the Mass is known as the consecration, and the congregation stands or kneels (depending on local custom) signifying the importance of the ritual. The church becomes very quiet, as people enter sacred time. The priest recites a short prayer of praise to God. A server may ring the altar bells three times as the people sing or pray the *Sanctus*:

> Holy, Holy, Holy Lord,
> God of power and might,
> Heaven and Earth are full of your glory
> Hosanna in the highest!
> Blessed is he who comes in the name of the Lord
> Hosanna in the highest!

The priest then begins the great prayer of petition and thanksgiving to God called the Eucharistic Prayer—the most important prayer of the Mass. During this prayer, the priest calls to mind the Last Supper; he takes the bread and says the words of consecration, *Take this, all of you, and eat it: This is my body which will be given up for you.* He elevates the bread above the altar to show to the congregation, and the alter server may ring bells. The bells are from a time before sound systems, when the priest had his back to the people. The bells signaled that the consecration had taken place. While looking at the Eucharistic bread, it is a common practice to silently whisper, "My Lord, and my God," or some other words of respect. When the priest sets the bread back down on the altar he genuflects in respect. He then does the same with the chalice of wine.

There are several versions of the Eucharistic prayer to choose from. The following reflects the liturgical imagery of the ancient Church.

Priest: "Lord, you are holy indeed, the fountain of all holiness. Let your spirit come upon these gifts (bread and wine) to make them holy so that they may become the body and blood of our Lord Jesus Christ. Before he was given up to death, a death he freely accepted, he took bread and gave you thanks. He broke the bread, gave it to his disciples, and said, 'Take this all of you, and eat it. This is my body, which will be given up for you.' When supper was ended, he took the cup, and again he gave thanks and praise, gave the cup to his disciples, and said, 'Take this, all of you, and drink from it. This is the cup of my blood, the blood of the new and everlasting covenant. It will be shed for you and for all so that sins may be forgiven. Do this in memory of me.' Let us proclaim the mystery of faith."

All: "Dying you destroyed our death, rising you restored our life, Lord Jesus, come in glory."

Priest: "In memory of his death and resurrection, we offer you, Father, this life-giving bread, this saving cup. We thank you for counting us worthy to stand in your presence and serve you. May all of us who share in the body and blood of Christ be brought together in unity by the Holy Spirit. Lord, remember your church throughout the world; make us grow in love together with our pope and our bishop and all the clergy. Remember our brothers and sisters who have gone to their rest in the hope of rising again: bring them and all the departed into the light of your presence. Have mercy on us all; make us worthy to share eternal life with Mary, the virgin mother of God, with the apostles, and with all the saints who have done your will throughout the ages. May we praise you in union with them and give you glory though your son, Jesus Christ. Through him, with him, in him, in the unity of the Holy Spirit, all glory and honor is yours, almighty Father, forever and ever."

Your Guardian Angel

Don't be shy about expressing peace with those around you, even if you don't know them. Don't worry, you don't have to kiss them; a handshake will do.

Breaking the Bread

The people then stand to say the Lord's Prayer together and share the "kiss of peace" with each other (usually not an actual kiss, but a handshake or a nod of the head). The priest breaks the host, symbolizing Jesus' broken body on the cross, while the people pray the *Agnus Dei:* "Lamb of God, who takes away the sins of the world, have mercy on us."

In an act of respect, the priest invites the people to join him humbly praying: "Lord, I am not worthy to receive you, but only say the word, and I shall be healed."

S'ter Says

Host is from the Latin *hostia,* meaning "victim," recalling the sacrifice of Christ. This term was used as one of several names for the Eucharistic bread in the Middle Ages.

The priest first eats and drinks the consecrated bread and wine and then invites the people to receive the sacrament. Those who are going to receive the Eucharist, usually most of the congregation, walk up the center aisle to the altar. They are given the option of taking the bread, now called the *host,* in their own hand and placing it in their mouth, or letting the priest place it on their tongue, as was the tradition for many years. Eucharistic ministers usually assist the priest by offering the chalice of consecrated wine. Real wine is used, and it is not necessary to take it. The sacrament is complete without the wine. As the communicants return to their seats, they kneel in prayer and meditation. Often, music is played or a song is sung in the background during the distribution of Communion.

The priest completes the Eucharistic ritual by washing the chalice and placing any unused consecrated hosts in the tabernacle. These hosts may be carried to home-bound parishioners or taken to the hospital and given to the sick. The priest sits after Communion and the church is quiet for a time of reflection. When he rises, it signals the people to stand for the conclusion of the service.

At the end of the Mass, the priest blesses the people and dismisses them with the "order," "Mass is ended! Go in peace to love and serve the Lord!" He sends them out into the world with a blessing, and the instruction to take Christ with them and make him known to whomever they meet. During his blessing, the people make the sign of the cross. The priest then ceremonially walks down the center aisle of the church preceded by the altar servers, while the people sing a final hymn. He usually stands outside and greets his parishioners as they leave the church.

It's More the Food Than the Talk: The Liturgy of the Eucharist

The main difference between a Protestant worship service and a Catholic Mass is the Eucharist. Not that Protestant churches don't serve Communion—many do—but the Catholic sacramental imagination makes it a unique ceremony. Catholics believe that through the priest's consecration and through the people's belief, the bread and wine actually become the body and blood of Jesus. This ritual is referred to as *real presence*. There is more about this very sacred and mysterious ritual in Chapter 11 in the discussion of the Eucharist as a sacrament.

You recall, Eucharist, the formal name for the Mass, has two meanings: it is a memorial of Jesus' celebration of the Last Supper and a memorial of his sacrifice on the cross. Let's take a look at each of these meanings in more detail.

Is It Real, or Is It "Memorex"?

The consecration ritual is very specific, it uses the same essential words and gestures each time it is done, in every church all over the world. Jesus told his followers to bless the bread and wine and think of him every time they got together for supper, and he would be right there with them. As Catholics follow the precise pattern used by Jesus at the Last Supper, they believe literally in the words of Jesus: that he is there with them. The Eucharist is a mystery, meaning it is taken on faith and can never be completely understood in the scientific way of knowing. It is possible, however, to catch a glimpse at how memory works in our lives, to begin to see how it is even possible to believe in real presence.

When a family or group of friends gathers and begins to recall memories of a departed member of the group—particularly a person they cared a lot about—that person begins to come alive in the mind and imagination (where memory is recorded) of the people. The stronger the emotional bond, the sharper the connection. As we talked about in Chapter 9, the memory is in the right hemisphere of the brain, where time is not linear. As the memories are recalled, people enter that sacred space where the past and present connect. Both modern day science and the ancient mystics agree that in that sacred space, God communicates with us. Memories are not locked in time, they are dynamic. Imagination is real and has substance. It is an internal reality, with chemical substance that flows through the body, becoming physical. This explanation does not capture the true mystery of the Eucharist, but the analogy can be helpful.

The presence of Jesus, as he gathered with the disciples at the Last Supper is recalled through the Mass and through the Communion ritual. As the communal memory of the congregation along with other congregations all over the world recall the same memory, it grows in power. When you then ask for insight on something going on in your life today, the real presence of Jesus can very much come alive for you. It is possible to feel his love, support, and comfort. He is there with you, as he was with his followers at the Last Supper.

Saints Preserve Us

Sts. Cosmas and Damian, September 26, Patrons of Druggists

St. Cosmas and St. Damian were brothers and were skilled in the science of medicine. They were filled with the spirit of Christian charity and never took money for their services. They were held in high esteem and greatly loved by the people of their town. When the persecutions broke out about the year 283, they were arrested because of their prominence. After undergoing various torments, they were finally beheaded.

The Eucharist ritual follows the Jewish tradition of remembering through story and ritual. Passover was one of the primary events in the Jewish story. It refers to the deliverance of the Jews from Egyptian slavery, and it is remembered with a ritual supper. This was the same Passover supper Jesus celebrated with his disciples as the Last Supper, the night before his death. Catholics believe Jesus declared that the sacrifice of his life would now achieve for all the deliverance of Passover. In declaring this, he fused the memory of these events, Passover and the Last Supper ritual.

The Meaning of Sacrifice

Why do Catholics call the Mass a sacrifice? Often we think of sacrifice as something we give up, even sacrificing a life for a cause, but as you look at the root word, it has a deeper meaning. It comes from Latin—*sacrum* meaning "holy" and *facere* meaning "to make." Sacrifice literally means to make something holy. Catholics use the word *sacrifice* when they talk about the Mass because they are bringing the gift of themselves to God at the altar to be made holy, to be blessed. The word "altar" comes from the Latin *adolere*, which means, "to burn up." Fire purifies, and sacrifices have been enacted by burning, symbolizing purification or transformation, since the beginning of time. Thus, the sacrifice has come to mean change, even molecular change—transformation.

In a sacrificial ritual, a person surrenders to God, he or she gives up the form in which they now exist, or the way they presently think about something, and willingly allows God to transform them. Jesus surrendered his will to God as he prayed in the garden of Gethsemane, as recorded in Matthew 26:39: " … Yet not as I will, but as you will." The events that followed took him to his death on the cross and to his resurrection (transformation). By remembering Jesus' surrender, Catholics surrender themselves to the will of God during this act of Communion.

Epiphanies

Each age has attempted to use language to express belief in the real presence of Jesus. **Transubstantiation** is a term from the Middle Ages. This term came to be used to more technically describe the belief that the priest's blessing during the Mass changes over (*trans*) the substance of the bread and wine to the substance of the body and blood of Christ. It expressed the difference between the appearance of the bread and its actual "substance," now believed to be Jesus' body and blood. It signifies that the change is real or substantial, not just accidental or surface, like changing water into ice. The importance of the act is the reality of the presence of Jesus in the Catholic spiritual life. The Church uses the term "transubstantiation" as a technical way to talk about the action of the Eucharist, but it is by no means the complete way.

Here's the Church, and Here's the Steeple, Open the Doors, and See All the People!

Catholics worship in a building called a church. As you enter a Catholic church, you can't help but notice the many sacred objects. From the holy water fonts on both sides of the entrance to the sanctuary lamp burning on the altar, there are many indications that you have entered sacred space. Catholic churches are generally quiet zones in our otherwise very busy and noisy lives, and it is the custom to observe silence when visiting a church. It is common practice for Catholics to visit the church when no service is going on and just sit in meditation in the presence of the Eucharistic bread in the tabernacle.

You'll see a long aisle with benches on both sides, leading to the sanctuary where the altar stands. The church has two basic spaces: the pews or the rows of benches with kneelers where the people worship, and the sanctuary where the priest, altar servers, and readers perform their respective tasks. The sanctuary and the pews face each other, and while the two spaces are defined as different, they interact. Let's go inside and take a look around.

Sacred Spaces

If you haven't been inside a Catholic church, the first thing you will encounter as you enter a pew is the kneeler. A pew may be long enough to comfortably seat 10 or more people. Each row of pews will have a *kneeler*, a cushioned board of wood hinged on both ends and attached to the bottom of the pew. When it is time to kneel, you put it down so it rests on the floor. When you need to move in and out of the pew, you raise it on its hinge so that the aisle is clear.

The sanctuary is a large space with several key pieces of furniture. There is an altar in the center of the sanctuary, typically a waist-high table or slab of marble, about 10 to 15 feet long and about 5 feet wide. The surface of this table is smooth and polished, with five Greek crosses engraved on its surface, one at each of the four corners, about six inches from both edges, and one in the center. It's covered with layers of cloth and will have candles burning during the liturgy of the Eucharist. Sometimes the candles are not on the altar but are placed around it. As you read earlier, the altar symbolizes Christ's sacrifice, or giving up of his will to God, and during the Mass, the followers will do the same.

The second item in the sanctuary is the *pulpit*, the stand from which the priest reads the Gospel and delivers the homily. The two parts of the Catholic Mass are celebrated around these two pieces of furniture.

Either on a shelf behind the altar or on a side altar, you will find a little marble or metal box called a *tabernacle*. It is covered with a cloth, and the door is locked with a key. The Eucharistic bread that has been consecrated at Mass is kept there in reserve. The sanctuary lamp sits or hangs near the tabernacle and is always lit, signaling God's presence in the tabernacle in the form of the consecrated bread, Jesus' body. As mentioned before, there is always a crucifix visible near the altar. Additionally, the Easter candle is prominently displayed. There is more discussion of sanctuary furnishings and sacramentals in Chapter 11.

Putting on Your Glad Rags

Those who participate at the altar during the Mass wear special ceremonial clothes. The priest's clothes (vestments) are the most elaborate and unusual. The different colors of the vestments correspond to the liturgical calendar and the seasons of the year. The rules that govern the proper form for the celebration of the Mass are contained in a book called the *General Instruction of the Roman Missal*. Here are some of the guidelines for the colors at Mass.

White and *gold* are used for important celebrations like Christmas and Easter. For funerals *white* is the regular color, representing Resurrection, although *black* (worn in the past) is still used in more traditional parishes. *Red* is the color for the feast of the Holy Spirit (Pentecost), as well as for the celebrations of the lives of martyrs. *Red* is sometimes used for ordinations and installations and for church dedications and anniversaries. *Purple* is worn during more somber seasons such as Lent and Advent, as we prepare for the feasts of Easter and Christmas. *Blue* is often used instead of purple during the season of Advent, as it conveys hope, the main mood of Advent. *Green* is used at all other times.

The Sanctuary. Christ the King Catholic Church, Nashville, Tennessee.

(Courtesy of H. L. [Dean] Caskey)

Altar servers also wear special clothes, either a white gown, like the priest, or a black one called a cassock with a white type of blouse over it called a surplice. Generally the lectors, Eucharistic ministers, and ushers don't wear special uniforms.

Who's Who at a Catholic Mass

Since Vatican II, the people are seen as participants in the Mass, not just observers. They make up the body of the assembled Church offering the Mass to God. The counsel document on the liturgy calls their role at the Mass "priestly." A priest presides, leading the congregation in offering worship to God. His words begin and end the Mass. He leads the prayers, reads the Gospel, and preaches the homily. He leads the praying of the liturgy of the Eucharist and says the words of consecration.

Often the priest is assisted by a deacon, or altar servers. Altar servers are boys and girls or men and women who assist by carrying items used in the service, such as the book containing the prayers and scriptures. They may also ring the bells during certain times in the Mass. There are also readers called lectors who read the Old Testament and Epistles, and the prayers following the homily. In addition, there are men and women who distribute the Communion bread and wine, consecrated as Lay Eucharistic Ministers. Altar servers, lectors, and ministers of the Eucharist are prepared for their jobs by special instruction. Serving outside the sanctuary are choir members and ushers. The ushers greet and seat people and take up the collection.

Your Guardian Angel

Being a lector at Mass can be a rewarding experience. The parish offers workshops to train lectors in public speaking and instruct them in the meaning of the Biblical texts. Don't be afraid to volunteer!

The key ministers in the whole service are the people.

Guess Who's Coming to Dinner: Is It Just for Catholics?

All are welcome at a Catholic celebration of the Mass. If you're not Catholic and you attend a Mass, you should feel free to sit during the service or join in all the gestures and prayers if you are comfortable doing that. Typically, there will be a booklet available to help you follow the Mass. Visitors to Catholic parishes often wonder why they may not join in receiving Communion because other churches don't have such restrictions.

Hopefully you'll forgive Catholics for what appears to be a lack of hospitality when it comes to this ceremony. The Eucharistic ritual involves the actual belief that Jesus becomes present at the consecration. It is therefore reserved for those who formally profess this important Catholic belief. It seems that all families welcome guests, and yet some gathering times are reserved only for members. This reinforces their family bond. Catholic Communion is just that, a sign of Catholic unity.

As a regular practice, Catholics do not share Communion at non-Catholic churches, although there are exceptions to this rule. While theologians and Catholic Church officials debate the possibilities for full Communion, many ordinary folks find themselves troubled by this separation, feeling the more unity Christians express, the closer all Christian churches will come to resolving differences, more closely modeling Jesus' words at the Last Supper: "that they may all be one." (John 17:21) Other Catholics want to maintain the existing rules around receiving the Eucharist to preserve its Catholic character, and to assure the bond of unity that is created by all who participate holding the same belief about its authenticity. When persons from another Christian denomination become Catholic, they are said to be received into full Communion. They are not re-baptized, but their participation in receiving Communion becomes the high point marking their transition into membership.

The Least You Need to Know

- The Mass is the primary worship service for Catholics.

- The consecration and distribution of Holy Communion is the central ritual of the Mass.

- Catholics believe that the real presence of Jesus is actually contained in Holy Communion.

- Although the priest presides, the people offer the Mass along with him.

Part  Catholic Identity: What Makes a Catholic?

We've looked at Catholics' biblical roots. We've looked at their sacramental life and practices such as incense, bells, and holy water. We've sampled their rich prayer life. Now in Part 5, we'll look at how they think and where they meet. When you consider the broad population base of Catholicism, what does it mean to identify Catholics as a tribe? Is there a process in which Catholic culture and thinking is formed? Is there a particular way Catholics engage the world? How does the Church maintain unity and diversity? Do Catholics all believe the same things? Do they all think alike?

In this part, we'll look at Catholic beliefs, examining some of the more controversial issues. We'll look at power within the Church: Who has it, and who does not. We begin, however, by looking at Catholics as a community.

Chapter 16

It's a Tribe

In This Chapter

- ◆ The communal nature of Catholics
- ◆ The parish: where the tribe meets
- ◆ The parochial school: discipleship and citizenship
- ◆ The Church's social face
- ◆ Getting in and getting out of the tribe

Catholicism has a distinctive cultural and ethnic mark that is more than the sum of its rules and beliefs. In this chapter, we'll look at where this ethos finds form, which is in the parish and the Catholic school that so often is an integral part of the parish. We'll look at the role Catholic schools play in forming Catholics as citizens.

A particular social sensibility is developed in the parish environment. It calls the faithful to the Biblical mandate to work for the transformation of all people, to bring forward the "reign of God." After looking at where Catholic identity is formed and where it is lived out, we'll end this chapter by looking at the process by which new people are initiated into the tribe.

Where the Tribe Meets

Catholic priest and sociologist Andrew Greeley describes the ideal form of a Catholic parish as an "organic community." He means that a Catholic parish will be successful to the extent that it can make the sacramental moments of the people's lives central to the life of the tribe. It is successful when it is able to connect the Gospel message to the lives of the people and link its members with the world beyond the parish.

The parish is the neighborhood. The tradition was that Catholics attended the church in the neighborhood in which they lived. Although less true today, in the past, the lines of parish distinction were as clearly drawn as those of voting districts.

Greeley believes that the Church should recognize the importance of establishing a religious base inside a local community. Especially now as the technological age advances, people need a sense of belonging to a community. The parish church can bring that sense of belonging. Church for Catholics is not in Rome nor is it at the level of the diocese, but it does exist down the block, on the corner. It's where you were baptized and where your older sister was married and where your grandparents' funerals were held. It is woven into your family history.

For many, Catholic churches also included Catholic schools. Approximately one third of all Catholic churches in the United States still have a Catholic school connected to them, and nearly half had one just 30 years ago. The school continues to be an important dimension of the organic sense of Catholic parish life. When the same beliefs and values are reinforced, a strong unifying statement is made through church, home, and school. The school is a forum to work specifically with the faith basis of peace and justice for the young people.

Parish: Center for Belonging

In the past, people often included Catholics in that infamous theoretical group addressed in the question, "Yes, but would you want your sister to marry one?" They would not have been the object of the Mr. Rogers musical question, "Would you like to live in my neighborhood?" In the predominately Protestant culture of America of yesteryear, Catholics were often not accepted into the larger community. They gained their much needed sense of belonging by gathering in their parish churches. Although times have changed, the need for belonging remains a strong human desire. Parish life remains the primary spiritual home and the touchstone of Catholic identity, where that identity is developed and experienced. From that base, Catholics find and belong to a variety of other organizations where men, women, and youth make face-to-face connections with others who have similar interests, backgrounds, or spiritual goals. Such organizations include the Christian Family Movement, Marriage Encounter groups, The Knights of Columbus, the Legion of Mary, programs for divorced and separated Catholics, Great Books clubs, Scripture study groups, Girl Scouts and Boy Scouts, the choir, various ministries to the sick and bereaved, and gatherings for seniors, to name just a few.

Play and recreation are at the heart of community and remain integral to spiritual and religious experience. You might call it "sacred play." Indeed, many churches have a gymnasium for basketball and volleyball, as well as an auditorium ready for dances and other social events, such as variety shows or a haunted house at Halloween. Many parishes sponsor golf or bowling leagues, card clubs, and quilting clubs. They offer ball fields, playgrounds, and grounds for church picnics.

Positive social bonding is a religious and spiritual affair. Social life in the parish allows Catholics to experience God as the unifying force in human relationships.

Parish: Center for Prayer and Sacraments

At the heart of the parish is the church where Catholics gather for the Mass. The varieties of celebrations of Mass reflect the different character of parishes. In Los Angeles, Mass is celebrated each Sunday in more than 50 different languages. Many Catholics still hold on to the Latin Mass, and a few parishes still offer it.

Music takes on the unique character of the parish. Depending on the preferences of the congregation and the church leadership, a parish might offer anything from folk music to Gregorian chant. Certain parishes might even offer a rock Mass performed by the youth choir. Music helps to set the mood and environment, which is a key focus in today's Church. Some parishes even offer choreographed lighting and sound. In addition, banners, sometimes made by the children or youth groups, decorate the church and mark the seasons.

The church is where the parish celebrates its sacramental life through baptisms, weddings, and funerals. People also come to the church for public and private devotions. Throughout the week, people make a *visit* to the church for private prayer. Until recently, Catholic churches didn't lock their doors. You could drop in at any time and expect to find a scattering of others sitting or kneeling quietly in prayer and meditation. Today, however, many city churches have found it necessary to lock the doors, but you'll still find the faithful in prayer once you knock. On weeknights, novenas, benedictions, and seasonal devotions, such as the Way of the Cross, are held during Lent. All of these ceremonies and rituals work to create a sacramental identity that is communally shared.

Parish: Launching Pad to the World

Ideally in the Catholic scheme of things, the parish contributes to the political and cultural life of its city and the world. It does this by organizing and focusing the power of the people. One way to accomplish these tasks is through committees at the parish level that educate members on issues and organize them to affect political policies on issues as diverse as taxes, medical practices, wages, or capital punishment.

Ironically, one of the things the larger culture often confuses is the Catholic allegiance to Rome and a lack of citizenship. Nothing could be further from the truth. In parochial schools, children are educated to be better Catholics *and* better citizens.

Your Guardian Angel

Send your kids to Catholic schools if you want to promote their social awareness. According to sociological studies, Catholics educated in Catholic schools are substantially more likely to be in favor of racial integration and tolerant of members of other denominations than are public school Catholics.

The school brings religious significance to skills and talents; learning is associated with bringing Catholic principles into being. In a way, Catholic students learn their ABCs and 123s in order to make a better world—which in Catholic terms means bringing about the reign of God. The point of interweaving values with those of the wider culture and social structure isn't about imposing the Catholic Church on others (although this has been the case at times), but rather it embodies basic foundational values such as Christian charity and justice for all. Catholic identity includes living the Gospel by being active in the world.

One man remembers how the very architecture of his Catholic grade school was influential in transmitting Catholic identity. The grades closest to the church building where the children were baptized were the primary grades kindergarten through three, then came the middle grades four through six, and finally grades seven and eight were located at a distance from the church. He felt this arrangement was a statement about life beginning in the security of the womb of the Church, moving through school, and then out into the world.

Growing up Catholic had a rhythm to it. Each age group had its own playground, and this series of playgrounds was important in terms of status and self-understanding. Different aspects of Catholic life were sampled at different grades: Second grade was First Communion time, while fourth grade funneled boys into either football or academics. Fifth grade was altar boy time, a time when young men were placed under the guidance of the priest. Being trained one-on-one as a Mass server meant being away from the tutelage of the nuns. In school, the nuns reigned supreme. Granted, Catholic culture is likewise subject to the limitations of the greater societal mores, as previously illustrated. By seventh and eighth grades, students were being prepared for the Catholic high school, and those who showed a particular interest in religion or church were encouraged to take up a vocation, as a life of service in the Church as a priest or nun. Students would begin to wear the insignia of the Catholic high school. In these grades, identification as a Catholic moved from the parish to the high school.

Of course, growing up Catholic today has a rhythm to it as well; it's just a different beat. Chapter 24 describes today's young Catholics.

Catholics' Social Face

The true measure of Catholic identity is how Catholics live their lives in the world. Jesus talked about bringing about the reign of God. The reign of God was not simply an idea to be expressed; it was an action to be taken. Jesus healed the sick, cared for sinners, and challenged the injustices in his society. His followers took on this mission from the start. The book in which the early doings of the Church were recorded is called the Acts of the Apostles.

Transformation of the structures of society is an ongoing response to the Gospel message and happens when organized movements confront injustice in all areas of society and culture: labor, human rights, the military, private corporations, and the government. From its earliest days to the present, the Church has taken on massive activities to bring about love and to effect justice. This work goes on at two levels: One is caring for people, and the second is seeking justice in the transformation of the structures of society.

The Church has expressed care for people in three primary ways:

> **For Heaven's Sake!**
>
> You can't be a good Catholic and pass the buck. Catholicism is a religion of action in the world. Being a good Catholic requires hard work; you are expected to be involved in your church and in the community.

- ◆ Health care for the community

- ◆ Education for the society

- ◆ Welfare for all those in need

Let's take a look at each of these concerns.

Catholic Health Care: More Than Chicken Soup for the Soul

From its earliest years in the United States, the Catholic Church has been vitally involved in health care. Currently, Catholic health-care institutions serve almost 80 million patients a year. Catholic hospitals constitute more than 10 percent of all hospitals in the country and receive about 15 percent of all hospital admissions.

Both lay and religious men and women respond to the vocation of healing the sick and comforting the afflicted. Catholic hospitals employ almost 750,000 people, about 15 percent of all hospital employees in the country; their total payroll is in excess of 20 billion dollars.

In a recent address to the Catholic Hospital Association of Wisconsin, Archbishop Weakland of Milwaukee reminded Catholics of the following:

> There is no doubt that Jesus was eager to heal physically those who were in any way infirmed. He did not make the distinctions that we would make today between physical illness, diabolical influences on people, psychological phenomena, and the need for spiritual healing. His approach was holistic in the best sense of the term. He saw all such wounds as hindering people from being the full entity that God would want them to be .... When he talks of salvation, it goes beyond but does not exclude these more physical and more measurably visible healings.

Most of the Church's health-care institutions are banded together in the Catholic Health Association (CHA), the largest single group of not-for-profit health-care providers. The CHA is organized to advance the health care ministry through advocacy, education, research, and development. It supports and strengthens health ministries in the United States and speaks out with one voice to address health issues.

Catholic Colleges: Rocking the Cradle of Thought

In the United States, more than 200 Catholic institutions of higher education educate two thirds of a million students. About 5 percent of these places are research universities, 10 percent are two-year colleges, and the remaining 85 percent are four-year universities and colleges, equally divided between liberal arts and more comprehensive institutions.

Saints Preserve Us

St. Vincent de Paul, September 27, Patron of Charitable Organizations and Prisoners

St. Vincent de Paul was a spiritual advisor to a wealthy woman in France. He became aware of the plight of the peasants and began his missionary work to aid them. He founded many orphanages and hospitals, the Congregation of the Missions (the Vincentians), and the Daughters of Charity. It was said that his way with wealthy women greatly enhanced the success of his work. He died in 1660. He is the patron saint of charitable organizations and prisoners, and his feast day is September 27. The charity that bears his name, the St. Vincent de Paul Society, was founded in Paris in 1833. It operates all over the world today.

Since the 1960s, both with Vatican II's openness to the world and the lessening of religious and ethnic identities in the culture at large, much has changed in these schools. Higher education in secular schools is no longer seen as a danger to the faith; in fact, many Catholic parents see it as desirable.

For the most part, Catholic colleges were founded by religious orders, such as the Jesuits, Dominicans, Franciscans, and Benedictines. As federal funding has required Catholic institutions to meet the test of independent control, most schools have moved to independent boards of trust that aren't controlled by the Church hierarchy. The religious orders have become sponsors, not owners. The faculty is diversified. Not only are there very few of the members of the sponsoring religious orders teaching, but the replacement faculty are not required to be Catholic.

These schools now must decide how to be distinctive Catholic institutions. Will these Catholic schools go the route of many of the other religious schools, such as Harvard, Yale, and Northwestern, for example, all of which were once church schools? Will they simply become a historical memory of the Church?

There are two reasons to believe that Catholic colleges and universities will retain their Catholic identities. For the most part, these institutions cannot successfully raise funds without making the case for their Catholic character and identity, which means that Catholics still want Catholic institutions of higher education to exist.

The other reason in favor of Catholic higher education is the pope's directive in the encyclical *Ex Corde Ecclesiae*, which means "From the Heart of the Church." In this letter to Catholic higher education administrators all over the world, the pope declared that the primary role of the Catholic university is to bridge faith and culture. This directive calls for the schools to develop highly credentialed faculties in the arts, the social sciences, and the natural sciences, in addition to the disciplines of theology and philosophy.

In the ongoing balancing act between how much is too much and how much is not enough, the present tendency is toward reasserting Catholic identity in Catholic colleges and universities. From the Vatican on down, the reins have been tightened on what can and can't be taught as Catholic doctrine, and to a degree, who can teach it. Recently, all Catholic theologians teaching in Catholic schools who want to maintain their status as a Catholic theologian have been required to sign

Your Guardian Angel

You can get a full education at a Catholic college. The primary goal of Catholic universities as most recently defined by Pope John Paul II is to mediate faith and culture. They do this by developing cultural understanding through the arts, social sciences, and natural sciences, partnered with theology and philosophy.

an agreement with the bishop assuring him that their teaching will replicate Catholic doctrine. Of course, this bumps into both religious and intellectual freedom, along with Catholic values. In an affirmative action kind of way, attention is being paid to how many Catholic teachers are on the faculty of Catholic institutions. At the same time, one has to wonder if faculty excellence will be sacrificed in the name of maintaining a distinctive Catholic identity.

Catholic Charities: More Than Just a Handout

Catholic Charities is the largest private network of social service organizations in the United States. It works to support families, reduce poverty, and build communities. Catholic Charities provides emergency and social services ranging from shelters and soup kitchens to day care centers, summer camps, centers for seniors, and refugee resettlement offices for more than 10 million people. Its annual budget exceeds two billion dollars.

Dorothy Day and the Catholic Worker Movement

Dorothy M. Day, who lived from 1897 to 1980, was an icon of the Catholic social faith in the twentieth century. A journalist, she converted to Catholicism, and her belief centered on a philosophy that stressed the value and dignity of each individual person. She founded an organization she called The Catholic Worker in which she attempted to make this ideal available to all who desired it.

The Catholic Worker was a Catholic presence that announced a concern for the poor and oppressed. In 1933, Day sold *The Catholic Worker* newspaper in New York's Union Square for a penny a copy. It has been in constant production since that time and is still sold at a penny a copy! Embracing voluntary poverty, Day worked tirelessly, establishing houses for the immediate relief of those in need and farming communes where each person worked to his ability and received according to his need. She modeled her organizations on early Christian communities. Day and her movement were a call to U.S. Catholics to reconnect to the Church history of caring for others.

Perhaps Day is best known for her proclamation of Catholic pacifism as the ideal response to war. Nonviolence was integral to her position, and her efforts at pacifism encouraged Catholics to change the social order by performing direct, albeit nonviolent, actions on behalf of peace and social justice. The pacifism of Dorothy Day and The Catholic Worker were at the heart of the American Catholic peace movement during the Vietnam War. The Catholic Worker movement spawned additional Catholic movements such as The Catholic Peace Fellowship and Pax Christi, U.S.A.

Dorothy Day reflected the Catholic's personal obligation of looking after the needs of fellow human beings as focused in the works of mercy. The works of mercy are seven charitable acts encouraged by the Church:

♦ Feed the hungry.

♦ Give drink to the thirsty.

♦ Clothe the naked.

♦ Visit the imprisoned.

♦ Give shelter to the homeless.

♦ Visit the sick.

♦ Bury the dead.

Hungering and Thirsting After Justice

Still alive and very well today, The Catholic Worker has served as a prototype to many movements for social transformation in the Church. Here are a few that might be of interest to you:

♦ **The Eighth Day Center**   In Chicago, various religious orders band together at this center to document major economic and political issues on a national as well as global scale. Similar centers exist all over the world. As international organizations, these centers are able to network broadly, quickly passing on information that will be used to bring about policy changes and create legislation in worldwide governments.

♦ **Volunteer groups**   One of the Church's best-kept secrets is that more than 300 Catholic organizations, such as the Jesuit Volunteer Corps, recruit college graduates for a year or two of service. Volunteers take their services into the community in the form of education in inner-city schools, job training, and finding housing for the homeless. At the same time, the volunteers live a community life of prayer and poverty, transforming their understanding of what it means to be in the world. More than 100,000 Catholics are involved in this work.

For Heaven's Sake!

Put your money where your values are! If you are lucky enough to have money to invest, you must be a good steward and choose a company to invest in that reflects your values. Remember, spirituality has practical applications.

◆ **The Jesuit Center of Concern** A policy think tank in Washington, D.C., the Jesuit Center researches the social implications of proposed legislation and thus provides a voice for justice in policy-making.

◆ **The Wall Street Group** Similar to the Eighth Day Center, Catholic religious orders have formed a Wall Street group that monitors the investments of their orders. They use their power as shareholders to call for corporate responsibility in the companies they have invested in.

"Mea Culpa, Mea Culpa, Mea Maxima Culpa"

The picture we paint in this chapter is the ideal, and there are many times and places when the ideal was met. Unfortunately, that has not always been the case. Putting Catholic values into action has sometimes suffered from bad translation! Throughout history and today as well, human limitations make a mess out of the attempt to "do the right thing." The Latin phrase above, "Through my fault, through my fault, through my most grievous fault," is a prayer said at Mass, and represents a permanent human condition. Even the best intentions are subject to human error. The fact that many people have suffered at the hands of a well-meaning Church cannot be denied. Examples abound.

While Catholic hospitals and charitable organizations provided safety for women and children, they likewise caused untold suffering by imposing misunderstood values. Women who were pregnant and not married were routinely "institutionalized" for their "own good" and for the "good of the baby." They were often lied to and pressured into signing adoption papers. Mothers and babies were separated cruelly, and continue to suffer because of these ill-designed policies. Practices have been changed for the most part, but the trail of broken relationships remains.

Another example involves the treatment of native people, from whom missionaries routinely took children out of their homes and "gave" them to other people or put them into homes across the country in the name of "Christianizing them." Not only were families destroyed, children were denied their language, customs, and spiritual practices. Stories of overly zealous nuns and priests and the resulting spiritual abuse have damaged many, and have likewise damaged the Catholic image.

Of course, the media have had a field day with these stories, making them front-page headlines along with stories of sexual abuse and cover-ups. Only through rigorous honesty on the part of Church officials and sensitive listening to members' stories will changes be made. Some efforts at healing these breaches have occurred already, and there's good reason to think such efforts will continue, due to publicity and financial damage to the Church. More on this topic in Chapter 25.

Getting In and Out of the Tribe

The majority of Catholics are born into the religion. Roughly 80 percent die Catholic as well. But there's another way of getting in and getting out: People can choose to join and leave as adults.

For those who were not born and baptized Catholic, the Church has designed a comprehensive process of initiation into the tribe. As we've seen, Catholicism is more of a culture than an organization, which means that the word *initiation* is more accurate than the word *join*. There is a period of time in which the initiate gets to know the tribe and the tribal ways. The process is called the Rite of Christian Initiation (RCIA) and includes socialization, instruction, and ritual celebration that lasts a minimum of a year.

Entering the Church is acknowledging the relationship God has with people. Do you remember our discussion of *covenant*, an Old Testament term that describes the nature of God's relationship to his creation? In this relationship, God claimed his people and told them he would never leave them.

Sometimes, people may find that their relationship with the Church does not fulfill their covenant relationship with God, and they may choose to leave. In rare cases and for the most serious of reasons, the Church may find it necessary to sanction the actions of one of its members. This would happen when the member's action threatens the unity of the Church's teachings and beliefs.

Joining Catholicism, Not a Quick Study

The Rite of Christian Initiation of Adults, commonly referred to as *RCIA*, is the process designed for adults to enter the Catholic Church. It's designed as a time of instruction and bonding with the community, culminating in receiving the sacraments of initiation and full membership in the Church. You may remember from the earlier discussion of sacraments that this process sometimes includes baptism, as well as confirmation, and the Eucharist, celebrated at the end of the process.

The RCIA came out of Vatican II, yet it reaches back in time to the early Christian communities for its model. The early communities emphasized bonding and a time for questions, instruction, and faith sharing, as well as preparation to receive the sacraments and admission into the Church, usually at the Easter Vigil. This very old tradition outlines the process for today.

Just as the early Church began with a time of getting to know one another, RCIA does, too. It begins with a year-long effort to welcome the stranger and to create a caring, cohesive community of believers. The individual determines how long the bonding needs to last.

For those who choose to move forward in the process, a period of inquiry begins, during which they meet with others from the parish. Everyone shares stories, asks questions, and learns about the basic beliefs of the Catholic faith. Someone from the parish acts as a sponsor and walks the journey with his or her candidate, the one seeking to join the Church.

When the candidate feels ready and when the sponsor and the community confirm his readiness, he is enrolled as a *catechumen*, the title used to describe those seeking instruction. During this more formalized period of learning, candidates usually participate in Sunday Mass, leaving after the homily (sermon) to attend their faith-sharing groups. At the appropriate time, generally the beginning of Lent, those who are ready to move ahead with the process will enter the final stages of preparation. The willingness of the candidate, the advice of the sponsor, and the acceptance of the community determine the candidate's readiness.

Ideally, the Easter Vigil is the time during which the candidates will receive the sacraments of initiation and be welcomed into full membership in the Church. After this, the *neophytes*, the new members, enter a period of reflection on their experiences of receiving the sacraments. They are then assimilated into the parish.

The success of the RCIA depends on the parish community's participation. Without a genuine spirit of welcome, the process is vulnerable to becoming nothing more than a time of instruction. The caring of the community gives the rite vitality and life. This participation offers a challenge to some parishes, especially large congregations where members tend to be alienated from the sense of community themselves. The benefits of the program are twofold: The catechumen is provided a community experience, and the community is drawn together to offer one.

Here is a summary of the process:

- **Time of welcoming** During this time, the candidate gets to know the community and experience the Gospel values it offers.

- **Acceptance as a candidate** During a liturgical ritual of acceptance, the candidate expresses desire, and the community responds. This ritual is the entrance into a more structured process of instruction and faith sharing.

- **A time of development in the Catholic faith** After the rite of acceptance comes this time of nurturing and growth in faith.

- **Election** This formal, liturgical rite is usually celebrated on the first Sunday of Lent. The candidates express their desire to join the Church, and the parish ratifies their readiness to receive the sacraments of initiation.

◆ **Celebration of sacraments of initiation**   Usually held as part of the Easter Vigil, the elect are initiated through baptism, confirmation, and the Eucharist.

◆ **The honeymoon**   After their baptism, confirmation, and reception of the Eucharist, the newly initiated reflect on their experience of receiving the sacraments, and they are integrated into the community.

Excommunication

Excommunication is a penalty that the Church uses to exclude a Catholic from full participation in the Church. Church authority imposes this penalty only for the gravest of reasons. Excommunication does not expel a person from the Church, but it does restrict that person's rights within the community.

Excommunication is not a moral condemnation of a person; it is the Church's firm response to an action that jeopardizes the integrity of the Church. The ultimate goal of this action is to safeguard the community as well as encourage repentance and reconciliation. Excommunication is the strongest censure the Church can make, and at the same time, it extends the spirit of forgiveness. Excommunication is like the big "time out." As parents may throw one of the kids out of the house, they can't really throw them out of the family tree, excommunication does not throw you out of the Church. It does, however, firmly enforce the boundaries.

S'ter Says

Excommunication is an ecclesiastical censure depriving a person of the rights of Church membership and excluding that person from full fellowship in the community.

The history of excommunication goes back to the beginning of the Church. References to it are found in the First Council of Nicaea in 325. Although the Church has received a lot of publicity regarding notorious excommunications in the past, such as those involving Galileo, Martin Luther, and King Henry the VIII, excommunication is not invoked frequently.

Excommunication is more likely to be used to control Church leaders than ordinary parishioners. Examples of behavior that might warrant excommunication include consecration of a bishop without papal mandate; a priest breaking the seal of confession (a priest is bound to confidentiality regarding a person's confession); profaning the Eucharist; or using physical force against the pope. Excommunicated people are not allowed to administer or receive the sacraments, and they may not function in any Church office.

The Church is hesitant about using excommunication, and officials consider a number of factors before resorting to it. Excommunication can be private, just between the person and his or her confessor. In public situations, the court conducts the excommunication process in a Church court. As in a civil court, mitigating circumstances such as culpability (full awareness of one's actions) may be cited.

Your Guardian Angel

Excommunication does not have to be forever! It's a big deal and is used only in very serious situations. However, unlike a military court martial, it can be repealed. If the offense was a public one, it requires a public apology. If it was a private matter, it can be resolved with your confessor.

Excommunication is lifted when the prescribed penance has been performed. If the matter was private, it is handled between the person and his or her confessor. If it was a public situation, the penance or admission of guilt and apology must be delivered publicly; the lifting of the punishment is also done publicly.

Other censoring occurs at official and unofficial level. Silencing is an example of official censoring. Silencing takes place after the pope warns someone several times to no avail, after which the offending person is forbidden to speak publicly or publish for a period of time, perhaps six months to a year. Such a punishment is generally reserved for Church officials such as errant priests, nuns, or teachers who are getting too far away from official teachings and thereby misrepresenting Catholic doctrine. It happens infrequently—in the last thirty years, only Charles Curran and Matthew Fox, both theologians who pushed the boundaries too far for Church authorities, officially received censorship.

Censoring happens unofficially fairly routinely, just like it does in any organization. Flexing the "holy" muscle can go a long way. Teaching positions can mysteriously close, speaking engagements can be cancelled, and so on, until the message is received. Presently, many critics of the Church's stand on birth control, women's right to choice, women's ordination, and the possibility of marriage for clergy, or celibacy by choice, have received unofficial censoring.

Maintaining Status: How Catholic Do You Have to Be?

As you may remember, we noted that 20 percent of Catholics leave the religion, and that the second-largest "denomination" in the United States consists of former Catholics. These statistics pose an interesting question: Just what do people mean when they say they are Catholic? Because of Catholicism's tribal nature and deep cultural identity, its character tends to remain with those who leave the religion. It is rather like being a German American, Mexican American, Asian American, or African American: Catholicism gets into the blood!

From the perspective of the Church, you are Catholic unless excommunicated. From the perspective of the individual, you are Catholic as long as you still practice or in some way identify yourself as such. Practice means going by the six precepts of the Church that we listed in Chapter 4.

It is not unusual to hear people refer to themselves as Catholics when they have not attended church for 20 years or more. What about them is still Catholic? Most of the time, these people have maintained Catholicism's sacramental and communal way of encountering God, a Catholic way of being in the world, and of relating to others—they keep their "Catholic wiring." They carry the Church within them.

For some people, this lingering connection can be problematic. Their encounter with Catholicism has been so wounding that they have to "recover" from it. They spend a lifetime trying to exorcise it. Others leave the Church because they feel it's not Catholic enough—or that it isn't big enough, too narrowly defined. Good or bad, the religion's tribal nature means its members carry it around in their bones.

Your Guardian Angel

If you have been the victim of abuse by someone in a leadership position in the Church, there is help available to you. Talk to someone you trust, someone who can help you get the spiritual healing you need. Many counselors are now trained in recognizing and treating religious abuse.

Broken Relationships

As we have seen, the Catholic Church leaves a deep imprint on its members. If this imprint has been negative, it poses a considerable problem. Unfortunately, a number of people's experience with the religion has been damaging, so much so that the term "recovering Catholic" has worked its way into the common language.

When an institution such as a large company, a government, or a church has enormous power in the lives of people, the potential for an abuse of this power exists. The Church members who are most vulnerable to this abuse of power are the children. Many Catholics remember nuns and priests with dread and fear because these members of the Church physically, emotionally, or sometimes sexually abused them. Betrayal by the very ones you're supposed to be able to trust leaves deep wounds.

A Call for Reconciliation

The Church has too often turned its back on the wounding of its members, ignoring them and even at times covering up for its leaders. Abuse is not to be tolerated, especially within the institutions that have the most influence in people's lives. At its core, most abuse is understood to be an abuse of power. With power must come a highly developed sense of responsibility. Leadership requires this degree of responsibility. As the power shifts in the Church and as the people begin to take more control in their religious lives, the potential for this abuse reduces.

Reconciliation requires that the Church educate itself on the nature of abuse and how to recognize when the potential for it exists in its ranks. Society in general is making strides in understanding the nature of power and the potential for corruption that goes with having power over others. We urge individuals who have been victims to seek counseling.

We've taken a look at the parish, some of the Church's organizations, its outreach, and its tribal nature. Regardless of how the Church identifies you—as a Catholic in "good standing" or a "backslider"—it is really your personal identity that is the important issue—you get to call the shot on this. How you choose to acknowledge or reject your alliance with the tribe differs with each individual. In the next chapter, we'll find out where Catholic teachings originate and how they become part of the traditions of the Church.

The Least You Need to Know

- ◆ Catholicism is more of a culture than an organization.
- ◆ Catholic education encourages students to take an active and informed role in society.
- ◆ Catholics have a strong presence in ministering to the sick and the needy.
- ◆ Catholics have a highly organized and effective network of people working for justice throughout the world.
- ◆ There is a comprehensive process of discernment to join the Church.

The Teaching Church: More Than Just a Slap with the Ruler

In This Chapter

- ◆ The sources of Catholic teachings

- ◆ What is the Catechism?

- ◆ How Catholic teachings are formed

- ◆ Liberation theology from base communities

- ◆ Who controls the truth in the Church?

One of the primary roles the Church has taken on is that of guardian of the truth. It has an elaborate means to decipher the meaning of Jesus' teachings and to protect and maintain their unity. In other words, to be a Catholic is to subscribe to a particular set of beliefs. In this chapter, we'll talk about the Church as teacher of the faith, examine the special book that lists the teachings of the Church, and then explore the process called theology from which new discoveries about truth emerge.

The Sources of the Church's Teaching: Scripture and Tradition

The two primary sources of Catholic beliefs are the Bible and tradition. The Bible is a closed text, meaning nothing can be added or taken away from its content. On the other hand, tradition develops with time.

Periodically, new interpretations are made, new information is discovered, or new insight is gained that affects established beliefs. Thus Catholic tradition is informed by what is called "ongoing revelation." Catholics believe God continues to speak. Councils have been called throughout history to define a belief or to examine new information that will eventually produce new Church teachings. Vatican II, which we discussed in Chapter 5, is a point in modern times where Church teachings changed direction considerably. However, once the Church establishes a direction, it must put specific teachings into place to move the Church in that direction. This involves encoding it into Church law—also called Canon law. As you will discover, there is many a slip twixt the cup and the lip!

The Authority of Tradition

When exercising their teaching authority, Church leaders first consider what the Church has traditionally taught about the topic in question. Such a way of deciding truth is also used in the American judicial system: When judges make decisions about cases, they must consult existing rulings to see how previous judges have ruled in similar cases. This process is called establishing and following precedent.

The process of interpreting traditional doctrines requires prayer, study, and dialogue. Church leaders take new facts and circumstances into account while remaining faithful to what God has already revealed. Often it takes decades or even centuries of prayer and discussion before the teaching authority is prepared to speak on a controversial matter. The tradition of the Church is not static, but for some it seems to move at the pace of a glacier.

Tradition is summarized in three places: the Nicene Creed, the teachings of the councils as collected in the council documents, and the encyclicals, or letters of the popes. The *Catechism of the Catholic Church* organizes and presents this material in a systematic form. We'll now take a look at the process the Church uses to shape its beliefs from where they originate in the Bible to the new teachings that are informing and changing the Church today.

Teachings from the Scripture

At the base of all teaching lies experience. As we mentioned in Chapter 7, the Church began because Jesus' disciples wanted to share a powerful new experience of the meaning of life with everyone they met. As the years passed, the various communities recorded their experiences in four Gospels, which marked the beginning of the teaching Church.

Defining and recording these Gospels served two important functions. First, the Gospels attempted to put the memory of Jesus into a written form so that folks who did not know Jesus or his followers could read about the experiences and relate to them. Even at the time of Jesus, many stories, some true and some misrepresentations, were circulating about him and his teachings. The early Church, made up of the followers of Jesus, chose what they felt were the authentic writings over those they considered to be less authentic stories. By doing so, they established the canon (official teaching), and thus the Church began to exercise its teaching authority over truth.

The Gospel stories relate these truths:

♦ God is revealed in Jesus, as one who loves us so intimately that we can call him "Papa (*Abba*)."

♦ The world is not the result of chance; it is the gift of a loving God, and there is a purpose to life.

♦ Death, that which we fear most, is overcome in Jesus and is not the end.

Just as the Church ruled on which Bible texts it considered authentic, so it also began to list what beliefs it considered authentic, and it continually updates this list. When *beliefs* are declared authentic, they are called *dogmas*. The truths and beliefs of the early Church were developed and written into what is called the Nicene Creed, which represents the Church's foundational beliefs.

S'ter Says

Belief describes a state of confidence in a person or idea. It is also a body of information held by a group to be true. **Dogma** is a word used to describe a formally stated official belief of the Church concerning faith or morals.

Teachings in the Creed

The first set of the Church's dogmas is called the Nicene Creed, which was officially adopted at the Church council in Nicaea in 325. The Nicene Creed is an essential part of the doctrine and liturgy of the Church. In Chapter 15 we presented the text of the Nicene Creed.

These foundational beliefs are gathered in the Nicene Creed:

◆ God is almighty, the Creator of heaven and earth.

◆ Jesus Christ is God's son; he was conceived by the Holy Spirit, was born of the Virgin Mary, was crucified, died, and was buried, and rose from the dead.

◆ The Holy Spirit is the third person of the Trinity and lives in the people, who are the body of Christ.

◆ The Church is one; it's holy, catholic, and apostolic. Its sacraments are the way to participate in the life of Jesus.

◆ There will be a resurrection of our bodies for a life everlasting.

Council Documents and Encyclicals (Letters of the Popes)

Since Nicaea, Church councils have continued to shape the beliefs of Catholics. So far, the Catholic Church has convened 21 councils. The first one lasted 2 months and 12 days and included 318 bishops. As we discussed in Chapter 5, the most recent council was the twenty-first, the Second Vatican Council called Vatican II. More than 2,600 bishops from all over the world attended. It lasted from September 1962 to December 1965. The decrees from each of these councils, as well as all those in between, form the body of teachings of the Church and are preserved in what are called the Council Documents.

S'ter Says

Encyclicals are letters written by the pope to instruct the people. The pope can issue an encyclical on any subject he believes the Church will benefit from. Encyclicals continue the tradition of Paul's letters to Christian communities back in the early days of the Church.

Your Guardian Angel

Find it in the Catechism! You can check the Catechism for a clear answer to almost any question you might have on Catholic beliefs. Feel free to get a copy, even if you're just learning about the religion. The Catechism isn't difficult to read and is chock full of helpful information.

Additionally, the pope issues documents and writes letters called *encyclicals*. When a pope writes an encyclical, he writes to all the Catholic churches in the world. Pope John Paul II has written about a dozen of them. A recent example is called *On Human Work (Laborem Exercens)*. This encyclical serves as a frame for examining work as a major sociopolitical question of the day. Pope John Paul II wrote it on the ninetieth anniversary of a famous encyclical by Pope Leo XIII called *On the Condition of the Working Classes (Rerum Novarum)*, which was written as a study of social conditions in the late nineteenth century.

Encyclicals are instructions for Catholics. For instance, Pope Leo's emphasis on social justice for workers marked a significant change from the traditional Church alignment with the aristocracy. On rare occasions, the pope will use the encyclical to declare certain dogmas, or required beliefs, of the faith. Church beliefs eventually find their way to the catechism. Let's take a look at it.

The Catechism

> **Q.** Who made us?
> **A.** God made us.
>
> **Q.** Who is God?
> **A.** God is our Father in heaven.
>
> **Q.** Why did God make us?
> **A.** God made us to know him, to love him, and to serve him in this world and to be happy with him in the next.

When asked these questions, every Catholic over the age of 35 will automatically give the very same answers. They learned them by heart in the *Baltimore Catechism*, the definitive religious textbook for all Catholic children in the United States from the end of the last century until the Second Vatican Council in 1960.

The Catechism is a text that collects the fundamental Catholic truths. They are stated so clearly that most people can read them without need of further explanation. As is true for so much about the Church, the Catechism has a long and interesting history. In ancient times and in the Middle Ages, the truths and the prayers of the faith were inscribed on tablets like the Ten Commandments and were displayed in the house or church where they could be easily seen so that everybody could understand their content.

Following the invention of the printing press sometime in the mid-1500s, what we know today as the Catechism was formulated. After the Council of Trent in 1566, *The Roman Catechism* was produced. It was a catalog of beliefs the Church determined Catholics needed to know so as not to "fall into the errors of Protestantism."

At the First Vatican Council in 1869, *The Roman Catechism* was updated and reissued. It was

For Heaven's Sake!

You don't have to read theology to be a good Catholic! Remember, Jesus didn't write any theology. He taught the people about God's love through his actions. He fed them, and he healed their illnesses. Through his attention, they were transformed. So if theology isn't your cup of tea, relax and read one of the many stories in the New Testament that tell of the works of Jesus.

translated into English in the United States in 1885 and became known as the *Baltimore Catechism*. One hundred years later, in 1985, the Church began putting together a new Catechism. This was the first such major gathering of the teachings of the Church since the 1500s! The whole Church, giving input through their bishops, participated in its preparation. The pope officially approved it on June 25, 1992, in effect retiring the old *Baltimore Catechism*. The new book is called the *Catechism of the Catholic Church*. As discussed, this edition of the Catechism has been our principle resource.

The *Catechism of the Catholic Church* is divided into four parts:

- ◆ **The Nicene Creed.** What the Catholic Church believes.

- ◆ **The Sacraments.** What the Catholic Church celebrates.

- ◆ **The Commandments.** What the Catholic Church lives.

- ◆ **The Our Father.** What the Catholic Church prays.

The new Catechism is characterized by its invitational style. It is less dogmatic in its approach; it shows truth in a more complex way, with much less absolutism. It shows the evolving nature of belief. On the other hand, it avoids opinions, that is, teachings by Catholic religious scholars whose thoughts have not yet made it into official Church teaching.

Theology: Formulating New Beliefs

Writing the Nicene Creed and the creation of other Church documents began with a process called *theology*, or talking about God. Theology is modeled on Greek philosophy, which means it uses concepts and abstract terms rather than stories or poetry, which Jews and other groups commonly used to pass on their teachings. Even as the Church selected which stories were to be gospels, theology began. Theology is also called reflection or interpretation.

Your Guardian Angel

Look beneath the surface for the meanings in the Bible. The teachings of Jesus changed people's lives, and they continue to have this power. He taught in parable form, meaning he told stories that had several meanings. People who have spiritual insight hear the deeper message.

Theology began in the Bible with the writings of Paul. Because Paul did not know Jesus during Jesus' lifetime on earth, his writings are "one time removed" from the experience: They are a reflection on direct experience. In the Epistles of the New Testament, Paul talks about God and explains the meanings found in the disciples' experience of Jesus. He was interpreting the events and giving them meaning, which is what theology is all about.

Theology began as an attempt to put the experience of Jesus into a language style that was understandable to the Greek and Roman mind. The Greek and Roman mind was formed in the structure of the classic scholars like Plato, Socrates, and Aristotle. Paul wrote of Jesus in a language that non-Jewish citizens of the Roman Empire would understand, not in Jewish stories and poetry as the Gospels do.

Starting with Paul, then, the Church began to use a new style of teaching. It moved from story to philosophical statements, or dogmas, which is a process that continues today. New experiences meet old stories and make new beliefs. As you've learned in this chapter, these beliefs are formulated in Church councils and in the tradition of letters begun by Paul.

Faith Meets Reason

Although the process of theology began in the Bible at the time of Paul, the Church didn't use the term until the eleventh century when Anselm, one of the early Church writers, provided this famous definition of theology: "faith seeking understanding." This definition is particularly helpful because it recognizes that theology is a philosophical process that uses reasoning, yet it clearly acknowledges that theology is grounded in faith. Some articles of faith are not "reasonable," meaning that they cannot be proven or understood by logic.

Saints Preserve Us

St. Anselm, Doctor of the Church, April 21

In case you thought metaphysics was a New Age concept, you might be surprised to know St. Anselm, born in 1033, was considered to be a metaphysician. Metaphysics is the systematic investigation of the nature of ultimate reality. In contrast to physics, which tends to be concerned with more practical issues like building bridges or highways, it is concerned with otherworldliness and the nature of being. Anselm is best known for his systematic argument for the existence of God. He entered monastic life at the age of 27 and died in 1109. He has not been declared a patron of anything yet, although he is a Doctor of the Church. Maybe metaphysicians might want to adopt him!

Theology begins with people's experiences of faith and talks about them in terms of the meaning they have for life. Its purpose is not to prove or disprove the faith experience, but to help people understand and interpret it. Theology builds a logical discussion about an experience, drawing spiritual conclusions that help people practice their faith in everyday life. Just as any meaningful discussion must follow logical form in order to be understood by others, theology uses a precise framework to express its ideas. Theology works with Scripture, Church tradition, and faith experiences and reason to bring spiritual insight to a situation.

Types of Theology—WWJD (What Would Jesus Do)?

Today, there are two basic types of Catholic theology: classical and contemporary. Classical theology begins its process with the truths of the Bible as interpreted by Church teachings and applies these truths to daily life to provide a moral guide. This type of theology reigned supreme in the Church until the twentieth century. Since that time, Catholic theology has followed a more contemporary approach.

A problem with philosophy and theology is the tendency of those espousing the ideas to build logical arguments on top of logical arguments on top of logical arguments until the conclusions are so far removed from everyone's life that the average person finds them difficult to connect with. Rather than building on abstract principles, contemporary theology starts with the lives of the people.

Contemporary theology begins with what is going on in the lives of the people, according to the people. This focus is the crux of the difference between contemporary and classical theology. The starting point in contemporary theology is the people's experience. The starting point for classical theology is existing doctrine. As the people talk about their lives, questions arise about how and why they are having a particular problem. For example, one contemporary problem is multigenerational poverty despite the fact that people work from dawn until dusk. Awareness of this situation raises questions such as: Is it God's will that the people should be poor? Are folks being paid a fair price for their labor? What part does the local government play in the situation? What is the role of the Church in helping or not helping the people? Through this process the people form a political and spiritual analysis of their situation.

After listening to the voices of the people as they ask questions and demand answers of their faith for the realities of their human condition, contemporary theology then goes directly to the text of Scripture where the experiences of the people today touch the experiences of the people of the Bible. This process opens Church teachings to new insight. It's a bottom-to-top model. In this approach, the human struggle of the people begins to inform leaders, and push them to discover new meanings from the traditional understanding of Scripture and Church teachings. Both the leaders and the people can end up getting stuck doing things the same old way—just because they've always been done that way. Everyone who has ever been in any organization recognizes that danger. But the process of using theology in this new way makes the Scriptures jump off the page, come alive. It supports people in changing both external conditions (political policies) and internal conditions (attitudes and beliefs) rather than simply accepting them. The stories of Jesus are brought face-to-face with the stories of the people when they ask their questions: How would he have responded? What is he telling us to do?

Scripture scholarship continues to improve, bringing new insight and deeper meaning to our understanding of the Bible. Catholic thinkers are constantly developing theology; the subject matter for it is unlimited. Through theology, Catholics understand their faith better; however, theology is a human endeavor and is never a substitute for faith. There is a difference between theological reflections and what will become part of the faith of the Church. Not every theology that is developed makes it to the level of Church teaching. The pope and the bishops alone are responsible for making the decision about which theologies become official teachings.

Your Guardian Angel

Theologians write theologies on any of a number of subjects: the nature of God, Jesus Christ, the Trinity, sin, redemption, the nature of the Church, politics, war, the economy, and ecology.

Feeding New Ideas into the System

We've mentioned the creation story of Adam and Eve a couple of times in the book. The creation story is a foundational belief of the Church, and many other beliefs are built on it. One of these beliefs is the Church's understanding of human nature. Then there is the doctrine of original sin. From this doctrine, Catholics understand human weakness. Sin calls for redemption, and redemption is God's grace in the form of forgiveness. Even Church teachings that death is the consequence of original sin are built on the foundational story of creation. A whole system of beliefs sits on top of a foundational belief in the story of creation.

What happens to a whole system of beliefs when the foundational base is challenged? The Catholic Church excommunicated Galileo because of his challenge to foundational beliefs. Later, you'll see how a theologian was silenced in more recent times because of his teaching.

But then, how do new ideas make it into Church beliefs? Right away, you can see that does not happen easily or overnight, but it does happen—and it did happen in this century with the concept of evolution.

As the culture gradually shifted to understanding creation in geological time rather than Biblical time, theologians had to rethink the doctrine of creation. Did they have to throw out the Biblical story of creation? No. The stories remain important ways that truth about God has been passed through history to us in the present time. The old way was to think of science as different than religion. Yet scientific truth and

Biblical truth are not inherently different; religion (from *religio*, meaning "to bind together") is the arena in which all areas of life come together.

Stirring the Pot of Change

How can Biblical teaching be realigned in the light of new truths? One way is by rethinking how the Bible functions. Many have come to see that the Bible is transmitting important truth to the people at the level of poetry and *myth*. It is following the old Jewish way of teaching through the use of story. The Bible is the faith story of the people of God. As new discoveries are made, and new understandings develop, basic beliefs about life are reformulated. New experiences of the people affect how the old stories are heard, so the meanings of the stories change. This is how the Biblical text continues to have meaning today.

S'ter Says

Myth is a story that tells the beliefs of a group of people regarding their origins, history, and destiny. Myth is neither historically true nor false. Myths transmit truths that cannot be understood apart from the story. In other words, you must look below the surface of the mythological story to find the meaning of it.

As we've stated earlier, a belief is a belief only when the people believe it. Church teaching changes as the people's beliefs change. Although the Church is slow to change, so is human consciousness. Yet they both change.

Who are the people who help stir the pot of change? In the secular culture they are called philosophers, and in the Church they are called theologians. They are the ones who make the creative connections between the people and the teaching and shape new thought and new Church beliefs.

Theologians affect the Church teachings in three ways:

- **As communicators** Communication requires both listening and speaking. Contemporary theologians have their ears to the ground; they listen to the people and to the culture and are able to speak effectively about what they hear.

- **As connectors** They connect the present-day people's truth to people's stories of yesterday by weaving the past to the present point in time.

- **As creative thinkers** Because of their skills and training, theologians hold the "big picture." They are able to listen to the people, and they also have a broad knowledge of Church teachings. They are the ones who can creatively connect the voice of the people (experience) with Biblical teaching (story) and weave it into Church teaching (tradition).

The Dynamic Triangle: The People, Theologians, and Bishops

Imagine a triangle connecting the theologians to the people and to the bishops. Let's make it a dynamic triangle, meaning that an exchange of energy in the form of ideas and power moves among the different points on the triangle generating creativity.

The movement begins with the experiences of the people. The theologians hear the people, and a dialogue begins between them. (Remember, theologians are the communicators; they have their ear to the ground, and they listen as well as talk.) New understandings about life and what it means to be human emerge. Theologians help formulate these understandings into ideas that can be presented to the bishops; the theologians act as spokespersons.

Your Guardian Angel

Not every idea in theology becomes a belief of the Church. The theologians' job is to come up with new ideas; the bishops' job is to sort through them.

Bishops, whose job it is to be the guardians of Church truth, act as moderators. They consider what the people are saying through the theologians and also what the Church has taught in the past. If the bishops feel strongly that the new teaching is in error, they will not accept it into official Church belief. If they see the truth of it, new beliefs are formed. Not every idea of the people, formulated by the theologians, will make it to the level of Church teaching, and the people will not believe every belief stated by the bishops.

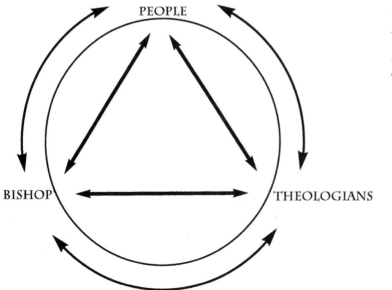

The Dynamic Triangle of Belief.

(Courtesy of Bob O'Gorman and Mary Faulkner)

A new teaching goes out to the people, usually in the form of a letter from the bishops. The people choose to accept the belief or reject it. Keep in mind that the Church acts as an advisor in matters of faith; it is ultimately up to the people to determine what is true for them and follow their conscience.

The Holy Spirit exists in every relationship; it is the glue connecting all creation. Whenever people are communicating, the Holy Spirit is present and is influencing the dynamics, bringing new insight and divine wisdom. The Holy Spirit connects the segments of the belief triangle. Whenever there is communication, the potential for divine revelation is present.

Bargains from the Border: Liberation Theology and Base Communities

Not too long ago in Latin America, a creative exchange in theology ignited and sparks went flying through society and the whole Church. The exchange produced two major additions to Catholic theology and Church structure: *liberation theology* and the birth of a new kind of church known as *base communities*.

Since the time of the Spanish conquest in the 1500s, Latin America had modeled its art, politics, literature, architecture, and theology on European traditions. Scholars from Latin America traveled to Europe for their training and returned to their own land to teach others the European ways.

S'ter Says

Liberation theology describes theologies that attempt to articulate the faith from the perspective of a group's experience of its struggle to overcome oppression. **Base communities** are groups of 10 to 20 people who gather together for Scripture reading and discussion and use these discussions to make decisions about the conditions in their community. They also hold Communion services in the absence of a priest.

The Mirror of Change

In the 1960s, the model for theology in Latin America radically changed. A crop of young seminarians studying in Europe at that time met French, Belgian, and German theologians, who changed the rules of the game. Here's our rendition of how that meeting might have happened. Imagine for a moment that you are a young man living in a small village. You have attended the mission church and school all your life—serving at Mass, tending to the chores of the missions, and studying hard in addition to working in the fields and performing the endless chores necessary to help your family. Your hard work and arduous studies have finally paid off. You have been selected to attend the university and then experience the exquisite honor of going to Europe to read the works of the Church's greatest theologians.

Your family and the entire village are proud because they have all worked to help you attain this great honor. They probably feel that they may never see you again, but they are rejoicing in the service you will be giving to God and the people and your opportunity to "make something of yourself" by escaping the poverty of the village and the limitations of village life. A hometown boy makes good!

Saints Preserve Us

Born in 1917, Oscar Romero was archbishop of San Salvador, El Salvador, and is remembered for his bold preaching on behalf of the rights of the peasants. Although he became the country's most respected and popular figure and was nominated for the Nobel Peace Prize, his decisive stand with the poor created a rift between him and the government. In 1980, a rightist death squad assassinated Archbishop Romero while he was preaching at Mass in the chapel of the cancer hospital where he lived. Many regarded his death as martyrdom. His cause has been introduced for canonization.

You have been prepared well by your teachers in Mexico City; you know what to expect, and you are looking forward to exploring not only the ancient and beautiful cities of Europe, but also the great classical texts of Augustine, Aquinas, Luther, and Calvin. As the first day finally arrives, you hurry to class along with the other young men from all over Latin America. You are yet unaware of the radically different situation that awaits you in the huge mahogany-paneled library of the university. Rather than being given the beautiful, leather-bound, gold-leafed books to read, you and your fellow students have been singled out for a different experience.

You are handed a mirror and are instructed to look into it! What is going on? The teachers want to show you the power of discovering God by looking at yourself. The teachers ask: "What do your experiences tell you of the nature of God?" You wonder, "What could this mean?" You begin your study of theology by looking at your own reality. It is difficult: To look at your life is to face poverty, enslavement, domination, and inferiority. You are not proud to bring these harsh and shameful realities to the light of reflection. You fear looking into the mirror.

In contrast to the traditional theological training, these men in the 1960s received much more. They learned how to work with the people to help them transform their lives through theology. Their new teachers insisted that the authentic study of God needed to start with "the present realities." Reluctantly, the young men began to look into the mirrors they held. They saw their own faces and the faces of their people, the faces of enslavement and poverty. The process had begun. For hundreds of years, when the peasants complained about their condition, the Church taught them that to be poor was to be more "Christ-like." They were told to accept their situation.

Epiphanies

Base communities are very popular in Latin America, Africa, and Asia. They began in Brazil in 1956 as "Sunday services without a priest" and spread like a revolutionary wildfire throughout parts of Latin America throughout the 1970s and 1980s. These groups grew during the oppressive military regime when the priests and bishops were repressed and could not be in contact with the people. The communities carried on the work of the Church. Today, Brazil has over 100,000 base communities. These communities are showing a new way of "being Church," and this vision is finding a home in North America.

Now they were being taught that their needs and the needs of their people were important, to be denied no longer. The reign of God was here and now. The seminarians were encouraged to search the Gospels for the saving message of "good news." They found it in the liberating message of the Gospel. Jesus had worked to end the oppression of the people. The word of God, for these young men and for the people they represented, became the promise of God's liberating action. Liberation theology was born.

These scholars returned to Latin America and, unlike their predecessors, did not impose classical theological teachings on the people. Instead, as their teachers had done, they began to listen to what the people were saying and search for a response in the Gospel. Over and over again, the Gospel told of good news for the poor and promised liberation. As the people realized that God had not abandoned them, the message began to heal the deep spiritual wounds caused by the Church and politics that they had lived with for many centuries.

Latin American theologians have contributed a substantial body of literature to Church teachings known as liberation theology. It set the tone for similar theologies to emerge that begin from the experience of the people: black theology, woman's theology, Asian theology, as well ecological theology, a theology that deals with the liberation of Earth itself. These theologies have begun to ask questions and make demands on the Church and the political structures to become more responsive to the needs of the people.

Church in the 'Hood

Liberation theology takes place in small, face-to-face gatherings of neighbors, where people talk about their lives and tell their stories. These gatherings are called base communities. Characteristically, the stories told are those of political or economic oppression. For example, a factory avoided paying into a health care plan and thus deprived the workers of benefits when they needed them. Other examples are low wages that make feeding a family almost impossible, or the lack of clean drinking water in the community. These everyday issues become the common story of the group.

The group then examines the Scripture for God's identification with their plight. They find new meaning in what they read and may be inspired to organize and take action.

This is a new sense of Church: A Church that is small and face-to-face and a Church that expresses salvation not in the future sense of heaven, but in the here and now of everyday life. This grassroots Church challenges the long patriarchal tradition of Catholicism.

Power, Power, Who's Got the Power?

There is major controversy regarding what gets taught as official Church doctrine and what does not. This controversy goes all the way back to the beginning of Church history, and issues of authority continue to be worked out in Church politics today. Dogma is decided in Church councils through a voting process. Theology informs the voters on the issues, but there are no guarantees on how it will go. On the other hand, bishops can silence theologians whose work they find to be too controversial or against church beliefs.

The Vatican maintains a watchdog office called the Congregation for the Doctrine of the Faith that constantly surveys the theologians and teachers and their published work. This office is the genetic remnant of the Inquisition, which we'll discuss later in Chapter 21. Checks and balances are healthy, but if it's only a check and there's no balance, many Catholics feel the pinch of Church politics.

As is true in any political arena, viewpoints in the Church tend to be polarized between liberals and conservatives. Control over what becomes Church teaching follows these lines as well. The decisions about the meaning of faith are not always worked out in the Church's offices and schools, however. The bottom line rests with the people. When all is said and done, a dogma or teaching of the Church is not a belief of the people unless they believe it.

In this chapter, you have seen how the Catholic Church exercises its role as teacher and how this role has developed and changed over the years. The next chapter examines the teachings themselves.

> **Epiphanies**
>
> A present-day example of a theologian being silenced is the case of Matthew Fox. In 1987, Fox, a Dominican priest, headed up a popular program in spirituality and ecology called The Institute for Creation-Centered Spirituality. He had an unorthodox curriculum and faculty, and his writings were on the cutting edge of ecological spirituality. Fox was reprimanded by Rome and given the option of closing his program or being silenced for six months. He chose to be silenced rather than compromise the effectiveness of his program and his staff.

The Least You Need to Know

- Catholics draw their beliefs from both the Bible and tradition.
- The Nicene Creed contains the basic beliefs of Catholics.
- Beliefs are developed through a dynamic process among the people, theologians, and bishops.
- The Catechism summarizes the Church's beliefs.
- The final decision about beliefs rests in the beliefs of the people.

Chapter

The Teachings of the Church: More Than Just the Party Line

In This Chapter

- ◆ Learn all about sin and forgiveness
- ◆ Find out about heaven and hell and who goes where
- ◆ Discover the relationship between sexuality and Catholicism
- ◆ Appreciate the "seamless garment of life"

It's been said that sinning is easier to do in Catholicism than any other religion because Catholics have so many beliefs, rules, and regulations. The Catholic Church focused its teaching and preaching on sin by listing every requirement or belief, and backing that up with the consequences each belief carried. "You better or else …" is often the first thing people think of when they hear the word *Catholic*, and this preoccupation with sin has been very self-destructive to the Church.

As a result, sex and sin became synonymous, and for some this connection is still true today. However, the good news is that for the most part, sin is no longer the major subject of the Church's teachings, and much has been done to repair the fractured relationship between sexuality and spirituality. In this chapter, we'll look at definitions of sin and free will, afterlife, human sexuality, and important Catholic social teachings that guide the faithful in their interactions in the world.

Sin After Vatican II

Post-Vatican II Church morality focuses on helping its members foster biblical virtues by promoting loving, peaceful relationships and working together to bring the reign of God forward for more people to enjoy.

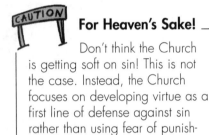

For Heaven's Sake!

Don't think the Church is getting soft on sin! This is not the case. Instead, the Church focuses on developing virtue as a first line of defense against sin rather than using fear of punishment as a deterrent.

Moving away from the emphasis on sin and punishment follows a general pattern of rethinking beliefs and redefining sin. New attitudes emphasize people's basic goodness and build on it. Yet remnants of the old thinking still remain. Certainly not everyone in the Church is living out the new definitions of spirituality and what it means to be a Catholic, but the direction has been established, and the trend is positive.

Sin: Missing the Mark

Sin is a religious term. In the Old Testament, sin is understood as a break in the covenant relationship with God. It's the result of not following the will of God as we know it in our hearts. Although sin is often thought of as a violation against God, it is actually a violation against ourselves, our neighbors, and all creation. Most often, when the term *sin* appears in the New Testament, it is used in the phrase, "forgiveness of sin."

In the past, Catholics saw sin primarily as disobedience to God and to "lawful superiors." Obedience became inextricably bound up with the Catholic identity; obedience was a Catholic's dominant *moral* characteristic, reinforcing loyalty to the tribe. The understanding of sin today is focused on the law of love and informed by the human sciences. Moral reflection is no longer centered on personal shortcomings but rather on the unconditional love of God. This change shifts moral reasoning from a reactive stance to a proactive one.

The new theology of sin teaches that sin enslaves, with the understanding that we are most God-like in our freedom. The new theology is based on the belief that God wants us to live creatively and be free to grow to our full potential. Sin, then, is whatever blocks our freedom to develop fully. Present teaching encourages Catholics to look at a wider context of social justice, because injustice limits the human spirit. If anyone is not free, no one is free. Catholics are encouraged to work for their own liberation and that of all others. Sin is that which violates human dignity and blocks freedom for others or ourselves.

Categories of Sins: Specks and Logs

Traditionally, there were two different kinds of sin in the Catholic Church: mortal and venial. Mortal sins are more serious than venial sins. An analogy might be that a mortal sin corresponds to a felony, and a venial sin is like a misdemeanor. The biblical references to the difference in the magnitude of sin come from two passages. Matthew 23:24 describes the difference between a gnat and a camel; Matthew 7:3 discusses the difference between a speck and a log.

Nowhere in the New Testament is there a list of mortal sins, nor is the punishment for them described. However, the Church has decided that certain extreme behavior should be classified as mortal or deadly sin. Mortal refers to the death a sin brings to the soul. Mortal sin constitutes a serious rupture in a person's relationship to God and to the community. In order to restore this relationship, those who have committed a mortal sin go to confession and work with their confessor to heal the damages caused by their actions. Three things are necessary for a sin to be classified as mortal:

- It is a serious offense.

- The person must have full knowledge of the seriousness of it.

- It is committed with full consent of the will and with no coercion.

For Heaven's Sake!

Guilt is a fire alarm. It tells you all is not right in your life. Find out what your part is in the problem. Forgiveness requires taking moral responsibility for your actions, and making the adjustments necessary to live in accord with what you know is right. When the fire is out, turn off the alarm!

Venial sins are described as lesser offenses. They do not cause a rupture in the relationship with God like mortal sins do. They are the everyday transgressions we are all subject to. However, any sin, like an illness in its early stages, can lead to more serious consequences if left unchecked. Paying attention to venial sins helps people locate troublesome patterns within themselves.

Newer approaches to understanding sin should not lead to laxity, but instead to a deeper sensitivity to the human condition and the development of compassion. When the definition of sin is broadened to include all the ways in which we might be refusing God by limiting our engagement with life, it is not easy to draw up a list of sins as was once the practice. Although the commandments and the laws of the Church are still part of the process of moral discernment (the process of identifying right and wrong), they in no way represent the whole picture. There's more on this topic in Chapter 11, in the discussion of the sacrament of Reconciliation.

Original Sin: One Day in Paradise

The concept of original sin helps to explain how evil can exist in a world created by a good God. Although there's no specific biblical mention of original sin in either the Old or New Testaments, it has always been a central Church teaching.

The name "original sin" did not enter into Church teachings until the time of Augustine. He identified original sin as a basic yearning for self-gratification that turns people away from God. His views on original sin became part of the official Church teachings in 418. During the Middle Ages, the interpretation shifted away from an emphasis on humans' corrupt nature to the break in the relationship with God that Adam caused by committing the first sin. Thomas Aquinas described original sin as a "weakened, disordered precondition." There has been little change in the theory of original sin up until present time.

In this pre-Vatican II teaching, it was understood that guilt also existed in all human beings. It existed prior to any wrongdoing on the part of the individual. Guilt was a condition of the soul that we inherited from our ancestors much as we inherit other physiological characteristics.

The doctrine of original sin is still a central dogma of the Catholic Church, and contemporary theologians struggle to keep its meaning relevant in the light of science and psychology. The underlying belief is that Christ's redemption, which is characterized by love and forgiveness, is at the very heart and soul of the divine plan. All humans are in need of the redemption he offers. The biblical story of Adam, Eve, the snake, and the tree is not a literal description of a historical first sin, but it is a description of what it means to be human. It is not necessarily telling what happened at the beginning of human history, but rather is reminding us of what is happening all the time in the human struggle.

When viewed this way, the story of the fall tells us of the inevitable mix of good and evil contained in human existence. Our highest motives at best are mixed and ambiguous. Human frailty leaves us vulnerable to lapses in good judgment, and we can be fooled by circumstances. The ultimate human dilemma is to exist in the midst of a sinful world, yet strive for goodness. Part of the struggle is to overcome a lower nature that sometimes wants to pull us off course.

The modern interpretation of original sin recognizes basic human qualities and world conditions. Most important, it recognizes God's participation with us in our struggles. To be human is to be in need of God's grace. In other words, we need the gift of God's help to navigate our earthly existence. The doctrine of original sin can be said to illustrate the adage, "Where sin exists there also does grace abound." See Chapter 25 for additional discussion on this.

The Seven Deadly Sins

The Church has determined that there are certain human impulses that are the root of our problems. They're called *capital sins*. The seven capital sins were immortalized in Chaucer's "The Parson's Tale" in *The Canterbury Tales* and in Dante's description of the terraces of purgatory in the *Divine Comedy*.

The seven capital sins are (1) Pride, (2) Envy, (3) Anger, (4) Sloth, (5) Greed, (6) Gluttony, (7) Lust.

These seven sins are said to be the wellspring from which all sins flow. The term *capital* comes from the Latin word *caput*, meaning head, and refers to capital sins being the source or headwaters for sins. These sins have also been called the "seven deadly sins." Although they are called sins, these seven characteristics are not sins in and of themselves. Instead, they describe tendencies toward sinning or character weaknesses through which sin occurs.

Good Guilt and Bad Shame

We conclude our discussion of sin with a look at good old-fashioned guilt and perhaps answer the question of whether Catholics have more than their fair share of it. Guilt is a subject for consideration both in the Church and in the world of psychology. Guilt, within the context of religion, is an intuitive understanding of wrongdoing. It seems to be an inborn feeling that helps to guide us in our choice of what to do and what not to do. As such, it is a healthy and helpful quality.

Guilt needs to be distinguished from shame. Guilt is innate; shame is developed. Guilt corresponds to a genuine violation of a value. Shame is the result of childhood conditioning. If a child has been punished about his or her normal developmental processes (like bed-wetting or thumb-sucking, for example), he or she may experience an inappropriate deep feeling of guilt that is better described as shame. In a perverse way, when a child has been badly mistreated, through sexual or other severe abuse, and the offending party does not take responsibility, the child is left with shame. The child believes he or she brought on the behavior, and cannot experience forgiveness.

Your Guardian Angel

Check your terms. Guilt is feeling bad about something you've done. Shame is feeling bad about yourself. There is a big difference!

When abuse occurs, a person is left with a broken relationship with God. Parents are our first understanding of what God is like. If parents fail to love and instead bring injury, the child's soul (psyche) experiences a loss of its natural connection to God, resulting in severely damaged self-esteem, which progresses to despair and self-hate. Despair is a spiritual condition in which you believe you are beyond help. Shame is a problem at the spiritual and psychological level and is best addressed by both a minister and a psychologist.

Free Will, Judgment, and Afterlife

Free will describes the human ability to choose a course of action. Both common sense and Church teaching agree that moral responsibility depends upon free will. The nature and degree of free will are the subjects of much theological and philosophical debate. Studies of human personality and development have shown that a person's free will is subject to his or her conditioning.

Catholic moral teaching functions much like civil law regarding free will. It teaches that free will can be greatly impeded by a variety of factors, such as fear, coercion, ignorance, emotional disturbance, passion, and the use of drugs, for example. In this regard, free will exists as an ideal. The human condition imposes limits to this ideal.

The Church teaches that consequences of our free will accompany us beyond death, that there is a direct relationship between moral action on earth and existence beyond death. It also assures us that God's judgment never exists separately from his mercy, meaning that God has the whole picture and knows both our heart and our struggles.

Evil: Bad to the Bone

As a direct result of the contemporary theology we discussed in the last chapter, the moral camera has turned to look at "corporate sin," also called structural sin. When corporate sin exists, it infects the structures of society. Catholic teaching on sin traditionally looked at the people's sins, not the institutionalized sin that existed in the Church as well as other social institutions. Corporate sin grows out of inequities in power that allow any one segment of the culture to perceive they have God-given rights over others. This inequity then is infused into all systems and structures, such as the right to education, fair wages, safe neighborhoods, adequate housing, health care, art, music, fresh air, and so on. How these social challenges get worked out depends on different cultural values. When the deep cultural value is that one group of people have more rights than another, corporate sin wins.

Horrendous examples of such evil are the massacre of the indigenous people of this country, the institution of slavery, and the Holocaust. In such cases, humans create a culture of evil, and free choice is severely restricted. The potential to do God's will is so greatly reduced that evil prevails temporarily. It is temporary because the Church teaches that good is stronger than evil. Evil exists only in a temporal way, meaning that it is limited. Good has an eternal quality.

The Devil Made Me Do It ... or Did He?

The Devil is often represented as a symbol of evil. Church teaching about devils maintains that they are spiritual creatures subject to God. Christ's death and resurrection overcame the power of evil in the world, and we can overcome evil by choosing Christ (living by Christian principles). The important theological point is that humans have free will, and you can't get by with saying, "The Devil made me do it."

Demonic Possession and Exorcism: Get the Hell Out of Here!"

Demonic possession has always captured the public imagination. Certainly William Blatty's book *The Exorcist* (HarperCollins, 2000) and the subsequent film fed this fascination with the bizarre. Many Church teachers do not believe in demonic possession, but most acknowledge that evil has a depth beyond human control. Exactly how this plays out, no one really knows for sure. The belief in demonic possession defines it as occurring when the psychic power of a demon takes over the personality of a human so that the human no longer has free will.

Possession manifests itself in strange ways, including hysterical behavior, incoherent speech, and uncontrolled physical movements, being self-destructive as well as destructive to others. Demonic possession is briefly mentioned in the Old Testament, and the New Testament tells of Jesus ministering to many who are possessed by demons. In the Gospel of Mark, Jesus exorcises a group of demons. He asks their names and casts them into the sea. (Mark 5:1–20)

Exorcism is a rite performed by the Church to expel evil from a person or a place. It involves prayers and specific actions. The Church proceeds carefully in cases of possession, requiring the person to undergo both physical and psychological examinations. When it does perform an exorcism, it chooses a priest who is known for his holiness and strength of character and who has received special training. The rite of exorcism is found in the Catholic book of rituals, called the *Roman Ritual*.

Death: The Last Good-Bye?

Catholic teaching on death is based in the resurrection and says that death is not the final state. Teachings from Vatican II state that God has created humans "for a blissful purpose beyond the reach of earthly misery."

The Greeks thought of the human soul as immortal. At death, the soul shed its body and was thus "freed" from the "prison of the flesh." Early Jewish belief portrayed death as a passage of the person from the land of the living to the dark and cheerless realm of the dead where there can be no happiness and no praise of God, known as *sheol* in Hebrew. (Psalms 6:5; Isaiah 38:18) Christianity follows a later Jewish tradition that death is not the last word, but an invitation to a more perfect union with God.

Your Guardian Angel

Fear not! One of the promises of living the good life is everlasting life in Christ. Although no one knows exactly how that works, we can trust that it is a good thing! In Catholicism, death is not the end, but a passage to perpetual life.

A contemporary Catholic teacher, the late Cardinal Joseph L. Bernardin of Chicago, provided his insight on death. He was featured on the cover of *Newsweek* with the headline, "He taught us how to die." In the article, Bernardin told how his struggle with cancer moved him from a fear of death to seeing death as a friend.

Hell: The Eternal Loss of God

Catholic teaching states that God's purpose in creation is for humans to form a personal relationship of love with him. Furthermore, the Church teaches that this relationship reaches its perfection in eternal life with God. Our free will allows us to cooperate or not to cooperate with God and to accept or refuse to enter into the loving relationship we are offered—thus the human struggle is described.

"Eternal damnation" is not attributed to an act of God, because in his merciful love, he can only desire our complete life with him. Hell is the pain produced by our choice of utterly and deliberately refusing to live in relationship with God, *if such a choice is even possible.* Hell is only a possibility because we take seriously the quality of free will God has created in us. It puts the punch into free will.

Speaking on the subject of hell, Pope John Paul II said not to consider it a place, but rather a state that the soul suffers when it denies itself access to God. To describe this reality, Scripture uses symbolic language. According to the pope, images of hell that appear in sacred Scripture are used as an analogy to show the complete desperation and emptiness of life without God: They are a poetic warning. The pope's remarks are directed at correcting the improper use of biblical images of hell that create anxiety and despair. Again, rather than a place, hell is a condition of the soul separated from God.

The pope went on to say that God has never revealed "whether or which human beings" are eternally damned. As stated earlier, damnation is the result of a serious sin and requires that the person absolutely knows what he or she is doing. The Church does not say this has ever happened to anyone. A good illustration occurs in the New Testament when Jesus does not condemn those who have participated in his crucifixion. Rather he says, "Father, forgive them, for they do not know not what they are doing." (Luke 23:34)

Epiphanies

The Bible often teaches with parables, stories, and metaphors, so the biblical images of everlasting fire are poetic warnings of what it would be like to be without God. Biblical images of hell abound: Matthew calls it a fiery furnace where people will "weep and gnash their teeth." (Matthew 13:42, 25, 30, 41) Mark says it is like Gehenna with its unquenchable fire. Mark (9:43) and Luke (16:19–13) tell the story of the rich man that explains hell as a place of eternal suffering with no alleviation of pain. Finally, the Book of Revelation (20:13) speaks of the "pool of fire."

The popular images of hell that have dominated Catholic thinking, although rooted in the Bible, were amplified and popularized in literature and art. Over the years, the poetic level of these images was lost, meaning that people forgot that the Bible tells stories to teach lessons. The analogous images of hell began to be interpreted as a real place. The pope has taken a bold step toward modifying the destructive fire and brimstone images of hell that have often limited our understanding of our relationship to God.

Heaven: "Where the Elite All Meet!"

Heaven is the word used to define the final fulfillment for which we were created. It describes the ideal relationship between creation and God. Heaven is revealed in Jesus' resurrection, which shows us God's plan for the future of the whole creation.

The Old Testament uses the term *heaven* in a variety of ways. It describes a vault in the sky as the dwelling place of God. Later, the physical heavens were seen to be symbols of divine triumph. Heaven is associated with both the first creation as described in Genesis and the future action of God, who would create a new heaven and a new earth in which the hopes of Israel would be brought to fulfillment.

Heaven (and hell) are Christian concepts; the New Testament explicitly associates heaven with Jesus Christ. The word of God comes from heaven to take flesh in Jesus. (John 3:13) After the resurrection, Jesus ascends to heaven to sit at the right hand of God. (Matthew 26:64; Mark 14:62; Luke 22:69; Acts 7:55) From heaven, Jesus reigns as Lord and Messiah, and from there he will appear again as the judge at the end of time.

Through revelation, Pope John Paul II says, we are taught that "heaven or happiness" is "neither an abstraction nor a physical place in the clouds, but a living personal relationship with the Holy Trinity." In attempting to describe ultimate realities, language always falls short, he reminds us. In so doing, he has shifted to the language of relationship from the abstractions of traditional theology. In the new interpretation, heaven is not a place of ideal real estate, but a description of the soul when it is in its completed form.

Human Sexuality: "Male and Female He Created Them"

Human sexuality refers to the state of being sexual, being in the world either as a female or a male. It includes anatomy, behavioral characteristics, bonding, and reproduction. Sexuality is a fundamental aspect of personal identity. Our sexuality enters into all aspects of our life and all personal interactions with one another and all aspects of self-expression and activity. There are no asexual or nonsexual human beings.

Your Guardian Angel

Think of your sexuality as part of your spirituality. God created human beings as male and female. Sexuality, then, is a gift of God. Sexuality and spirituality cannot be separated. Both are calls to intimacy, and therefore two sides of the same coin.

The role of the Church regarding sexuality is to help the faithful understand their sexuality and act in sexually responsible ways. This is an ongoing process of assessment and discernment that Church teachers have addressed from the earliest times. Increasingly in recent times, lay people have added their voices to these teachings.

Vatican II called for the renewal of Church teaching in light of new knowledge from the physical and social sciences. In this section, we'll look at some of the issues in human sexuality that Catholics are struggling with today: birth control, homosexuality, and celibacy.

Birth Control: The Church's Big Headache

Contraception refers to the ways in which men and women can prevent formation of a new life as a result of sexual intercourse. The Church's moral stand on contraception is based on important values regarding sexuality. One value is propagation, or having children. Until the twentieth century, the Church taught that having children took precedence over all other sexual values. All attempts to block sexual action from the intention to procreate were considered wrong, considered to be against *natural law*.

Vatican II introduced important changes on sexuality, and the mutual self-giving that is possible through sexual intercourse became a key value. Teachings began to recognize that sexual intercourse strengthens the unity between couples, and also recognized that married couples had both the right and duty to limit the size of their family to correspond to their situation.

Following Vatican II, Pope Paul VI gave a strict interpretation of these teachings in an encyclical called *Humanae Vitae* (Latin for "of human life"), declaring, "Each and every marriage act must remain open to the transmission of life." *Humanae Vitae* set the Church spinning. Questions from bishops, theologians, pastors, and congregations abounded—many still have not been answered.

Sociological data reveal that approximately 80 percent of practicing Catholics do not follow the Church's official and authoritative teachings on birth control. However, abstinence in rhythm with a woman's fertile cycle is the only acceptable form of birth control. The rhythm method, as practiced in the past, was often called "Vatican roulette" as an indication of how well it worked.

For hundreds of years, Christian churches of all denominations prohibited the use of any type of birth control, citing the concept of *natural law*. Natural law maintains that it is immoral to frustrate the natural processes of the body, including sexuality. At the beginning of the twentieth century, most Protestant denominations broke away from this philosophy, leading many Catholics to believe that the Catholic Church's teaching would change, as well. Pope John XXIII created a Birth Control Commission in the 1960s, which issued a report in favor of "artificial" methods of contraception. The Commission's report had a serious impact on the Church, as it suggested that God created sexual intercourse with two purposes in mind. The commission defined sexual intercourse as a unifying act in which a husband and wife are brought closer together and bonded in a spiritual way, and also a procreative act, in which the married couple and God are co-creators in bringing forth new human life.

Pope Paul VI responded to the Commission's report in 1968 by issuing the controversial encyclical *Humanae Vitae*. Although the encyclical agrees with the Commission's characterization of married sexual intercourse as both unifying and procreative, it maintains that such an act can never be divorced from its biological implications, namely procreation. The encyclical's message was that the Church would maintain its prohibition on "artificial" methods of contraception, despite the Birth Control

Commission's recommendation. Many Catholics felt disappointed and frustrated by the encyclical. Others commended Paul VI's commitment to traditional Church teachings, and appreciated the theology of openness to life he employed to write it.

The issue of contraception continues to divide the Catholic Church. Sociological data reveal that a very small percentage of practicing Catholics follow the Church's teaching on contraception. Many Catholics choose to employ "artificial" contraception, and report that their parish priests support them in the decisions they make in this matter, despite the Church's teaching.

Natural Family Planning: It's Not Your Grandma's Calendar

Many today, however, use Natural Family Planning (NPF), the Church-sanctioned form of birth control. This method is also known as the "sympto-thermal method." The woman observes and charts her temperature upon awakening, along with the consistency of cervical mucus and changes in the position and texture of the cervix. The charts allow couples to know when the woman is fertile and thus when to abstain. The time of abstinence can be seven or eight days. This process is much more involved and accurate than the old rhythm method but is estimated to be 97% accurate before ovulation, the fertile portion of a woman's cycle, and 99% accurate after ovulation.

An added benefit to couples who use NFP is having fewer chemicals and preservatives in their bodies, such as result from the birth control pill. Those who have side effects or can't take the pill along with other medications also use it. Data also indicate that couples who use NFP have a divorce rate of only 5 percent—far below the national average. A couple was quoted as saying, "You have to communicate when you do this, and that seems to be one of the biggest stumbling blocks for couples. This requires you to talk about something very personal, which seems to make it easier to talk about other things."

Homosexuality: Yes and No

For the most part, the Church has taken the position of "love the sinner, hate the sin" toward homosexuality. According to Church beliefs, to be a homosexual is not in itself sinful, but to practice homosexuality is considered immoral. The Church bases its belief in Scripture (Genesis 19 and 20:13, Romans 1:24–27, 1 Corinthians 6:9–10, and 1 Timothy 1:9–10) and moral tradition based on natural law reasoning. Natural law reasoning is a process the Church uses to examine human acts according to the "nature of things."

Some teachers in the Church have attempted to propose a Catholic approach to homosexuality. This approach would remain faithful to the traditional teaching about the two goals of sexuality (procreation and love) and at the same time be a genuine response to the nature of homosexuality. These people argue that because a change of orientation is out of the question (it is generally accepted that a person does not deliberately choose their sexual orientation), homosexuals should be given the same moral choices as heterosexuals: celibacy or permanent exclusive partnership. The Church, however, has not altered its position at this time. Although it mandates understanding and compassion toward homosexuals, it holds a firm line against them acting on their sexual inclinations.

Celibacy: Giving It Up for God

Celibacy is sexual abstinence. Sexual abstinence is defined as refraining from sexual intercourse or any other use of the sexual faculties. Celibacy describes a temporary choice married people make for spiritual purposes, the state of unmarried persons, or the permanent choice made by those taking religious vows (priests, nuns, and monks).

Celibacy of the clergy in the Western Church grew more out of custom than law. It began in the 300s, continued to be shaped through time, and was reaffirmed in the 1500s at the Council of Trent when the lives of virginity and celibacy were declared superior to the married state. It is recognized that rules regarding celibacy are Church laws, not divine laws. They can be changed if the Church ever decides to change them.

The rules for celibacy have been questioned in the light of Vatican II. Arguments in favor of celibacy center on its pastoral effectiveness and its relevance for spiritual development. Arguments against celibacy generally focus on mandatory celibacy include the following:

> **Epiphanies**
>
> St. Paul, writing in the early years of the Church, urged his congregations to consider celibacy. Scholars now tell us the reason for Paul's teaching was the Church's belief at that time that the end of the world was coming soon. Therefore, it was not the time to bring new life into the world. Additionally, for Paul, celibacy provided him unrestricted opportunity to be of service to the Church.

- Celibacy is based on Church tradition, not divine law, and Church laws are subject to change.

- Greater understanding of human psychology has led to questions regarding the impact of celibacy on the human development of the clergy.

- Many non-European cultures view celibacy negatively.

Several situations assure a continued debate regarding celibacy. One is the declining number of priests in active ministry. Another is the exemption from celibacy for married clergy who enter the Church after having been ordained in other churches. A third is that in various parts of the world, especially in Africa and Latin America, celibacy is not observed. In Chapter 25, we look at arguments about the role celibacy potentially plays or doesn't play in clerical sex abuse.

The Seamless Garment

S'ter Says

The **seamless garment of life** refers to Jesus' robe, which legend has it was seamless. In applying this ethic, one recognizes that protection of life is the basis for determining the morality of war, capital punishment, and abortion. In other words, under this ethic, it would be difficult to be in favor of capital punishment and against abortion.

Cardinal Joseph L. Bernardin of Chicago called for the use of a consistent ethic of human life. This ethic would be applied to the issues of abortion, capital punishment, modern warfare, euthanasia, and socioeconomic issues of food and shelter for all. His teaching recognizes the relationship between these social issues and the obligation to respect human life and dignity in all arenas. According to this principle, abortion and euthanasia (pro-life issues) and social ethics (human rights, peace, social justice, and capital punishment) must all be viewed in the same light. In other words, Cardinal Bernardin's teachings ask for moral consistency in what he has called the *seamless garment of life*. Let's take a look at each of these issues.

Euthanasia: Say No to Dr. Death

Euthanasia comes from the Greek and means "good death." Today, we use it to refer to intentionally ending the life of a terminally ill person. Other terms used to describe euthanasia are mercy killing, assisted dying, and recently, aid in dying. The 1980 Vatican *Declaration on Euthanasia* defines it as "an action or omission which of itself or by intention causes death, in order that all suffering may in this way be eliminated."

The issue of euthanasia boils down to the difference between taking an action to bring about death versus allowing a person to die naturally. *Killing* is a human act carrying moral responsibility for causing death. *Allowing to die* refers to withholding or withdrawing treatment so that the illness can run its course, the outcome of which may be death.

The Church teaches that one is not morally obliged to use "extraordinary means" to stay alive, for example, to have surgery, or chemotherapy, or radiation, or be force-fed, or live on a ventilator, or seek a transplant. All of these can be seen as "extraordinary." One is only bound to the ordinary: shelter, comfort, and food and water if eating and drinking are possible. The capacity of modern technology to ward off death brings more pressure to individuals, families, and caregivers; this and their inability to accept the inevitability of death are factors that contribute to the choosing of extraordinary and often futile treatment.

The Catholic Church recognizes life as a precious gift, humans as mortal, and God as supreme. Euthanasia violates the sanctity of life and the sovereignty of God by assuming ownership over life. The Church views the legalization of euthanasia as a threat to the common good; its teaching affirms the role of health-care providers as stewards of healing and caring. It upholds the hospice movement as a model for health care. Hospice sends health-care professionals into the homes of terminally ill people with the objective of making the people as comfortable as possible while they die a natural death without prolonging or hastening the process.

Can War Be Justified?

The Just War Doctrine claims that, despite its destructive character, war is morally justifiable in certain circumstances and limitations. The doctrine has its roots in the Hebrew Scriptures and the Greek and Roman world. Augustine formulated it in the 400s when he stated that war is love's response to a neighbor threatened by force. Thomas Aquinas in the 1200s claimed the legitimacy of war waged in self-defense. These teachings came before the rise of modern warfare.

The Just War Doctrine has two purposes: First, it is a reminder that war is always a moral matter, not simply a political one. It requires serious consideration. Second, although the doctrine can judge certain circumstances for war as just, violence must be limited. The doctrine recognizes that regardless of its justification, war is a serious matter and must be mourned.

The eight criteria used to determine a just war are the following:

- ◆ It must be a just cause. Traditionally, to be a just cause, a war must have as its goal the protection of people from unjust attack, the restoration of rights that have been taken away, or the restoration of just political order.

- ◆ It must be led by a competent authority, which means that declarations of war must be made by competent authorities following established criteria, or due process. This principle has recently come under scrutiny.

- ◆ It must be a last resort after all possible peaceful solutions have been explored.

- ◆ It must involve comparative justice to remind both sides that neither is absolutely just.

◆ Its ends must be proportionate to its means: Even a just war for a just cause cannot be pursued if the evils to be suffered significantly outweigh the good.

◆ It must have a right intention, which means it cannot be motivated by vindictiveness or hatred, but must be for the purpose of establishing a better and more peaceful existence.

◆ There must be a probability of success; if there is no possibility of winning and many people will be killed in the process, then it cannot be a just war.

The Just War Doctrine includes an additional principle of right conduct within war. Justice must rule conduct within war. Attacks against civilians are forbidden, and there must be ethical treatment of the wounded or surrendered.

The Just War Doctrine has been an important part of Catholic moral teaching. However, because of the development of nuclear weapons of mass destruction, theologians are now questioning whether war can ever be justified. In 1983, a pastoral letter by U.S. bishops, *The Challenge of Peace: God's Promise and Our Response*, reaffirmed the Just War Doctrine, but with the additional comments that in no cases could nuclear war, even limited nuclear war, be justified.

For Heaven's Sake!

Church teaching about war has said that because of the enormity of the destruction, nuclear war is not to be used under any circumstances.

The matter of establishing competent authority has also come under scrutiny. Many are unwilling to give the state the authority to determine whether justice is being served by war. Church teachers realize that governments are prone to interpret the situations in their favor, using the Doctrine of Just War to justify war. It falls to the Church community as a dedicated and informed body to be a voice for peace against the strong cultural presumption of violence as a solution.

Abortion: A Tough Choice

Few issues are more emotionally and morally charged than *abortion*. In this discussion, we're defining abortion as the intentionally induced termination of a pregnancy. Abortion is legal in some form in most countries in the world. The United States has the most unrestricted laws regarding abortions, having made abortion on demand both legal and available to any woman who can afford to pay for it.

The controversy surrounding abortion centers on identifying the time at which a new life is said to become human. At this time, scientists disagree regarding this very important point. The Church had found it to be the most reasonable and prudent

NOT TRUE   HAD?

position to accept conception, the moment when the sperm fertilizes the egg, as the beginning of human life. The Catholic Church opposes unrestricted abortion for the following three reasons:

- The Church sees God as the author of life and views the conception of a child as a gift to be welcomed into the community. The Catholic response to pregnancy is to care for both the mother and child.

FALSE

- There is no clear scientific agreement to determine when life begins. The Church has taken the stand that it begins at the moment of conception.

- Because life is sacred and because there is no reason to believe it does not begin at conception, the fundamental value of life must be awarded the soul in the womb.

The Church believes no one possesses the right to take the life of the fetus. Although the right to choose is an important concept within the Church, it exists only before conception. Cases of pregnancy due to rape or to coercion or ignorance pose difficult problems for Church teaching; these issues have not been fully addressed. Objections posed by theologians and others look at the absolutist nature of the abortion rule, pointing out that it does not meet a requirement of Catholic theology—that of critical nuance. Nuance means that circumstances count when weighing moral decisions.

The Church recognizes the difficulty of many women who are faced with the painful decision of whether or not to terminate a pregnancy. A seamless garment of life teaching about abortion would require that the social, cultural, and economic issues affecting the unequal status of women come into focus in the analysis. However, the official teaching remains that the only time abortion is permitted is when it is necessary to preserve the mother's life, which is covered under the concept of the lesser of two evils.

FALSE — DIRECT ABORTION — NEVER!

Capital Punishment: A Call to Reconciliation

Catholic teachings hold to the sacredness of human life and teach that it must be respected from conception to death. Although Catholic teaching allows life to be taken through the Just War Doctrine and in cases of self-defense, Church leaders have increasingly brought the wisdom of capital punishment into question. The growing sense of the image of God present in all people presents a distinct spiritual obstacle to taking a life, even where serious injustice has occurred. Arguments against capital punishment are based in the following religious principles:

- Jesus' command to love your enemies and to be reconciled to them calls on society to find spiritual solutions.

- The Gospels provide bountiful evidence of God's absolute love for every person. Jesus did not avoid sinners in his ministry, but focused on the abundant mercy and gracious forgiveness of God.

- There is a foundational Catholic belief in the potential for moral conversion present in all people, even the worst sinners.

For these reasons, many Christian churches have denounced capital punishment as incompatible with Christianity. Although the Catholic Church has been reluctant to condemn it in principle, most of the recent popes and bishops have spoken out against its use. The pope recently made a strong social statement against capital punishment in St. Louis, where he personally met with the governor and requested that the sentence of a man condemned to die be commuted. His request was honored.

For Heaven's Sake!

Be consistent! Catholic teaching has come to identify a "consistent ethic of life" that questions taking life in any circumstances, including abortion, just war, euthanasia, and capital punishment.

We've taken a look at the major teachings of the Church and gained an understanding of the process of how Church teaching evolves. In the next chapter, you'll learn more about the inside workings of the Catholic Church and about some of the career officers of the religious orders and the Church hierarchy.

The Least You Need to Know

- Catholic moral teaching has shifted toward developing virtues and promoting loving response and away from what you are doing wrong.

- Current teaching about heaven and hell says that they are states of the soul brought by a personal relationship with or by separation from God, not physical places.

- Catholics are reconstructing their understanding of human sexuality and healing from some misunderstandings of the past.

- Catholics are urged to follow a consistent ethic of respect for all life in their teachings on abortion, euthanasia, capital punishment, social justice, and just war theories.

The Church: Moving from Steeple to People

In This Chapter

- How does the Church structure work?
- What is a vocation? How would I know if I had one?
- Religious orders: Who does the work of the Church?
- Can regular folks have vocations, too?

The Catholic Church is in the midst of change. It's moving from the hierarchical structure developed at the time of Constantine into a more communal model with shared power, one more representative of the Church in its earliest years. Blueprints were drawn at Vatican II, and the changes have begun to take place. The Church is moving from a centralized power base with authority at the top to a concept of hierarchical communion.

The Catholic Church is governed by the College of Bishops with the bishop of Rome, the pope, at its head. It's one of the few Churches that maintains a centralized authority, which means that almost every major decision has to be cleared through Rome. As mentioned earlier, the pope exercises full authority over the Church's teachings through the doctrine of papal infallibility. However, the new Vatican II blueprint calls for collegiality, meaning that the pope teaches infallibly only when he consults with the College of Bishops. Each bishop has the authority to teach in his own diocese. Rome restricts that power in only a few cases. The appointment of bishops is the big one.

Blueprints for Change

The Church is not one big corporation with joined assets. The Holy See administers its own funds, including money contributed by individuals around the world. These funds support 25 major administrative offices that employ more than 4,000 people. Collectively, these offices are known as the *Roman Curia*. The Holy See does not administer any other property, other than in exceptional cases. Each diocese, which contains individual parishes, functions with a high degree of financial autonomy.

S'ter Says

The **Roman Curia** is the bureaucracy that assists the pope in administering his duty of pastoring the Catholic Church. It was formally organized in 1588. It was last reorganized in 1988 by John Paul II.

In the Catholic Church, the parishes are grouped under the guidance of a bishop. Each diocese is a complete unit. It makes local decisions but the decisions must be in conjunction with Rome.

The Church of Rome is like any other diocese, although its bishop, the pope, presides over the other dioceses. This structure is somewhat similar to the United States, with Washington, D.C., presiding over the other states. Washington, like Rome, is the seat of government; each state has a governing structure and independence.

The hierarchical communion model of the Catholic Church is a union of churches expressed as "one." This expression of "oneness" happens through each diocese's connection to the diocese of Rome. There is a tension or balance constantly being struck between the federal government and state government, and in the Church there is the same tension between diocesan control and the control of Rome. Depending on which party is in power, it can go either way.

We have shown this post-Vatican II structure with the diagram in Chapter 6 labeled Hierarchical Communion, which better describes the emerging notion of Church. The old hierarchical pyramid of power is shown as well.

The Roman Curia

Continuing our parallel between the Church and the United States government, the Roman Curia would be similar to the president's cabinet, but with greater power.

The Roman Curia is headed by cardinals who make decisions that affect the other diocesan Churches. They handle such things as the appointment of bishops, regulation of worship, Church missionary efforts, and oversee who teaches and what is taught. One of the major offices in the Roman Curia is the office of the Secretariat of State. Through this office, the Vatican maintains ambassadors to almost every nation in the world.

Many of the Church's decisions about teaching come from the office called the Congregation for the Doctrine of the Faith. This office was originally started in 1542 as the Congregation of the Holy Inquisition. In 1908, the name was changed to the Congregation of the Holy Office. In 1967, it received its present name, the Congregation for the Doctrine of the Faith. The purpose of this office is to …

- Promote and safeguard the faith and morals of the Catholic Church by investigating writings that seem contrary or dangerous to the faith and issue warnings and admonishments.

- Respond to new initiatives in science and culture.

- Assist bishops in their role as teachers.

The relationship of the Curia to the pope is a hard one to nail down. The Curia makes many decisions that are never seen by the pope. Some are specifically approved; others are allowed to be published under his name without his explicit approval. It differs with the issue being decided upon. Again, this can be compared to the authority given by the president to his cabinet members.

Your Guardian Angel

The Church's authority is in flux. It has sustained the Church through the years as an organization, and at the same time it has caused most of its troubles. The splits with the East and with the Protestants were over the issue of papal authority.

Who's Who in the Church

As we've said, the new model is a hierarchical communion. The hierarchy still exists. All power is in the office of bishop. The pope is a "big bishop." He leads the other bishops and acts as their spokesman. The hierarchical order of the Church consists of the following offices:

- **The pope**   The structure of the Church begins at the top, with the pope, the bishop of Rome. The College of Cardinals elects the pope.

- **Cardinals**   The College of Cardinals is a group of approximately 120 bishops who have been elevated by the pope to the rank of cardinal. Membership in the College of Cardinals is divided between those who hold office in the Vatican (the Curia) and those who are bishops of major cities in the world. For example, the United States has eight cardinals from cities such as New York, Chicago, and Los Angeles.

◆ **Bishops**   Bishops are priests nominated by other bishops in their country and appointed to office by the pope.

◆ **Priests and Deacons**   The bishop ordains priests and deacons.

Everyone below this level is considered part of the laity of the Church. An unofficial hierarchy exists within the laity. It might be represented in the following way:

◆ **Seminarians**   Those who are in training to become priests.

◆ **Nuns**   Women in religious orders.

◆ **Brothers**   Nonordained men in religious orders.

◆ **"Lay" professionals**   Directors of Religious Education, pastoral ministers, ministers of music, and chaplains, for example.

◆ **All the rest of the folks**

In the spirit of Vatican II, every person has a role in all the missions of the Church, and none is more important than another. The impetus is toward a more communal power structure. However, at the risk of being repetitious, change comes slowly, which is true in societal structures as well as the Church.

Vocation: No Family Is Complete Without One

In Chapter 11, you read about the sacrament of Holy Orders; now you'll read about the vocation of the priesthood. You remember, the word *vocation* means calling. For Catholics, vocation has always been synonymous with a calling to Church service, and a lot of pride and respect is connected with being an "official" servant of the Church. A big part of growing up Catholic means being open to the possibility of becoming a priest or a nun.

Vocation to religious service starts at baptism, when everyone is called to work for God. The traditional use of the term *vocation*, however, describes a professional level of Church service with special commitments. Those following a religious vocation give themselves completely to the service of the Church as a full-time endeavor; they do not hold other jobs. A religious vocation is considered very important because this person will have influence over many people. Consequently, the time of preparation is lengthy and rigorous and can last from 5 to 15 years.

Religious vocations include becoming a priest, nun, or brother. We'll look at these vocations and different religious orders, including what characterizes them and the work that they do. We'll begin with the vocation to the priesthood.

Priests: The Guys on the Front Line

The first choice a person entering the priesthood makes is whether to be a diocesan priest or join a religious order. Diocesan priests work directly for the bishop and often head up parishes as pastors. "Order" priests belong to specific religious communities and their jobs vary. Often they are teachers or missionaries.

The three ministries of the diocesan priest are preaching, teaching, and administrating the business of the parish. He celebrates Mass, administers the sacraments, visits the sick, marries, and buries. He is in charge of the buildings and finances and organizes the various parish ministries. He reports to the bishop. Priests promise celibacy and obedience to their bishop.

Order priests join a particular religious community and take vows to their particular religious order. A religious order is a group of people who have joined together to live in a religious community. The concept of a leader with an identity separate from other members of the Church did not develop until the end of the first century, when the Church moved away from Judaism and began to form its own identity as a separate religion. In the beginning, the first leaders were called bishops. Later, bishops delegated some of their duties, especially the celebration of the Mass, to people who were called priests.

The belief that priests had liturgical power to change bread and wine into the sacrament of the body and blood of Christ added to the priestly mystique and remains at the core of the priestly image today. Their relationship as members who lived in the community of the faithful diminished as their positions of power over the community became established.

In the 1500s, the Council of Trent formally established the Church hierarchy, drawing clear lines of distinction between the priests and the people, institutionalizing this popular image of the Catholic priest as a man "set apart." The priest's defining role centered in the Eucharist and the Mass, rituals that still characterize Catholicism in the eyes of the world. The people saw him as a celibate person who was called to distinctive liturgical service. More and more spiritual power was turned over to the clergy, until it was commonly believed that they stood between the people and God. All religious business had to pass through the priest's hands. This privileged role remained in effect until Vatican II, an event that began a process of rethinking the priestly ministry in relationship to the ministry of the people as a whole.

Vatican II has begun the process of balancing the role of priest as clergy and the priestly aspect of the laity. Since then, a new understanding of the priesthood continues to emerge. However, people are slow to give up their idols. Vatican II reaffirmed that the entire community of the baptized is a priestly people and is able to relate directly to God, as Jesus taught. For the people, this means taking more responsibility for their spirituality, and also Church ministries.

Your Guardian Angel

The proper way of addressing a bishop is "Your Excellency." The written form uses the title "Most Reverend."

The post-Vatican II shift is away from the priest as the one who presides over the Eucharist and toward the position of priest within the community. This new emphasis reaffirms his role as being with the people rather than as having power over the people. The priest and the people are now seen as having a more equal partnership.

Bishops: Shepherds of the Flocks

In the rank and order of the Church, a bishop is in charge of a diocese, which is made up of many parishes. He is the administrator of the business of the diocese, assigns priests to parishes, and they report to him. As priests are pastors to their parish, he is the pastor to his diocese. He presides over feast day Masses and special ceremonies from his church, called the cathedral. He travels to the parishes in his diocese to administer the sacrament of confirmation and leads special events throughout the diocese, such as the dedication of a church or the installment of a new parish priest.

The bishop supervises all the charities and educational institutions within his territory. He represents the Church in civic matters, and he is the principal teacher for his diocese. Just as the pope writes encyclicals to the whole Church, the bishop writes letters that teach and direct his people. Bishops are nominated by a group of other bishops from the same country. Following an elaborate process to determine eligibility for the office of bishop, the pope makes the final approval of all bishops.

Religious Orders: Know Your Players

Other religions and denominations have priests, nuns, and monks, but in the popular imagination, they are most often pictured as Catholic. The organization to which these religious, as they are called, belong is called a religious order, made up of groups of men or women living in separate communities in which they practice a particular form of spiritual life. The Catholic Church has a number of religious orders. Most of them are celibate communities, in which the members join with the intention of staying for life, similar to the commitment others make to marriage (without the sex).

Religious life focuses upon a community of prayer and service. Some orders live in seclusion from the world, even raising their own food, keeping a few animals, and making food products to sell. Other orders serve in the world by running schools, hospitals, and other social services. Orders have been a constant tradition in the Church. Some date almost from the beginning of the Church history; others have begun in the past century.

There is a saying in Alcoholics Anonymous that all it takes to start a new meeting is a grudge and a coffee pot. Similarly (slightly stretching the metaphor), religious orders often arose over a disagreement with the pope as a way to bring balance into the mix. When a particular religious leader felt something needed to be done in society, and the pope wasn't doing it, he or she could form a religious order to attend to it. As these orders grew in popularity, they did influence the larger Church. Religious life has traditionally been characterized by the vows of poverty, chastity, and obedience. Chastity means celibacy or virginity. Poverty generally means that all money is held communally. Obedience means the individual takes direction from his or her religious superiors regarding the nature of work assignments and living arrangements. Since Vatican II, the interpretations of the poverty and obedience vows have become less strict. Many members of religious orders keep some personal money, and many choose to live on their own.

There are two basic types of religious life: active and contemplative. Active religious members are characterized by their work in the world. Contemplative life describes the life of those who choose solitude, silence, prayer, and penance. The contemplative tradition goes all the way back to a second-century Church movement called the Fathers and Mothers of the Desert. This tradition reflects the values of prayer, meditation, and work and is characterized by separation from the world. Contemplative spiritual life is focused in the earth. In living away from the world and worldly concerns, members are especially attuned to nature's rhythms. The essence of contemplative life is the chanting of the Liturgy of the Hours, where the passing of the day and night are marked by special prayers. (Chapter 14 has more information about the Liturgy of the Hours.)

After the renewal of Vatican II, religious life was updated. The Church urged religious communities to reexamine their original connection to Christ and to live the Gospel, to recapture the spirit of their founders, and adapt it to the contemporary world. This radical shift resulted in many leaving their communities. Now, years later, new ways of forming religious communities have developed, and ministries have been created that are more in tune with the times.

Today, much of the polarization between contemplative life and active life has been deemphasized. Both are seen to have their own action. Where once the divisions between internal life and external life were seen to be very deep, the Church now acknowledges that all expressions of religious life contribute to the wholeness of spiritual life. New religious movements and groups are increasingly open to single and married people. Several groups are embracing non-Catholic members.

The essential elements of religious life today are still rooted in a response to living the Gospel by following Christ and being in service to others, and with a high value placed on community, just as it was in the early Christian communities. Religious life is based on a deep commitment to the community to which you belong, personal and communal spiritual development, prayer, and meditation.

Monks, Nuns, and Brothers

Preparation to become a monk, nun, or brother begins with a one-year *novitiate*. This is a time of intense spiritual formation in which candidates learn about the order they are preparing to join and spend time assessing their call to religious life. This time is followed by a profession of the vows of chastity, poverty, and obedience made in accordance with the traditions of the community they are joining. At that time, the candidates make a permanent commitment to God, to the religious life, and to the community they are entering.

The term *monk* refers to any member of a male religious community who lives a solitary life of prayer and contemplation. The word means "one who lives alone." The Camaldolese, for instance, are members of a community that live in total silence. Many people have heard of Benedictines and Trappists, communities with unique characteristics, but all are working toward the same end. Some monks are ordained as priests, and some are not. Technically, all members of religious communities who are not ordained as priests are considered part of the laity of the Church.

S'ter Says

Cloister means a place of religious seclusion. Members of a cloistered order limit their interaction with the world, remaining behind closed doors for the most part, where they lead a life dedicated to prayer, fasting, and meditation.

Is there a difference between "nuns" and "sisters"? Well technically, yes, nuns are cloistered and stay with the same abbey and always make an eternal profession of their vows, but not so for all sisters, who move about more in the world. Both are part of the "laity." The confusion arises because people address both nuns and sisters as "Sister [name]."

A popular image shows women dressed in recognizable outfits called *habits* and living in homes called *convents*. Since Vatican II, many religious orders have modernized both their styles of dress and their interaction with the world. All orders of nuns are committed to living the spiritual values of the Gospel in some manner. Just how those values are adhered to differs with each order. There are more than 500 orders of nuns in the United States alone, including 83 orders of Franciscans and 11 different orders of Dominicans, among others.

Brothers are male members of religious orders who take the vows of poverty, chastity, and obedience. Like nuns, they are lay members of the religious community. The call for brothers is to live the Gospel in community, with a deep sense of commitment. In the post-Vatican II Church, brothers, like sisters, have moved into a wide variety of ministries, especially in the area of peace and justice needs. Traditional arenas of education and health care remain at their core, and they have expanded their ministries to better meet the needs of the times.

Your Guardian Angel

Most nuns take a new name when they enter the convent. It is correct to refer to a nun as "Sister" followed by her religious name, if you know it, or simply as "Sister" if you don't.

Benedictines: Behind Closed Doors

The Rule of St. Benedict is the basis for thousands of Christians who belong to the monastic movement. As you may remember from earlier discussions, monasteries are places where people go to practice a particular form of spiritual life, and they are a part of most world religions. Benedict, a religious man in the late fifth century, wrote a set of rules governing monastic life that is so remarkable for its wisdom and clarity of language that it remains the practice of many religious orders even today.

Monasteries and convents often existed as closed societies, living on the edges of civilization, in the hinterlands. The farther away they got, the more apt they were to fall prey to strange spiritual practices. We've all heard the stories of hair shirts, inordinate fasting, and self-flagellation. Benedict created a form for religious life that reflected balance and good healthy practices. The Rule of St. Benedict teaches basic monastic virtues such as humility, silence, and obedience, as well as directions for daily living. Benedict suggested times for common prayer, meditation, reading of sacred Scripture, and manual labor. He recommended moderation for his monks, believing

Your Guardian Angel

Make sure your after-dinner drink is a Benedictine! The famous liquor was named for the Benedictine orders. At Christmas, buy your cheese and fruitcake from the Trappists, who support their order by making and selling these items.

in principles of sound health. He imposed limits to the fasting and all-night prayer vigils that had become extreme in many monasteries. He recommended working with the hands about six hours a day and having leisure for reading and common prayer.

The Rule of St. Benedict remains the backbone of Christian monasticism today. Many religious communities follow it, if not by the letter, definitely in spirit. Its particular recipe for prayer, fasting, and service assures the values of the Bible are lived in a balanced way. Each Benedictine monastery is a local institution and has a high degree of autonomy. A person who joins the order usually remains in one place for life. Many monasteries were formed during the Middle Ages by nobility, but they began to wane at the end of the twelfth century when newer orders, such as the Franciscans and Dominicans, developed. By the close of the eighteenth century, Benedictine numbers were very small. Over the next century, Benedictines experienced a revival.

Benedictine Sisters are a branch of the Order of St. Benedict and, amazingly, have been around since the 500s. They were formed by St. Scholastica, Benedict's sister. Their work includes agriculture, hospitality, education, skilled crafts, scholarship, counseling, and parish ministry. Many of their monasteries observe strict seclusion. The Benedictine Sisters came to the United States in 1846 and are actively involved in education and justice service ministries. Benedictines have the initials O.S.B. (order of St. Benedict) after their names.

The Rule of St. Francis

The Franciscan order is the common name of the Order of Friars Minor (O.F.M.). The members of this order follow the rule of life written by its founder, Francis of Assisi. They remain rooted in the call to a life of poverty and reflecting St. Francis's peaceful and gentle love of all, especially the poor. The rule was written in the early 1200s, and it embraces complete poverty not only for all its members, but also for the order itself. Over the years, Franciscans have negotiated a more moderate and practical interpretation of their rule, changing it to meet circumstances and pastoral needs more in tune with the times.

The Franciscan order originated in the late twelfth and thirteenth centuries along with many movements of lay people who were seeking to return to the life characterized by the early Church of Jesus and his followers. Members chose to live simply, to counter the emerging culture of the commercial towns of central Italy with their growing wealth and social status. The Franciscans supported themselves by whatever trades they knew, devoting their lives to living the Gospel in simplicity and preaching its message to others.

The order became enormously popular, and it soon demanded a more sophisticated structure. The friars (the English pronunciation of the French word for brother, *frère*) were forced to abandon their rural lifestyle for the most part, and settle into urban monasteries known as friaries. The training schools for the orders, located in centers such as Paris and Oxford, produced some of the greatest masters of theology of the Church. Franciscans have remained in the forefront of intellectual Catholicism and were the primary missionaries who brought the religion to the New World.

Saints Preserve Us

St. Clare, August 11, Patron of Television

St. Clare, born in Assisi, is said to be St. Francis's spiritual daughter because she very much followed in his footsteps. Born in 1193, she felt her calling from childhood. Under the guidance of St. Francis, she entered a Benedictine convent. She persisted in her desire to live an even more austere life, further separated from the world, and finally succeeded in founding the Poor Clares, or the Second Order of St. Francis. Her order soon spread across Europe. Clare inherited a great sum of money, which she gave to the poor, and she would accept no revenues for her monastery. She died in 1253 and was made a saint two years later. She was named patron saint of television because she was a woman of vision, and because she had visions!

Although the Prayer of St. Francis may or may not have been written by him, it captures Francis's spirit and the spirit of the Franciscans. It has been handed down over the ages and is a beloved prayer of Catholics and other Christians as well:

> Lord, make me an instrument of your peace;
> where there is hatred, let me sow peace;
> where there is injury, pardon;
> where there is doubt, faith;
> where there is despair, hope;
> where there is darkness, light;
> and where there is sadness, joy.
> Grant that I may not so much seek to be
> consoled as to console;
> to be understood as to understand;
> to be loved as to love;
> for it is in giving that we receive;
> it is in pardoning that we are pardoned;
> and it is in dying that we are born again in
> eternal life.

For Heaven's Sake!

Don't think that all religious communities live isolated from the world. Many of them are active in the world and maintain a life of prayer as well. For example, the Dominicans and Franciscans practice both prayerful meditation and service in the world.

Dominicans: Telling It Like It Is

The Dominican order, officially known as the Order of Preachers (O.P.), is a religious community founded in 1216 by St. Dominic de Guzman for the intention of teaching and preaching the Gospel message. Their founder believed that in order to be effective as preachers of the Gospel, members must return to the "apostolic life," meaning the life as led by the apostles, where members lived in communities, free from worldly concerns such as maintaining property. They could then travel and preach without being caught up in their material responsibilities.

Traditionally, Dominicans lived a contemplative life, dedicated to prayer and poverty, devoted to the study of the word of God. The order was further shaped by one of its well-known members, Thomas Aquinas, whose vision is best summed up by his words: "To gaze with love on God, and then to share what has been seen with others." Catherine of Siena (1347–1380) brought a social dimension to the order, infusing it with a concern for human rights. This concern is still very much a part of the Dominican life today. The Dominicans' outward focus is balanced by their strong tradition of inward-looking spirituality.

The Dominicans were established in the United States in 1805. Although they've undergone changes over the years, they continue to be characterized by a commitment to poverty, prayer, and study. After Vatican II, the order revised its constitution and renewed itself in the democratic spirit of its founder. Dominicans publish periodicals, conduct schools of theology, and work in dozens of parishes, hospitals, and universities all over the world. The order now includes cloistered nuns and sisters in active ministry, as well as non-vowed members, who, in fact, are the largest number in the order. Although Dominican organizations function autonomously, they are united as the Dominican Family under the master of the order, who resides in Rome.

Jesuits: The Pope's Foot Soldiers

Jesuit is the popular name for the Society of Jesus (S.J.), a religious order founded by St. Ignatius of Loyola in 1540. The Jesuits' motto is "For the greater glory of God." Ignatius, a military man, imbued the order with his fighting spirit. It was started with the purpose of engaging in an active ministry to "quell the heresies" of the day. The Jesuits marched to Rome and put themselves at the disposal of the pope, declaring that they would not be "chanting Office," like the other religious orders. Instead of chanting, which represented to them a passive type of spirituality, they declared that their work would be action for the advancement of Catholic doctrine and life. They vowed to go anywhere in the world the pope chose to send them. In addition to poverty, chastity, and obedience, Jesuits have a special vow of obedience to the pope.

Like the Dominicans and Franciscans, the Jesuits have a social ministry and have established many orphanages and other agencies for social assistance. Following a principle from their founding constitution, to "see God in all things," Jesuits are seen as more worldly than some of the other orders. Earlier in their history, they became explorers of the New World both in North and South America as well as Asia. They helped organize large numbers of American Indians whose communities were destroyed and whose land was taken through European expansion.

Jesuit spirituality is grounded in its founder's spiritual exercises and the values he communicated. These values include the following:

♦ **The centrality of Christ**   Christ is the preeminent focus of Jesuit spirituality (compared, for example, with the Dominicans, who have a great devotion to Mary). The spiritual exercises are designed to deepen the bond with Christ within the person who practices them.

♦ **Collaborative action with God**   This principle is based in the belief that God is vigorously at work in the world and needs human help to accomplish his work.

♦ **Spiritual discernment in decision-making**   This principle means using the exercises to choose options that support collaboration with God.

♦ **Generosity of spirit**   The exercises were developed in Spain in an environment of chivalry and romance, and that spirit is expressed in the Jesuits' willingness to be of service.

♦ **Fraternity and companionship**   Early Jesuits called themselves "friends in the Lord," and this community bond is an important part of their practice.

♦ **Seeking God in all things**   Spiritual integration is the primary theme of the Jesuits. This integration of prayer and service, contemplation and action, and effect and reason marks their spirituality.

> **Epiphanies**
>
> The Society of Jesus, popularly known as the Jesuits, is the largest religious order in the Church. It numbers some 25,000 members on six continents and in 112 nations. Among these members are 18,000 priests, 3,000 brothers, and 4,000 men preparing for the priesthood. They serve under their general superior in Rome, who is immediately accountable to the pope.

Lay Vocation: What About the Rest of the Folks?

We opened this chapter by saying that Catholics traditionally used the word *vocation* to talk about priests, monks, nuns, and brothers. Since Vatican II, the terms *lay vocation* and *lay spirituality* have worked their way into Catholic-talk. The terms refer to the individual ways members live out their religion in their everyday life by elevating common endeavors to the status of vocation. The common understanding of the word *lay* is "a nonprofessional." Catholics use the term to mean those who are not ordained.

S'ter Says _____

In Catholic terms, **lay** refers to Church members who are not ordained. The status of the laity has been greatly enhanced since Vatican II.

Your Guardian Angel _____

Get active in your parish! It is a Catholic tradition to participate in service work, and there are many ways to do this at your local parish. Consider starting a new group that meets your needs and serves others. The main thing is to belong by being active.

Christian spirituality is faith in action, and it takes many forms. It means living the Gospel values in whatever arena one is invited to enter by grace or the Holy Spirit. Post-Vatican II thinking is that full participation in Catholic life as a layperson exists side-by-side with the spirituality of the religious and ordained. Like the ordained clergy, the laity are called to bring Christ into the world. Historically, they had come to accept themselves as passive people who left the spiritual and religious matters to the clergy and expected to simply "pray, pay, and obey." A concerted effort has been made in the post-council Church to redefine the role of the laity and encourage the idea of its shared responsibility as the people of God.

We'll now take a look at some of the ways the laity participate in their religious calling. We'll describe the responsibilities that the nonordained, nonvowed Catholics take in the Church, specifically focusing on volunteer work. We'll also explore the revolution within the Church that now allows the laity to take professional leadership positions.

There Is a Job for Everyone

Although the Church has always relied heavily on volunteers, the following ministries reflect a growing process of the people sharing in the sacramental ministry and the governing of the Church:

- Eucharistic ministers are people who distribute Communion during Mass as well as take it to the homes of the sick.

- Lectors read the first two readings of the Mass.

- Song leaders are members of the congregation who announce hymns, teach new songs, and lead congregational singing.

- Offertory gift bearers bring the bread and wine up to the altar.

- Altar servers are often young boys and girls who light the altar candles, hold the book for the priest to read from, ring the bells at the important times during the Mass, assist at Communion, and in other ways help with the celebration of Mass.

- Parish council members are elected by the parish to serve on the advisory council to the pastor in the operation of the church. Council members head up committees, such as the finance committee, the committee for the liturgy, and more. Lay people also serve on diocesan pastoral councils.

- Social action enlists the aid of many volunteers. The parish may operate a shelter for the homeless, soup kitchens, or a food basket program. The parish might also spearhead education and social action on topics like capital punishment, abortion, peace, and justice.

The following represent traditional lay ministries:

- Ushers greet people as they enter the church, show them to their seats, take up the collection, and generally assist the congregation.

- Ministers of hospitality welcome new members to the church and arrange the refreshments and coffee following Mass.

- Catechists teach the Sunday school religion classes.

- Youth ministers organize and gather the adolescent members of the church for social outings and spiritual reflection.

- Ministers of care are assigned to visit the sick and homebound.

- Prayers are the faithful who often attend daily Mass and are called on by the parish when it has a particular prayer to offer.

In addition, volunteers do a myriad of jobs ranging from cleaning the altar on a regular basis to providing transportation for elder members.

> **CAUTION**
>
> **For Heaven's Sake!**
>
> Give everyone his or her due respect! No one's job is any better than anyone else's. Jesus was a carpenter, a day laborer. Peter was a fisherman. Luke was a doctor. Matthew was a tax collector. The women were homemakers, prepared food, and had leadership positions. Yet all had equal respect in the community.

Lay Vocation: Ambassador to the World

The Jews have a word, *napesh*, which means "how you are in the world." This word is a good definition for spirituality, or how your spirit affects the world. Catholic laity is reclaiming its true vocation as the people of God in the world. A recent letter from the United States Catholic bishops called *Everyday Christianity* acknowledges Catholics' vocation in the world. "Catholicism does not call us to abandon the world," reads the letter, "but to help shape it. This does not mean leaving worldly tasks and responsibilities, but transforming them."

The kingdom of God moves forward by increments. People who join the Jesuit Volunteer Corp or go to India to work with Mother Teresa's house for the dying, for instance, certainly advance the kingdom. So do conscientious workers in all fields: bricklayers, mothers, musicians, trash collectors, and high school biology teachers. Faith sees God's presence in ordinary human interaction. It is played out in the midst of life's everyday hustle and bustle. The moment is rich with sacred potential; the holy is deeply contained in the ordinary.

For Catholics, transformation is enhanced by a certain spiritual sensitivity. It is developed through prayer and meditation and carried out into the world in everyday activities. Vatican II's embrace of the world encouraged the Church to pay attention to this "spirituality of the mundane."

The Catholic lay spirituality is not dependent on job or position, but in the dignity you bring to the work and to the people you meet. Spirituality exists in our jobs, families, and neighborhood interactions as we bring love, justice, integrity, and care into them. The laity is the heart and spirit of the Church and shares its heart and spirit in the world. Lay vocation is not a vocation to the Church, but a vocation to the world.

Your Guardian Angel

Begin to think of your job as your spiritual vocation. You will be amazed at how much this thought can improve your attitude and your relationships with fellow workers. You are also more likely to receive the spiritual assistance or grace you need in overcoming difficult situations. Just try it for one day!

The vocation is lived through Catholics' engagement with the world as corporate executives, migrant farm workers, senators, welfare recipients, university presidents, parents, day-care workers, farmers, office and factory workers, union leaders, small business owners, teachers, scientists, bankers, salespeople, artists, and entertainers. All are called to partner in God's creative action in the world.

Faith in Action

To reinforce the connection between Church and world, some parishes have begun to hold ceremonies in which a person and their vocation is blessed. For example, during Mass one Sunday, the pastor called recent graduates of a nursing program to come forward. He prayed with them, saying: "God, you are the Great Physician, be present with these young people as they go about the work of healing. Bless these caps and stethoscopes, symbols of their service as a nurse." He then anointed the nurses' hands with holy oil.

One church has specified the following days as jubilee days for specific occupations to honor workers for their contributions to the life of the Church and the world and to "reflect on the challenges these workers face in living the Gospel."

♦ **February 18** Jubilee for artists

♦ **May 25** Jubilee for scientists

♦ **May 29** Jubilee for the military

♦ **June 4** Jubilee for journalists

♦ **September 4** Jubilee for building trades

♦ **September 10** Jubilee for teachers

♦ **November 5** Jubilee for government employees

♦ **November 12** Jubilee for agricultural workers

♦ **November 19** Jubilee for police

As you can see, the updated version of Catholicism reflects the trend toward more respect and equality within the ranks, thus moving us all from steeple to people.

Having looked at what's happening today, in the next chapter, we'll revisit the Church's early years to gain a deeper understanding of its long history.

The Least You Need to Know

♦ Vatican II drew the blueprints for a new model of Church with shared power.

♦ Vocation is shifting from a call to privilege to a call of service.

♦ Religious orders have played an immeasurable role in shaping the Church, and they continue to do so today as they have for 1,500 years.

♦ The new model of the Church empowers the laity to play a more active role.

♦ Ministry is becoming recognized as one's occupation in the world.

Part **6**

The Church's History

Here we look at how Catholicism parallels the story of the Western world. We describe the different periods of history shaping the Church: its identification with the Roman Empire, the establishment of its centralized authority, its concern with unity, and how it became a European Church and then a truly world Church.

You'll learn about two big splits in the Church: first, between the Latin Church based in Rome and the Eastern Church based in Constantinople; second, between much of Northern Europe and Rome, which resulted in Protestantism. You'll learn the story of Christianity's bloody arrival onto the shores of the American continent, brought by soldiers and missionaries, and finally, how the new religion incarnated in the Hispanic New World with the special assistance of the brown Lady of Guadalupe.

Chapter 20

The Roman Establishment

In This Chapter

♦ How the Church became the darling of the Roman Empire

♦ The price the Church paid for privilege

♦ The monasteries of Europe and the spread of the religion

♦ The rise of the Holy Roman Empire

Back in Chapter 6, we left the story of the early Church just as it was getting established. This chapter returns to those early days to describe some of the key players and important events in Church history. We resume the story in the fourth century with a look at two remarkable men, one an emperor and the other a bishop—with two remarkable mothers.

From Underdog to Top Dog

As you may remember from previous chapters, the early Church was an outlaw religion. For the first 300 years of Catholicism, Christians faced the very real threat of having to choose their religion over their life, and many of them died for their faith. Despite these dangers, however, an unusual and interesting thing happened: The Church not only survived, but it also grew in numbers. The Church's core message of liberation appealed to a growing number of people inside the Roman Empire.

As the Church entered the fourth century, two men—and their mothers—would have a great impact on its development. The first was Constantine (288(?)–337 C.E.), the Roman emperor who gave his protection to the new Church, effectively ending the persecutions. In the early years, the Church consisted of small communities of members who met in individual homes. Rituals were simple and intimate. This organization began to change when the important leader Constantine began to embrace the Church.

The second man to strongly influence the emerging Church was Augustine (354–430 C.E.), active just a few years later than Constantine. Soon after the Scriptures were recorded, Church leaders (known as "Fathers of the Church") began to write down their thoughts and reflections, and Augustine was the most significant figure in this theological tradition. One of the great systematic minds, he established the Church's intellectual foundation.

Constantine: The Church Gets a Break

In the year 312, Catholicism got its first big break. Constantine from Gaul (which is modern-day France) took control of the Roman Empire and became its new leader. He then made a decision that altered the course of history. He legalized the Catholic Church and supported it personally.

Saints Preserve Us

St. Helena, August 18, Patron of Converts and Divorced

St. Helena was born in England. She married Constantius, an officer in the Roman army, and gave birth to Constantine. Shortly after her husband was given the title of Caesar and took over the governing of Gaul and Britain, he divorced her to marry another. Helena later converted to Catholicism and influenced her son regarding his favorable treatment of the Church. He made her an empress, and she used both her wealth and her power to help the poor and to build churches. At the age of 80, she went to Jerusalem to find the Holy Cross, the one upon which Christ was crucified. Legend says that she found it. She built a church there and used her considerable wealth to take care of those in need. She died in Rome in about 326.

Although Constantine himself was not baptized a Catholic until his death, two forces drove him to endorse this new religion. The first was the influence of his Catholic mother, and the second was a dream he had just before going into a battle at the Mulvian Bridge over the Tiber near Rome. In the dream he is said to have seen in the sky a flaming cross inscribed with the words, "In this sign thou shalt conquer." He accepted the cross, Catholicism's major symbol, and won the battle. His victory became one of the most decisive moments both in the history of the Catholic Church and the history of Western civilization. Eventually, under his protection, Catholicism became the favored religion.

Constantine affected both the external and internal structure of the Church. First, his favors took the form of both land and tax incentives. Second, Catholics, no longer fearing persecution, stopped meeting in homes and started holding services in newly converted public buildings, a major work of his mother, St. Helena. Finally, he influenced the Church's internal structure by finding a way to settle disputes of faith.

Epiphanies

Keep in mind that although the edict of toleration ended the Roman persecutions, the Catholic Church has been systematically oppressed in many other countries over its 2,000-year history. England in the sixteenth century, Ireland in the seventeenth, the United States in the nineteenth, and the Soviet Union in the twentieth are just a few places where the property, rights, and even lives of Catholics were threatened. As we'll see, there have been times when the Church has sanctioned similar behavior toward those who disagreed with it. The Declaration of Religious Freedom issued at Vatican II in 1965 held that religious freedom was both a natural and a civil right for all persons.

Constantine began the tradition of Church councils, in which members assembled to discuss differences and make decisions by majority rule. This method assured that the Church would always speak with one voice. He called the Church's first council, the Council of Nicaea (325 C.E.), as you learned in Chapter 17. Constantine was an administrator who was familiar with both military and political organization. He gave the Church a political form, emphasizing the collective authority of the bishops. This structure gave the Church the stability it needed in the early years, which enabled it to grow, but the structure also gave the Church its authoritarian character, which has brought it much controversy.

Almost from the beginning, worldly considerations influenced Church structure, and it gradually adapted to the Roman world around it. Within the next 100 years, household Church communities became a thing of the past. The role of women in the Church, once so apparent during the time of Jesus, was all but eliminated as its all-male structure developed. Rather than being associated with service, Church office began to be associated with status and power.

Increasingly, Church and state finances mingled, and the Church became not just a vocation but a prosperous career for many people. Church leaders eventually lived like members of the secular aristocracy, often enjoying wealthy splendor. The simple communal meal that once characterized Catholic Communion gradually gave way to massive and ornate altars, where bread and wine were laid out ceremoniously. The separation between the priests and the people grew. In the centuries to follow, separation from the people, worldliness, and opulence would bring many problems to the Church.

On the other hand, there were positive changes that stemmed from the Church's relationship with the Roman state. The Church was able to exert a more humane influence on the empire. The state began to apply a more Christian understanding of social responsibility by feeding the poor and taking care of the sick. Most of all, the Church was able to grow and remain one communion that could transcend vast cultural differences—a cultural miracle that characterizes the Catholic Church up to today.

Although its decline had begun in the West, the Roman Empire was still vast and powerful, and Catholicism, now a favored religion, spread to its four corners. The Church suddenly began to acquire many new converts. When a chief of a tribe of people within the Empire converted, his whole tribe came with him.

Augustine: Lover and Loser

Like Constantine, Augustine was also greatly influenced by his mother. He was born in North Africa in what is now Algeria in 354 and grew up to become a writer, teacher, philosopher, and one of the most influential people in the Church's early history. His father was a pagan and his mother, Monica, was a Catholic. Augustine had an inquiring mind and explored many of the philosophies and theologies of his time before being drawn to Catholicism. Once a very worldly man, he founded a religious community as a safe haven from what he called "the decadent world," where he prayed and wrote extensively. He was made a bishop in Hippo (near present-day Annaba, Algeria) and worked tirelessly for the Church by preaching, writing, and administering. He believed in the power of education as a way to reclaim the soul's lost goodness. His vast body of writings on many subjects has been admired from his time through today.

Augustine left Christianity a mixed legacy. His deep love of the Church and of spiritual matters cannot be denied. He wrote beautifully and poetically about how the human spirit will only be satisfied when it falls in love with the will of God: "you have made us for yourself, O Lord, and our hearts will not rest until they rest in you." On the other hand, he was highly influenced by Plato's understanding of human nature and was caught up in a belief of the time called Manichaeism. Manichaeism taught that matter was separate from spirit and was in fact evil. It went even further to imply that there were two gods, one of good and one of evil. Although he eventually abandoned this philosophy and returned to the Church, he was never able to completely reconcile Manichaeism's dualism of good and evil. This led to Augustine's writings on original sin, which we discussed in Chapter 18.

Saints Preserve Us

St. Monica, August 27, Patron of Mothers and Widows

St. Monica, the patron of mothers and widows, was born in 333. She married a pagan man described as having a "high temper." Her patience and gentleness influenced him, and he converted to Christianity before his death. Their son, Augustine, who was only 17 at the time of his father's death, was a bit of a playboy around old Algeria. Monica prayed long and hard and with great fervor for his conversion. When he left to go to Italy, she followed him and, along with St. Ambrose, the bishop of Milan, had a positive influence on him. However, it took another 15 years before he converted. In 387, she witnessed his return to God as he was baptized by his good friend Ambrose. Monica died soon afterward. Many a Catholic mother has prayed to St. Monica!

Augustine's most influential book was called *The City of God.* In it, Plato's ideas show up in Augustine's views about the relationship between the Christian community and the larger world. Augustine was also writing in response to the sack of Rome in 407. For him, this world-shaking event demonstrated the frailty of human endeavor. Only the soul endures forever in Augustine's view. His dualistic thinking showed up in his understanding of the relationship between the Christian community and the larger world. He believed that the Church should strive to form a "perfect society," a religious society separate from the material world around it. He believed humans' only purpose in life is to form this "City of God" on earth.

Augustine's idea of the relationship of religion to the state greatly influenced how the Church saw itself. It laid the foundation for medieval society, a society more concerned about the welfare of the soul than the welfare of the body. The difficulty resulting from Augustine's theories was the separation between the Church and the world around it. The Church adopted his beliefs on original sin and his views on separating spiritual matters from worldly concerns.

Even today, this dualistic view haunts Catholics as they sort their material and spiritual priorities. The redefinition of the relationship between the Church and the world was one of the primary shifts of Vatican II. Since Vatican II, the Church has made major efforts to improve its relationship with the culture around it.

Christianity Comes to Your Hometown

For the most part, Western Europe of the 400s to the 800s was an unstable patchwork of towns, villages, and settlements, some of which were Roman and some of which were Germanic. The period was characterized by almost constant power struggles and fighting. Tribes coming from the northern and eastern areas of Europe were pouring into its settled parts searching for land and riches. By this time, the old Roman Empire had lost much of its power in the West and no longer offered the people protection against the invading tribes. In the Roman Empire's absence, the Catholic Church became the stabilizing force in Western Europe. The religion prospered and was characterized by its missionary work, building an elaborate system of monasteries and convents. These places provided safety, education, and support in an unstable time.

Monasticism: Attraction Rather Than Promotion

Monasteries and convents brought Catholicism to non-Christian Europe. Monastic life is a tradition in the Catholic Church that goes back to the desert with St. Anthony and his followers in the third century. As early as 250 C.E., hundreds of Christians were living as religious "hermits" (monks) in the deserts of Egypt, Israel, and Syria. Antony (or Anthony) was converted to Catholicism (271 C.E.) and moved into the Egyptian Desert as a religious hermit after hearing the words: "If thou wilt be perfect, go and sell all that thou hast." He is often spoken of as the "Father of Christian Monasticism." As we learned in Chapter 19, St. Benedict in 510 shaped monastic life under what is called the Rule of St. Benedict, which became the template for Western Christian monasticism.

Monasteries and convents housed communities in which religious life developed, away from "the world." As mentioned in Chapter 19, men who belonged to these early Church communities were often called monks; women were called nuns. From these communities came the *missionaries* who went out and lived among the tribes, helping to convert many tribal people to a new way of life.

S'ter Says

Missionaries are Church workers who are sent to foreign countries to do religious or charitable work. At times, they have been criticized for imposing values and beliefs on other cultures without an open exchange of ideas. In recent time, however, missionaries offer medical and educational assistance while working within the cultural beliefs of the people they serve.

The monasteries were cradles of art, sacred writing, and theological thought. As the invading tribes spilled down into Europe, the monasteries became safe harbors for the people and their culture. While continuing the work of conversion begun by the founding missionaries, some monasteries grew extremely wealthy and powerful. Their abbots (the name given to the head of a monastery) became some of the most influential figures in the area.

St. Patrick: Three Cheers for the Irish

Missionary work was an important part of the early Church. If ever there was a giant among missionaries, it was St. Patrick. He is called the "apostle of Ireland" and remains its patron saint. Dates of his birth differ between 432 and 456, and his death is given as 461 or 493.

One of the best-loved stories about him says he drove the snakes out of Ireland. This story may be a reference to converting Ireland from the Druid religion, because snakes were one of its sacred druidic symbols. He used the shamrock to teach about the Trinity, which is why it is the sacred plant of Ireland. The Druids burned ritual fires throughout the countryside as part of their spring rites. Another legend says St. Patrick lit the Easter fire in defiance of this pagan custom.

The story goes that raiders from the sea captured St. Patrick from his home in Britain when he was 16. He was taken to Ireland where he worked as a slave for the next six years. He eventually escaped and went back home to Britain. He became a priest and later a bishop. He was haunted by a dream in which he believed God was calling him back to Ireland. He eventually followed his dream and went back to the Irish and never left. He carried out massive missionary work, implanting the Catholic faith so widely and deeply in Ireland that it became one of the most Catholic of nations.

Many Christian texts were stored and copied in the monasteries of Ireland. For hundreds of years, the invading tribes from the "uncivilized" northern regions invaded Europe, eventually capturing and destroying Rome. Works of literature and art were hidden in the monasteries, thus preserving them from the invaders.

The term Celt has come to be associated with the Irish, but it refers to many of the people who lived across middle Western Europe. Their conversion to Catholicism was gradual. The old Druid religion existed side-by-side with Catholicism in most of the Celtic lands for many years. Catholic churches were built on the old holy sites of the Druids, and often the names and images of the old gods were carved into the stone walls. The Celts retained the holy days of the old religions and rededicated them to Catholic saints. Ceremonies to acknowledge the new holy days were often similar to the ceremonies of the deities they supplanted. The holy days were celebrated

Epiphanies
Did you know that the Irish are credited with saving Western civilization? Invading barbarians were destroying towns and villages throughout Europe, and the art and books of both the Greek and Roman civilizations were in danger of being lost. Many of them were hidden in the Irish monasteries, and so the boast has been made that the Irish saved Western civilization.

with songs, dances, and ceremonies of the old religions. This process of appropriation was very common in the spread of Catholicism.

As the Church replaced Druids with bishops and priests, the people transferred their love and loyalty to them. Some of the magical world of Celtic mythology was translated into the rich Catholic stories of the lives of the saints. The Celtic religion had many goddesses, such as the Great Mother called Anna who would eventually be found in different forms in the various Celtic cultures of Europe. In Christian times, she lived on through the veneration of St. Anne in Brittany, St. Non in Wales, and St. Brigid in Ireland.

As a rule, Celtic and other indigenous religions held the female principle in equal if not higher regard than the male. You'll often hear reference to the Catholic Church as the "Mother Church," both in everyday language and in official documents. This designation represents the feminine or nurturing aspect of God. It refers to the Church as a womb in which the members grow and develop. The Church is the spiritual home, and home is the domain of the mother. The spirit of the Celtic people infused Catholicism with a sense of story, a love of song, and a strong community spirit.

Celtic monasticism was characterized by an independence of spirit and generally had little or no use for the politics of the Church in Rome. The clergy of the Celtic monasteries was able to get along well with the barbarian royalty. Their style was to mingle with the dignitaries, and they made every effort to respect local values. The intense era of Irish missionary activity throughout Europe lasted for roughly 100 years, from approximately 550 until 670.

Saints Preserve Us

St. Brigid of Ireland, February 1, Patron of Dairy Workers, Nuns, and Scholars

Sometimes called the second St. Patrick, St. Brigid of Ireland was born in 450. She established communities all over Ireland, which helped the growth of the Church. Many miracles are attributed to her. One story says she once turned water into milk, which is why she is the patron of dairy workers. Her symbol, St. Brigid's Cross, is a straw cross, which is kept in the homes of Irish country people. This cross appears in pre-Christian art forms as well, giving substance to the idea that Brigid is an adaptation of the Celtic goddess, Brigit. Most likely, attributes of the pagan Brigit were transferred through folk memory to Brigid. Some scholars suggest that St. Brigid was the first bishop of Kildare, although this has not been proven. She is buried at Downpatrick with St. Patrick.

In addition to the still vibrant churches in the East, two very different ideas of the Catholic Church existed side-by-side in central Europe during the first millennium. The Celtic version was an independent and decentralized form of Catholicism; the

other Catholicism was a very Roman-centered Church, which saw itself as the authority in religious matters.

German Christianity

In the countryside that would eventually be known as Germany, people lived in small
villages and settlements and practiced pagan religions. The Catholic Church was
extending its missionary efforts into the area. Boniface (673(?)–754), one of the leading missionaries of the time, was to Germany what Patrick was to Ireland a couple of
hundred years earlier. He brought Catholicism to the German people.

Boniface was born in Devonshire, England, and from the age of 13, monks in a
monastery in Exeter, which he later joined, educated him. One of the stories about
Boniface tells of an encounter he had with a pagan chieftain. Boniface felled a sacred
oak tree that the people believed belonged to Thor, the thunder god. When he was
not struck dead, as the local people believed he would be, many of them converted.
He built a church out of the oak tree. However, the pagans may have had the final
say. A few years later when traveling near the same place, he and his 52 companions
were attacked and murdered by a band of locals. His grave soon became a sanctuary
where many gathered to pay respects to him.

Earlier missionary activity in Germany had left converts to Christianity without the
adequate support to maintain their faith in the outposts of civilization in which they
lived. Boniface was able to bring support to these stranded Christians and bring many
more converts to the Church. He did this by establishing monasteries that were centers for the faith, in which people were educated and instructed in the ways of the
religion. He and his female cousin, Leofgyth, instituted a series of monasteries, which
became anchors for the faith. These monasteries lasted for over 1,000 years, and
many of them are still in existence today. The Church's missionary zeal did not con-
fine itself to Germany, but was extended to Hungary, Russia, Denmark, Sweden, and
all parts of Europe.

From Rationality to Mysticism

The Roman world, influenced by the Greek culture, had carried many of the classical
Greek thoughts and ideas, as well as its mysticism, into Europe. As the Empire ended,
so did the time of classic learning. The period that followed, known as the Dark Ages,
lasted until the 1100s. However, it's important to recognize that many things lumped
together under this period's moniker are not necessarily "dark." Catholicism prevailed, for instance, to become the popular religion of the land despite constant power
struggles and wars.

During this time, the Church defined many of the practices and rituals with which it is so strongly identified today. For example, the Rosary was introduced, and statues and paintings of the saints sparked devotions. Feasts were celebrated with processions of colorful vestments, flags, and music. Morality plays and religious dramas were acted out publicly. Catholicism stabilized into the form it would keep for the next 1,200 years.

Epiphanies

Just as Ireland has Patrick and Germany has Boniface, many European nations have a missionary saint sent from the Eastern Church in Constantinople who first established Catholicism within their borders. Here are a few such saints with the approximate dates they began their missionary work:

- St. Severinus of Austria, 470
- St. Columba of Scotland, 560
- St. Ansgar of Denmark, 830
- St. Cyril of Russia, 860
- St. Methodius of the Czech Republic, 870
- St. Sigfrid of Sweden, 1,000

A New Empire Is Born

Roman culture continued to influence both politics and the Church's identity. Like the Roman Empire, the Church was headquartered in Rome and developed a centralized power structure. In the absence of the Roman state, the Church found itself existing as both a spiritual and often a civil authority, not entirely because it wanted political control, but because the people looked to it for leadership.

For Heaven's Sake!

Don't confuse the Holy Roman Empire with the Church whose headquarters are located in Rome. The empire was a political structure. The Catholic Church and the kingdoms of Europe partnered for a thousand years, during which time the difference in roles between church and state was often unclear.

When Pope Leo III crowned Charlemagne emperor on Christmas in 800, the marriage between the Church and state became official. Charlemagne was the leader of a tribe in central Europe called the Franks. As he was crowned, he accepted the role of protector of the Church. The religious and political foundation for the later Holy Roman Empire was laid.

Let's summarize and clarify this important relationship between Catholicism and the Roman Empire. Initially,

Catholics were outsiders and a threat to the Roman state. Then they became not only tolerated but also favored by Rome, which was losing its power to invading tribes at the time. The popes in Rome became the ones who could hold government together, and the Church began to exercise both civil and religious authority.

When Charlemagne was crowned emperor, civil power and Church power again became separated, that is to say, there were again two distinct leaders, the pope and emperor, but there was still one agenda: to build Augustine's City of God. This new child of the marriage between church and state, called the Holy Roman Empire, would last 1,000 years. For centuries to come, Christian Europe was torn by wars between kings and princes. Contrary to the Church's intentions, the Holy Roman Empire never succeeded in bringing about the City of God.

By the time of the Dark Ages, the Church had adopted an authoritarian model and was wedded to the state. Problems of money, power, and authority infiltrated its structure. In the next chapter, we will look at the corrupt practices that resulted from these problems.

The Least You Need to Know

- The organizational structure of the Church given to it by Constantine stabilized it and allowed it to grow.

- The indigenous tribes of Europe provided the Church with a rich, colorful heritage rooted in the earth.

- Monasteries were stabilizing influences on European culture, and spread the values of Christianity throughout Europe.

- The problems of power, money, and authority came with the Church's marriage to the Roman Empire.

21

Division, Debauchery, and Reform: The Church's Second Millennium

In This Chapter

◆ Catholicism splits in two

◆ Crusades, Inquisitions, and Indulgences

◆ Martin Luther, Henry VII, and the Protestant Reformation

◆ Catholicism reforms during the Council of Trent

The preceding chapter explained how the Catholic Church spread across Europe organically connected with the developing political powers of the time. In this chapter, we'll look more closely at some of the problems that would haunt Catholicism for the next 1,000 years. We'll look at the reforms within the Church that brought it into modern times.

As the new millennium dawned, trouble that had been brewing for some time was about to boil over. First, the Greek Church split from Rome over differences in politics, ritual, and language (Greek versus Latin). Then a couple of protesters, one of them a friar (Martin Luther) and the other a king (Henry VIII), turned against the Church, taking big political portions of Europe with them. These events finally forced the Church to examine its practices and its role in the lives of the people. Although Church leaders instituted major reforms, the Church never again captured the unifying power it had. Let's take a closer look at these changes.

Catholic and Orthodox: The Church's Y1K Problem

So far, we've concentrated our primary focus on the development of the Catholic Church in the West, headquartered in Rome. However, the East has a vibrant history as well. In addition to Rome, there were major Catholic churches at Alexandria in Egypt, Antioch in Syria, and the well-known Church at Constantinople, as well as, historically, in Jerusalem. Until the fifth century, these five regions of the Catholic Church, each headed by a *patriarch*, were considered to form a ruling "patriarchy." After this period the Church at Rome assumed supremacy as these Churches maintained less and less unity.

S'ter Says

Patriarch is the chief bishop of the Churches in a particular region of the world. The word is from the Greek *patriarches*, which means the father or chief of a race (*patria*, is Latin for a clan or family). In the Hebrew Scriptures Abraham, Isaac, and Jacob, as the fathers of the Jewish family, are revered as patriarchs. Patriarchy then refers to the territory governed by patriarchs. Today, mainly the heads of the Eastern Churches use the title.

Although the first lasting separation in Catholicism didn't occur until 1054, tension had been building for several centuries. The Catholic Church in the East, centered in Constantinople, and the Catholic Church in Rome argued over differences of language and theology. They eventually became locked in a power struggle. Rome's way of handling the problem was to excommunicate (expel) the Patriarch of Constantinople. In turn, the Patriarch of Constantinople excommunicated Rome, thereby breaking off from Roman rule. The rest of the Eastern churches followed suit and as a group they became known as the Orthodox Church in Russia, Greece, the Ukraine, Romania, Turkey, and other parts of Eastern Europe.

Over the next 400 years, there were major attempts (with some successes) to mend this tear in the fabric of Catholicism. Essential practices and much of the theology of the Churches remained the same. Today, it would be difficult to identify the differences between them. However, except for some of these Churches, which reunited with Rome, they remain distinct Churches. Efforts to reunite the Orthodox Church and the Catholic Church continue. Pope John Paul II, the present pope, is from Poland, which borders on and, which having had missionaries from Constantinople, is influenced by the culture of Orthodoxy. He has made the rejoining of the Churches one of the aims of his pontificate.

Catholicism's Dark Side

Although the Church felt the loss of its Eastern members, growth throughout the West more than made up for it, and the Church remained a major power in the Western world. Due to some unhealthy developments, which we'll examine in this chapter, the Church found itself rolling in money and basking in power. Such a combination was extremely damaging for an organization whose mission was to proclaim God's reign and to do good works. Over time, the Church strayed far from its humble beginnings in the small towns of Galilee where Jesus walked the dusty roads with the people and taught about his Father's love. We'll look at three particular practices the Church employed that took it further away from ministering to the people: the *Crusades*, the *Inquisition*, and the selling of salvation in the form of *indulgences*.

Epiphanies

Simony refers to both the buying and selling of Church offices (the office of bishop, for example). This practice was originally condemned in the Acts of the Apostles, when Simon Magus tried to buy the apostles' power of blessing through the laying on of hands. Despite repeated efforts by the Church to extinguish this process, it was a recurring problem until the sixteenth century. Major offices of the Church, such as appointment to the position of cardinal, were bought by wealthy and influential political figures who wished to control Church decisions and finances.

At the time of Christ, the Church's liberating message called for an end to political oppression. Ironically, the Catholic Church conformed to the patterns of the very society it was supposed to transform, the Roman Empire. In modeling the worldliness of the Roman Empire, opulent displays of wealth became the norm for the Church. Church leaders often lived like princes, holding court balls and hosting great banquets. Membership in the clergy carried privilege to the degree that Church offices could be bought and sold, a practice called *simony*. The organizational structure of the Church became a hotbed of infighting and jockeying for position. At one time, three different people claimed to be pope. The following sections take a look at practices that have caused problems for the Church even into current history. Although it has made steps toward change, the Church still struggles to come to grips with its past.

Crusades: Holy War or War on the Holy?

Crusades are the name given to the "holy wars" launched by the Church mainly for the purpose of liberating the sacred places of Palestine from the Muslims, who are the members of the Islamic religion. Islam began to develop in Arabia under the direction of its founder, the prophet Muhammad. The spread of Islam after Muhammad's death in 632 has had no match in history. For the next 29 years, it expanded north of Arabia to Damascus and Jerusalem, east to Persia, west to Egypt, and farther on to the northern coast of Africa. By 715, Islam had reached Spain. The spread of Islam left the great centers of Eastern Christianity cut off from the Roman Empire. Lines were eventually drawn, and a peace was established that lasted for some time.

By the middle of the eleventh century, Islamic leaders closed the Holy Land to Christian pilgrims. The pope saw this action as an opportunity both to unite the Catholic princes of Europe against a common enemy and to liberate the Holy Land. He called for the first of a series of Crusades that stretched from the late 1000s to the late 1200s. Although the first of the Crusades did open up the Holy Land for Christian pilgrims, the net effect of the Crusades was destructive. This section provides a quick look at some of them.

Epiphanies

Did you know that Islam is the fastest-growing religion today, with about a billion believers? Its population centers are in Indonesia (161 million), Bangladesh (100 million), Nigeria (100 million), and India (100 million). Its name comes from the Arabic word *Salaam*, meaning "peace." Membership requires surrender to God: "There is no God but Allah, and Muhammad is his prophet." This basic belief is accompanied by the practice of good deeds prescribed in their holy book, the Quran. Islam's history begins with Abraham of the Jewish Scriptures, and is monotheistic. In this regard, Judaism, Christianity, and Islam are akin to one another.

The First Crusade lasted from 1097 to 1099. In it, Christian armies defeated Turkish armies, capturing the ancient city of Antioch and occupying Jerusalem. Their motto was *Deus vult*, "God wills it," and by this time, no one doubted it! Their victory, which was a complete slaughter, came at the expense of the inhabitants of the area, including Jews and Eastern Christians whose skin was darker than the Europeans. The Second Crusade (1148–1149) failed. Jerusalem fell back into the hands of the Muslims about 40 years later. The most romanticized crusade, the Third Crusade

(1189–1192), began when Europe's three most powerful rulers, Emperor Frederick Barbarossa of Germany, King Philip Augustus of France, and King Richard Coeur-de-Lion of England (Richard the Lion-Hearted) "took the cross." This phrase described the fact that the shields of the crusaders bore a cross. Tales of Richard became legend, but nothing much was accomplished. The Muslims kept Jerusalem, and Richard was stuck in an Austrian prison, waiting to be ransomed.

The Fourth Crusade (1203–1204) resulted in the complete sacking of Constantinople—a Christian city! After robbing, murdering, and raping the inhabitants, the out-of-control crusaders divided the spoils. The pope was furious at the crusaders.

The Children's Crusade in 1212 was perhaps the most bizarre one of all. Thousands of children followed a boy from Cologne who believed God wanted him to liberate Jerusalem. The main group was over 7,000 strong. The Crusade failed, and while many of the children made it home, Christian merchants sold countless others into slavery and prostitution.

The Church promised crusaders rewards for their efforts. If they died in battle, their sins would be forgiven, and they were assured of going straight to heaven. If this inducement were not enough, they also were allowed to divide the booty of the war, an incentive that led to the pillaging and looting of property and the rape and murder of innocent people. These military expeditions put blood on the hands of the Church, because tens of thousands of innocent people were slaughtered in its name.

It is ironic that in our day both the image of a crusade to liberate Islam from "despot" rulers and a "Holy War" or Jihad, which assures the martyr of instant paradise, are still as powerful today in the very places they were employed almost 1,000 years ago.

Good Out of Evil

Despite the negative consequences of the Crusades, there was an unintended positive by-product for the West. There was a reconnection to the great learning of the ancient world and an influx of new ideas from the Islamic world, such as astronomy and chemistry. The Islamic world gave the West the Arabic number system and introduced the concept of zero, which made higher mathematics possible. In fact, *algebra* is an Arabic word.

One of the major beneficiaries of the rediscovery of classical learning was Thomas Aquinas. Taking the previously lost works of Aristotle, the great mind of the Greek Classical period, Aquinas incorporated his logical method into the theology of the Church. His methods of teaching, thinking, and talking about God have remained a bulwark of Church education up to the present time.

Saints Preserve Us

St. Thomas Aquinas, January 28, Patron of Schools

Thomas Aquinas (1225–1274) was born in Italy and was sent to the monastery of Monte Cassino at age five for education. He joined the Dominicans in 1244 and taught in Paris. Despite the fact that the bishop of Paris condemned him and had his works burned, he was named a saint in 1567. In 1880, Pope Leo XIII made him the patron of all the Church's schools and required all seminary students to study his thought as the one official philosophy of the Church. He is acknowledged as the greatest master of Church thought.

Inquisition: Ask Me No Questions, and I'll Tell You No Lies!

People have questioned Church teachings since the Church began. Among the teachings that seemed to raise the most doubt were beliefs about the results of the fall from grace, original sin, heaven and hell, Jesus' divine nature, the virgin birth, and the real presence of Jesus Christ in the bread and wine of the Mass. The Church did not always deal well with questions or dissent. It felt that heresy threatened its unity and the duty to keep the teachings of Jesus pure. Alignment with the political sector gave the Church the opportunity to use civil authority to employ physical force against dissenters, whom it identified as *heretics*.

The Inquisition was a court system set up by the Church for the purpose of tracking down heresies and punishing heretics. The word *inquisition* means "to question." At the same time, however, the Inquisition involved more than Church authorities. Secular authorities had an interest as well. Both groups wanted to minimize dissent and disruption, and neither tolerated much diversity. The Catholic Church was still smarting from the loss of the Orthodox Church, and its ideal of one faith. In an attempt to hold it all together, the Church and the secular authorities joined to exert control over the religious world around them.

Priests of the Inquisition, led by the Dominicans, traveled throughout Europe preaching the faith. Following their sermons, they would ask the question: "Does anyone disagree with these Church teachings?" People were encouraged to come forward to report any wrong thinking or wrongdoing they might know about. Usually, no one would admit that they had any doubts about the religion themselves, but quite often they would declare a neighbor or enemy a heretic. Under torture, those who were accused and found guilty by the Inquisition were fined, imprisoned, and their lands and goods confiscated. If they refused to renounce their false beliefs, and often even if they did, they were cruelly tortured and killed.

The courts of the Inquisition were Church courts, and the crimes for which people were tried, specifically heresy and related offenses, were religious in nature. However, the power to punish was in civil hands. Those suspected of heresy by the Church were handed over to the civil authorities for punishment. In so doing, the Church attempted to stay above the consequences.

Saints Preserve Us

Joan of Arc, May 30, Patron of France

Joan of Arc was caught in both the politics of France and England and the Inquisition. Born on January 6, 1412 in France, she heard the voices of St. Michael and St. Catherine from an early age. When she was 17, the voices told her to go to the king of France and help him recapture his kingdom, lost to the English. She was captured in battle, and the French did nothing to save her. After many months of imprisonment, she was tried by a local court and found guilty of heresy, sorcery, and adultery. The judges declared Joan's visions and voices to be "false and diabolical." Joan was burned at the stake on May 30, 1431. She was only 19 years old. Thirty years later, she was exonerated of all guilt by a court constituted by the pope. She was declared a saint in 1909.

There were three distinct Inquisitions, spanning hundreds of years. Unfortunately, historical accounts of the Inquisitions are affected by a religious bias that hinders the gathering of accurate data. The avowed purpose of an inquisition was to protect the faithful from heresy. Although the Inquisitions originally were launched against heretics, they later became directed against Jews and Muslims. In many areas of Europe, women became a favorite target of the Inquisition. In 1484, the pope issued an order that allowed an inquisition of those suspected of witchcraft.

Epiphanies

A remnant of the Inquisition called the Congregation for the Doctrine of the Faith exists in the Church today. (We talked about this group in Chapter 19.) It safeguards and promotes authentic Catholic teaching throughout the worldwide Church. It investigates controversy and holds extensive studies regarding questions surrounding matters of Church doctrine. It evaluates theological opinions and may admonish those regarded as incorrect or harmful to Catholic teaching. It also examines books and provides the authors the opportunity to defend themselves.

The most notorious of the Inquisitions was the Spanish Inquisition, which began in about 1480, at the time Islam was driven out of the peninsula. Unlike the others, which were under ecclesiastical (Church) control, the Spanish Inquisition was an instrument of secular power, the Spanish crown. The goal of the Spanish Inquisition was to search out converted Jews and Muslims suspected of practicing their "old" religions. The Spanish Inquisition was used against political opponents. The Inquisition lasted in Spain for almost 400 years until the 1800s. The Spanish conquistadors exported the tradition to the New World and used it against the native people. They demanded loyalty to Spain and to the Church under penalty of torture and death.

Indulge Me, One More Time

Nobody knows when the practice of selling indulgences began, but it blossomed during the 1400s and 1500s. *Relics* of the saints were often displayed for a price and sometimes sold. Relics were a popular religious sacramental of the time. They consisted of pieces of wood, said to be from the authentic cross, or pieces of cloth, hair, or bone that were believed to belong to one of the saints. Money from the sale of these goods was used to finance the building of the cathedrals and fund the extravagant lifestyle of the clergy.

Indulgence is a term that describes the remission of punishment due for sins. The Church supported its belief of what was right and wrong with the idea of punishment in the afterlife. It assigned a spiritual value to certain practices or prayers. The performance of these practices or prayers is said to erase spiritual debt. If a sin were committed, an indulgence could balance the books. An indulgence is like a "get out of jail free" card from Monopoly. This practice went on until it was officially condemned in 1562, but not before it became the proverbial straw that broke the back of the Catholic Church. Indulgences are still a part of the Church today; however, they are not sold. They are a physical connection to persons who led lives of spiritual value, prayer, and good deeds.

Problems, Protest, and Protestants

The Church, having partnered with the state in the Inquisition, employed increasingly more authoritarian means to thwart any diversity of thought or question of its dogma. Its use of power and control, albeit for the intended end of protecting the teachings of Jesus, had taken it far from its original mission.

Against this backdrop of corruption, a sound could be heard, a tap, tap, tap in Wittenberg, a small town in Germany. The sound came from a hammer banging against the large cathedral door. When the sun rose on that October morning in 1517, it shone upon a large piece of paper known as the *95 Theses* on which were listed 95 complaints against the Church. The man who wrote the paper and nailed it to the door was Martin Luther. It was not long before the document was discussed all over Europe, and the *Protestant* Reformation was born.

On the heels of Luther's protest, Henry VIII, the king of England, broke with Rome and declared himself head of the Church of England. The differences in the beginning were political rather than religious, a quarrel between the king and the pope, which was not unusual in the Middle Ages. However, this quarrel went on to result in a permanent schism. Let's take a look at both of these influential men and how their actions affected the Catholic Church.

S'ter Says

A **Protestant** is any Christian belonging to a sect that seceded from the Catholic Church at the time of the Reformation. Lutheran, Episcopal, Methodist, and Baptist are some of the Protestant denominations.

Martin Luther: The Hammer Heard 'Round the World

Martin Luther, a German friar, began the Reformation. He was an Augustinian priest who was sent on a mission to Rome in 1510 and returned indignant at the corruption and worldliness of the Church. The following year, he became a professor of theological studies, a position he held until his death. Luther's studies brought him to the belief that people are saved by faith alone. They could not earn salvation through actions or prayers. As a result, Luther was particularly outraged at the selling of indulgences, which violated this core belief. He attacked this practice and others in his *95 Theses*.

Luther followed his first list of complaints with his treatises of 1520, in which he questioned papal authority and other official Church doctrines. He was excommunicated in a document issued by Rome, which Luther promptly burned in the public square. Soon, the emperor summoned him. Luther defended his beliefs eloquently and refused to recant. He was outlawed and sought refuge in the castle of Wartburg under the protection of Frederick, an official of the area. Luther translated the Bible into German. He also organized the Lutheran Church and wrote essays, sermons, catechisms, and hymns, including the famous Protestant hymn, "A Mighty Fortress Is Our God." The creation of the Lutheran Church, which was formed around the teachings of Martin Luther, resulted in the Catholic Church losing its followers in a major portion of Germany.

Henry VIII: Love and Marriage

The man known as Henry VIII was not only one of the most colorful rulers in the history of England, he also maintains an important place in Church history as well. Henry was more practical than idealistic; his actions were motivated by his desire to divorce his wife and marry another. The Church refused to grant him the annulment he desired. Henry defied Church doctrine and authority by remarrying in 1533, and was duly excommunicated. In response, Henry instituted the Church of England and declared himself its head. As a result, Catholicism lost most of its English members. The Church of England, better known as the Anglican Church, exists as the Episcopalian Church in the United States.

In addition to the Lutheran Church and the Anglican Church, many other churches were founded in the 1500s in protest of the Catholic Church and its various practices. These splits weren't entirely about the selling of indulgences or the Catholic Church's prohibition of divorce. The emerging states of Europe were gaining power and wanted their independence from the old empire. They resented the fact that Church money from their regions was channeled into Rome. The Church and the state were so intertwined that political independence came at the cost of religious independence, and many wars would be fought throughout Europe for centuries because of it. Further splits with the Catholic Church occurred in France, Switzerland, and other Northern European countries. Generally, the southern countries remained in Rome's fold.

Trendy Trent: Going to Reform School

Both Martin Luther and Henry VIII packed a big wallop, and the Catholic Church felt the sting of its losses. It realized that it had better make some changes, or it was going to lose even more members. The birth of Protestantism gave the push for the reform that many had been urging for hundreds of years. The pope finally called the Council of Trent. During the years 1545 to 1563, bishops of the Church met to clarify doctrines and to pass reforms that would redirect the course of the Catholic Church for the next 400 years. The results of this council essentially sounded the death knell for corrupt Church practices, and Church leaders got back to business—religious business.

Scripture and Tradition Upheld

The Protestant Reformation sparked what is called the Counter-Reformation, in which the Catholic Church began to define its authority. It reaffirmed its stand that revelation is found in both revealed Scriptures and lived traditions. The Church had always claimed that a person couldn't interpret God's truth simply by reading the Bible. It has always believed God's revelation continues to unveil itself through the teachings of the Church. This idea, which was unacceptable to the Protestants, allowed bishops to continue to formulate Church teaching on more than just what was revealed in the Bible. The Church continued to decline to approve new translations of the Bible that were in the people's everyday language. This seemed to justify the Protestants' claim that the Catholic Church was afraid to have people read the Bible and do their own interpretation of God's will. The gulf between Catholics and Protestants was widening.

By the time the Council of Trent closed in 1563, it had dealt with many of the abuses cited by the Protestant Reformers, and it ended the corruption in the Catholic Church. The changes included a prohibition on the sale of indulgences, a crackdown on simony, a reformed liturgy, the establishment of seminaries for the proper training of priests, and more local control given to bishops.

The Council of Trent did not, however, address the important issue of the nature of the Church's relationship to the modern world then emerging. As you've seen, that subject became the focus of the most recent council, Vatican II.

> **CAUTION**
>
> **For Heaven's Sake!**
>
> Be careful about how you use the word Protestant. This is a generic term Catholics (and other non-Protestants) often use to refer to non-Catholic Christians. Baptists, Presbyterians, or Episcopalians, for example, would not refer to themselves as Protestants, but instead use the specific name of their denomination.

Lines Drawn: Them and Us

The Church began to define itself over and against Protestantism. Catholicism was no longer the only game in Christendom, and by the end of the Council of Trent, firm boundaries were established between the Catholic Church and Protestantism. There were five primary differences between them, and these differences remain in effect even today:

- Catholics maintain that moral authority comes from both Scripture and tradition. Remember, the Catholic Church bases its authority to declare truth both in Scripture and in its interpretation of the Scripture, which it calls tradition. Protestants believe that Scripture alone holds moral authority.

- Catholics hold that Christ is truly present in the consecrated bread and wine of the Eucharist. Protestants, for the most part, see the Eucharist as a symbolic memorial of Christ's Last Supper.

- For Catholics, the sacraments are celebrations of the salvation achieved by Jesus Christ, which God offers us as a gift. Sacraments are Catholics' participation in this reality. Protestants believe that salvation comes through faith in biblical Scripture alone, and was accomplished once and for all time in the Calvary sacrifice of Jesus.

- Catholics believe in mediation, the establishment of a relationship between one person and God through the efforts of another person. The mediator can be a priest or a favorite saint. It can be other persons who pray for them. They themselves can be mediators, as they pray for others, the souls in purgatory, for example. Mary is the favorite Catholic mediator. Protestants believe in an immediate and direct relationship with God, and shun intermediaries, for the most part.

◆ Catholics keep the traditional seven sacraments: baptism, reconciliation, the Eucharist, confirmation, Holy Orders, marriage, and anointing of the sick. Protestants, de-emphasizing the role of a priest mediator, for the most part practice just two sacraments: baptism and the Eucharist.

The Church Turns Its Face to the New World

The Protestant Reformation caused much of Germany and England to leave the Catholic Church. The result was that the Catholic Church lost its position as the primary religion. While the Catholic Church was losing its hold on Europe, a Catholic country, Spain, was opening up a new world. The New World provided an opportunity for the Catholic Church to establish the "City of God" one more time. That's what we'll discuss in the next chapter.

The Least You Need to Know

◆ The ideal of one religion for all was shattered with the separation of the Orthodox Church.

◆ The involvement of the Church in money and power caused a loss of identity and integrity.

◆ The Protestant revolt spurred the reform of the Catholic Church.

◆ The Catholic reformation assured the Church's survival as a religious institution and brought it into modern time.

The Birth of the Church in the New Land

In This Chapter

- ◆ The conquistadors meet the Aztecs
- ◆ Christianity in the Americas begins with an apparition
- ◆ A new race is born: the brown face of the Catholic Church
- ◆ Hispanic American Catholic heritage

In 1492, a Catholic Italian explorer named Christopher Columbus claimed America for Spain. Well, that's almost true. Actually, Columbus claimed America for both Spain and for God—in 1492, Spain's official religion was Catholicism. Thus, Catholicism in America and America itself share a common birthday.

Spain had just ended hundreds of years of war against Islam and was determined to solidify its kingdom. The Spanish believed in the unity of church and state, and a strong alliance had been forged between the crown and the cross. In this arrangement, the Church sanctioned the activities of the state, and the state promoted the authority of the Church. This unity, combined with a high degree of military expertise, became Spain's double-edged sword, and explorers carried this sword with them into the New World.

In this chapter, we'll take a look at the drama that was the establishment of Catholicism in the Western Hemisphere. We'll look at the religions that were already here and the effect that Catholic missionaries and soldiers had in the spread of Catholicism. This story involves missionaries, apparitions, exploitation, poverty, discrimination, and new beginnings. Indeed, a lot happened to Catholics and for Catholicism after October 12, 1492.

Colonization: Ready or Not, Here We Come!

We often think of the New World as New England first and then the rest of the United States. However, the term *New World* describes the continents of South America and North America, including Central America and the Caribbean. Historically, the story of Catholicism in America begins in Mexico. Catholicism was exported from Europe on the same ships that brought the conquistadors. Conquistadors were the soldiers sent by Spain to conquer the people of the New World and establish European rule, which included European religion.

The indigenous people of the New World were architects of beautiful cities. They built canals, temples, and observatories. They knew mathematics and had accurate tools by which they measured the movement of the stars. They had a high degree of technological, artistic, religious, and scientific development. What they did not have, however, were the sophisticated tools of war that the Spanish and Portuguese brought with them. The finely tuned European war machine eventually overwhelmed the indigenous people of the Americas.

It is impossible to separate the spread of the Catholic religion from the effects of exploration and colonialism on the native cultures. Franciscan missionaries accompanied the soldiers into the New World. The soldiers and the priests each had their own agenda: to find gold for Spain and to baptize converts for Catholicism. This era of European expansion lasted for hundreds of years. During this time, the ideas, economies, and religion of Europe were transplanted to the New World.

Europe Comes to Mexico

The first areas of the New World conquered by the conquistadors were the Caribbean islands, Mexico, and the countries of Central America. Critics of European conquest cite many incidences of inhumane treatment of the native people. Massacres and, in some cases, the complete annihilation of whole cultures occurred. The arrival of the

Europeans and the imposition of their civilization left many of the original inhabitants poor, hungry, and suffering from the many illnesses brought by the explorers.

For the most part, the Church turned its back on the atrocities of the armies, accepted the legitimacy of conquest, and apparently had no trouble combining the practice of slavery with the practice of Christianity. It seems as though the Church was satisfied with the belief in the "natural" superiority of the Europeans to these strange, apparently "barbaric" pagans.

At the same time, Mexican historians have noted that it was the missionaries who extended the few acts of kindness and who challenged military practices. It seemed that although the "big" Church was indifferent—and by its indifference was a partner in the atrocities—the "little" Church took a stand against the prevailing practices.

One of the ways the missionaries attempted to assist the people was through the establishment of missions. Missions, not unlike the monasteries described in Chapter 20, were like small villages containing schools, churches, infirmaries, and shelter. Native language, customs, and religious beliefs were replaced with European language, manners, and values. In theory, the missions provided safe havens and were an attempt to socialize the native people into European culture. Many missionaries made little effort to understand the beliefs of the native people, to learn their language, or to engage their culture in any positive way. However, some missionaries did learn the language of the people and even adopted many of their ways.

Saints Preserve Us

Blessed Bartolomé de las Casas (1484–1566)

Born in Seville, Spain, he was a missionary to Latin America and the first priest to be ordained in the New World (1512). He was a Dominican who worked to improve conditions of indigenous people and to end their enslavement. The king of Spain named him Protector of the Indians. Bartolomé's efforts influenced the pope to declare that American Indians were rational beings with souls and their lives and property should be protected. His efforts led to the "The New Laws" adopted to protect the native peoples in Spanish colonies. He was the first bishop of Chiapas, Mexico. A scholar and historian, he has been called "the father of anti-imperialism and anti-racism." He knew Columbus and edited his journal. He is called Blessed, a step on the way to sainthood.

The Beliefs of the Indigenous People

Europe met three main cultures in the New World: the Mayans, the Incas, and the Aztecs. According to historian and theologian Virgilio P. Elizondo in *La Morenita*, the Mayans had a well-developed culture and were great traders. The Incas had a closely-knit society that insured the equal redistribution of goods throughout the empire. The Aztecs were ruled by a monarch and had a hierarchical society. All three cultures were polytheistic, with both male and female deities, including an Earth Goddess and a Sun God. The concepts of an underworld and an afterlife were present, and human sacrifice featured in all, to a greater or lesser degree. The Mayan pantheon was particularly interesting; the dual nature of their deity represented the duality of life and death, with stories of death and resurrection figuring prominently.

In the indigenous religion, Ometéotl, the name of "Great Spirit," was both the Lord and Lady of all creation. Ometéotl's feminine aspect was known by many names. She was the mother of earth, mother of the gods, mother of wisdom, and the heart of earth.

The indigenous religions had many similarities to the Catholicism of Europe, which, after all, had roots in the practices of the old tribal peoples. For example, both the religion of the Indians and the religion of the missionaries had sacred rituals, a calendar of religious feasts, a sacred language in which to speak to their God(s), and a well-defined priesthood with vestments, temples, and processions. The Indians also expressed their religious beliefs through poetry, song, and symbol. In the Indian religion, Elizondo explains, "Nothing is unrelated." As we saw in the Old World, Mary intertwined with symbols of existing deities. The feminine aspect of the Indian's Great Spirit, Ometéotl, resurfaced in the coming of Christianity to the New World, as we will see later in this chapter.

Spanish America

Even though the Aztecs did not possess the essential tools of war that the Spanish had, such as horses, steel weapons, and guns, they could have been a formidable force. However, it only took six years for Spain to conquer this major civilization. Three factors contributed to the success of the Spanish leader Cortés and the demise of the Aztec leader, Montezuma.

Epiphanies
Hernán Cortés (1485–1547) was a Spanish explorer and conqueror of Mexico. In 1519, he was welcomed into the Aztec capital by Montezuma II (1466–1520), the last independent Aztec emperor. Montezuma mistook Cortés for the incarnation of the Aztec god Quetzalcòatl, whose return had been prophesied. Four years later, Montezuma was fatally wounded in a battle against the army of Cortés.

Many Indian tribes felt that the Aztecs' use of human sacrifice was a corruption of the religion of Quetzalcòatl, which was based on the dignity of life, simplicity, and prayer. Other groups of Indians especially disliked the Aztecs, who used brutal methods to hold their empire together, and they joined the conquistadors in a popular uprising against them.

A second factor giving Cortés an advantage over Montezuma was a religious one. In both the Mayan and Aztec cultures, the prophets had read many signs and had begun to prophesy the end of their civilization. The end had been predicted to occur in 1517 and 1519. In a very powerful coincidence (or perhaps as the fulfillment of their prophecy), Cortés landed on the Yucatan Peninsula in 1517 and arrived in their land in 1519.

A further prophecy given to the Indians by their priests predicted the return of Quetzalcòatl, a spiritual figure central to the religion of many Central American cultures. The prophecy foretold that he would come as a bearded white man out of the East. When the Indians saw Cortés, bearded and white, approaching from the east, many of them believed they were seeing the return of their god, and they began to follow him.

After Cortés took over the Aztec capital, the Franciscan priests met with the Aztec priests for a brief period of time. After the Catholic priests examined the religion of the native people with its blood sacrifices, they concluded that the religion should be destroyed. So Cortés and the soldiers not only brought down Montezuma, but they also plundered the temples. In their frenzy, they caused the massive destruction of all aspects of the Central American culture. Towns were destroyed, women were raped, and subjection and slavery were instituted. In the wake of the conquest, the oppression of the native people would last a long time.

The Incas and Mayans experienced similar fates. When the conquistadors arrived in modern-day Peru in 1532, they betrayed and murdered the Inca emperor, and were able to wipe out all resistance in just five years. The Mayan civilization was in an advanced state of decay by the time of the conquistadors, yet they still held out against the technologically superior Spanish for nearly 20 years (1527–1546), defeating them on several occasions. After they were overcome, both cultures suffered the same treatment the Aztecs had received.

Missions and Conversion

As we stated earlier, the relationship of the missionaries to the people tended to be different from that of the conquistadors. The missionaries' underlying belief was that all people should have access to God. They believed the God of Jesus was the true God. However, they respected the people and defended them against the soldiers whenever they could. The native people came to see that the missionaries were sincere, simple men who literally walked barefoot among them. The missions became "sanctuaries" against the soldiers, and the missionaries protested the military's brutal treatment to the civil authorities.

Frailes e Indigenas, a Representation of the Comparison of the Bible and the Aztec Codex (the Aztec's sacred writings) by Spanish and Aztec Holy Men. Federico Cantù 1959.

(Courtesy of CONACULTA— I.N.B.A.—PINACOTECA VIRREINAL, Mexico City)

However, in spite of an improved relationship between the missionaries and the natives and despite the missionaries' most zealous efforts, the missionaries still were unable to convert the Indian people to Catholicism in any significant numbers after 10 years. Broken and powerless, the native people weren't buying into the new religion!

A New People Emerges

Although the Church failed at first in its efforts to convert the masses, some remarkable developments changed the face of Catholicism in the New World forever. Many who have examined the details of these happenings believe that they were a new incarnation of Christ. Let's take a look at these amazing events.

The Brown Lady of Guadalupe

On December 12, 1531, a native peasant named Juan Diego Cuauhtlatoatzin had a religious experience that profoundly affected the development of the Catholic Church in the New World. It occurred as he hurried up Tepeyac Hill just outside of Mexico City on his way to Mass at a Franciscan mission. Suddenly, a vision of the Virgin Mary appeared before him. In his vision, she was a young Indian woman, brown and pregnant. As he saw her, she stood in front of the sun, but she did not obliterate its light. Rather, it glowed all around her, illuminating her. Her face radiated compassion, and she spoke to Juan, telling him she was the holy virgin mother of the true God. She spoke in Nahuatl, the Indian language of the conquered people. She told him that she wanted a temple to be built in her honor on the very spot on which she appeared. From the temple, she would help the people. She then sent Juan to the bishop to tell him of her request.

Juan went to the bishop with the message the Virgin gave him, but he was refused admission and sent away. He left feeling sad about failing in his important task. He went back to the hill where he had seen the Virgin, and to his surprise, she came to him again. Juan asked her to please find another more important man to deliver the message, because the bishop would not see him. The Virgin assured him that he, "the smallest of my children," was the one she wanted to bring this powerful message.

Juan went back to the bishop, and this time he was finally granted an audience. The bishop asked him many questions, and he told the story of the Virgin, right down to the smallest detail of his experience. The bishop did not believe him and asked for a sign that would prove it was the Virgin who had sent him.

Juan went back to the hill, where Mary appeared to him once again. He explained that the bishop wanted proof in the form of some kind of a sign. She told him to come back the next day and promised to give him proof. The next day Juan was detained due to the illness of his uncle. He was rushing to get the priest, and in his hurry, decided to not stop at the place where he had seen the apparition. As he passed by the place, Mary called out to him. He was embarrassed, but he stopped. She told him that his uncle would recover and that she would have a sign for him at the top of the hill. He went where she directed him to go and

Your Guardian Angel

Flowers and music often accompany apparitions of Mary. It is believed that these things are the supreme, most perfect means of communicating the presence of God. Likewise, honor is paid to Mary by bringing her flowers and through playing music, such as the many versions of the Ave Maria that have been composed for her.

was astounded by what he found. There were exquisite roses where they should not be growing at this time of year. She told him to gather the roses inside his cloak and to show no one but the bishop.

Juan went to the bishop, and at first his servants ignored him. Eventually, the aroma of the roses began to spread throughout the office, and they went to tell the bishop something unusual was happening. Juan was invited in, and the bishop asked to see what he was holding inside his cloak. As Juan opened his cloak, beautiful roses of many varieties and colors spilled out onto the floor. The bishop was amazed. But even more astonishing was the exact image of Juan's vision of the Virgin that had been imprinted on his cloak. The bishop fell to his knees in prayer.

Elizondo tells us the appearance of the Virgin Mary had profound significance for the Indian people. In discussing the symbolic meaning of the appearance, he goes on to say that perhaps most important was that the mother of God came to them not as a Spaniard but as one of their own. Her skin was brown, the exact color that the conquerors told them was "inferior." Unlike the typical European images of her, the Virgin was obviously an Indian woman of native Mexican heritage.

It was significant to the Indian people that the Lady stood in front of the sun. The Sun God was the main god in their pantheon. Her position in front of it showed that she came as a new representation of the divine, growing out of that which came before her. In this way, she connected the symbols of the old religion to the new religion of Christianity.

There were further symbols, as well. The Lady's dress was a pale red, the color of the blood sacrifices of the old religion and the color of the blood of the people that had been spilled by the conquerors. Red is also the color of the East, and it represented new beginnings to the people. Her blue mantle told them she was of royal descent, possibly a deity. The stars in her mantle echoed the prophecy given 10 years earlier that told of a comet signaling the end of their civilization. Perhaps most significant was the black maternity band stretched across her belly, in the center of which was the Aztec cross. The Lady was clearly offering her child to the New World. This vision would come to be understood as a new incarnation of Christ in the Americas.

Word of the Lady's appearance spread rapidly across the land. Crowds began to gather at the bishop's home to see the cloak that held her image. It was placed above the cathedral altar and later in the shrine that was built on the site of her appearance, as she had requested. The "Brown Lady" became the new symbol of the Mexican people and a new symbol for Catholicism as well.

The image of Our Lady of Guadalupe, as she is called, fused European Christianity with the spirit of the native people. Because the Indian people could see themselves in her, their own spirituality could translate into Christianity. To this day, the image remains brilliant in the Basilica in Mexico City, which was built on the site of the original appearance of the Lady. Millions of people visit this site every year.

As brilliant as the image hanging in the Basilica is, it lives even more intensely in the hearts of the people. The merging of symbols in this image—the Aztec Sun God and the God of the Christians in the womb of the Virgin Mary—transformed both Catholicism and the indigenous religions. For the Indians, the new religion of Catholicism was no longer seen as something foreign, but as something growing out of their own religion. They believed they had entered the next phase of their spiritual story. Rather than seeing the end of their civilization, they saw a new beginning. For Catholicism, this image offered an opportunity for renewal.

La Nueva Raza: The New Race

In the beginning, the Church opposed what they referred to as the Guadalupe incident, fearing that it was a ploy by the native people to reinstate their own religion. Although the grassroots Franciscan missionaries understood the importance of the devotion to Guadalupe, the Franciscan intelligentsia fought it vehemently. However, the archbishop reaffirmed his official support of the devotion. He had ordered the building of the basilica, and he was convinced of the importance of the image.

A picture of Our Lady of Guadalupe *as imprinted on the cloak of Juan Diego in 1531.*

(Norberto Mujica)

In the long run, the Church could not deny the remarkable effects the Lady of Guadalupe had on its mission to spread the word of Christ to the people. Unlike the first 10 years of the Spanish presence in the New World, the second 10 years were marked by the conversion of a phenomenal number of Indian people to Catholicism. It was as though the Mexican culture sprang back to life. Festivals, pilgrimages, and dances are still a huge part of Mexican Catholicism today. A mingling of cultures amongst the Spanish, the African slaves they brought over, and the indigenous Indians occurred. From this mixture, a new race of people was born called *La Nueva Raza*.

S'ter Says

La Nueva Raza, the new people, is a Spanish phrase that describes both the mixing of the Spanish, African, and Indian blood, spirituality, and culture, and the resulting new culture that was produced.

The "official" Church waited many years before ruling on the miraculous nature of Juan Diego's vision. In 1754, a little over 200 years after the vision, the pope knelt in front of a painting of the Virgin and declared Our Lady of Guadalupe the patroness of Mexico. He instituted a Mass and prayers in her honor. What this meant to the people, in effect, was that the Virgin's appearance had become "dogma." Pope John Paul II canonized St. Juan Diego on July 31, 2002. His feast day is December 9.

Saints Preserve Us

St. Martin de Porres, November 3, Patron of Hairdressers

St. Martin de Porres (1579–1639) was born in Lima, Peru, the son of a Spanish gentleman and a freed African slave. He is one of the few saints of color recognized by the Church. At age 15, de Porres became a Dominican lay brother and became known for his rugged humility. God worked extraordinary wonders through him. He spent his life in service to his community both as a barber and a farm laborer. It was said that God rewarded Martin for his humility with the gift of great spiritual wisdom. Bishops sought his advice, and he resolved many theological problems of the day. St. Martin de Porres became the patron saint of hairdressers because hairdressing was one of the duties he performed for his brothers in the friary to which he belonged.

Cultural Contributions to Today's Catholicism

Firmly planted in the New World, the Spanish and Portuguese culture flowered, as did the Church. The scope of the lands these countries would come to control was immense. It stretched thousands of miles from the tip of the South American continent, across Central America, the major islands of the Caribbean, and from Florida across the South and Southwest to the western shores of California. The heritage of these Catholic lands continues to exist today in place names such as St. Augustine, San Antonio, Santa Fe, and San Francisco.

This heritage goes beyond names on a map. Today, Catholicism exists in large numbers among Hispanic Americans, who are estimated to actually comprise nearly 50 percent of the total United States Catholic population. As the number of Latin American Catholics increases, the face of Catholicism in the United States is changing. The Catholic Church, once dominated by Europeans, struggles today to understand the hearts and minds of these "new people." Communal by nature, and still remembering the poetic-symbolic religion of their ancestors, these people embody a spiritual aspect of religion that offers balance to the more "rational" side of the European Catholic Church.

According to the official 2000 Census, there are 35.3 million Hispanics (or Latinos, as they are termed in the census) in the United States, or 12.5 percent of the total population. They are 37.5 percent of the U.S. population under age 18. Since 1990, the nation's Hispanic population has increased 58 percent, up from a total of 22.4 million in 1990. In 2020, the Hispanic population will be approximately 52.7 million. In 2040, this number will grow to about 80.2 million. In 2050, with a population of approximately 96.5 million, Hispanic Americans are projected to constitute 24.5 percent of the U.S. population, one out of every four U.S. Americans.

The Hispanic people have a strong sense of family and family values. They bring particular religious and cultural practices to the United States Catholic Church in the form of *liturgical rituals* that strengthen family values.

The *Posadas* is a ritual enacted at Christmas in many Mexican American parishes in Texas, Chicago, California, New Mexico, and elsewhere. It involves a house-to-house procession in which a couple, playing the role of the two Galileans, Joseph and Mary, walk through the streets, knocking on doors seeking shelter. Over and over again, they are refused. After the young couple has been rejected a number of times, someone finally listens to what they are saying and offers them a place to stay. As they are received into a home, there is much joy and celebration.

S'ter Says

Posada, the Spanish word for "shelter," is used to describe a house-to-house procession at Christmas time in which the drama of the Galilean couple Joseph and Mary is enacted.

The two key themes of this Gospel re-enactment are the rejection of the poor and the joy that comes to those who open their home and heart to the ones whom others have rejected. In a remarkable connection, this faith ritual relates beautifully to the current Mexican American experience. Risking their lives by crossing the border to find work to feed their children, Mexicans meet rejection. Like the holy couple who is carrying the child Jesus, the hope of the future, with them, they do not give up.

As in the ritual enactment of the Posada, the second important part of this real-life Mexican Posada involves a request to the people of the United States to open the border, share their wealth, and receive the gift of joy that is the completion of the ritual.

In this chapter, you've met some of the indigenous cultures that were living in the area now known as Central America and Mexico and have heard how Catholicism arrived in the New World. In the next chapter, you'll see how Catholicism spread in the North through European immigration.

The Least You Need to Know

- ◆ There were well-developed cultures on the American continent when the Europeans arrived.

- ◆ The colonization and evangelization of North America and South America was accomplished with pain, death, and a great loss of native culture.

- ◆ The appearance of Our Lady of Guadalupe transformed the European assault into a new revelation of the face of God.

- ◆ Hispanic American Catholics play an important role in shaping the new face of the Catholic Church in the United States.

Chapter 23

Catholics Earn Their Citizenship

In This Chapter

- ◆ Catholics and the American Revolution
- ◆ Five million Irish sail into U.S. ports
- ◆ Germans keep their language and faith
- ◆ The Catholic Church becomes American
- ◆ Crises of faith and citizenship

In this chapter, you'll see what happened north of the border in the New World. At first, the 13 colonies of New England barely noticed Catholicism. Soon, however, following an enormous wave of immigration, Catholics became major players in the construction and expansion of the United States. The reaction of the established Protestants to the immigrants was not altogether favorable, and Catholics suffered a great deal of prejudice and discrimination. They reacted by building a fortress Church and developing a strong Catholic identity of separatism.

As time went on, their prosperity in the middle of the twentieth century allowed them to become part of mainstream America and to become champions of democracy. The reward was the election of one of their own, John F. Kennedy, as president. Before they were able to bask in this new glory, however, his assassination, the Vietnam War, the cultural revolution, and Vatican II's redefinition of Catholicism put American Catholics in a tailspin. This chapter explores these developments.

Catholicism and Colonial America: There Goes the Neighborhood!

Catholicism's journey took a very different route north of Mexico. The first English colonists were Protestant: Puritan, Quaker, and Anglican, not Catholic. At the time of the American Revolution in 1776, the proportion of Catholics in the British Colonies was estimated to be less than 1 percent. Slowly but surely, however, Catholicism entered mainstream American life.

Breaking Into the Protestant Club

The colonial adventure began in 1607, when a small number of colonists, mostly from England, settled in the new land. They had endured the difficult migration across the Atlantic and survived the challenges of the first years of homesteading. Houses had been built, and the village church had been roofed. The essentials for life in the New World had been secured.

Put yourself into this picture and imagine that you and your family were living there. The hard hours you had spent in your small candle-making business in downtown Boston had begun to turn a profit. Life was good. The promise of America stretched out in front of you like the vast sea you had recently crossed, and it was filled with hope and expectation.

You were part of a group of Protestant reformers who left Europe to come to a new land free of the trappings of the Old World religion. You saw this land as a "New Jerusalem," "A City on the Hill" that would be both politically and religiously free from the Old World and its Roman ways. Here was the definitive break from Rome, both the state and the Church.

All too soon, word began to reach you and the other pioneers that the Catholic colonists from Spain were advancing northward, stretching out across the plains. So much for keeping the Puritan New World to yourselves!

At the same time, another situation was all too rapidly becoming apparent in the marketplace of Boston and other ports along the Eastern seaboard: a marked increase in the number of French Catholic traders selling furs. All over the coast of eastern Canada and northern Maine, French trappers and their families were arriving, bringing their version of the Catholic story with them. They brought Catholicism to the northern regions where they trapped and moved down the trade route of the Mississippi River to the port of New Orleans. Like the Spanish in the southern part of the continent, the French intermarried with the native population, sowing their culture and religion into the native soil.

Saints Preserve Us

Blessed Kateri Tekakwitha

Kateri Tekakwitha (1656–1680) had a Christian Algonquin mother, and her father was a chief of the Mohawk. She converted to Catholicism and was rejected by her people. She ran away to the Christian Indian village of Sault Ste. Marie, near Montreal. She dedicated herself to Christ and led a life of holiness and austerity. She died at the young age of 24. She was known as "Lily of the Mohawk," and the faithful have credited her with many miracles. She has been beatified, meaning that she is called "blessed," which is a step in the process of becoming a saint.

No doubt, the British Protestant population felt squeezed between these two sets of unwanted "invaders," the Spanish and the French. In this unfriendly and somewhat hostile environment, Catholicism, for the most part, was met with prejudice, fear, persecution, and eventually laws that discriminated against it. Indeed, discrimination and prejudice against Catholics would have a long history in Britain's original colonies and throughout much of modern American history. The Protestants were there first, and the Catholics were forced to earn mere acceptance, to say nothing of respect. For instance, early copies of *The New England Primer* were filled with images that would persuade any young reader that the Catholic Church was the Devil incarnate.

Catholics and the Revolution

Back home in England, in an effort to civilize the Irish and rid the country of its popish religion, Britain had strengthened its Penal Laws. These laws discriminated against Catholics, even to the point of forbidding the celebration of the Mass. England extended these laws to its colonies in America. Catholics, although few in number, were forbidden to own land or hold office in the New World. Without land, they could not build churches or schools. In spite of the prejudice they faced in colonial America, however, Catholics joined their Protestant neighbors in the revolution.

They had a specific interest in it because the British penal laws threatened their religious survival. They became fervent supporters of independence.

Once the Revolutionary War was won and the U.S. Constitution ratified in 1789, the Catholic Church had the freedom to officially establish its first diocese, which it did in Baltimore, Maryland. The Catholic Church in America then elected its first bishop, John Carroll.

As Catholics began to own land and start businesses, they came to be regarded as good citizens, and as a result, their Protestant neighbors more readily accepted them. For the first time, Catholics felt welcome in the new United States. All that would change, however, during the nineteenth century, when Catholic immigrants began to arrive in record numbers, upsetting what had been a delicate balance among the new country's citizens.

Coming in Droves: The Immigrant Experience

The words *foreign, Catholic,* and *poor* became synonymous in the minds of the original Protestant settlers. The relationship of "native" Protestants to "foreign" Catholics entering the United States in the nineteenth century was similar to the way our body tries to fight against what it perceives as disease: by rejecting foreign matter that enters it.

The story of immigration is told in the population statistics. During the century after 1790, the Catholic population grew from a mere 1.1 percent to a significant 14.4 percent by mid-century. Most of these immigrants were Irish or German, and they tended to congregate in the cities. The number of foreign-born Catholics in major U.S. cities was staggering:

- Philadelphia: 30 percent
- New York: 49 percent
- Chicago: 50 percent
- St. Louis: 60 percent

Catholic Hispanics, French, Irish, and Germans immigrated to the United States in significant numbers during the first part of the 1800s. Italy, Poland, and Eastern Europe sent even more Catholics at the end of the 1800s and the beginning of the 1900s. More than two million Italians and more than a million Poles and Eastern Europeans came to the United States between 1900 and 1925. These immigrants formed ethnic neighborhoods and parishes often staffed by the clergy and nuns who accompanied them in their migration. They built schools, convents, hospitals, and orphanages. These "ethnic" neighborhoods still characterize cities such as Chicago, St. Louis, and New York.

Due to American farmers' need for harvesters between the 1920s and 1960s, Mexican Catholics increased their migration to the United States. In the 1970s and 1980s, Catholic refugees from Vietnam, Cambodia, Laos, Guatemala, El Salvador, Nicaragua, and Haiti came to the United States as a result of political unrest in their home countries.

Potatoes, Poverty, and Discrimination: The Irish in America

The Irish potato crop failures in the late 1840s sent huge waves of Irish, most of whom were Catholic, to the United States. In a relatively short period of time, Ireland's population was reduced by half. Thousands died of starvation at home, and many more died in the "coffin" ships that brought them to America. More than five million Irish emigrated to the United States in the nineteenth century.

If you were living in New York in 1840, imagine how you would react to the dirty, disease-ridden ships as they pulled into the harbor and disgorged their cargo of impoverished, illiterate, and often desperate people onto the streets in staggering numbers. Barely able to hold on to their lives, much less a job, these immigrants created an incredible strain on the existing population, posing a real threat to health, social stability, and the economy. The reaction of the citizens to this overwhelming situation was unfortunate but predictable.

Political cartoons, rampant discrimination, derogatory literature, and even physical assaults occurred. By the end of the century, acts of political and economic discrimination were prevalent. For a time in Philadelphia, the bishop had to close all the Catholic churches, dispensing people from their Sunday obligation in order to protect his flock from physical harm. Protestants were attacking and burning the churches in reaction to the Catholics' challenge of the use of the Protestant version of the Bible in the city's schools.

Epiphanies

After the Protestant Reformation, English-speaking Protestants used their translation of the Bible known as the King James version. As we discussed in Chapter 7, "the Protestant Bible differs somewhat from the Catholic version. Public schools of the day used the King James Bible and prayed Protestant prayers, sang Protestant hymns, and required attendance at Protestant services. This situation made Catholic children feel like second-class citizens.

In New York, the bishop armed his Catholic flocks with stones and brickbats for the first and some of the most severe urban riots the United States has ever experienced. The sheer numbers of Irish Catholic immigrants, their poverty, and the perceived threat to the Protestant Bible laid the groundwork for a century of prejudice.

A national political party, popularly known as the Know-Nothings, was formed in the middle of the nineteenth century to oppose Catholics and other foreigners. Their standard-bearer, Millard Fillmore, was a former president of the United States. Several state legislatures had a significant number of Know-Nothing representatives who passed many laws discriminating against Catholics and their schools. One of the most notorious of these laws was the Convent Inspection law. This law required nuns to open their doors to state-appointed committees to ensure that no woman was being held there against her will. During the immigration of Italians and Poles at the turn of the century, the infamous Ku Klux Klan widened its scope of bigotry to include Catholics.

Despite the difficult situations the Irish faced in settling in their new home, they survived and strongly influenced the character of the Catholic Church in America, not only by their sheer numbers, but also by their indomitable spirit. They brought a love of family, a sense of humor, and a deep respect for the clergy. Since they lacked other political representation, they elevated their priests to the status of the old tribal chieftains of their beloved homeland.

Sauerkraut and Sausages: Germanic Education and Liturgy

German Catholics also had a strong influence on the course of Catholic history and culture in the United States. At one time, the German immigrants instituted a movement whose purpose was to make German a second language in the public schools. When this movement failed, they sought an alternative. They began to promote and champion what was then only a small movement— the Catholic school system—to preserve their language and culture.

An abiding question for the Church during this time of growth and adjustment was just how much it should participate in the dominant Protestant American culture. There were those Catholics who favored assimilation and those who fought to keep the Church separate. The hierarchy spent much time in its national meetings debating the "school question," that is, whether or not Catholic children could be educated in the "common" or public schools. By the end of the century the question was decided at the Third Council of Baltimore (1884). With German agitation and support from Rome, the council decided that every parish had to build a Catholic school and that parents had to send their children to the Catholic school under the sanction of mortal sin.

As the twentieth century began, the only question Catholics had about their schools was how much better than the public schools they could make them. As Garry Wills, popular Catholic author, points out in *Bare Ruined Choirs* (Doubleday, 1972), the decision of Baltimore III had many implications: It meant that a poor body of immigrants would make great sacrifices to build their own school system, and with no support from the taxes they paid to build the public school system. It meant that a massive work force of religious nuns and brothers would be recruited and trained, not to be contemplatives or instructors of the upper classes as in Europe, but to be teachers of all classes. It meant that nuns would have as much if not more formative influence on young Catholics as priests did. It meant that U.S. Catholicism would be child-centered with a feminine piety. And, most significantly, it meant that the Church would concentrate most of its resources on this system.

For the first two thirds of the twentieth century, Catholicism could be described as "the Church that was a School." The Irish-dominated hierarchy granted an important concession to German immigrants and to other non–English-speaking Catholics who longed to hear the sound of their faith expressed through the prayers and hymns of their mother tongue. They permitted the establishment of national parishes, which are parishes based on ethnicity rather than geography. Germans and other non–English-speaking Catholics were able to keep their language both in the schools and in the churches.

If you were a German-speaking Catholic, you were allowed to become a member of a German-speaking parish, which might lie outside the normal parish boundaries for your home. By 1912, there were more than 1,600 national parishes: 346 German, 336 Polish, and 214 Italian. Today, as a remnant of this policy, you might find two Catholic churches standing side by side: one that served an English-speaking Catholic congregation and the other that served a German-speaking one.

Another contribution made by the German Catholics were the monasteries in the heartland of Indiana and Minnesota, where the vibrant Catholic liturgy was kept alive in this country. The German tradition of monasteries goes back over 1,000 years to the time of St. Boniface, as we saw in Chapter 20.

S'ter Says

A **national parish** is a parish that is not based on geographic boundaries, but which belongs to an ethnic group. Such parishes, where English was the second language, were common in the United States during the years of immigration.

Poles: Pierogi, and Patriotism

Large-scale Polish immigration to the United States began in the 1870s. The early settlers attended Irish or German Catholic parishes until they could found their own. Soon, however, they established lay committees to raise funds and lobby the bishops to provide Polish parishes and schools. With the parish came other Polish organizations providing insurance for illness and death, promoting Polish religious observances, and sponsoring youth activities.

Polish financial contributions were among the highest in the U.S. Catholic Church. In 1870, there were about 15 Polish parishes; by 1930, there were more than 800. By 1920, there were more than 400 Polish American Catholic schools, and more than two thirds of the Polish American children attended them. The role of the Polish priest was that of the undisputed religious and civic leader. He was spiritual leader, temporal leader, teacher, legal counselor, business advisor, and mediator between the immigrant and American society. In the parish schools, classes were generally taught in Polish, and English was taught as a foreign language.

U.S. Church authorities exercised strict control over national parishes. They demanded title to all property and the authority to assign priests. This denial of lay participation in decision-making conflicted with the Polish experience of Catholicism back home. It also conflicted with their dreams of American democracy. A foreign, mainly Irish, clergy and hierarchy controlled the most important Polish institution in America, the parish church. Despite Polish pleas for the appointment of Polish American bishops, it was not until 1908 that the first Pole was ordained bishop. He was an assistant to the archbishop in Chicago.

By 1904, however, several Polish priests and parishioners had seceded from the Catholic Church and formed what later would become the Polish National Catholic Church, which does not accept the pope as its head. This church immediately began to celebrate Mass in Polish, added "the word of God, heard and preached" as a sacrament, and permitted priests to marry. Currently, this Church has four dioceses in North America with more than 150 parishes. This was the first schism, or independent movement, in the U.S. Catholic experience. Presently, talks between the Polish Catholic Church and the Roman Catholic Church are underway in the hope of possible reunification.

Although the overwhelming number of Polish American priests and parishioners remained members of the Catholic Church, Poles, perhaps more than any other ethnic group, saw the mission of the Church as the transmission of a Polish identity to an increasingly Americanized and secularized group of Polish immigrants. In 1980, only 38 percent of German national parishes were still functioning, but more than

75 percent of Polish national churches were. Today, Poles are the fastest-growing immigrant group in Chicago and continue to swell the ranks of U.S. Catholicism.

Italians: Pasta and *Festa*

In 1870, Rome, the last vestige of the Papal States, fell, and the pope retaliated by forbidding Italian Catholics to participate in national politics. The Vatican denied recognition to the kingdom of Italy. With the accompanying political, social, and economic unrest, millions of Italians left their homeland. By 1900, more than 100,000 Italians were migrating annually to the United States. Four fifths of these immigrants were from southern Italy, and 75 percent of those who came were working-age males. For the most part, these immigrants were poor and illiterate.

Saints Preserve Us

St. Frances Xavier Cabrini, November 13, Patron of Immigrants

Born into a farming family in Italy, the youngest of 13 children, St. Frances Xavier Cabrini (1850–1917) founded a religious order called the Missionary Sisters of the Sacred Heart of Jesus. She sailed to New York with Italian immigrants in 1898 and opened Columbus Hospital there. She became a citizen in 1909 and took her works of mercy to all parts of the United States. At the time of her death, 3,000 of her nuns lived in 70 convents. She founded more than 50 hospitals, schools, and orphanages. She is the first American citizen to be canonized a saint, and she is the patron of immigrants.

The Irish-dominated Church in the United States saw its task was to turn these Italian immigrants into church-going, law-abiding Catholics who would demonstrate to U.S. Protestants the compatibility of Catholicism and American patriotism. Their aim was assimilation. Few Italian priests migrated to the United States, and those who did were generally not accepted by the American bishops, who regarded them as incompetent and avaricious. It wasn't until 1954 that the first Sicilian-born bishop was ordained in the United States. It was mainly the Italian religious orders, such as the Franciscans and the Scalabrini Fathers

Your Guardian Angel

You can attend the annual **festas,** commemorations of the patron saints of particular villages or areas of Italy, in many United States cities. They are popular, citywide celebrations. Perhaps the best known is the feast of San Gennaro in New York, which runs for 11 days in September and attracts over three million visitors.

(a special order that was founded in 1887 to minister to immigrants), who served as missionaries to the Italian Americans.

The assimilation goals of the U.S. Catholic Church succeeded with the Italian immigrants. They stand in marked contrast to Italians in Italy, who are not regular churchgoers and are at times downright anticlerical. They take great pride in the many Italian American Catholic men and women who serve the United States as mayors, governors, cabinet members, and members of the Supreme Court.

African Americans: Soul Food, Clapping, and Justice

Catholicism is the largest religion in the world for people of African descent, and there are more than 200 million black Catholics worldwide. However, Catholics make up less than 6 percent of the African American population. Presently, there are 2.3 million black Catholics in the United States. The history of African American Catholics goes back to the oldest Spanish settlement in the United States: St. Augustine, Florida in 1565.

The Church's relationship with its African American members has not always been ideal. The Church's position on slavery was disturbingly conservative and cautious. For example, the bishop of Philadelphia during the time just before the Civil War stated that he regretted the consequences of slavery, but at the same time, he cautioned his church members that the public law must be obeyed. Catholic landowners, including priests, owned black slaves as early as the 1600s. The practice was not widespread, but it continued until the end of the Civil War. On the positive side, the pope sent missionaries to the United States from England to open the schools and seminaries to black membership. Also, some bishops, like the bishop of Cincinnati, used his religious authority to call for emancipation.

> **CAUTION**
>
> **For Heaven's Sake!**
>
> You're making a mistake if you think that Africa hasn't played an important role in the Catholic Church from its beginning. Sts. Augustine, his mother Monica, Benedict the Moor, Moses the Black, Cyril of Alexandria, and Simon of Cyrene who helped Jesus carry his cross were all African. So were three popes!

By the late 1800s, the black Catholic population was approximately 200,000 out of a total black population of 7 million. There were 20 churches, each with its own primary school, and 65 other schools. The schools were staffed primarily by two orders: the Oblate Sisters of Providence in Baltimore, Maryland, founded by Elizabeth Lange, and the Sisters of the Holy Family in New Orleans, Louisiana, led by Henriette Delille and Juliette Gaudin.

Father Patrick Healy, Ph.D., born in 1830 of an Irish father and a mother who was an emancipated slave, was the first freeborn African American priest. This remarkable man became the president of Georgetown University in 1868. Born in 1854, Father Augustine Tolton was the first slave-born priest in the United States. Because no American seminary would permit his entrance, he was educated and ordained in Rome. Upon completion of his studies, he was supposed to be sent to work in Africa. In a surprise decision and possibly to test the United State's claims of being an enlightened nation, Rome sent him to America. He served in a parish in Quincy, Illinois, and later in Chicago.

Although still underrepresented in the Church leadership, today African Americans are visible in all areas of the U.S. Catholic Church. The highest concentration of African American Catholics is in Louisiana and in the Baltimore-Washington, D.C. area. African American Catholics make up 15 percent of the Louisiana Catholic population, 13 percent of Maryland's Catholic population, and 7 percent of New York's Catholic population. There are 250 priests and 13 African American bishops in the United States, one of whom is the president of the U.S. Conference of Bishops.

Their presence, and the presence of many other black leaders (deacons, sisters, seminary professors, and heads of religious communities), has created many positive results. Their lively liturgies are a joyful expression of the African soul. Their commitment to justice is a living example of the Church "walking its talk" on a variety of social issues. The emergence of an effective cadre of Black Catholic scholars has resulted in the following contributions:

♦ Insights about black culture and black theology have been introduced into mainstream scholarship.

♦ Ministry to black parishes and social programs has increased.

♦ Infusion of spirit-filled liturgy to the rest of the Catholic Church.

♦ A new emphasis on black lay leadership and spiritual formation has developed.

♦ Strides to end racism in the Church have been made.

As a result of the efforts of these black scholars and others working for racial equality in the Church, a hymnal entitled *Guide Me: The African American Catholic Hymnal* (G.I.A. Publications) was published in 1987. That same year, the first black Catholic congress in the twentieth century was held in Washington, D.C. These have become annual events. Shortly afterward, Catholic bishops issued a pastoral letter on racism called "Brothers and Sisters to Us," and the black bishops issued their own pastoral letter on evangelization, "What We Have Seen and Heard."

Perhaps the ministry valued most by the African Americans is the Church's commitment to inner-city Catholic schools. Big-city dioceses heavily subsidize education for African Americans who make great sacrifices to enroll their children. Religious affiliation is not a requirement of acceptance into these schools. In fact, the number of Catholics enrolled is less than 30 percent in some schools. Nor are these schools seen as a means of recruiting new Catholics. They are a perfect fit between a Catholic Church that values good teaching and African Americans who value good education.

Infallibility in the Land of Liberty

The nineteenth century, the intense time of Catholic immigration, was a difficult time for the Church in Europe. The monarchies of Europe began to fall as governments transformed into modern nations. The mutually beneficial relationship between church and state, which Constantine had formed with the Church way back in the 300s, was long gone. The key question for the Church became how to exist in the age of democracy and nation-states. What would its new relationship to the world be?

S'ter Says

Modernism was a heresy condemned by the pope in 1907. The term refers to the Church's condemnation of modern scientific thinking that said truth changed. The Church believed truth was eternal and unchanging. Up until 1967, Catholic priests were required to take an oath against modernism.

Since the Council of Trent in the mid-1500s, the Church had lost more and more of its influence over the world of politics. It went its way, and the culture went another. The world looked to science rather than religion for truth. The Church reacted by dismissing the progress of the world. It wouldn't accept new ideas, scientific developments, or the fact that religious truth and doctrine evolve. It was protesting against what it called *modernism*. Modernism is a term used to describe the fact that people had turned to the world rather than religion to solve their problems; they became self-sufficient.

The Church took a strong stance against the modern culture, especially on any of the emerging notions of religious freedom. It developed a defensive attitude. This stance came to a head in a declaration of papal infallibility in 1870 at the First Vatican Council. This teaching said that the pope has the special protection of the Holy Spirit and cannot err when he officially defines a doctrine of the faith or moral behavior.

In sharp contrast to Rome, many of the U.S. bishops opposed the definition of papal infallibility. For more than 100 years, they had carefully woven relations with their Protestant neighbors to prove that Catholicism was not contrary to democracy. The absolute authority of papal infallibility would only lend fodder to the feelings of anti-Catholicism that were just beginning to tone down.

Due to the threat of war in Europe at that time, several bishops sailed home early from the council and did not register their votes before leaving, so the true extent of disagreement may never be known. Fifty-five bishops signed a letter to the pope saying they would absent themselves in order to avoid voting against it. However, two negative votes were cast. One was by the bishop of Little Rock in the United States. The headlines at home read: "Little Rock Attacks Big Rock." "Rock" refers to Jesus' statement to Peter, "Upon this Rock, I will build my church," which is the Scripture passage on which Catholics based the supremacy of the pope.

The doctrine of infallibility gave the Church a feeling of internal security and perhaps the sense of regaining some of its lost power. However, it further alienated the Church from a secular world that generally found such a position totally untenable. As Catholicism came kicking and screaming into the twentieth century, the Church became trapped by its own absolutism. The transforming event of Vatican II was yet to come. It would teach the Church to embrace the world's development and accept change as a fact.

> **CAUTION**
>
> ### For Heaven's Sake!
>
> Don't think sheer numbers created a Catholic culture in the United States. Although by 1850 the Catholic Church was the largest single denomination, the character of the culture in the United States remained Protestant well into the twentieth century.

A Checkered Church Solidifies

If you look at a penny, you'll find imprinted upon it the Latin phrase *E Pluribus Unum*, "one people out of many," which became the motto of the United States. If the Catholic Church in the United States minted its own pennies, they might read *E Pluribus Unum Catholicum*: "one Catholic Church out of many people." The U.S. Catholic Church faced a major challenge, namely to maintain an essential Catholic identity characterized by oneness under Rome within a culturally diverse America. This Catholic identity was fed by a diversity of ethnic customs, with an emphasis on emotional practices and devotions of the faith, such as celebrations of Mary, feast days of saints, novenas, public processions, and benedictions. Immigrant Catholicism was characterized by dependency on clerical authority and strong ties to Rome.

The Catholics' first experience in the United States was a positive one. In the American Revolution, they won their freedom of religion and the right to own property. They ended the nineteenth century in great numbers, but were rejected by the larger society. The Catholic reaction was to develop a siege mentality and form a cultural fortress within the cities. The Irish had broken the ground of immigration in the new country. The next waves of immigrants, the Germans, the Italians, the Poles, and the Eastern Europeans, benefited from this sod busting, but they also inherited the anti-Catholicism that was so strong in this century.

Immigrant Catholics Dig In

By the 1920s, Catholics made up about 20 percent of the U.S. population, and this figure remains about the same today. In the first half of the century, the Church focused on securing its internal structures, unifying its practices, and firming up its relationship with its new home, the United States.

Catholics, persecuted in the nineteenth century, became champions of what America could become and what a Catholic immigrant could become in America in the twentieth. Catholics and Protestants had resolved many of their differences, having bonded in the foxholes of World War I. These Protestants and Catholics, who might have had differences at home, found themselves fighting side by side. Catholics, whose patriotism had been doubted, proved by their action in war that they were true Americans. The war had the effect of leveling differences between Americans.

Protestants, still the majority, began to open economic and social doors to Catholics, and Catholics saw in America the best chance for the Church since Jesus told the apostles to go out and baptize all nations. It seemed that the seeds that Jesus planted were coming to fruition in the United States.

> **Epiphanies**
>
> Al Smith, a Democrat, was governor of New York. In 1928, he became the first Catholic to run for the presidency. He lost to Herbert Hoover in a campaign marred by anti-Catholic bigotry. The slogan "A vote for Smith is a vote for the Pope" was frequently heard. Born on the Lower East Side of Manhattan, Smith used to joke that he graduated from the Fulton Fish Market. Smith made a commitment to religious liberty and freedom of conscience.

Many of the immigrants who came to the United States after World War I came from a Europe that was birthing communism. The Church found itself face-to-face with an ideology that rejected all religion. For almost 400 years, the Catholic Church had withdrawn from the contemporary world, distancing itself from the needs of the common people. Communism rose to fill that void, and it had no use for God or the Catholic Church. In the first papal letter in modern time dealing directly with social issues, *Rerum Novarum* (the opening words and the title), Pope Leo XIII in 1891 called the Church back to the needs of the people. He proposed a Catholic stand on the conditions of the working class that contrasted with communism.

Catholic Prosperity

Although Catholicism prospered, it still remained separate from the mainstream. Instead of merging into the public American world, Catholics built a parallel world of Catholic-run hospitals, orphanages, and welfare agencies that provided food, heating fuel, clothing, and money. There were homes for the aged, schools from elementary through university levels, professional organizations, social charities, and even Catholic cemeteries.

During the 1950s, a Catholic building boom exploded across America. Catholic churches and schools filled the land from Maine to California. In numbers never before experienced in the history of the Church, Catholic parents sent their sons and daughters into religious service as priests, sisters, and brothers. They became the work force that built the strong identity of the Catholic tribe in the United States. Upward of 70 percent of Catholics attended church every Sunday, and one half of all Catholic children were educated in parish schools. In the evenings, families across the country gathered around their radios to listen to Father Peyton broadcast the family Rosary. Bishop Sheen delivered his weekly TV message to millions of Catholics (and Protestants). The Catholic Church was comfortable in the 1950s.

Every Catholic classroom in the United States displayed an American flag, a picture of the president of the United States, and a picture of the pope. Class began with prayers, followed by the Pledge of Allegiance and four verses of "My Country 'Tis of Thee." Students were taught that good citizenship was an important part of good Catholicism. There was an optimistic spirit and a sense of well-being that went with being Catholic in America. An entire generation had climbed out of the poverty of the immigrant years and could now put money away for their children to attend Catholic colleges. The spirit of the day seemed to say to Catholics that they surely were in the right place at the right time. It fostered their belief that they were citizens of the one true country and that they held the one true faith.

The Loss of Innocence

In 1960, in a history-making event, John Fitzgerald Kennedy became the first Catholic elected to the highest office in the land, which further fanned the embers of Catholic faith. The odds of Kennedy, a Catholic, winning the nomination and then the presidency of the United States were poor to say the least. Anytime a Catholic aspired to public office, anti-Catholicism showed itself to be lurking just below the surface. Although Catholics had certainly achieved a respectable number in the population, they could not elect a president by themselves. Any candidate would have to win a considerable Protestant vote to make that happen. Protestants feared that a Catholic's allegiance to the Church in Rome superceded allegiance to the United States Constitution.

In a famous speech to the Houston Ministerial Alliance, candidate Kennedy convinced his audience that this fear was unfounded. Although elected by the most narrow of margins, it showed the world that Catholics had "made it," even if just barely. Kennedy was bright, attractive, and promised Americans that life would be good. In so doing, he redeemed a generation of older Catholics from the humiliation of Al Smith's brutal defeat in 1928.

Bubbling beneath the surface of society, however, were stewpots of unrest. As those pots began to boil over in the decade of the 60s, the certainty of the 1950s gave way to questions for all Americans. This experience would ultimately affect Catholics as well. The changes during this decade challenged accepted notions of what it meant to be a United States citizen and what it meant to be a Catholic.

Kennedy's assassination after just 1,000 days in office—along with the assassinations of other political and religious leaders, including Martin Luther King Jr., Robert Kennedy, and Malcolm X, in the years that followed—abruptly ended the innocence of the time and set the nation spinning. For Catholics, it was an especially tough time. The changes in society seemed to go against every tenet of their faith: the use of drugs, protest against the government's involvement in Southeast Asia, the sexual revolution, the advent of the birth control pill, and the possible legalization of abortion. The expectation that they would be the new carriers of America's promise to become the "New Jerusalem" was being sorely tested.

Catholics Come of Age

Jack Kennedy broke through the religious barrier and seemed to free Catholics' access to higher office. If you examine the lists of the candidates at the top of the ticket during the 60s, 70s, and 80s, it seems that it was almost a requirement to include a Catholic on the ticket: Tom Eagleton, Sargent Shriver, James Miller, and Geraldine Ferraro are all examples of prominent Catholic candidates. The numbers of Catholics in the president's cabinet continued to grow, and their leadership in Congress increased.

Social research showed that Catholics were among the best-educated people in the United States. They were capturing major executive positions in business, and they were moving to the suburbs. What had been a poor, immigrant, illiterate, disempowered minority who had built a Catholic fortress was now truly becoming an organization of the first citizens of the land.

In the 1960s, however, Catholics received a double whammy. Vatican II was called to take a serious look at the definition of the Church. It created questions in the minds of many Catholics. In so doing, it knocked out a major pillar they had come to rely on: the notion that their Church was the perfect, one true Church. In the political arena, anti-war and anti-patriotic demonstrations in the form of burning flags and draft cards knocked out the other pillar that held up many citizens: the idea that the United States was the perfect state. These two blows shook the U.S. Catholic identity. The 40 years since the crumbling of these pillars has been a tough time of reconstruction.

Movin' on Up

For Catholics, moving into the suburbs meant moving away from the tight-knit, ethnic neighborhood parishes. In the suburbs, Catholics lived side by side with "other" Americans. Often, the parochial school did not follow them to their new suburban parishes. This happened for a couple of reasons. Although Catholic wealth increased dramatically, the cost of building new schools increased even more dramatically. In addition, the suburban public schools that served these Catholics were extremely well-financed and clearly superior to the ones in the cities from which the Catholics had come. Catholics who now had their sights set on upward mobility would turn to these public schools for the sake of socially and financially bettering their offspring. It became clear that post-Vatican II Catholicism would no longer be primarily fostered in a Catholic classroom.

At the time of Vatican II in the 1960s, there was a massive system of primary, secondary, and higher education with the Catholic University of America in Washington, D.C., as the symbolic capstone. By 2000, however, even though the U.S. Catholic population increased from 40 million to 60 million, Catholic school enrollment dropped from its high water mark of 5.5 million grade and high school students to 2.7 million children, reflecting Vatican II's openness to the larger culture.

The Transference of Leadership: The Baton Is Passed

Not only did the profile of parishioners change in the 40 years following Vatican II, but so, too, did the leadership. The council introduced a new word to Catholicism: "ministry." In the 1960s and 1970s, as the clerical and religious leadership began to digest Vatican II, people saw a new opportunity for service in the Church. Nuns, whose work had largely been confined to education and health care, went back to school and retooled themselves for work as *pastoral ministers*, rather than schoolteachers. In their absence, both the teaching core and the leadership of Catholic parochial grade schools and high schools shifted to the lay members of the Church.

Throughout the Church's history, a wide gap had existed between the clergy and the people. Vatican II seriously challenged this division between the sacred and the secular. Consequently, a great number of priests and sisters re-examined their state of life and the basis on which they had made the choice to "leave the world." Priests left the priesthood, and sisters and brothers left the religious life in great numbers. In 1965 there were 60,000 priests in the United States and in 2000 there were 45,000, despite an increase of 20 million U.S. Catholics. The post-Vatican II climate affected the new supply of leadership coming into the Church as well. Enrollment in seminaries by the end of the 1960s plummeted in a more dramatic fashion than the stock market crash of 1929. In 1960 there were 41,000 U.S. seminarians. By 2000, that number was down to 3,400. On the other hand, while in 1960 there were very few lay people preparing for professional Church ministry, in 1985, there were 10,500, and by 1996 that number had almost doubled. In 2000 there were over 35,000 lay Catholics enrolled in programs preparing for professional Church ministry, more than 10 times the number of seminarians preparing for the priesthood!

These pastoral ministers perform many of the works that were exclusively done by priests and nuns in the past. While Catholic schools have less and less influence on the increasing number of Catholics, the actual works of pastoral ministry have multiplied. Many of these ministers work in the new youth programs of the parish. More lay ministers work with the sick and dying. Many parishes have bereavement ministers who contact the family as soon as news comes of a death and help that family grieve the loss and prepare the funeral celebration. In fact, lay ministers now make up the majority of professional Catholic chaplains in hospitals. And, of course, many of these lay professional ministers administer and coordinate the spiritual and physical operation of the over 3,000 U.S. Catholic parishes that do not have a resident pastor. All of these pastoral ministers are in addition to the 150,000 lay teachers and administrators in the Catholic elementary and grade schools.

The non-ordained serve at the level of diocesan leadership as well as in such positions as chancellor (manager of the bishop's office), chief financial officer of the diocese, and judges in diocesan church courts. Women comprise more than 85 percent of this leadership. Administrative and pastoral responsibilities in the post-Vatican II Church in the United States have become virtual female arenas.

Vatican II gave the Catholic Church a new character. For the first time in its history, it was forced to find ways to tolerate dissent. This change took place during the information age, which meant that the press reported every move of the council to the world. With the veil of secrecy lifted from a Church council, everyone could see the significant amount of debate and contention that goes on when leaders deal with the word of God. The openness and the intensity of the debates at Vatican II confirmed that dissent was not only possible, but also invigorating.

The Catholic Church represents a broad spectrum of beliefs today. There are those small groups that tenaciously reject the changes, but polling surveys of Catholics today provide the following data:

- Ninety-three percent believe the Church should end the ban on artificial birth control.

- Eighty-five percent dissent from the Church's rule on remarriage after divorce.

- Sixty-nine percent disagree with the Church's stance on abortion.

- Sixty percent favor the ordination of women to the priesthood.

- Eighty percent favor ordination of women as deacons.

- Seventy percent would allow priests to marry.

Catholicism's Emerging Identity

Catholic identity is less and less defined by specific practices such as abstaining from meat on Friday, going to weekly confession on Saturday, or attending Mass every Sunday. Catholics are continuing these practices out of choice, not obligation. Present-day Catholic identity is shaping itself in a myriad of ways. Catholicism is no longer the "one-size-fits-all" model of the past. There is much greater personal liberty in moral decision-making. Both liberal and conservative activism is much more pronounced. The spirit of religious freedom from Vatican II has for the most part ended the notion that only those who accepted the Catholic Church as the one true faith could be saved. Church authorities are no longer seen as the final word for many Catholics. Today's dissenters do not leave the Church; they stay on their own terms.

For many in this country, the post-Vatican II Church captured a spirit of justice and gave voice to hope. Idealism among Catholic youth today finds its outlet not just in the few who might enter religious life. A large number of Catholic young people join programs such as the Peace Corps, Jesuit Volunteer Corps, and hundreds of other volunteer programs sponsored by the Church and religious orders. It is typical for these young people to spend a year or two living a life of poverty in service to the community. They feed the hungry, work with the homeless and jobless, teach skills to inner-city children, and become a witness for justice and civil rights in many arenas. The Jesuit Volunteer motto, "Ruined for Life," is an apt description of the counter-cultural transformation that these young people undergo. As they re-enter the culture from which they came, they do so with a value system that is remarkably different than the norm.

In the spirit of Vatican II, the U.S. bishops reorganized themselves as a national body. Since Vatican II, they have met in sessions one or even two times each year. A primary focus of the sessions is the internal operation of the Church, but the sessions have become a platform for prophetic teaching as well. These teachings from the bishops' councils include the pastoral letter on peace and nuclear warfare and the pastoral letter on the economy, to name just two.

In the years following Vatican II, there has been a return to centralization. This centralization seems to be in conflict with the Vatican II call for a sharing of power. Present Church leadership seems to favor restoring the old model of authority. Many of the decisions in recent years from Rome have reversed the directives to share control, especially with the bishops in their various countries and cultures.

At times, the top at Rome has had to settle even the simplest of issues, such as the use of inclusive language in the English translation of the Mass, rather than allowing such decisions to be made locally. Seemingly, Rome is restraining the reforms of Vatican II through its appointment of bishops. As the progressive bishops who served at Vatican II retire, more conservative bishops who work from the top-down model of decision-making are replacing them. For the most part, however, the Catholic Church is a revitalized Church, with more participation at deeper levels than ever before, perhaps since the very earliest days of Jesus.

We've seen how the Church was brought to the United States with the immigrants, how it became accepted, and how it eventually became mainstream. In the next chapter, we'll look at some of the challenges the Church faces and opportunities it offers in the new millennium. We'll address the question of what the Church might look like in the years to come.

The Least You Need to Know

- An American checkered Church characterizes the growth of Catholicism in the United States.

- Immigrants from Ireland, Germany, Italy, Poland, Mexico, and many other countries have contributed their cultural traditions to the United States Catholic Church.

◆ *E Pluribus Unum Catholicum:* One Church out of many people would be a good motto for the Catholic Church in the United States.

◆ The results of Vatican II are more participation in the Church by greater numbers of people.

◆ Dissent by Catholics who remain in the Church is much more the practice today.

Part 7

A Look to the Future

Finally, we look at the Church of the future from the spirit unleashed at Vatican II. We focus this future through the classic marks of the Church—*one*, *holy*, *catholic*, and *apostolic*—to see how these enduring qualities speak to the Church and to the culture. We look at inequity between men and women, divisions between culture and the earth, competition between European values and values of a worldwide Church, and the power struggle between the institutional Church and Church as community. We look at who the U.S. Catholics of 2025 will be.

Additionally, we take a hard look at the festering wound of sex abuse that has plagued the priesthood for more than a generation, now lanced by the laser light of the media. Taking a Taoist view, we see this as both crisis and opportunity.

We're optimistic about the future. We see the rich resources of the Church's lived tradition as bread for the journey.

Chapter 24

Face-to-Face in the Third Millennium: The Church Looks to the Future

In This Chapter

- ◆ A new name for a "new" Church
- ◆ Challenges the Church faces in the new millennium
- ◆ Strength and values that transcend time
- ◆ Generation X meets Generation Ñ

Ecclesiastes reminds us that there is really nothing new under the sun. However, each age seems to have its own version of the same old human story; each time brings a "unique" set of challenges and opportunities. In this chapter, we'll take a look at four challenges we believe the Church now faces as the new millennium unfolds. At the same time, we see resources and traditions within the Church that can meet these new situations with creativity.

Recap: Past, Present, and Future

Pope John XXIII told the Church to turn and face the culture, to engage it, embrace it, learn from it. This advice represented a drastic reversal from the past—it sounded a new note in Catholicism, the beginning of a whole new symphony. The new journey required a new self-image. For many years, the Church thought of itself as "The City of God," a perfect society with a separation between members and clergy. It also took the clergy out of the trenches, out of the human struggle, and placed them a rung up on the ladder. It did nothing to create good relations with other faith communities. The Second Vatican Council retrieved an old biblical image, Church as "The People of God," a much more inclusive image—it speaks to community, and says we're all in this thing together.

It is no small thing to change one's image. In the case of the Church, the change reverses all interactions between the institutional Church and members, and likewise with the larger world community. It is no surprise that it meets resistance and takes time. However, there are characteristics of the Church that endure. You may recall them from your catechism; they've been around a long time. They're called the four marks of the Church: one, holy, catholic, and apostolic. In this chapter, we'll follow the new identity in the culture to see how these four marks are reflected at this time in history.

The Tectonic Plates Shift

As the Church turned to face the world, one of the first things it discovered was that democracy had given rise to a new era. The common people had access to education (thanks in large part to the proliferation of Catholic schools and universities) and other amenities previously reserved for the upper class. There was a new kind of Catholic sitting in the pew more educated than his counterparts in the previous generations. She is feisty, full of Yankee ingenuity and entrepreneurial chutzpah, and by now, used to having a say in things. It's all part of a new *paradigm*.

S'ter Says

A **paradigm** is a model, or a very clear example of something. It helps us to frame our thinking. To change our paradigm requires a major shift in how we see things.

Paradigms are ways looking at society, ways of organizing reality. When a paradigm changes or shifts, it's like an earthquake: not necessarily destructive, but definitely rearranging the landscape! Previous paradigm shifts in Western history include the ending of tribal life, the building of city-states, and the demise of many monarchies.

Democracy radically changed the way people thought of themselves, the demands they put on their leaders, how they interacted with government. As a result, all the institutions of the culture began to change. We say *began* to change rather than changed, because it takes time for such a radical turnabout to come through all the layers of society. The term paradigm shift entered mainstream culture about forty years ago, and it is still being integrated into our minds and institutions.

An Ever-Changing World

A term that came with the paradigm shift is "quantum," a word first used by Einstein. For many years, physics understood that matter was made up of tiny particles: the neutrons, electrons, and nuclei you learned about in science class. Scientists developed quantum theory by observing the behavior and interactions of these elementary particles and noticing that the particles also contain wave properties. Today, under this theory, scientists have determined that everything is made up of both particles (solid) and waves (energy) and that these two states exist at the same time within each "individual piece" or "quantum." And because things are really both solid and in motion we now understand the universe is alive and expanding, that creation is still happening!

The significance of quantum theory is inestimable. When Einstein, one of the most brilliant men in history, realized what his calculations meant, he closed the books on them and turned away. To accept his findings would require completely rethinking everything. It was other scientists who, using Einstein's work, later developed the field of quantum physics.

Einstein admitted that turning away from his discovery was perhaps the greatest mistake of his life—and his experience illustrates an important point. When new information is discovered, it can be so overwhelming that the human mind can't take it all in at one time. It can take many generations to integrate the really big changes.

Science had been organized on the old paradigm or model called the mechanical view, which considered the universe to be non-living, something that the creator wound up like a clock, set in motion, and then stepped back. Thousands of years of Western thinking was organized on the mechanical universe assumption. This thinking pitted science and religion against one another. Science wanted to take God out of the equation, and considered the material world devoid of spirit or life; God was no longer relevant as creation was a finished product. Religion maintained the belief that God was present in creation, which science considered to be a "magical" understanding, and thus the two branches of thought set out on different paths.

To summarize: The paradigm shift of quantum physics shows that everything is both what it is in the solid state, and at the same time, is fluid and changing, expanding, still creating. Time, of course, makes a huge difference when it comes to keeping things at least appearing to be solid: The more dense the thing, the slower it moves. What does this have to do with the Catholic Church? For example, we just used the words: solid, fluid, changing, expanding, and time! There you go! The Church has all of these qualities in spades.

Science and Religion Kiss and Make Up

Today, science and religion have forged a new partnership. They are expressing the same ideas, each in their own language. Quantum theory tells us in scientific terms that the universe is a unified field. Everything is really all made out of this one substance.

Now, again, what has this got to do with the Catholic religion? Science has just described what you learned in first grade religion class:

Q. Where is God?

A. God is everywhere.

What they're describing is God's omnipresence.

Science tells us that we are really all one, that there is no "higher" order in the way of separation we have thought about higher in the past. There are greater degrees of complexity, but not a ranking system in the old way. It is also supporting the idea that we are all connected. The gazillion different forms these "quanta" take, from a tiny seedpod to the secretary of state, is a tribute to the vastness of the mind of the Creator, a tribute to God's unlimited power. Just think of it!

New understandings in theology emphasize *process*: seeing the Church as a community of believers who are in the process of discovering God and establishing God's reign. It is highly dynamic, an arrangement that is always being worked out. Accord, or peace, doesn't necessarily come and stay, it's happening on a moment-by-moment basis. It's a living arrangement, a give-and-take that is constantly being negotiated.

Think of family life. How much do you wish you could get it all nailed down? Quite a lot, no doubt. How nice would it be if you didn't have to reconfigure who gets what, why, and when? Very nice. That's the very reason why we came up with the answer, "because I said so!" And sure enough, in the constant interplay among the people of God's creation, there are times when law and order is called for. We can't reinvent the wheel at every corner. That very important impulse to stabilize, to hold the line, is negotiated with the impetus to grow and change. The dance goes on!

The Voice of Wisdom Speaks

Church leaders rightly caution Catholics against falling prey to what they call "New Age" thinking, a contemporary movement they describe as a naîve way of looking at the world through magical glasses. This can result in a lack of responsibility. The Church is concerned with watering down the essential Christian message, and turning Christ into a universal panacea, an Alka-Seltzer in the sky that can be taken whenever a bromide is called for. They fear it negates the importance of Jesus as the saving grace of humankind, and places too much focus on human accomplishment.

On the other side, many Catholics are concerned that the Vatican might throw the baby out with the bathwater by lumping together many ideas and dismissing it all as New Age bunk. In expressing this concern, they are claiming their ability to critically analyze current philosophy and discern what is appropriate to Catholic thought. A skill learned at the hands of Catholic scholars at Catholic universities.

The new paradigm is one of connectedness. It breaks through the dualistic thinking that has characterized Western thinking since early times. The new paradigm thinking no longer separates the sacred from the world, matter from spirit, clergy from the people. It is non-hierarchical, and non-patriarchical. The following table shows how four principles—authority, power, order, and the divine—change with the new paradigm. Many lay and clergy theologians understand the principles of the new paradigm to be the same as those reflected in the teachings of Jesus. They believe that it takes us past the dualism that has impeded many from grasping the true Christian message.

Here is how Christian principles look when translated into nondualistic principles.

Old Paradigm	New Paradigm
Either/Or	BOTH
Institution/Private	Mutual
External/Internal	Cooperative
Transcendent/Immanent	Here and There
Hierarchy/Anarchy	Holarchy

Let's now turn away from the culture and back to the Church to see how the enduring character of Catholicism meets the needs of a contemporary world.

The Church Is One

Today, we hear the term *globalization* in almost every area of life. We hear about global education, global communication, and global economy, to name just a few.

S'ter Says

Globalization means understanding the world as a community. This worldview emphasizes the interconnectedness of people, economies, and resources.

How is the Church responding to globalization and the diversity it brings? Closer to home, in the United States, women have moved into the mainstream in almost every political and social sector, with the notable exception of the Catholic Church, where the key positions of leadership remain unavailable to them. How will the Church respond to the inevitable feminization of this previously all-male bastion?

A phrase that one hears today that describes our shrinking world is "global village." It describes a way of perceiving ourselves in relationship to the rest of the world. It recognizes our oneness or unity with others when it comes to economic issues, the use of Earth's resources, sharing power, and the sharing of knowledge. It calls us to relate through our common qualities rather than focusing on differences. In the process, we don't see differences as problems to overcome but value them as unique expressions of God's diversity. Scientists, economists, ecologists, and theologians from many traditions are coming together and recognizing interconnectedness. To think that any one group has found the "right" answers for all other communities, or that the actions of any one community does not have an effect on other groups of people, has become a thing of the past.

Today you can board a plane in Kansas and get off in Singapore all in one (long) day. We can pick up the phone and talk to someone across the globe as fast as we can dial it. The Internet itself has become a metaphor made real: the information highway that can transmit a thought around the world in four seconds. It is almost as though we are speaking face-to-face while living 10,000 miles apart. We truly are experiencing the globe as one village.

How do we participate in the global village? When we meet each other eye-to-eye, what style of relationship will we use? As we've seen from the beginning, the Church has pursued a vision of unity. The quantum worldview brings with it the potential for realizing that vision. Not in the old way of overtaking a culture and imposing values, but in true mutual respect, a give-and-take exchange in which all parties win. As we learn to be less fearful of differences, seeing them as God's diversity, we can look for how we are alike and recognize the presence of the Holy Spirit in all people.

Women in the Wings

It is an understatement to say that one of the major areas of pronounced difference in the Catholic Church has been in the arena of gender. Women have been shut out of decision-making leadership since the second century. This issue presents the Church with an important opportunity to step into the lead as society searches for religious values to determine the right action in regard to the equality of women.

In fact, the Church actually has a history of supporting female leadership. From the early years when convents and monasteries first developed to the present time, there has been a strong Catholic tradition of religious women (nuns). These women have always made their own decisions and set their own policies, making Catholic women among the first in Western culture to occupy executive roles.

In modern times, women have been the CEOs in three major arenas within the Church: the educational system, the health-care system, and the governing of their religious orders. In this regard, the Church has been ahead of the culture. If you were to look at college and university presidents in the 1950s, you would find very few females, but those you would find would very likely be Catholic nuns.

Today, women remain a primary resource for the continuing life of the Church. They are in the forefront of religious scholarship. The majority of students in the ministry programs at Catholic colleges and universities are females. At many Protestant seminaries, Catholic females make up an increasingly large proportion of the student body. They are studying in the fields of theology, pastoral ministry, as chaplains, and religious educators. They are in every way preparing to be leaders and decision-makers in the Church. Thousands of parishes in the Catholic Church today are without a priest, and women are pastoring them.

Catholics have well-educated women theologians, teachers, and pastoral ministers who are ready to become partners with men in leadership. However, ordination is the only gateway to decision-making. As these women prepare to take ministerial responsibilities in a variety of areas, some are preparing for ordination. At this time, however, the doors of the Catholic seminaries, and therefore ordination, remain closed to them.

Epiphanies

Sister Mary Madeleva, C.S.C., president of St. Mary's College in Notre Dame, Indiana, was a champion of women's education in the Church. In 1949, she presented a groundbreaking paper in which she proposed an educational reform program for American nuns. Until this point, they had been put into the burgeoning Catholic schools before they had a chance to finish their own education. The pope called the major superiors of religious women to Rome and urged them to offer programs of professional education and spiritual formation before sending sisters to their assignments. This movement changed the identity and set the direction of Catholic nuns, making them some of the best-educated women in the country.

In the past, when the U.S. Catholic Church refused to admit black students to the seminaries, the Vatican opened Roman seminaries and ordained them. The Church does have precedents and resources for dealing with change regarding cultural and societal inequities.

From its first council in 325 C.E. to the present time, the Church has held 21 councils in which beliefs and policies for all its members have been established. However, no woman has ever had decision-making authority at any of these councils. Strides toward partnership were made after the council of Vatican II, and women have been allowed to participate in several official ministries. However, ordination is not one of them. Papal statements since Vatican II have continued to uphold the ban against women's ordination.

To gain insight into the issue of women's exclusion from partnership in the decision-making process, let's use the power of the imagination. Imagine that a woman is the pope of the Catholic Church. The entire College of Cardinals is composed of women; all the bishops are women; and all the priests, deacons, and seminarians are women. Let's imagine that only recently have men been allowed to be altar servers.

Imagine that this all-female decision-making body has had enormous power in the society in which you live and over your soul as well for 2,000 years. Imagine how disconnected this organization's decisions would be from a man's needs. How would such a structure be fair to men?

As you experience this exercise, you are able to see what it is like from the other side. The point of the gender concern is not a shift in who is the dominant one, but a call for a new paradigm of partnership. Let's use our imagination again to gain insight into how a partnership model might function. Imagine men and women working side by side to make decisions that reflect the true nature of being human. In this model the concerns of all are considered; participation is based on the biblical reminder "In his image … male and female, he created them."

The Church Is Holy

As Church membership moves away from defining itself by adherence to tightly bound beliefs and strict rules of behavior, it moves toward a more spiritual understanding of the human journey. Indeed, almost one half the people in the United States meet at least monthly in some sort of a small group that defines its purpose as a spiritual quest. This is a startling shift from a few years ago, representing a transformation not only of our sense of community but also of our sense of the spiritual.

As the twenty-first century dawns, there is a tremendous interest in spirituality in the culture at large. There is greater material consumption now than in all preceding centuries put together, yet the call to spirituality has never been heard more loudly. People who would not have imagined ever joining a church or belonging to a formal religion talk about being on a spiritual quest. You can go into any bookstore and see the shelves of material being written about spirituality—retreats, seminars, and workshops on spirituality abound. Coursework at any given Catholic university shows a decided proliferation of classes on inner growth and self-discovery as well as spirituality and the spiritual classics, such as Hildegard of Bingen, Catherine of Siena, Teresa of Ávila, John of the Cross, and others in the Catholic mystic tradition.

While this overlap of psychology and spirituality concerns some, others see it as inevitable. The word "psyche" itself means soul. Psychology, like the other sciences, separated from religion for a time; but now the movement is reclaiming its original connection to assisting people in discovering their souls, the inner dwellings of the spirit. Whether the message is coming from the human potential movement as "self-actualization," or the U.S. Army as "Be all you can be," underneath the slogans is a desire to develop the self and to incorporate the spirit.

Previously, there were two specific camps regarding spirituality. One group had a scientific orientation. To them, the only thing that was real was the material world. The other group separated themselves for the world; they saw spirituality as "otherworldly," believing that holiness would be found later in heaven. We looked at the origins of this camp in the early Church in Chapter 20 and St. Anthony's move to the desert. The world was a distraction, a temptation to be avoided. They saw God as outside of the world of matter.

The once great distance between these two camps is now just a stone's throw. They are meeting in an understanding that matter and spirit are one and the same. As these two opposite worldviews connect, both are sensing the presence of the spiritual in the everyday. With this growing sensitivity, there is an awareness of connectedness. We have coined the phrase *quantum spirituality* to describe this, because quantum is about realizing that there is one field of energy unifying both matter and spirit.

S'ter Says

Quantum spirituality is a spirituality that calls us to recognize the holiness of the world and be involved with it creatively, as Jesus did in becoming human with us.

The Quantum View

Quantum spirituality is a celebration of our partnership with God's creative will in an expanding universe. Through it, we are called to embrace the world and its creative process, not as separate from the life of the spirit, but as the context where the life of the spirit is encountered. Redemption is seen as part of divine creation, not as necessitated by sin. Quantum spirituality's origins are embedded in the ancient spiritual traditions, especially the matriarchal and indigenous societies whose cultures modeled the solidarity among nature, humankind, and the divine. Current expressions of this spirituality are mending the dualism of Western spirituality that sees these as separate. Quantum spirituality is incarnational because it proclaims the divine presence in both matter and spirit.

Some Church authorities are concerned about how contemporary thought flirts with pantheism, the heresy of identifying God with nature. These concerns come from Catholic doctrines such as God's omnipresence, the incarnation, the presence of the Resurrected Lord, and the movement of the Holy Spirit. Lively dialogue is happening between the various theologies that have always been intrinsic to Catholic belief.

In the ongoing balancing act between stabilization and movement, between dogma and mystery, the emerging spirituality is not so concerned with Church doctrine or rules but with experience. People are sensing spirituality in nature, in relationships, in communities, and as they reach out to help others. In so doing, spirituality is located less in particular beliefs and established traditions and more in the everyday interactions in the world in which we live. Following quantum spirituality is about recognizing the mystery in life. It creates a mystical awareness of being alive and a sense of the goodness of life.

Sacramental Life: Back to Our Roots in the Earth

The new interest in spirituality draws Church members back to their Catholic identity in the sacraments. As they reconnect to their sacramental roots in the physical elements—earth, air, fire, and water—consciousness of the presence of the sacred in all creation is awakened. As senses are sharpened, they are reminded as the Jesuit motto says, "Christ is present in all things." Quantum spirituality retrieves the Catholic understanding of the sacredness of life.

A revitalized Church imagines sacraments in a new way. For example, a group of people might gather on a Saturday night for a communal dinner. They bring ingredients and spend time together baking bread. As the dough is kneaded, rolled, and punched, the kitchen becomes dusty with flour, and stories are shared. "I remember when I was a kid …" "The smell of the bread reminds me of …" "This is just like the time when …" They connect. When the bread is ready and they sit down to dinner, they might break it ceremoniously, giving thanks for the grains of wheat and the warmth of friends gathered together around the table that will nourish them. They experience Eucharist.

Likewise, a family outing to the lake can become the occasion to have an intimate relationship with baptismal waters. Paddles dip into cool water as the canoe slides across a still lake. A child trails her fingers in the water, mesmerized by the small wake it creates. A paddle bounces across the water, splashing the children. Catching an opportunity for a game, one of them splashes back. Laughter rings out across the lake, and the worries of the week are washed away. A moment in time has been made holy. Later in the evening, as the parents sit by the water's edge, they reflect over the experiences of the day. They feel the intensity of being alive and the goodness of it all. They are overcome with gratitude, the kind that spontaneously wells up from a deep place inside when you give it the time and space to do so.

At Mass on Sunday, the Eucharistic bread now tastes different because of the spiritual connection between baking bread on Saturday night with friends and receiving Communion on Sunday morning. The priest's sprinkle of the holy water has a renewed experience. A day on the lake with the family is a blessing, a baptism in which all are renewed. The spiritual connection between the sacraments and the world tells Catholics that God is present. Quantum spirituality connects us.

The Church Is Catholic

The four marks of the Church were first written in Greek, and then were later transcribed into Latin, as it became the official Church language. It is significant to note, however, that the term "catholic" remained in its Greek form as the official name—*katholikos, kata* or "toward" plus *holos* or "whole." Catholic is often translated as universal, meaning the Church is for everyone and it is found all over the world. This is true. Let's explore the difference between these two understandings.

Universal: All Over the Map

Today, there is no place on the globe where Catholicism is absent. What was once an essentially European Church now finds itself surpassed in size by the Church of Africa, Asia, and the Americas. As you read in Chapter 2, more than one billion of the world's six billion people are Catholic. Of this population, Africa represents 12 percent; Asia, 12 percent; the United States and Canada, 6 percent; Mexico and Central America, 14 percent; South America, 28 percent. Together, these areas of the world add up to 72 percent. Europe represents the other 28 percent. Clearly, Catholicism is no longer a European Church, although at the beginning of the twentieth century, more than 75 percent of the Catholic population was in Europe, as it had been for 15 centuries.

Global ministry has long been a major part of the Church. Catholics have set up schools and hospitals, and created diplomatic alliances all over the globe in an effort to bring the Church to other cultures. However, in doing this, missionaries often went with the understanding that bringing the Church to the people meant converting the people to the European understanding of the Church, rather than learning the ways of the people. This method resulted in the destruction of many other cultures. This old way was to understand "catholic" as *a universe*, with lines of distinction between itself and the larger world. In that way of thinking, others must enter the existing "universe," an understanding that does not challenge the existing membership to learn and grow—to expand and embrace. It's a one-way relationship.

Speaking a Universal Language

You recall how the Holy Spirit came to the apostles and disciples on Pentecost, and when the disciples went out to speak to the people, the people could understand them in their own language. It is important to note that the people didn't necessarily understand the language the apostles were speaking, but rather it was the other way around. It was as if the apostles were speaking the people's native tongue. One way this can happen is through the language of symbol. The deeper understanding of "catholic" is "toward the whole." It means opening to embrace, not forming a closed circle.

The new missionary approach requires a deeper understanding of Christianity, an ability to relate through the symbols of faith, rather than the strictly literal understanding of the Christian message. The Church now realizes its job is to act as translator, finding common expressions of the sacred within different cultures.

New missionary outreach respects local autonomy. Missionaries adapt to the culture they have come to serve. Religious orders organic to the cultures are founded—clergy are native people and are increasingly selected as bishops and archbishops. In 1978 there were 3,714 Catholic bishops; in 2002 there were 4,439. The bulk of that increase can be attributed to Africa. Rather than becoming the means of instilling European values, indigenous religious orders relate to specific needs of the local people. The Mass thus becomes a celebration of the culture. Colors, fabrics, flags, and other sacramentals relate to the symbols of the people, rather than the overlay of European symbols. Church architecture is no longer imported from Europe, but instead churches are made of local materials, designed by the people according to the styles of their culture.

In the "quantum church," the Gospel message is grounded in the political, economic, social, and spiritual realities of the local area, rather than those of Europe. Perhaps most importantly, in a transformed understanding of the Church's mission—to bring the Good News—the Church offers itself as a symbol of the coming together of people, loving one another, and sharing resources as the early Apostolic communities did. It does this by expanding itself to embrace others, to celebrate diversity, to enlarge their own understanding of the Gospel.

The Church Is Apostolic

The word "apostolic" applies both to the institutional Church and to the members of the Christian community. Most Catholics are more familiar with the term "apostolic succession," referring to the institutional application of the word, describing papal lineage, connecting the office of the pope to Peter. The other use of the term describes the experience of a community of people who, like the communities of the first apostles, are devoted to keeping the occurrences of knowing Jesus alive.

These two concepts of Church, expressed in Chapter 4 as The Big Church and the Little Church, really are two aspects of the same thing, following the same pattern we have seen throughout history. The institution of Church has tended to overshadow the Church as community. Rather than see itself as supporting the community, it has viewed the community as supporting the institution. A quantum understanding of Catholicism connects these two "separate" functions again, seeing them as both vital and necessary.

Partnership: From Power over to Empowerment

"Quantum Catholicism" brings partnership to power and decision-making that reaches back to apostolic time and reclaims the "new" understanding of power that was the original good news. As the Church shifts from the mechanical world to the quantum world, it is shifting from the hierarchical model to relational power. In the relational style, many groups are included in decision-making.

As you have seen, the strong emphasis on the hierarchial ordering in the institutional Church is based in a pre-Christian governing structure. It located the seat of power exclusively in the governing structure, and separated the leaders from the people.

As we've seen, the Church's highly centralized idea of power and its absolutism has gotten it into trouble more than once. The traditional objection from within the Church to a shift in the flow of power is: "The Church is not a democracy." This is true. Nor is it an aristocracy or a dictatorship. Instead, it is a community. As the Church moves farther into this next thousand years, it is modifying its structure to include both a way of talking with the people and a way of listening. This feedback loop will make decisions more communal.

Celebrating Natural Order: Holarchy

We turn again to the intersecting world of science and spirituality to learn about an organic organizing structure present in all of nature. Philosophers of science today refer to *holon* theory to look at how the world is organized. All of nature organizes according to a pattern. Simpler organisms, called holons (being whole and complete), join with other organisms, also whole and complete, and become a new, more complex substance, also whole and complete.

For example, two hydrogen molecules combine with an oxygen molecule and become water—a new substance, whole and complete. Water is a more complex structure dependent on the individual elements to be what it is—water. We would say water is *more significant*, but not more *essential* than the elements within it. In forming the larger unit, a process of *adaptation* goes on—the larger unit will have an identity separate from the individual holons.

Holy Holon: A Church in Process

When this model is applied to people, it means that individual people (or groups of people) have an innate need to bond into a larger community. At the same time, they need to maintain their individual identity. The larger group that they form is both more complex and is dependent on the individuals within it. There is a mutual give-and-take within the bonding and expanding process necessary to make it happen.

Father Cletus Wessels, O.P., is a Dominican friar who has applied holon theory to the Church to deal with structures and tensions between the institution and the people. His model shows that the institutional Church is dependent on individual members. At the same time, individual members have an innate desire to bond into larger groups and there is *interdependence*. We naturally gravitate toward becoming "more" than we are. In short, Big Church and Little Church need each other.

In the give-and-take of maintaining individuality and group identity, there is tension. How much can individuality be sacrificed to the group, and how much diversity can the group handle and still maintain group identity? This tension need not be destructive—if we allow nature to instruct us, and trust the inborn (God-given) senses we have, a creative relationship is assured. However, it will never be "nailed down"; it will always be evolving.

According to holon theory, organizing structures are natural, but not in the way they have been used in Western culture, where the larger organism is seen to have more power than those below. This new order is called *Holarchy* (versus hierarchy) and each individual part of the structure is seen as whole; interdependence is recognized.

The role of leadership in a holarchical Church is not to control but to assist members to discover and articulate the guiding vision and beliefs. Such leadership will free the community to discover the internal movement and guidance of the spirit. This authority will work effectively only when the leaders' authority is granted and accepted by the members of the community. As in any self-organizing system, leadership will emerge but this should be dependent on community recognition. As such, then, the whole community is the guardian of apostolicity.

Sharing the Bread

The Church has a powerful resource within its tradition to accomplish partnership. This resource is Jesus, the man who came out of Galilee 2,000 years ago and gathered together communities for sharing, a purpose that was ritualized in the Eucharist.

Jesus, a Jewish teacher, did not center his teaching in the Jewish temple. He showed the people how to honor the "kingdom within." As he taught them to go within themselves and connect with the God inside them, he changed the rules of how power flows. In every action, in every word, in every way, he told his followers that they had the power. "The Kingdom of God is within you," he said.

Jesus also changed the flow of power in another significant way. He turned the Church structure upside down, creating a bottom-to-top model of sharing power. He did not direct his teaching to the temple authorities. He did not tell them they should treat the people differently; he told the people to understand themselves differently. The challenge to build partnership models in the Church of the next millennium is a challenge to the people, rather than to the leaders. As the paradigm within the Church shifts, the challenge to its members is to accept their power and take responsibility as full partners.

The ultimate survival of the Church, of course, depends on the generations to come. Following our theme of Quantum Catholicism, how will the Church of the future meet the challenges of the next generation?

Your Guardian Angel

Prayer is an equal opportunity event! According to Vatican II, the new image of the Church challenges any notions of spiritual elitism, which have been fostered by differences between clergy and lay people. The spirituality of the common people is not to be considered in any way lesser than priestly, religious, or monastic spirituality.

The Next Generation: Passing the Cup

No one can tell the story of Catholicism's future, but we do know it lies in the hands of the next generations. Who are these young people? How are they responding to Catholicism? When we look to the Catholic future, it might be helpful to do a quick survey of the present.

Pre-Vatican II Generation are Catholics who came of age prior to Vatican II and comprise approximately 22 percent of Catholics born before 1943. They've upheld the institutions of twentieth-century Catholic life and they exhibit a loyalty to the institutional Church.

Vatican II Generation—Baby Boomers were born between 1943 and 1960 and are more likely to be concerned with individual self-fulfillment than the institution. They comprise about 43 percent of the Catholic population.

Post-Vatican II Generation were born between 1960 and 1980 and have almost no lived experience of the pre-Vatican II Church. They are estimated to be 41% of the adult Catholic population.

Popular culture has described this generation of young adults in the United States with two images: Generation X and Generation Ñ (pronounced *EN-yay*). Let's see who these folks are.

Generation X

Generation X is largely made up of the descendants of the European immigrants. An article in the July 1999 issue of *U.S. Catholic* describes them as the first generation of "latch-key children" who learned early to fend for themselves in day care and after-school programs. Many Generation X'ers are seeking family and beyond that, a community. They have spent far less time with their parents than the generation before them; community is formed around a common spiritual purpose and commitment. They describe an ideal community not unlike the New Testament family whom Jesus identified when he was asked who his brothers and sisters were. He replied, "Those who hear the word of God and do it."

This generation has a healthy irreverence and skepticism of all institutions, including the Church. They recognize God's presence in the broadest sense and see God in all communities, all religious traditions, all races. Their God is not bound to one sexual identity. This generation is more comfortable crossing cultural barriers than any of its predecessors.

Generation X'er receiving Communion.

(Courtesy of Tom Wright)

They share a bond of diversity and tolerance is their ethic. They are at home on many spiritual paths: Catholic, Protestant, Hindu, Buddhist, Jewish, Muslim, Native American, and more. They move in and out of many cultures: Black, Caucasian, Asian, Latino, and more. They do not define people by their sexual preference or political alignment: gay, lesbian, straight, Republican, or Democrat.

For them, church is not an end in itself, but a symbol and they refuse to idolize it. Religion is not about words; it's about love in action. They want the Church to be a role model and live out its beliefs.

This generation has not been schooled in religious education in the traditional ways. Many are unfamiliar with the Catechism, and their heroes and role models are not found in the lives of the saints. They are unfamiliar with the history of the Church. Although they may attend Mass and partake of the sacraments, they do so without a deep connection to the traditional meanings.

The symbols are drawn from the pop culture; life's meaning is conveyed to them through music, movies, sitcoms, and comic book characters. A large portion of this pop culture, by Generation X'ers' own admission, is meaningless, yet a part of it does carry meaning and even creates inspiration. Generation X'ers seem to be asking for the Church to help them in sorting out the mix.

One Generation X'er described his idea of church in the following way, "The Church in the next millennium will welcome all, as did our role model in the first-century Palestine, regardless of their physical and social situations. Church is not an institution for dispensing grace. Church is people who have accepted grace and are striving to live in harmony with each other and creation."

Generation Ñ

The term *Generation Ñ*, coined and copyrighted by Bill Teck and used in a July 1999 issue of *Newsweek*, describes young *Latinos* who, like their counterparts in Generation X, are in their twenties and thirties, but feel that the phrase "Generation X" does not completely describe them. They come from as many as 22 different countries of origin. Many are white, some are black, and most are in between. They are a global culture. Some of their families have been in the United States for centuries; some have only recently arrived. They are the descendants of the conquistadors and the Indians of the New World culture.

More than being simply bilingual, they are rediscovering their roots and inventing a new bicultural identity, meaning that they exist in both worlds without losing the sense of who they are. They weave a complex web of relationships with their elders, other cultures, and with one another. They show no signs of assimilation or "Americanization." Rather, their strong identity influences the culture.

Epiphanies
The terms **Hispanic** and **Latino** are used interchangeably to define a diverse people. The terms refer to Mexicans, Caribbeans, Cubans, Puerto Ricans, Dominicans, the Andean people, and people from the American Southwest. The diversity of the Hispanic community is its strength. The religious spirit of these people blended with the Catholic faith. Their spirituality is expressed in love of God, love of neighbor, and love of self; this love binds the people together fashioning *el pueblo de Dios*, the people of God.

For the most part they are Catholic, and like Generation X, their faith is more unstructured. As one member of Generation Ñ put it, "We respect and honor Catholic traditions, yet are not bound to the old practices." Their Catholicism is cultural as well as religious, and it is integral to their Hispanic identity. They are aware they come from a rich culture and history, and they want to celebrate it. Like Generation X, they are less tolerant of the male dominance over females than the previous generation. Both Generation X and Generation Ñ believe in religion, but the affluence of their lives has reduced their dependence on it. In a marked contrast to Generation X, Generation Ñ draws a strong part of its religious values and identity from family. The people in Generation Ñ often grew up living together with aunts, uncles, cousins, and grandparents, all attending church together.

Quantum Generation: Generation Q: Identity Chosen, Not Commanded

As the Church enters the new millennium, it does so with a generation for whom all things are alive, filled with spirit, and connected. We might call this new generation of Catholic youth the Quantum Generation. They are inheriting a globalized vision of what it means to be human, and are carrying the values that can bring in their vision.

Epiphanies
Demographically, about 60 percent of Catholics under 20 are Latinos and Latinas, many of whom were not born within the U.S. borders. A good number of these kids live in the West and Southwest, not the Catholic institutional bastions of the Northeast and Midwest. They are big city dwellers for the most part. It is less likely for them than their grandparents that both their parents are Catholic and that they were married in a Catholic church. Also unlike their grandparents, 50 percent of whom attend Mass once a week, only 25 percent of their parents do. Only about 60 percent of their parents are registered in a Catholic parish versus almost 80 percent of their grandparents.

Those in the Church who work with these young people say they are looking for ways to be involved and that it is important that they feel invited. They want to be with others of like values. They don't have the traditional structure of growing up their parents and grandparents had, and they desperately want to form relationships. The Church is attractive to them for that reason, but they have to be invited. While they sense a spiritual hunger, they don't seem to know where to have that satisfied. If the Church is to be a place to nourish this hunger, it will have to be perceived as having something important to give. Service to others is very attractive to them. They will join in when offered the opportunity.

Epiphanies
One of the most successful programs for the young is "Theology on Tap." It is an opportunity for the young to gather to share their faith concerns, along with a meal and company. The format is generally a series of evening events that are simple and relaxed, gathering in a restaurant, listening to a presenter, and then sharing. These programs are popular in many dioceses around the United States.

The third millennium will contain major challenges. The story of the Catholic Church will be lived and written by the Church's greatest asset: the next generation. From our point of view, it is in good hands.

The Least You Need to Know

- The Church's new identity and new name for itself, "The People of God," harkens back to its origins as a community.

- The Church of the future moves beyond dualism, healing the separations of the past: mind/body, male/female, and toward wholeness.

- The new Church will be less religious—bound to fixed dogma and rules, and more spiritual—open to grow and expand.

- Catholicism will draw on its identity as embracing the whole and less on its identity as a separate universe.

- There will be a shift in the order between community and organization. The institution will support the people rather than the other way around.

- The Church is in good hands. The present generation already is carrying the values for its transformation.

Chapter 25

Catholic Sexuality: The Church's Dirty Little Secret?

In This Chapter

- ◆ Sex scandals: How could this happen?
- ◆ Clerical collars and clerical culture
- ◆ Catholic sexuality: out of order
- ◆ Seeking wholeness: rethinking the Incarnation

This chapter speaks to an issue we did not anticipate two years ago when we first wrote this book, but which has done what kings through the centuries could not do—brought the Catholic Church to its knees. That issue is sex.

Beginning 30 years ago as a whisper, and now reaching a deafening crescendo, sex scandals have damaged the faithful, clergy and laity alike. The Church finds itself skating on the edge of financial bankruptcy. Broken trust, like shards of broken ice, cut away at its structure and threaten the faith of the people. Or does it?

Shocks stop us in our tracks; they make us pay attention. In that process, we discover things that we thought were true, aren't. Many Catholics believed that their leaders were sexless. Our reference to Father O'Malley

(Bing Crosby) in Chapter 3 represents the myth of "a nonsexualized version of male power." We found out that they can have sex problems like everyone else.

This chapter looks at the abuse and the attempted cover-ups by Church leaders to try to answer the underlying question: How could this happen? In search of insight, we'll look at the history of Catholic sexuality and the development of a clerical culture to see its relation to a climate of abuse. Out of this catastrophe, the people seem to be claiming a new sense of ownership of their religion. We'll end with a look at the dawn of a new era of faith and what it means to reclaim Catholicism.

Sex, Lies, and Vatican Tapes

In the closing years of the twentieth century, and continuing into the twenty-first, we have been blasted with news about sex scandals within the Church. One couldn't open a newspaper or turn on the television without hearing of further discoveries of pedophilia by priests and cover-ups by bishops. These problems eventually led to the unprecedented resignation of the senior cardinal of the U.S. Catholic Church, Bernard Law of Boston.

The Church has always kept a tight moral muzzle on the people's sexuality: The nuns warned girls about such dangers as panties being reflected in patent leather shoes and priests pounded respect for virginity into the boys, who were threatened within an inch of their lives if they attempted to lead a Catholic girl into premarital sex. Catholics can't divorce, use birth control, or seek an abortion (regardless of the circumstances). However, this time the moral camera is on the clergy rather than folks in the pews.

> **CAUTION**
>
> **For Heaven's Sake!**
>
> There is much dissent in the Church regarding sex and authority. A growing chorus of voices in the Church (lay and clergy alike) are voicing the need for more autonomy in making moral decisions. These dissenters can't be categorized as marginalized; they are well educated and well spoken. Just like any other family, the Catholic family has many views on most subjects, particularly sex.

In addition to thousands of lawsuits filed against the U.S. Catholic Church, reports of further abuses began to pour in from the four corners of the world. Nuns in AIDS-riddled Africa raped by priests wanting "safe" partners and young women seeking entrance into religious life coerced into having sex with priests. Day by day, our idols fell. As victims and parents began to come forward and expose these violations, they were assured by their pastors and bishops that the offender would be effectively dealt with by the Church. They were told to "trust the Church." In fact, however, superiors played a shell game, transferring offenders to other parishes where the abuses continued for years. What became apparent in the civil investigations, as the scandal unfolded, was a pattern of cover-up in diocese after diocese. The figures continue to rise, and few Catholic parishes in the United States are free of accusation.

"Safe" Sex: The Episcopal Cover-up

As the rubble pile grew higher, deeper questions began to surface. The focus shifted from the victims and priests to the bishops. How long had this been going on? Who knew? How was it kept quiet, and why? Catholics believe their clergy is a special breed—well educated, dedicated, and a cut above the regular guys. Catholics are also used to leaving Church business to the "professionals." With a "don't ask, don't tell" arrangement, the people trusted Church officials to take care of business. This arrangement created a climate in which secrecy would become a dangerous tool, eventually used by the leaders who employed it to cover up the sexual misconduct of the offending priests. In a closed culture the group makes a conscious or subconscious decision to overlook each other's deeds that are detrimental to the body as a whole. Thus, the pedophile, the womanizer, the sexually active homosexual, and the substance abuser cover for each other.

Everyone—bishops, priests, victims, and parents—turned to Rome for instructions as they always had. The pope met the situation with aloofness: It's an American problem, his demeanor seemed to suggest. The bishops, pressured by parishioners, lawyers, and the press, grew impatient. In June of 2002, they broke usual form and called their own meeting to discuss the problem and discern an appropriate response. In doing so, the timeless code was broken and a new note sounded: People were holding their leaders accountable.

Is Sex Abuse a Catholic Issue?

The scandal is far from resolved. Resignations continue. Some people believe the Church will collapse into financial ruin, as millions of dollars are extracted for settlements in diocese after diocese. As for the sexual abuse crimes, much is still to be discovered. What makes such an incomprehensible set of crimes possible? What makes a sexual predator? The exact social or genetic factors aren't fully known. Nor are the long-term results of these abuses on the victims known, although experts have testified to the extensive damage and the slow, painful time of recovery.

For the most part, there are many more questions than answers. We won't attempt to address the dynamics of sexual abuse, but we will explore the climate within the Church, examining age-old beliefs and practices to see if they have created an environment in which sexual abuse was able to incubate, grow, and eventually become systemic. One question that gnaws away at the heart of many is whether or not sexual abuse is a Catholic issue.

Pope John Paul II reads his message on the clergy sex abuse scandal to American Cardinals gathered in the Vatican, April, 2003.

(AP/Wide World Photos)

The sexual abuse of children has been a part of life for thousands of years. Different societies at different times in history have identified it and dealt with it in different ways. There isn't enough information at this time to know if the Catholic community has a disproportionate amount of abuse in their ranks compared with other segments of the society. At the same time, experts agree that certain components are common to the history and profile of all kinds of abuse, including sexual abuse. The agreed-upon ingredients are power inequity, secrecy, and the strong likelihood of previous abuse. Again, the question arises: What role (if any) does the Church play in contributing to the problem of sex abuse?

To begin to answer the question, let's take a look through the rearview mirror at the history of sex in the Catholic Church.

Our Legacy: Dualism and the Mind/Body Split

As we gaze into the rearview mirror, we see a man in a hair shirt, another wearing the robes of bishop, and the third in monk's clothing. They are Anthony, Augustine, and Aquinas. These three men, spanning time from two centuries after Christ up into the 1200s, formed the Church's understanding of human sexuality. We have talked about this many times throughout the book, and it comes into play again here, as it forms the rationale for patriarchy, hierarchy, and finally celibacy, all of which shape the character of the Church's *clerical culture*. From the beginning of the institutional Church, sexuality was rooted in the split between body and spirit, resulting in a belief in the body's innate sinfulness, distorting the basic understanding of human sexuality.

S'ter Says

Clerical culture is the beliefs, customs, practices, and behaviors of the clergy who live a life distinct from the lay people.

The Soul of a Cleric: Anthony and Augustine

Many of the Church's ideals regarding spiritual life were developed in the Egyptian desert during the third century, under the influence of Anthony (251-356), the founder of Christian monasticism. You read about this in Chapter 20, so we'll just remind you that desert spirituality involved men and women living away from the world in separate communities in which they practiced celibacy and virginity, along with a life based on prayer and fasting. They believed spiritual transcendence depended on subduing the flesh. Thus, spiritual perfection was based more and more on celibacy, not Christian charity. As time went on, these celibate communities became the primary source for clergy from which popes and leaders were then selected.

Augustine (354–430), following Anthony's teachings, articulated the Church's primary rationale for both celibacy and marriage. Augustine believed that original sin was passed through the genitals during sexual intercourse. Out of this philosophy, the Church became fixated on genital sexuality and failed to see intercourse in the context of love, devotion, and family life. Marriage was seen as a necessary "evil," a lesser state, reserved for those who could not control their "lower" nature. It took a back seat to the celibate life. Thus the foundation was laid for marriage and also for the clerical culture, a culture reserved for men separate from the world of families and children.

The Slippery Slope of Celibacy

Celibacy was not an easy mountain for the Church to climb. For the first several hundred years, clergy exercised the right to choose marriage and family. A first official step toward mandatory celibacy occurred as early the Council of Nicea, in 325, when a papal decree was issued insisting that there was to be no marriage after ordination. Candidates for the office of bishop who had wives and children were required to sign a statement protecting the Church from any inheritance claims.

A thousand years passed in the Western Church, and the struggle to achieve mandatory celibacy continued. In the tenth and eleventh centuries, papal documents pretty much solidified its practice in the Western Church. The religious world of the clergy separated further from the world of marriage, and their involvement in family life was limited to the experiences of their own childhoods. They failed to come to see sex as part of a complex set of relationships between human beings based on love and caring for one another. They saw it as an independent act disconnected from anything other than procreation.

Spawning Ground for Sin Legislation

Thomas Aquinas (1225–1274) became the next reigning theologian, upholding the teaching on sexuality exclusively for procreation by adding his Natural Law Theory as the new basis for moral reasoning. The crux of Aquinas' theory is that natural laws exist governing all creation, including the activities of animals and humans. By observing nature, we are able to determine God's will, and live in harmony with it. The Church used Natural Law Theory to arrive at its conclusion that there can be no artificial interference in sexual intercourse. Thomas, basing his theory in Aristotle's philosophy, believed there were universal moral absolutes. Therefore, today, Catholics uphold that their sexual teaching applies to them and to everyone else as well.

Natural Law has definite limitations, which are quite obvious. For example, through its application the Church deduced that although fornication, adultery, incest, and rape were serious sins, they did, in fact preserve the "natural order," (they could result in procreation) and thus were lesser sins than artificial interference during sexual intercourse (birth control) or masturbation.

During the Middle Ages, these theological "conclusions" became the source for the education of the clergy and laity lasting well into the twentieth century. Definitions of exactly what act resulted in which sin and the recommended penances were detailed in a little black book called a *penitential*. This book listed sins and the required penances. The penances reflect the excessive concern for sexual sins—100 days on bread and water for the first masturbation, one year for further transgressions—a fast of 10 years for using contraception. Anal and oral sex were considered unnatural acts because they couldn't result in procreation, and demanded fasts lasting up to 15 years—more severe penances than imposed for murder. As we know, once any thoughts, beliefs, or practices enter the Church system, they tend to get locked in. So while the penitentials no longer are used, many of the attitudes about sex represented by them live on.

S'ter Says

Penitentials were handbooks of penances, or punishments, circulated in Ireland, England, and on the Continent, from the sixth to the twelfth centuries prior to the institutionalization of confession as a sacrament by decree at the Fourth Lateran Council (1215). Penitentials provided a broadly based and normative code of sexual behaviors among very diverse early medieval societies.

Sex Education: "Thou Shalt Not ..."

The primary message was about keeping sex "under wraps." Under wraps, of course, meant bridled, harnessed, boxed, or subdued in some fashion. The Catholic link between sex and sin was thus forged—the body was declared sinful—spirituality was considered otherworldly and characterized by an ethereal quality of sexlessness.

In ruling on sexual matters, the Catholic Church has continued to adopt a Natural Law ethic to guide its members (and all of society) on sex, contraception, and homosexuality. It continues to interpret the primary purpose of sex as procreation and anything that prohibits the natural outcome of sex is seen as a barrier to the fulfillment of the sexual purpose. Thus contraception, oral and anal sex, masturbation, and homosexuality are all understood as activities that prevent procreation from happening and are condemned as unnatural.

Vatican II brought a development to Church teaching on sexuality (see Chapter 18) placing value on the bonding through mutual self-giving that intercourse creates for couples. For clerics, who are denied the bonding of a lasting sexual union, the Church's teaching on sex is theoretical rather than being grounded in experience, which raises the question as to how well the official teachers understand the Church's new attitude on sex.

> **Your Guardian Angel**
>
> Catholic sex education still is focused in "don't." Religious educators are calling for a comprehensive theology to be written on Christian sexuality that would be directed toward understanding human sexuality. They see sex education as a lifelong process affirming the sacredness of love, the body, and sexuality.

Our legacy of "pure" soul and "vile" body influenced Church theology from the get-go. Just as the association between sin and sexuality was made early in Church history, the link was infused early into the young Catholic's life: Everything sexual was sinful. By way of a hazy reference, we all learned "down there" was off-limits. Many older Catholics can remember the dating drill. While a song from the popular film *Casablanca* reminded us, "You must remember this, a kiss is still a kiss …," that tidbit of cultural wisdom was not true for Catholics, for whom a kiss was more likely to be an occasion for sin. Kissing was allowed, under various circumstances (such as accompanying an engagement ring); however, the occasion for sin always lurked nearby, and if unchecked, could easily slither into the bad deed itself. How long was long enough, and how long was too long for a Catholic kiss filled many religion class discussions.

Although these teachings don't occupy classes today, they remain as trickle-down attitudes from parents and teachers and continue to have influence over younger generations of Catholics. For the Church officials, sex was a series of isolated individual acts—lusting, kissing, petting, intercourse—each bearing its own moral price tag. It wasn't taught (perhaps it hadn't been discovered yet, in the pre-Kinsey world) that sexuality intrinsically belonged to being human, that to break off bits and pieces of sex was like chipping off a piece of Michelangelo's David to teach about art. So few learned how to be sexual beings.

Clericalism: The Secret Culture

Going back to the question we asked earlier in this chapter about whether sexual abuse is a Catholic thing, perhaps a clue to the answer can be found in one word, *clericalism*. Clericalism describes the power and influence of the clergy. In its extreme it results in a clerical culture, a composite of the beliefs, customs, practices, and behaviors of a particular class of people who live a life distinct from the larger society, in this case the clergy.

In the Catholic Church, this culture is set apart from the general membership. Formation for the priesthood occurs in seminaries, where young men are separated from their families and friends to spend the next four to eight years in a spiritual incubator. The word "seminary" is from the Latin *semen* and means "seedbed" or nursery. The purpose of seminary formation is to cultivate a special or distinct way of life different from the culture left behind.

The clerical culture has spiritual power over the members. It makes the Church's rules and sets its norms, and this is done in the Vatican chambers, behind closed doors. The clergy's decisions have enormous influence over the larger membership, yet it has no accountability to them. No accountability involves secrecy.

The Power of Secrecy

The enormity of this secrecy recently came to light when U.S. bishops were required to turn their records over to the civil authorities. Many in the public were shocked to realize the Church existed outside society's laws. Church authorities were not always required to report cases of abuse. Even when they were, the clout of their sacred power was so great that civil authorities hesitated to act; they were more apt to go along with bishops who promised they would take care of this business. Many centuries of clerical culture conditioned both the clergy and the people to accept this privileged discretion with few questions.

The clerical collar is a symbol of trust with sacred power. Catholics have traditionally had great love and respect for their priests and bishops. For the most part, the clergy lives up to their reputation. That is why Catholics as well as many others were shocked to discover these enormous transgressions. What happens when the priest, wearing the sacred symbol of priestly position, has a very "human" sexual problem? Common sense questions such as this escaped the imagination for a long time because these men were regarded as living in a different world—a world removed from the mundane—a secret world.

Secrecy has power.

Bishops: Stewards and Shepherds

As you might remember from earlier discussions on the role of bishops, they perform a twofold job. They are both shepherds of the flock and stewards of the Church. Now, looking back over the events of the last few years, this conflict of interest sits at the heart of the cover-ups; it represents a decision to protect the institution at the expense of the children. The effects of this decision—which was not made just once by one bishop, but over and over again by many bishops—is immeasurable.

At the same time that the actions of Church authorities were being investigated, a similar dynamic exploded in the corporate culture and news of financial scandals shared the spotlight with the Church pandemonium. Although these corporations wield a lot of power over our financial lives, the Church claims eternal power over our souls. In short, for believers the stakes are much higher. But in both cases, the dynamics are the same—a cover-up to protect the institution at the expense of the people.

In human interactions, secrecy can be a dangerous thing; whoever has the most information has the advantage. When leaders within an organization are allowed to "handle" problems that affect others, when they have a stake in the company, and they are forced to choose between the needs of the people and their need to keep the organization going, accountability often goes out the window. It's the same dilemma that has been nibbling away at the integrity of all institutions, and dining on the integrity of the people forever, it seems. Morality has always been about taking responsibility. When people give their responsibility away to institutions, the institutions grow fat on power, and the people become spiritually, as well as financially, bankrupt. As the British Lord Acton said regarding popes, "Power tends to corrupt and absolute power corrupts absolutely."

Sexually abusing children is an emotional or mental sickness. It requires treatment. Covering it up, leaving children in danger, giving parents false information, and denying priests the help they need indicates moral decay. It requires treatment.

Peeking Under the Cleric's Robe

Celibacy, a requirement for the priesthood, is surrounded by controversy. As the heat builds regarding sexual abuse in the Church, there is a strong temptation for those who oppose mandatory celibacy to jump on the scandal and attempt to co-opt the emotional charge to help energize their cause. The Church has rightfully made the point that there is no direct correlation between celibacy and sexual abuse. While this is true, there is the tendency of those who advocate for celibacy to refuse to look to see if anything might be discovered about child abuse in the clerical culture. Yet, below the surface of these two opposing theories exists the possibility of a deeper connection between celibacy and abuse, the link between celibacy and power.

Celibacy is the glue by which the clerical culture is held in place. A pious but powerful image of the priest that has endured over time is that he is "in the world, but not of the world." Yet, the great poet T. S. Elliot wisely reminds us of our humanness in his poem "The Hollow Men," in the line: "Between the idea and the reality ... falls the shadow." Celibacy is an idea, an ideal. It has seldom (perhaps never) been practiced perfectly. Yet, the Church has presented priestly celibacy as a *fait accompli*, as if it were perfectly lived. Although stories of priestly infidelities have always circulated, such idle gossip has generally been interpreted as anti-Catholic and even slanderous by mainstream Catholics.

Generally the Church does not talk about *attempting* to live a celibate life or pursuing it as a virtue to strive for. Catholics seldom get a sermon preached where the priest begins with a statement like, "Boy, isn't this sex thing a bitch?" Rather, the discussion about sex focuses on the people in the pews. Many feel that it would be better if we knew that the priests were having problems living up to their ideals, that we were all in this together. We'd know up front that they are sexual beings, too, and stop thinking of them as superhuman. We'd know what we were dealing with, and we could help each other more. More importantly, parents might be less likely to place children in what might become a dangerous situation, if we were not so naïve on this issue.

Yet, priests do struggle with celibacy. They sometimes win the struggle and sometimes lose and submit to a variety of clandestine sexual relationships: with women, with men, and apparently with children. Does this struggle mean there is a relationship between celibacy and sexual acting out? No, but understanding the struggle allows us to shed light on the situation and then be able to recognize and deal with deviancy. When sex is surrounded by lies, cover-ups, shame, and guilt, an unhealthy climate begins to build—sex and secrecy isn't generally a good mix.

As stated previously, "Whoever has the most information has the advantage." If the clergy knows its members are not actually being celibate, if a variety of informal sexual arrangements are ignored or allowed, and if the real issue is that priests are not permitted to establish lasting relationships, but a few indiscretions are treated with a wink and a jab, yet the people think they're celibate, the clergy has more power. In such

> **Epiphanies**
>
> Data from the field of psychology indicates a positive correlation between a person who was sexually abused as a minor and the likelihood of later becoming a perpetrator. Alarmingly, it is estimated that those former victims who do become sexual abusers will abuse 117 others. This statistic underscores the obvious need to intervene as soon as possible when abuse is reported. The perpetrator needs treatment, and needs to be kept away from other potential victims.

an environment, when all the sexual encounters are swept under the rectory rug, is anyone sorting through it? Are there different classifications established so that when someone crosses a big line—like having sex with a minor—someone flags it?

When the institutional Church has something to lose, be it its own image of itself, the trust of the people, or the power that is secured through secrecy, the tendency for denial is great. The decision to sweep this volatile situation under the rug is like storing nuclear waste in the refrigerator: It has a half-life that won't go away.

Protecting Patriarchal Power

Almost since the beginning of the Church's history, all authority has been located in the clergy, and the clergy has been all male. Even in the world of religious orders, the structure and rules for women's communities are subject to the approval or disapproval of the male leadership. All too often women are seen only as "servants of the Church," which quickly translates to servants of the male clergy, and children are simply invisible. Rectory dinners seem to magically appear out of nowhere, empty coffee cups are quickly replenished, and wine is poured by invisible hands; floors glint and silver glistens—all quite anonymously. Certainly this is not true in every rectory, but significantly and historically so—and the higher the office, the more padding.

There are no women present in the clerical halls of Rome where the decisions are made. There are no children running down the stairways, needing supper, or leaving grimy little handprints on the art. Which goes to say that the attitudes, definitions, and rules about life and, pertinent to our present discussion, the rules about sex, are formed by celibate men who are isolated from the world of women, children, and family men. Further to the point, decisions about sexuality have not changed significantly since the fourth century. The rules were made when people still thought the world was flat and the question of whether women were human was debated in religious and intellectual circles. Clerical celibacy assures that women, children, and family men remain quietly outside the inner circle. To be "outside the circle" means you have no power. In this case, it also means no access to law-making. Celibacy has power.

Over the centuries, the clerical culture has presented the ideal of celibacy and closed ranks on its members who fall short of the mission. Power is maintained through keeping the secret. Do they do this to protect the power?

Sex and the Single Seminarian

Paradoxically, Catholic clergy are among the best educated of any group of people in the world in most areas of their preparation. Seminarian training often begins at college level and lasts for seven or eight years. It includes Scripture; Church History; Canon Law; Fundamental, Dogmatic, Systematic, Moral, and Pastoral Theology; Liturgy; Preaching; Teaching; and Pastoral Care. Entrance includes psychological testing and extensive interviews with spiritual directors, educators, and psychologists. Instruction of these young men includes emotional, intellectual, and spiritual development. Time is devoted to understanding celibacy as a spiritual discipline; perhaps, though, not enough time is spent understanding their own sexuality. Understanding ourselves sexually requires interaction between the sexes; we learn from each other. Seminary education that keeps young men isolated from women (and other men) doesn't address the deeper issue of human sexuality.

Another factor in the debate about celibacy is consideration of the growing Catholic population, particularly in parts of Africa and Latin America. Celibacy is not culturally accepted, and high numbers of clergy (estimated some places to be as high as 80 percent) live with women in various marriage arrangements. Bishops, including the bishop of Rome—the pope—tend to ignore the situation, employing the Clinton directive of "don't ask, don't tell."

While no direct link can be made between the practice of celibacy and the sex scandals, the climate of repressed sexuality woven through the Catholic clergy, combined with secrecy, and power—all earmarks of the clerical culture—creates a potent mix. Experts will be looking closely at all aspects of seminary training and clerical life in their quest to understand what has gone wrong with the Church.

Gay Priests: Scapegoats?

Since the sex scandals most often have focused on men having sex with young boys, the question arises sooner or later: Is this a gay priest issue? There is a gay priesthood; experts in the Church estimate that between 25 and 80 percent of the present clergy is homosexual, a situation that some would rather ignore. The Church attracts gay men for the same reasons it attracts "straight" ones: They are drawn to ministry, ritual, and the service of others. In addition, however, the priesthood can offer gay men an opportunity to escape from the expectations of family and society regarding dating, marriage, and family.

For some troubled seminarians, celibacy and the other disciplines of Catholic priesthood help provide boundaries for their potential sexual problems. In the Catholic Church, practicing homosexuality is forbidden. The policy is "to love the sinner, hate the sin," but there is no ban against being a homosexual. For the most part, Catholics don't discriminate against priests based on sexual orientation, probably because they don't think of the priest as a sexual being.

Homosexuality is a sexual identity, but pedophilia is an indication of a severe disturbance and it is a crime. Pedophilia technically refers to having sex with pre-adolescent children, often the very young. In many of the cases being investigated, the minors involved are boys in their mid-teens, creating a gray area that must be further investigated.

Statistics are being compiled, and much more study will be needed to determine whether homosexuality is a factor in the abuse cases. The data isn't in yet. It is important to avoid the temptation to attribute the sex abuses to any one segment of the population, and gay priests would make handy targets. The human condition makes us want to point the finger at others, to blame a problem on a group that is a minority, and homosexuals remain a minority population.

Sexual Imagination (Thou Shall ...)

Catholic sexuality among the Church officials seems confusing at best, somewhat disturbing, and downright destructive at times, as we are currently bearing witness to. And sex education has been responsible for implanting ideas about the sinfulness of sex to the exclusion of sex as bonding and nurturing.

How does this perplexing sexual story play out in the Catholic bedroom? At first thought, it would seem to follow that Catholics would be hopelessly messed up in the sex department. However, that does not seem to be the case. According to research by sociologist and Catholic priest Andrew Greeley, Catholics have good sex—in fact, better than the rest of the U.S. population—measured by everything a sociologist can measure. In addition, Catholics place a high emphasis on family, and generally hold women in high regard. In light of the weird messages that have pervaded Catholic teaching and the popular image of sexually repressed Catholics, how can this be?

The Paradox: Lousy Laws, Good Sex

The answer to the paradox lies in the rich Catholic tradition of sacramental ritual, the penchant for smells and bells that is intrinsically Catholic. (See Chapter 9.) Ritual transmits meaning at a deeper level than written or spoken teaching. Catholic people have traditionally put more emphasis on ritual than on the other forms of Church teachings. Earlier we talked about the writings of Anthony, Augustine, and Aquinas and the *rational* tradition of theological writing directed to the intellectuals. At the same time, a sacramental tradition based in symbol and ritual was passing information to the rest of the people. Fed by the indigenous tribes of the European continent who were not historically connected to the Greek-Roman dualism, the people maintained a healthy relationship with the body, including a lusty sense of sexuality as something to be enjoyed. This earthy kind of spirituality fed into the rituals, and formed the Catholic people.

Smells and bells, along with other sensory stimulants such as vestments and banners of bright colors, oils, candles, and pageantry, form the basis of sacramental life. They are the symbols of ancient people, encoded with their inborn sense of the sacredness of life and the earth. As you no doubt know, Catholics are sprinkled, rubbed with oil, and otherwise anointed throughout life. This spiritual and sensory liturgical life sharply contrasts to the dualistic theology that separates spirit and body and it negates conflicting messages that tell us the body is sinful.

Remember, only 10 minutes of the weekly Catholic Mass is dedicated to transmitting the Word through preaching. The rest is all sacramental ritual. Beliefs transmitted through ritual sink deeper into the soul than the written word—they deliver a stronger teaching.

A question begging to be asked is: "Why, then, aren't Church leaders positively influenced by the rituals they perform?" A possible answer is that they probably are, at least on an intellectual basis. However, the spiritual message isn't reinforced through practice and thus it doesn't get into the body. At the top, leaders, already distrustful and intolerant of their own physical nature, are invested in maintaining the structure as it is. At the bottom, people, enlivened by earth-based liturgy, live a religious life that is not separate from the physical body, sex, and family life.

Passing the People's Tradition

The popular tradition is passed from generation to generation through family rituals, Church rituals, and the heritage of art and music—another spiritual expression of the people. All through the Middle East, and across Europe, cathedrals dedicated to Mary abound. Throughout history, *Ave Marias* bounced off these cathedral walls, filling the ear, reverberating the Christian story in music and sound. Year after year, Christmas pageantry pronounces the arrival into our midst of the Son of God, born of woman.

In countless holy pictures, Mary, young, vulnerable, pregnant, rides on the back of a small donkey, led through the night to Bethlehem by Joseph. It is into his care that Jesus and Mary are placed, completing a picture of family life that is the central premise of Christianity.

The *Pieta*, echoing the ageless theme of mother and child, still stirs the heart of all who see it. Faithful to the end, Mary is left with the broken body of Jesus, her child, laid to rest once again across her body, as he was the day he was born, this time for the last time: flesh, holding flesh, comforting, mourning, refusing to give up this precious body to the grave. Later the women came to anoint his sacred body and found him missing; he again took physical form to announce to his worried followers that life continues after death. Thomas, the doubting apostle, is convinced only after he pokes and prods the wounds. The Resurrection is taught to us through physical presence: We know by touching.

Bad Laws or Poor Process?

Theologians point to the tendency toward authoritarianism in how rules are made and issued from the inner chambers of today's Vatican. Moral laws are dictated as black and white mandates that both lay theologians and some clergy find troubling. For one thing, commanding goes against the Catholic tradition of addressing moral issues from a larger perspective. Theologians call it nuance. Which means that decisions must be looked at in the context in which they are made. In other words, circumstances count. For example, in the wake of the heavy focus put on abortion, a bishop was once asked what ever happened to the Church's social justice agenda. He replied by saying that until a child was safe in its mother's womb, nothing else mattered. Such a position does not take into consideration that because of social conditions, many women in the world are not safe—therefore their unborn child is not safe either. Circumstances count.

The worldwide epidemic of AIDS has unquestionably altered the rules on human sexuality, and moral law must discern the right response to new realities. Currently, Church law refuses to allow even married couples the use of condoms when one or both are infected. Such a stand, of course, forbids the use of condoms by the rest of the population, too, which shuts off a way to stem the spread of the disease.

A case can be built both for and against these particular moral decisions; it is the manner in which they are being declared that is problematic. Many feel that the Church's authoritarianism reflects a clergy that lives in a separate culture called clericalism. They are protected from the realities of those who are different, particularly women and children. This is not unlike the old European world where monarchs lived behind gated walls, above the people.

Some argue that Church doctrine must be preserved, but just what constitutes Church doctrine is not agreed on by Church officials, nor is the exact interpretation of doctrine always the same. Some fear that the Church will water down morality and serve up a weak soup just when a strong broth is called for. There is a long-standing misunderstanding that the Church does not, cannot, change. That if it were to change its position on something, it might break into pieces like Humpty Dumpty. But the Church isn't a hard-boiled egg, sitting on a garden wall. It is made up of flesh and blood people, struggling to do God's bidding to help initiate the reign of God. The fact is, Church teaching does change—it has changed, and it continues to change.

As the Church moves to participatory decision-making, liberals chomp at the bit and call for hijacking the hierarchy. Conservatives shudder and quake, and call for duct tape for all who disagree. However, middle ground suggests a compromise.

The everyday running of the Church could remain in the hands of competent professionals whose lives are dedicated to that service, with regular, required consultation and advisement among men and women laity. When laws are made by an isolated group of people, and don't flow out of the experience of the community, it may not be possible that the laws will serve the people. The question then follows, do they represent the will of God, or the will of those who made them? Just like John XXIII in the middle of the twentieth century called for the windows to be opened to air out a stagnating Church, the doors behind which decisions are made and secrets are kept now must be unlocked.

In this chapter, we've placed the sexual abuse scandal in a larger context. We've looked at secrecy and how it creates separation between priests and the people and builds a clerical culture. Clerical culture or not, the truth is, we're all in this thing together. Out of the terrible pain and suffering that both the people and the clergy are experiencing, a new relationship can be formed. This new way of being together is living out the bodily richness of the sacramental life.

Hope Born and Reborn

The events that precipitated the writing of this chapter are still fresh in the minds and hearts of both the readers and writers. So much seems to have happened so fast. Yet, below the surface of this immediate tempest, a compelling story rings true. The Creator of this vast universe took form as a tiny baby, and walked among us. He delivered a simple message that spoke of loving and a love demonstrated by feeding each other and caring for the needs of the world. It is ironic to think that his arrival into the human story should be interpreted as anything but encouragement and an indication that this is a good place and we are good people. It is hard to believe that the very folks who most celebrate his coming, even name themselves after him, might miss the point.

During a recent U.S. presidential election, the slogan "It's the economy, stupid!" circulated. A way of adapting that phrase to this situation might be: "It's the Incarnation, idiots!" For a long time, the Church has been focused on the Resurrection. It claims special status as the Church of the risen Lord. In doing that, it puts more of an emphasis on God's otherworldliness. Not a bad thing for a religion to do. However, balance calls us to look more closely at the Incarnation. Not just to settle questions about whether Jesus saved us, paid our bill on sin, or showed us how to live; those kinds of theological debates go on forever. Who can really know the mind of God? Balance might come in a simpler, easier way. What does any family do when a baby is born? They celebrate. It might be time to celebrate the Incarnation, rather than attempt to figure it out.

In that spirit of celebration, we conclude the second edition of this book, with gratitude to all who have read the first edition, and many who have written to us to let us know what was missing, as well as what they really liked. Over the last three years, the book has given us the opportunity to meet many people and hear about their faith struggles and victories. The old way was to think we were all separate, and that at the time of death, some would be sent one way and others a different way—and we all had our fingers crossed! In listening to the people, it becomes clear that we are all in this thing together and we sink or swim as a community. As imagined differences fade, as rank and privilege erode, we see ourselves reflected in one another's eyes—we move closer to the promised wholeness.

The Least You Need to Know

◆ Sexual abuse by priests is one element of the recent sex scandals, and the cover-up by bishops is a second and more destructive element of the scandals.

◆ While Church history gives a picture of a flawed understanding of the body and spirit, the sacramental life celebrates the presence of the spirit in the body.

◆ Not everything is known about the causes of abuse; however, it is known that power inequities and secrecy are factors.

◆ The Church is called toward being a community, where the primary concern of the institution is to assure the safety of the whole flock.

Appendix A

Glossary

abortion, clinical Intentionally bringing about the termination of a pregnancy to cause the death of the fetus.

absolution The power the priest has through the sacrament of reconciliation to extend God's forgiveness to contrite people.

altar From the Latin *altare*, akin to Latin *adolere*, which means to burn up: An altar is a raised structure on which the Eucharistic elements are consecrated in the sacrifice of the Mass and incense is burned in worship.

apostolic One of the four classical marks of the Church, which characterizes the connection of the Church for all time to the tradition and experience of the first followers of Jesus, the apostles. The term designates the authenticity of the tradition.

angels Purely spiritual creatures with intelligence and free will, acting as messengers and protectors in service to God.

Ascension Jesus' return to heaven after his death and resurrection to be reunited with God and to prepare a place for his followers.

Assumption When the Blessed Virgin Mary's earthly life was completed, she was taken up body and soul into heaven, where she shares in the glory of her son's resurrection.

baptismal font Large container for water often made of marble and placed at the entrance of the church that is used in the sacrament of baptism.

base communities Small groups led by laity who gather together for Scripture reading, discussion, Communion services, and community action; this movement started in Latin America.

belief An expression of faith accepted as true even in the absence of scientific proof; it may or may not be part of official Church teachings (see *dogma*).

Bible The sacred texts of both the Old Testament (or the Hebrew Scriptures) and the New Testament (the material written after the time of Jesus).

Bible vigil Post-Vatican II Church ceremony during which the Bible is honored on the altar and passages are read and reflected upon.

bishop The highest order of ordination in Church hierarchy; this person is ordinarily in charge of a group of parishes called a diocese.

canon (biblical) The word is used to designate those writings that came to be accepted as authentic biblical texts; it also is used to designate the most solemn part of the Mass including the consecration of the bread and wine—the "canon of the Mass."

Canon law From the Latin "rule": The rules governing the Church. One refers to Church law as Canon law.

capital sins Not actual sins, but thoughts and behaviors that the Church has determined to be the human conditions that are dispositions toward sinning. They are pride, covetousness, envy, anger, lust, gluttony, and sloth.

catacombs A system of tunnels beneath the ground outside of Rome and other ancient cities often used by early Catholics as hiding places when they were being persecuted. Many saints are buried there; they are visited as sacred sites.

Catechism The book containing the official teachings of the Catholic Church for the instruction of children or adults interested in the Catholic faith.

cathedral From the Greek *cathedra*, meaning "bishop's chair" or "throne," cathedrals are churches in which a bishop ordinarily celebrates the sacraments.

catholic The word from the Greek *kata or* "toward" and *holos or* "whole" is one of the four classical "marks" of the Church. In its original Greek sense it expresses the ideal of Jesus that "all" are to be embraced as God's people. From its Latin translation, it means universal, an emphasis as extending all over the earth, as a church for all; all its believers follow a set of common beliefs and practices.

celibacy Promise made by those entering religious service to abstain from sexual relationships.

ceremony A formal practice or custom established as proper to honor a special occasion.

Christ The Greek word for "anointed"; Kings were anointed in the Old Testament. Applied to Jesus as the anointed one of God.

Christian Term first used (disparagingly) to describe the followers of Christ in Damascus as early as 40 C.E. Later adopted by these followers in the second century.

Church A specific community of the faithful, usually determined on a territorial basis, local or regional, that carries on the mission of Christ in the world to reconcile humankind to God.

clergy   Those ordained to perform the sacramental functions of the Church.

clerical culture   The beliefs, customs, practices, and behaviors of the clergy who live a life distinct from the lay people.

clericalism   Describes the power and influence of the clergy.

cloister   Place of religious seclusion for prayer and meditation.

College of Cardinals   A group of select bishops that offers counsel to the pope, elects new popes, and governs in times between popes. They are the chief administrators of the Church. They are the bishops of major dioceses and/or head up the various Church agencies. The pope appoints them.

colonization   A process by which one country occupies another for the purpose of economic exploitation.

communion of Saints   An expression of unity linking all the people of God, living or dead, through all ages, into one eternal community.

contemplative   A meditative form of prayer developed in the monasteries.

co-redeemer   An unofficial but popular title celebrating Mary's part in the Redemption.

council (ecumenical)   A worldwide assembly of bishops called together by the pope for the purpose of setting policy and making decisions.

covenant   An agreement used in the Old Testament to describe the relationship between God and the people. It establishes that God will not abandon the people even if they fail to live up to their side of the agreement.

creation   The unfolding of all God's plans. Creation is in a state of movement toward an ultimate perfection as destined by God.

cross   Two planks of timber, one placed across the other; an instrument of execution in Roman times. Jesus was put to death on a cross.

crucifix   A cross that holds the image of Jesus crucified, used for devotion in Catholic churches and homes.

Crusades   Military expeditions undertaken by the Christians of Europe in the eleventh to the thirteenth centuries for the recovery of the Holy Land from the Muslims.

dogma (doctrine)   A formally stated official belief of the Catholic Church concerning faith or morals.

dualism   The view that reality consists of two basic opposing elements, such as mind and body or good and evil.

ecclesial or **ecclesiastical**   Pertaining to the Church.

ecumenical   Of worldwide scope or applicability, concerned with promoting unity among churches.

encyclicals   Letters written by the pope to instruct the people.

epiphany   A sudden intuitive perception or insight into the essential meaning of something.

Epiphany   The feast when the kings or wise men visited the Christ child in Bethlehem. It is celebrated January 6. The birth and the baptism of Jesus are considered epiphanies.

Eucharistic ministers   Parishioners who assist the priest in the distribution of Communion during Mass.

evil   That which motivates or results from morally bad or wrong choices.

excommunication   Censure by Church authorities excluding a Catholic from participation in the sacramental life and from the exercise of any Church office.

existentialism   Twentieth-century philosophical movement emphasizing a person's radical aloneness, personal freedom, and personal responsibility for decisions in one's existence.

Extreme Unction   Former name of the sacrament now called "Anointing of the Sick." "Extreme" refers to the deathly condition of those who are receiving it, and "Unction" means "anointing with oil."

faith   Our belief in the basic goodness of God's plan for us. In faith, we believe and act as if what we hope for will be granted. It also refers to the acceptance of Church teachings or the content of those teachings.

First Communion   Reception of the sacrament of the Eucharist for the first time.

free will   The human experience that governs our actions and gives us the freedom to make choices regarding our full expression of God's love.

globalization   Understanding all the world as a community and seeing the interconnectedness of people, economies, and resources.

God   The supreme divine being, the Creator of all that is, the fullness of being and of all perfection. God is without beginning and without end. God is love, the binding force in all that is.

Gospel   The good news that Christ has come. The Gospel, as read at Mass, is taken from the biblical books of Matthew, Mark, Luke, and John.

grace   From Latin *gratia* or "gift": the gift of God's life in our souls, which moves us toward right choices.

heaven   State of fulfillment after our life on earth where we are in God's presence for eternity.

hell   State of our existence without God; once understood as the eternal fires in which the damned suffered forever.

heretics   Catholics who engage in any deliberate, persistent, and public denial of some article of revealed truth of the Catholic faith.

hierarchy   Literally, "a holy order": the term refers to Church government by the ruling body of clergy organized into orders or ranks, each subordinate to the one above it; also, it designates a graded or ranked series of Catholic values.

Holy Orders   The process of ordination by which a man becomes a deacon, priest, or bishop to minister to people's spiritual needs and safeguard the rules and regulations of the faith.

Holy Spirit   The third person of the Trinity—Father, Son, and Holy Spirit; God's eternal presence to us opening our hearts and minds, guiding us in our actions, and otherwise assisting us on our journey.

homily   A sermon centering on scriptural text.

holarchy   A holarchy is a hierarchy of holons.

holon   Comes from the Greek *holos*, "whole," and *on*, "part" or particle. A holon asserts its individuality in order to maintain the order of a structure, but it also submits to the demands of the whole structure in order to make the system viable. Holons are self-contained, autonomous pieces. The holon has a "self-assertiveness tendency" (wholeness) as well as an "integrative tendency" (part). This duality is similar to the particle/wave duality of light.

host   One of several names for the Eucharistic bread. From the Latin *hostia*, meaning "victim," it recalls that Christ was sacrificed for us.

Humanae Vitae   Latin for "of human life," this is the document written by Pope Paul VI continuing the ban on the use of artificial birth control.

Immaculate Conception   Dogma that Mary was conceived in her mother's womb free from original sin to enable her to be a pure vessel through which Jesus would be brought into the world. Do not confuse with "virgin birth," which refers to Jesus' conception in Mary's womb, without Mary giving up her virginity.

immanence   God's presence here and now that can be experienced by humans.

Incarnation   The event in which God took human form and entered the human journey.

indulgences   Prayers or actions performed to remit the afterlife punishment for sins.

infallibility   A dogma stating that the pope speaks without error, on behalf of the Church, in union with the bishops when he proclaims an article of faith or morals.

Inquisition   Official investigation by the Church of suspected heresies.

intercessor   Christ's function as the mediator between God and the people. This term is also applied to his mother, Mary, because she was a necessary link in God's plan to send his son as an intercessor. Saints act as intercessors, too.

Jesuits   A religious order established in the 1500s by St. Ignatius of Loyola, dedicated to work for the pope. Their official name is the Society of Jesus.

Jesus   Hebrew name meaning "God saves," expressing both the identity and the mission of the Son of God born of the Virgin Mary.

La Nueva Raza   Spanish phrase, "the new race," describing the mixing of the Spanish, African, and Indian blood, spirituality, and cultures through which all of the cultures are changed.

lay people   From the Greek word *laikos,* meaning "of the people." Church members who are not ordained.

liberation theology   An array of theologies that articulate the faith journey from the perspective of the people's experience of their struggles.

liturgical practices   Church services and ceremonies, readings at Mass, Communion, the sacraments, prayers, rituals, and celebrations.

liturgy   The prayers and rituals of the Church.

magisterium   The Church's teaching function.

martyrs   Those killed for their faith. Martyrdom automatically results in sainthood. That is to say, a martyr's soul goes directly to God.

Mary   The mother of Jesus, the Son of God.

mechanical view of the universe   Sees the universe as nonliving, something the creator wound up like a clock, set in motion, and left on its own.

miracle   An event that breaks the laws of nature; an extraordinary happening that gives us a glimpse of God at work in the world.

missionaries   Religious workers sent to foreign countries to do religious or charitable work.

missions   Agencies such as schools and hospitals established and maintained by the Church in areas new to the Church's influence to assist people to meet their everyday needs.

modernism   A heresy condemned by the pope in 1907 referring to modern scientific thinking, which believed that truth changes.

monasticism   Tradition of taking oneself away from the mainstream of society for the purpose of developing spiritual practice.

monstrance   Ornate golden vessel containing the Blessed Sacrament under the form of bread, pressed between two pieces of clear glass. It sits on the altar for Eucharistic devotions.

moral (noun)   A concisely expressed belief or rule stating what we believe is right or wrong.

moral law   A sense of right and wrong that is part of an inborn and informed conscience. It is based in the understanding of a rational order established by the Creator that gives us guidance in making moral choices.

mysteries   Beliefs taken on faith, which can never be fully understood by reason.

mystic   From the Greek meaning "mystery," this term describes a person who engages in the practice of meditation from which he or she experiences a relationship with God and gains spiritual insight.

mysticism   Going within yourself to a quiet place where it is possible to experience the mystery of God.

myth   A story that tells the beliefs of a group of people regarding their origins, history, and destiny. Myths transmit truths.

national parish   A parish not based on geographical boundaries, comprised of an ethnic group who celebrate the liturgy with special attention to their native customs.

Natural Family Planning   A practice which requires a couple to restrict intercourse to naturally occurring times of infertility within the woman's cycle. It works with the nature of human sexuality by respecting the biological reproductive imperative rather than attempting to alter it through barrier and chemical methods. The Church endorses this method of birth control.

natural law   The way the natural world works. It makes itself known to us by our awareness of the natural order of things. It represents a common-sense understanding of the world.

New Age   The *New Age* takes its name from cycling into the astrological Age of Aquarius as the 2,000-year-old Age of Pisces draws to a close. It is seen as a moment in history when people are between certainty and uncertainty relating to religion, political institutions, and formal medicine. In the *New Age*, there is a search for alternative institutions. Religion is internalized, celebrating the sacredness of the self. God is reduced in certain *New Age* practices so as to further the advancement of the individual. Freedom, authenticity, and self-reliance are all held to be sacred.

novena   From the Latin *novem*, meaning "nine," this is a devotion repeated nine successive days.

omnipresence   One of the characteristics used to describe God; it describes God's presence everywhere.

ordination   Entrance rite into the order of deacon, priest, or bishop.

original sin   An inherited state of reduced power that we endure because of being separated from our original state of unity with God. It is part of being human.

Orthodox   Describes the Greek or Eastern Churches that are not under the direction of the pope.

paradigm   From the Latin for "to compare." It is a model of something. It designates the set of assumptions, concepts, values, and practices that frame a culture's vision. To change our paradigm requires a major shift in how we see things.

parish council   A post-Vatican II development in the Church's governing structure made up of church members who are elected or chosen to plan ministries and secure the resources for the parish.

parochial schools   Elementary and high schools supported by the parish, which provide a general education and instill Catholic ethics and values.

pastoral ministers   Church workers who have taken on various roles that once were filled by priests or nuns.

patriarchy   Means controlled by men. The opposite is matriarchy, which means women are in charge and are the head of families. Much of patriarchy has its roots in Catholicism.

pedophilia   Sexual activity of an adult with a child.

Pentateuch   The "book of the five scrolls" known as the Old Testament Torah. Moses commanded that the Torah law be placed in the Ark of the Covenant to be kept safe during the wilderness journey of the Hebrew people.

Penitentials   Handbooks of penances from the sixth to the twelfth centuries prior to the institutionalization of confession as a sacrament that provided a code of sexual behaviors among very diverse early medieval societies.

Posada   From the Spanish for "shelter," this term describes a house-to-house procession at Christmas in which the drama of Joseph and Mary is enacted.

priests   Ordained clergy of the Church.

prophetic tradition   Old Testament warnings about the consequences of actions. Some of the prophets were Isaiah, Jeremiah, Amos, and Micah.

Protestant   A Christian belonging to a sect that seceded from the Catholic Church at the time of the Reformation. Lutheran, Episcopal, Methodist, and Baptist are some Protestant denominations.

pulpit   From the Latin *pulpitum*, this is a staging platform from which the priest proclaims the Gospel reading of the Mass and preaches the homily.

purgatory   A state of the soul after death in which it progresses toward its final union with God. The soul in purgatory can be aided in this journey through prayers and good works of the living.

quantum spirituality   The call to recognize the unity of the world and be involved with it creatively.

quantum worldview   Holds that everything is made up of both particles (solid) and waves (energy) and that these two states exist at the same time within each "individual" piece or "quantum." This is an understanding that everything is connected by way of a unifying field of energy. It is in contrast to the mechanical worldview that perceives a separation between the physical and spiritual worlds.

RCIA   Stands for the Rite of Christian Initiation of Adults. It is a process of entrance into the Catholic Church.

real presence   A dogma that Christ is present in the sacrament of the Eucharist, physically and spiritually feeding the body and soul.

reason   Our ability to know the existence of God with certainty through our hearts and minds.

Reconciliation   The sacrament by which sins are forgiven and we are reconciled with God and absolved from guilt. A common name previously was confession or the sacrament of penance.

relics   Any part of the physical remains of a saint or items such as clothing that have touched the body of a saint.

religion   From the Latin *religare*, meaning "to bind back," religion is concerned with making connections between the sensate world and that which exists beyond. Religion operates from a faith basis rather than reason.

religious liberty   A Vatican II doctrine affirming the natural right to be free of coercion in one's religious beliefs.

Renaissance   The rebirth in Europe of the classic Greek and Roman architecture, painting, sculpting, music, and literature during the fourteenth, fifteenth, and sixteenth centuries.

Resurrection   The faith event of Jesus' rising from the dead on the third day after his crucifixion, demonstrating his victory over sin and death and eternal life that is available to people.

revelation   A source of knowledge available to us beyond the reach of normal knowing; it is divine insight or inspiration by which God speaks to people of the divine plan.

ritual   See *ceremony*.

Roman Curia   Bureaucracy that assists the pope in administering his duty of governing the Catholic Church.

Roman Ritual   Liturgical book of the rites and blessings commonly performed by the clergy. Since Vatican II, this book has been called the *Book of Blessings*.

sacramentals   Objects used to connect Catholics to spiritual experiences. Rosaries, candles, bells, and statues are common Catholic sacramentals.

sacred Scripture   The sacred writings of the Old (Hebrew) and New (Christian) Testaments that are believed to be inspired by the Holy Spirit and written by human hand.

salvation   God's loving action through Jesus that guides us and moves us toward what is good for us and away from that which would harm us.

seamless garment of life   An ethic recognizing all created things are connected to and by the Creator in a whole and unbroken relationship. It requires a consistent ethic of respect for the value of life across the board in the areas of access to food, shelter, health care, education, capital punishment, war, abortion, and euthanasia.

seminary   From the Latin *semen* and means "seedbed" or "nursery"; is a theological school for training priests.

sexual abuse   Forcing unwanted sexual activity by the use of threats or coercion.

"signs of the time"   Phrase used by Pope John XXIII in opening Vatican II that told the Church to look at the world and to learn from it.

simony   Refers to the sin of both the buying and selling of Church offices.

sin   Behaviors or intentions that are against God's will for us. It has been described as "missing the mark" or falling short of our potential.

social justice   A concept holding that all members are free to participate fully and receive the just benefits in the society in which they live.

soul   Our individual spiritual self, the breath of life, the indwelling of the Holy Spirit. Not separate from the body, but integral to it, it connects us to God, to one another, and to all of creation. Our souls live on when our physical lives are finished.

spiritual director   One trained to work with people spiritually, much like a psychologist works with someone emotionally.

tradition   Church teachings that have developed over the years based on the teachings handed down from Christ and the apostles.

transcendent   Beyond the ordinary range of human experience or understanding. The full nature of God is transcendent.

Triduum   The liturgy celebrated on the three days prior to Easter Sunday: Holy Thursday, Good Friday, and Holy Saturday.

Trinity   The mystery of faith expressing one God in three persons. The divine persons, the Father, Son, and Holy Spirit, do not share the one divinity among themselves, but each is a distinct personality of God, whole and entire.

Viaticum   Latin meaning "on the way with you," the name of communion when it is being given to a dying person.

virginity   In ancient times, a state of independence or autonomy, referring to a woman who made her own decisions. When used to describe Mary, it means she said yes to God of her own free will, acting independent of any influence or coercion. Commonly, it means a woman or man who has never had sexual intercourse.

virtues   Right ways of acting, habits that guide us in the way of good sense and good faith and govern our relationships with others.

visit   Catholic custom of stopping in to the church for a few minutes during the day to say a quick prayer.

vocation   From the Latin *vocare*, meaning "call," this term refers to a calling to the priesthood, religious life, or other spiritual paths.

vows   Binding promises made when one goes into a religious order. The principal three are poverty (giving up private ownership to the community), chastity (giving up the right to marry and have an intimate sexual relationship in order to devote oneself to the Church), and obedience (submitting to the authority of one's superiors for assignments).

Western world   Lands west of Istanbul, Turkey. Lands to the east of Istanbul are called the Eastern world.

Appendix B

Recommended Readings

Altemose, Sr. Charlene. *Why Do Catholics?: A Guide to Catholic Belief and Practice*. Burr Ridge, Ill.: WCB/McGraw-Hill, 1990.

Cahill, Thomas. *Pope John XXIII*. New York: Viking Press, 2002.

Carroll, James. *Toward a New Catholic Church: The Promise of Reform*. Boston: Houghton Mifflin Co., 2002.

Cozzens, Donald. *Sacred Silence: Denial and the Crisis in the Church*. Collegeville, Minn.: Liturgical Press, 2002.

Dumestre, Marcel J. *A Church at Risk: the Challenge of Spiritually Hungry Adults*. New York: Crossroad/Herder & Herder, 1997.

Elizondo, Virgilio P. *Galilean Journey: The Mexican-American Promise*. Maryknoll, N.Y.: Orbis Books, 2nd edition, 2000.

Faulkner, Mary. *The Complete Idiot's Guide to Women's Spirituality*. Indianapolis: Alpha Books, 2002.

———. *Supreme Authority: Understanding Power in the Catholic Church*. Indianapolis: Alpha Books, 2002.

Greeley, Andrew. *The Catholic Imagination*. Berkeley: University of California Press, 2001.

Groome, Thomas. *What Makes Us Catholic: Eight Gifts for Life*. San Francisco: Harper San Francisco, 2003.

Kennedy, Eugene. *The Unhealed Wound: The Church and Human Sexuality*. New York: St. Martin's Press, 2002.

Meara, Mary J. F. C., Jeffrey A. J. Stone, Maureen A. T. Kelly, and Richard G. M. Davis. *Growing Up Catholic: An Infinitely Funny Guide for the Faithful, the Fallen and Everyone In-Between*. New York: Broadway Books, 2000.

Weigel, George. *The Courage to be Catholic: Crisis, Reform, and the Future of the Church*. New York: Basic Books, 2002.

Whitehead, Evelyn and James. *The Wisdom of the Body: Making Sense of Our Sexuality*. New York: Crossroad/Herder & Herder, 2001.

Wills, Gerry. *Papal Sin: Structures of Deceit*. New York: Doubleday, 2001.

——. *Why I Am a Catholic*. Boston: Houghton Mifflin Co., 2002.

For In-Depth Reading

Encyclopedia and Catechisms

Bunson, Matthew (Editor). *2003 Our Sunday Visitor's Catholic Almanac*. Huntington, Ind.: Our Sunday Visitor, 2002.

Catechism of the Catholic Church. Washington, D.C.: United States Catholic Conference, 2nd edition, 2000.

The Companion to the Catechism of the Catholic Church. San Francisco: Ignatius Press, 1994.

Flannery, Austin P. (Editor). *Vatican Council II: Volume 2: The Conciliar & Post Conciliar Documents*. Collegeville, Minn.: Liturgical Press, 1998.

Glazier, Michael and Thomas J. Shelley (eds). *The Encyclopedia of American Catholic History*. Collegeville, Minn.: Liturgical Press, 1997.

Glazier, Michael and Monika K. Hellwig. *The Modern Catholic Encyclopedia*. Collegeville, Minn.: Liturgical Press, 1994.

McBrien, Richard P. *Catholicism: New Study*. San Francisco: Harper San Francisco, 1994.

McBrien, Richard P. (editor). *The HarperCollins Encyclopedia of Catholicism*. San Francisco: Harper San Francisco, 1995.

New Catholic Encyclopedia Second Edition (15 Vol. Set). Waterville, Maine: Gale Group, 2002.

Catholic Beliefs and Practices

Anderson, Bernhard W. *Understanding the Old Testament* (Fourth Edition). Paramus, N.J.: Prentice Hall College Div., 4th edition, 1986.

Beaudoin, Tom. *Virtual Faith: The Irreverent Spiritual Quest of Generation X*. Hoboken, N.J.: John Wiley & Sons, 2000.

Berry, Thomas. *The Great Work: Our Way into the Future*. New York: Harmony/Bell Tower, 2000.

Boff, Leonard. *Ecclesiogenesis: The Base Communities Reinvent the Church*. Maryknoll, N.Y.: Orbis Books, 1986.

Cooke, Bernard J. *Distancing of God*. Minneapolis: Fortress Press, 1988.

Dulles, Avery. *Models of the Church*. New York: Image Books, 1991.

Elizondo, Virgilio P. *Guadalupe: Mother of the New Creation*. Maryknoll, N.Y.: Orbis Books, 1997.

———. *La Morenita*. Liguori, Mo.: Liguori Publications, 1981.

Greeley, Andrew. *The Catholic Myth: The Behavior and Beliefs of American Catholics*. New York: Collier Books, 1997.

Happel, Stephen and David Tracy. *A Catholic Vision*. Minneapolis: Fortress Press, 1988.

Haughton, Rosemary. *The Catholic Thing*. Springfield, Ill.: Templegate Publishers, 1980.

Hellwig, Monika K. *Understanding Catholicism*. Mahwah, N.J.: Paulist Press, 2002.

O'Murchu, Diarmuid. *Quantum Theology: Spiritual Implications of the New Physics*. New York: Crossroad/Herder & Herder, 1997.

Sawicki, Marianne. *The Gospel in History: Portrait of a Teaching Church: The Origins of Christian Education*. Mahwah, N.J.: Paulist Press, 1988.

———. *Seeing the Lord: Resurrection and Early Christian Practices*. Minneapolis: Fortress Press, 1994.

Wessels, Cletus. *The Holy Web: Church and the New Universe Story*. Maryknoll, N.Y.: Orbis Books, 2000.

Wills, Garry. *Bare Ruined Choirs: Doubt, Prophecy and Radical Religion*. Garden City, NY: Doubleday, 1972.

Catholic History

Carroll, James. *Constantine's Sword. The Church and the Jews: A History.* Boston: Houghton Mifflin Co., 2001.

Coffey, Kathy. *Hidden Women of the Gospels.* Maryknoll, N.Y.: Orbis Books, 2003.

Davies, Oliver and Fiona Bowie. *Celtic Christian Spirituality: An Anthology of Medieval and Modern Sources.* New York: Continuum, 1999.

Davis, Cyprian. *The History of Black Catholics in the United States.* New York: Crossroad/Herder & Herder, 1995.

Dolan, Jay P. *In Search of an American Catholicism.* New York: Oxford University Press, 2002.

Gilkey, Langdon Brown. *Catholicism Confronts Modernity: a Protestant View.* New York: Seabury Press, 1975.

Küng, Hans. *The Catholic Church: A Short History.* New York: Modern Library, 2003.

Morris, Charles. American Catholic: *The Saints and Sinners Who Built America's Most Powerful Church.* New York: Vintage Books, 1998.

O'Gorman, Robert T. *The Church That Was a School: Catholic Identity and Catholic Education in the United States Since 1790.* Washington, D.C.: The Catholic Education Futures Project, 1987.

O'Murchu, Diarmuid. *Reclaiming Spirituality: A New Spiritual Framework for Today's World.* New York: Crossroad/Herder & Herder, 1998.

Pennick, Nigel. *The Sacred World of Celts: An Illustrated Guide to Celtic Spirituality and Mythology.* Rochester, Vt.: Inner Traditions Intl. Ltd., 2000.

Thompson, Mary R. *Mary of Magdala: Apostle and Leader.* Mahwah, N.J.: Paulist Press, 1995.

Catholic Culture

Brinkmeyer, Robert H. *Three Catholic Writers of the Modern South.* Jackson, Miss.: University Press of Mississippi, 1985.

El Dia de los Muertos (The Day of the Dead). San Antonio: Institute of Texan Cultures, The University of Texas at San Antonio, 1991.

Giles, Paul. *American Catholic Arts and Fictions: Culture, Ideology, Aesthetics.* New York: Cambridge University Press, 1992.

Icher, Francois. *Building the Great Cathedrals*. New York: Abradale Press, 2001.

Massa, Mark Stephen. *Catholics and American Culture: Fulton Sheen, Dorothy Day, and the Notre Dame Football Team*. New York: Crossroad/Herder & Herder, 1999.

Smith, Huston, David Wakely, Thomas Moore, and Ismael Fernandez De La Cuesta (eds). *Gregorian Chant: Songs of the Spirit*, (book and CD). San Francisco: Bay Books, 1996.

Walker, Barbara G. *The Woman's Dictionary of Symbols and Sacred Objects*. San Francisco: Harper San Francisco, 1988.

Catholic Prayers and Saints

Alberione, James. *Queen of Apostles Prayerbook*. Boston: St. Paul Editions, 1976.

Bauer, Judith A. (ed). *The Essential Mary Handbook: A Summary of Beliefs, Practices, and Prayers*. Liguori, Mo.: Liguori Publications, 1999.

Bielecki, Tessa. *Teresa of Ávila: Mystical Writings*. New York: Crossroad/Herder & Herder, 1994.

Chittister, Joan D. *The Rule of Benedict: Insights for the Ages*. New York: Crossroad/Herder & Herder, 1992.

Cohen, J. M. (translator). *The Life of Saint Theresa of ávila by Herself*. New York: Viking Penguin Books, 1957.

Delaney, John J. *Dictionary of Saints*. New York: Doubleday, 1980.

Ebertshäuser, Caroline H. *Mary: Art, Culture, and Religion Through the Ages*. New York: Crossroad/Herder & Herder, 1998.

Heywood, W. (ed). *The Little Flowers of St. Francis of Assisi*. New York: Vintage Books, 1998.

Hoever, Hugo. *Lives of the Saints for Every Day of the Year*. New York: Catholic Book Pub. Co., 1999.

Sandoval, Annette. *The Directory of Saints: A Concise Guide to Patron Saints*. New York: Penguin Books, 1997.

Tetlow, Joseph A. *Ignatius Loyola: Spiritual Exercises*. New York: Crossroad/Herder & Herder, 1992.

Tobin, Greg. *Saints and Sinners: The American Catholic Experience Through Stories, Memoirs, Essays and Commentary*. New York: Doubleday, 1999.

Trouvé, Marianne Lorraine. *Favorite Prayers and Novenas.* Boston: Pauline Books & Media, 1997.

Warner, Marina. *Alone of All Her Sex: The Myth and the Cult of the Virgin Mary.* New York: Knopf, 1976.

Internet Resources

Catholic Information Center on Internet
www.catholic.net

The Holy See
www.vatican.va

Natural Family Planning
www.billingsmethod.com
www.ccli.org

Official Catholic Sites on the Web
www.georgetown.edu/centers/woodstock/links/links_official.htm

Religious Orders
http://employees.csbsju.edu/roliver/orders.html

Chart of Symbolic Elements

This chart shows how the religious symbols that are the basis of the rituals in the Catholic Church connect through time to Europe's old religions.

Elemental Symbol	Corresponding Symbols	Symbolic Meaning	Implied Meaning	Catholic Beliefs and Practices
Earth	Winter; night; north; black	Death and gestation; nurturing; physicality; creativity; female	What appears to be dead is gestating and will be reborn; food and shelter; Earth as sacred; physical body as sacred; wisdom; the mystery of life	Jesus' physical presence on Earth; Jesus' birth in the manger; Mother Mary; Jesus' healing ministry (feed the hungry, heal the sick, raise the dead); Jesus' death on the cross and burial in earth; altar; holy oil; ashes (dust to dust); Sacraments: Holy Eucharist, Anointing the Sick, Marriage (procreation)
Air	Spring; morning; east; white; green	Birth; life and breath; new beginning; movement; promise; mind/meaning; male	The gift of life; hope; renewal; communication; thoughts as sacred	Incense; bells; prayers, songs, and chants; Declaring the Word; Holy Spirit as dove; preaching and teaching; hope reborn; resurrection; Sacrament: Holy Orders (as preaching and teaching)
Fire	Summer; noon; south; red; orange	Transformation; strengthening the will; in the action world; willing into being; fruition and abundance	Holy Spirit as fire; zeal; missionary work; Christ's Passion; use of miracles	Candles; sanctuary lamp; Catholic action (do the right thing); Sacraments: Holy Orders and confirmation
Water	Fall; evening; west; blue	Inner depth; quieting; soothing; waters of the womb; emotions; female	Cleansing; initiation; reflection; fulfillment; universal solvent	Holy Water; blessings; mediation; contemplation; intuition or door-way to wisdom; Sacraments: baptism and reconciliation

Appendix D

The Poop on Popes

There have been more than 260 bishops of Rome since St. Peter, with dozens more antipopes (pretenders claiming to have that title) in the nearly 2,000-year history of the Church. They have been a mixed bag, some extraordinary, some unremarkable, some great, and some just plain awful. What follows is a baker's dozen of past popes.

St. Linus (66–78). Hardly anything is known about St. Linus, who was St. Peter's, the first pope, immediate successor. He may be synonymous with the Linus mentioned in the Second Letter from Paul to Timothy. If so, he has the distinction of being the only pope other than Peter to be named in the New Testament.

St. Damascus I (366–384). Described as a charming but forcible, even arrogant, man, St. Damascus's distinction is that he saw Christianity proclaimed the state religion of the Roman Empire and Rome established as the head of the Church. He worked to enhance the appeal of Christianity to the Roman aristocracy. He believed in converting the women, with the expectation that they would soon bring their husbands over as well. The opulence of his reign left a bad taste in the mouths of some, and he was not without his critics. At one point, his enemies accused him of adultery, a charge he was acquitted of by a synod of 44 bishops.

St. Leo I (440–461). One of only two popes to be referred to as "the Great." He defined the doctrine that each pope inherited his authority directly from St. Peter and thus could not be tainted by the questionable acts of a previous pontiff. The emperor confirmed the pope's authority over other bishops. He is probably best remembered for his confrontation with Atilla the Hun in 452, when he successfully persuaded him to withdraw his armies and not invade Rome. He was successful in further negotiations with Vandal leaders and lessened the damage caused by their invasions.

St. Gregory I (590–604). The first monk to rise to the papacy, Gregory criticized the lack of discipline he saw in his fellow bishops and urged the need for higher moral standards, especially with regard to clerical celibacy. He was the first to use the term *ex cathedra* to define the bishop's authority to speak on matters of doctrine. He sent missionaries to Anglo-Saxon England and is probably best known today for the chant that bears his name (although he may have had nothing to do with its composition).

Times had changed for both Rome and the papacy. The empire that provided structure and order was now falling. Somebody had to fill the void. Gregory organized plague relief and the disbursement of food to the hungry. To deal with invading Lombards, he also arranged for the city's defense, paying the troops out of the Church's treasury and eventually negotiating a peace.

Gregory began his life as an aristocratic civil servant and rose to the position of prefect of Rome. But then he became a monk and, reluctantly, pope. He was, however, the right man for this role. Although not necessarily a great intellect, he was an administrator *par excellence*. It is in this role as a temporal ruler that Gregory most clearly shaped the future of the papacy.

Stephen VI (896–897). Stephen was about as bad a pope as could be imagined. He was apparently motivated by equal parts political favoritism and a bizarre need for revenge. He exhumed the body of an earlier pope, Formosus, and put the corpse on trial for imagined misdeeds. The body was dressed in papal vestments, and a deacon was forced to provide the voice. After the corpse was found guilty, the three fingers that the dead man had used to administer blessings were cut off, and the body was delivered to a cemetery for the homeless. A couple of days later, it was thrown into the Tiber River.

Unrest in Rome, partly due to his horrifying behavior, soon led to Stephen's imprisonment. While in prison, he was strangled. Assassination and violent death were all too frequent dangers to the popes of this era, and Stephen died in a manner befitting the way he had lived.

Sergius IV (1009–1012). About the only thing Sergius, the son of a shoemaker, is remembered for is establishing the tradition whereby the pope chooses a new name upon his election. In the past, a pope might take a new name under special circumstances (for example, he might have a given name of a pagan deity, such as Mercury), but in the nearly 1,000 years since Sergius, only two have retained their original names. Sergius seems to have had two reasons for changing his name. His given name was Peter, and Peter would be a rather presumptuous handle for any pope to merit. In addition, he probably wanted to have a new name so people would stop using his nickname of "Pig-nose."

St. Gregory VII (1073–1085). A stubborn, forceful individual, Gregory fought hard for his ideals. He pushed ardently for Church reform, especially clerical celibacy. He battled with the Holy Roman Emperor over the buying and selling of Church offices (simony) and the power of lay rulers to name bishops within their own territory. Gregory lost the battle and was driven into exile, where he eventually died. The emperor seized Rome and installed his own antipope. However, Gregory won the war. In 1122, the Concordat of Worms cemented the principles for which Gregory had struggled.

Adrian IV (1154–1159). The only English pope, Adrian (also known as Hadrian) probably owed his accession to the influence of the English King Henry II, the most powerful monarch in Europe. It was common for both local (Roman) and European politics to have a powerful effect on papal elections. In a document, he urged Henry to subdue Ireland and reform the Irish Church. Whether this document meant giving Ireland away to the English crown forever is a matter of some debate, but it was the catalyst to the violence that still affects that island today.

Alexander VI (1492–1503). Alexander certainly was the most notorious of the popes. His uncle, an earlier pope, made him a cardinal at the age of 25. He used lavish bribes to secure his election as pope. A Borgia, he fathered at least nine illegitimate children, the most infamous of whom were his daughter Lucretia and his son Cesare (whose exploits inspired Machiavelli).

Alexander's reputation for extravagance was exaggerated to X-rated proportions by generations of later Protestant critics. He greatly extended the practice of selling indulgences, particularly when he declared a Jubilee Year in 1500 in order to increase the number of pilgrims and donations flowing into Rome. He used these monies to finance his son's military adventures.

Despite his immodest behavior, Alexander is also remembered as a great patron of Renaissance artists and a capable administrator. He neatly divided the New World between Spain and Portugal (favoring his fellow Spaniards) simply by drawing a line on a map. Although his death was probably due to fever, the old legend that he accidentally consumed the poison he had arranged for a rival cardinal cannot be discounted.

Adrian VI (1522–1523). Adrian was the last non-Italian pope prior to the election of John Paul II in 1978. He had three daunting challenges in front of him when he assumed power: Lutheranism, the Ottoman Empire, and reforms needed in a Church whose leadership viewed him as an outsider to begin with, and which was determined to hold on to its many perks. Adrian's acknowledgement that the Roman Court had been the fountainhead for all corruption in the Church won him no allies. He died after only 20 months, but 20 years probably would not have been enough to accomplish these tasks.

Pius IX (1846–1878). Pius was considered liberal when compared to his immediate predecessor, who, for example, considered railroads to be an invention of the devil. Pius was forced to deal with the inevitable crisis of the modern age. His reign saw the loss of the Papal States and a corresponding loss of the temporal power that had been a part of the papacy for 15 centuries. Pius's reaction to this occurrence was to insist on absolute authority in the spiritual realm. He declared the doctrine of papal infallibility. His 32-year pontificate is the longest in history.

John Paul I (1978). The penultimate pope, John Paul was pontiff for only 33 days. He seemed to promise a breath of fresh air, and his first two acts suggested a new pope for a new era. Upon his election, he broke precedent and chose a dual name to honor his two predecessors, Paul VI and John XXIII. Typical of this man's humility, he refused the traditional crown of the popes and instead wore only a bishop's miter. During his short reign, his charming personality earned him the nickname of "the smiling pope." His unexpected death, so shortly after his accession, shocked the world and gave bogus ammunition to conspiracy theorists everywhere.

And the ever popular ...

Pope Joan (855 or 1087?) No list of popes would be complete without the mythical Pope Joan. As the thirteenth-century legend has it, Joan was a devout and learned woman who disguised herself as a man and earned the admiration of all for her keen intellect and holiness. After the death of the preceding pope (either Leo IV in 855 or Victor III in 1087, depending on which version you believe), Joan was elected pope, taking the name John. It was said that she ruled wisely and well for a couple of years, but her secret was revealed in disastrous fashion. One day while walking through the streets of Rome with her cardinals, she gave birth. Her legend was enjoyed for centuries, and no amount of Vatican denials could stifle it. The story was especially popular with Protestant reformers, because it seemed to prove the debasement of the papacy. The myth wasn't thoroughly disproved until the seventeenth century, and even today she is still better known than the vast number of real popes.

Index